AF386180

# Carpow in Context

*In memory of John George Alexander Strachan*
*(1924–93)*

'There is a sort of river of things passing into being, and Time is a violent torrent; no sooner is a thing brought to sight than it is swept by and another takes its place, and this too will be swept away.'

*Augustus Meditations*, Book 4 section 43

'Time seemeth to be of the nature of a river or stream,
Which carrieth down to us that which is light and blown up, and sinketh and drowneth that which is weighty and solid.'

*The Proficience and Advancement of Learning*, Book 1, Francis Bacon

'So we beat on, boats against the current, borne back ceaselessly into the past.'

*The Great Gatsby*, chapter 9, F Scott Fitzgerald

# Carpow in Context:
# A Late Bronze Age Logboat from the Tay

DAVID STRACHAN

*with contributions by*
Michael Browne, Peter Clark, Gordon Cook, Trevor Cowie, Mike Cressey, Anne Crone,
Sue Dawson, Damian Goodburn, Mark Hall, Seán McGrail, Paula Milburn, Robert Mowat,
Rob Sands, Theo Skinner, Steven Timoney, Richard Tipping and Sarah Winlow

*and illustrations by*
David Hogg and Leeanne Whitelaw

Edinburgh 2010
SOCIETY OF ANTIQUARIES OF SCOTLAND

Jacket image by David Strachan

Published in 2010 by Society of Antiquaries of Scotland

Society of Antiquaries of Scotland
National Museum of Scotland
Chambers Street
Edinburgh EH1 1JF
Tel: 0131 247 4115
Fax: 0131 247 4163
Email: administration@socantscot.org
Website: www.socantscot.org

The Society of Antiquaries of Scotland is a registered Scottish charity no. SCO 10440.

ISBN 978 0 903903 25 7

Society of Antiquaries of Scotland gratefully acknowledges support of this volume from

Design and production by Lawrie Law and Alison Rae
Typesetting by Waverley Typesetters
Manufactured in Spain by Graphicems

# Contents

# Foreword

No two estuaries are alike. The River Tay is Britain's foremost river in terms of discharge, and its estuary is a Scottish gem, remarkable in many ways. In its upper reaches, above the confluence with the River Earn, the channel is incised along the axis of what is the finest example of a rift valley in the country. Indeed, its geological and geomorphological features, like the extensive sand dune systems of Buddon Ness and Tentsmuir at the seaward end, are of national and international importance. The inter-tidal flats of the middle and lower reaches support nationally important populations of wading birds. Together these account for the numerous conservation designations bestowed upon the estuary. Furthermore, its predominantly rural character is a rarity amongst Britain's major estuaries and this has helped to maintain the Tay as one of the least polluted such water bodies in Europe.

The undeveloped character, however, is not without the influence of human intervention. On the north bank of the estuary, what is today the largest continuous reed bed in Britain, which supports nationally important populations of reed bed birds, is the consequence of a 19th-century endeavour to combat erosion and induce land claim. In contrast, the relative lack of development and human intrusion on the southern shore has played an important contribution to the outstanding preservation of the archaeological find that is the subject of this volume.

Until its discovery in 2001, the $c$ 10m long oak hull of the Carpow logboat had lain undisturbed for perhaps 3,000 years, almost completely buried within the muddy and peaty inter-tidal deposits of Carpow Bank near the mouth of the River Earn. To date, this is the eighth logboat known to have been recovered from the Tay; the other seven (of which only one remains) were discovered in the 19th century. The Carpow vessel is the second oldest dated logboat to be found in Scotland and the best preserved thanks to the lengthy protection afforded by its shallow grave in the Tay's sediments. Erosion was, however, beginning to expose the hull, hence its discovery, and there was a real threat to the structure that was to stimulate a high-profile programme of rescue, excavation and ultimate recovery.

Natural scientists, engineers, geologists, botanists, archaeologists, amateurs and professionals have been studying the Tay – its tidal flows, sediments and biota – for some two hundred years. Indeed, one of the most fundamental of scientific discoveries that is the underpinning basis of our understanding of estuarine water and sediment dynamics was made offshore from the beach of the nearby parish of Flisk, in a channel that must surely have been graced repeatedly by the passage of the Carpow logboat centuries before. Hereabouts in 1813 the Reverend John Fleming, the parish minister, collected water samples at differing water depths and stages of the tide, which he evaporated to dryness and weighed the crystalline salt residues. Thus, the Tay Estuary was the site of the first recognition of estuarine salinity stratification and these pioneering observations (Fleming 1816) were the forerunner to estuarine classification on the basis of mixing characteristics. Coincidentally, it was Fleming (1822) who also made the first discovery of what he called a 'submarine forest' in the Frith (*sic*) of Tay, to the west of Flisk, a buried landscape comparable and likely contemporaneous with that of the eroding inter-tidal peat with *in situ* tree stumps in the area of Carpow Bank.

The early 21st-century find of the logboat is important not least because it highlights the potential for further inter-tidal archaeological study in the estuary. Undoubtedly the Tay still has many more secrets to reveal with the passage of time, but she divulges these sparingly. This excavation and recovery project is a fine example of multi-disciplinary partnership working; bringing together local, regional and national bodies to a common goal. It has also provided an opportunity to undertake the first detailed synthesis of Bronze Age evidence for the Tay Estuary area for almost four decades, since the work of Herbert Coutts (1970; 1971), then Keeper of Antiquities and Bygones at Dundee Museum.

In 2009 the Tay Estuary Forum (2009) Local Coastal Partnership launched its voluntary, non-statutory Management Plan with the over-arching aim to secure and promote for future generations the wise and sustainable use of the Tay Estuary and adjacent coastal waters. Nested within the plan's 'Environmental Strategy' is a priority to protect and enhance the cultural heritage in all its diverse forms within the TEF region. The Carpow logboat project is entirely in harmony with this priority and the resulting volume, for which it is my privilege to write this Foreword, is a splendid account of a remarkable vessel; a multi-faceted study of a piece of our cultural heritage and a story that embraces a marriage of context, discovery, excavation, recovery, conservation, science and landscape. Moreover, it is a reflection of the passion, commitment and determination of all those involved.

ROBERT W DUCK
*Chair, Tay Estuary Forum*
Professor of Environmental Geoscience
School of Social and Environmental Sciences
University of Dundee
Dundee

# Preface

It needs no evidence to prove that the men who navigated our shores and rivers, in canoes hollowed out of single trees, had made but little progress in the constructive arts.

Laing 1876

So begins an introduction to the prehistory of the Tay Estuary by Alexander Laing, whose lasting memorial, The Laing Museum, remains on Newburgh High Street to this day. While Laing's view of logboats as primitive craft was not uncommon at that time, antiquarian interest in logboats was considerable and had been triggered by numerous discoveries resulting from both the exploration of crannogs (Stuart 1866; Munro 1882; 1885) and the dredging and increased economic exploitation of estuaries (Buchanan 1854a; 1854b). Indeed, all of the logboats from the Tay Estuary, prior to the Carpow example, were discovered in the 19th century, and the majority were found by either fishermen or workmen (Chapter 9, p 125). Logboat studies received little attention in the first half of the 20th century, however, and interest was only revived due to further discoveries (Feacham 1959) and the development of dendrochronology and radiocarbon dating in the second half of the century (Mowat 1996, 1). The main corpus of Scottish logboats, originally published by Stuart (1866), was a Victorian creation, and the 20th century saw only occasional additions to the established distribution.

The opportunity to study the Carpow vessel came fairly soon after my appointment with Perth and Kinross Heritage Trust in 2000. This followed a period working on inter-tidal archaeology on the Essex coast (Strachan 1998), which had highlighted to me the value of the waterlogged resource (which very often remains unrecorded) to be found along our coastline. The evaluation excavations in 2003 demonstrated that Carpow was a well-preserved Bronze Age vessel that retained an *in situ* fitted transom at the stern: only the second example from a prehistoric logboat from the British Isles. Monitoring of the exposed bow subsequently indicated that the boat was eroding as a result of tidal action and it soon

became clear that full excavation and recovery of the vessel was the most appropriate course of action. The execution of the project was not undertaken lightly. The scale of the vessel and its location beneath the UK's largest river (in terms of freshwater discharge) made for a formidable task. The considerable logistical challenges involved required a multi-disciplinary team of archaeologists, commercial divers, conservators, palaeoenvironmentalists and salvage operators. The result was a successful, if challenging, excavation and the project developed an innovative and effective method of recovery, involving floating the vessel from the site to a quayside and road access.

The cultural significance of Carpow can be measured both in terms of its contribution to logboat studies and our understanding of the contemporary archaeology of the area. These were very much the themes of the 2007 conference, entitled *Tales of the Riverbank: the Carpow Bronze Age Logboat in Context*, held at Abernethy, overlooking the excavation site. The vast majority of British logboats are in poor condition in comparison with Carpow and tell us little about techniques of manufacture. Furthermore, relatively few have been dated (Mowat 1996, 129) and the true significance of Carpow in terms of the diffusion of logboat manufacture in Europe (Lanting 2000) will only be understood following radiocarbon dating of a selected but significant sample of the Scottish examples, as has recently been carried out in Northern Ireland (Fry 2000). The wider value of Carpow as an artefact has been as a catalyst for discussion about landscape archaeology. As methods of transport, logboats and their sewn-plank counterparts (Chapter 14) provide a rare insight into how prehistoric people moved around, traded and exploited the varied ecotones around them. A tendency persists for studies of terrestrial sites to take interaction between prehistoric communities for granted, with travel and transport seen as mundane 'means to an end' without considering movement in prehistory directly (Cummings & Johnston 2007, 1). Carpow has offered an opportunity to discuss directly aspects of the dynamics of transport, albeit of one form, in the area at the end of the Bronze Age.

Given the archaeological potential of Tay Estuary, it is unfortunate that to date there has been no systematic programme of inter-tidal survey as has been carried out on estuaries on the east coast of England (Wilkinson & Murphy 1995; Van de Noort & Ellis 1995). As a result, the archaeology of the estuary remains largely unknown and it is likely that a variety of sites survive, in numbers, awaiting discovery. While the Tay Estuary Forum now provides a good basis for future management of the historic environment of the estuary, this baseline data is necessary to make that aim possible. Beyond that, the research framework for the Greater Thames Estuary (Williams & Brown 1999) illustrates a way forward in considering priorities for future study, whether through academic research or via developer-funded archaeology.

It is fair to say that the display of logboats has long presented a challenge to museums and many of the examples recovered in the 19th century, gnarled, shrunken and barely recognisable as boats at all, have been displayed with little context and minimal information. Fortunately, the only other surviving logboat from the Tay Estuary, Errol 2 (Fig 151), is an exception. While it appears to have been on display in Dundee almost continuously since it was found in 1895 (Donald pers comm), it is reassuring that at the time of writing, following a major refurbishment, it is awaiting redisplay in The McManus, Dundee's Art Gallery and Museum. Furthermore, the great success and popularity of the Dover sewn-plank boat display (Chapter 14) is an indication of the extent of public interest in early watercraft. Hopefully the forthcoming display of the Carpow vessel at Perth Museum and Art Gallery will also contribute to a wider appreciation of logboats and what they can tell us about Bronze Age life.

Finally, it was my great pleasure to organise an educational project in August 2009 that involved the manufacture of a 9m-long logboat on the banks of Loch Tay under the instruction of Damian Goodburn, one of the key contributors to this volume. With a team of volunteers, including archaeology students, a 12m-long Douglas Fir log was transformed into a boat over a three-week period, primarily using replica Bronze Age tools and the techniques outlined in Chapter 7. While not of oak, many of the features from the Carpow vessel, such as the footrests and moss caulking, were incorporated in the Loch Tay vessel, which was paddled across the loch in a memorable 20-minute journey to the Scottish Crannog Centre. The reconstruction project validated many of the ideas within this volume. In addition, the experience of using replica bronze axes, adzes, chisels and gouges offered the team insight into and appreciation of the skill and ingenuity of the original boat-builders that would be very difficult to achieve in any other way. So, in conclusion, and to address Laing's deprecating opening statement, the aim of this volume is to document the skill and proficiency of the craftsmen who manufactured the Carpow boat, and to suggest how, and why, it was made and used all those years ago.

DAVID LEWIS STRACHAN
Perth
June 2010

# Acknowledgements

The project, from discovery in 2001 to the planned date for display in Perth in late 2011, will have taken a decade and has proved challenging, rewarding and memorable in equal measures. Understandably there are many people to whom I am indebted for their contributions towards bringing this publication to fruition.

A partnership project from the outset, the work could never have taken place without the funding partners – Perth and Kinross Heritage Trust (PKHT) and Historic Scotland (HS) – who jointly funded the field work, and the in-kind contributions from the National Museums of Scotland (NMS) and Perth Museum and Art Gallery (PMAG), who both contributed staff during both the excavation and conservation process. In addition, expertise from the project's contracted partners, CFA Archaeology (CFA) and Moorings & Marine Services (MMS) was essential to the success of the venture.

Particular thanks are due to the excavation and recovery team. The project was difficult in many respects and often involved short, intense bursts of activity in very arduous circumstances. The archaeological team from PKHT – Sarah Winlow, Lindsay Farquharson and Steven Timoney – were competently supported by CFA Archaeology Ltd, with Chris O'Connell and Alasdair Curtis under the able supervision of Bruce Glendinning, and with Mike Cressey and Len McKinney conducting the palaeoenvironmental study. Jim Ferguson, Donny Macleod and Scott Macleod of Moorings & Marine Services provided invaluable expertise of submarine and inter-tidal logistics, and with local knowledge of the Tay Estuary engineered the floating and lifting of the vessel under the supervision of the author as Project Manager. From the initial evaluation work, a team of conservators and museum staff worked alongside the excavation team on site: Theo Skinner, Alison Sheridan, Jane Clark and Colleen Healey (NMS) and Mark Hall and Fiona MacKenzie (PMAG). In addition, the NMS contributed the video recording of the project, for use in interpretation and display, by Circa Media of Edinburgh. Thanks are also due to volunteers Scott McGuckin, Keith Emerson, Ricky Blake and student Jake Streatfield-James who were involved in various stages of the operation, and to David Dawson of KOREC Group for his digital survey work. I am also indebted to the owners of Carpow Bank, the Millar brothers of Jamesfield Farm, who gave the permission to excavate.

The task of publication has proved an equally epic adventure, and once again I am indebted to the funders – PKHT, HS and the Society of Antiquaries of Scotland (SAS) – and to Philip Robertson and Noel Fojut (HS) and Erin Osborne-Martin (SAS) in particular. I would like to thank all of the contributors to the publication and the illustrators Leeanne Whitelaw (CFA) and David Hogg. Thanks are also due to Andrew Driver for his AutoCad model of the boat, and to Sarah Winlow and Steven Timoney (PKHT) and Sara Ann Kelly, Local Studies Librarian with the A K Bell Library, Perth, for their help with the preparation of this text.

I am extremely grateful to Bob Mowat (RCAHMS), Pete Clark (Canterbury Archaeological Trust), Professor Colin Martin, Damian Goodburn and, in particular, Professor Seán McGrail for numerous and invaluable discussions on various aspects of early boat building and the study of Carpow. Finally, the opportunity to carry out this project has been possible only through the backing of the Executive Committee of Perth and Kinross Heritage Trust, and my gratitude is expressed to Sue Hendry, the present Chairman, and in particular to the Reverend Fergus Harris, who was Chairman throughout much of the project, and whose continual encouragement and support is always very much welcome.

# List of contributors

MICHAEL BROWNE
British Geological Survey
Murchison House
West Mains Road
Edinburgh

PETER CLARK
Canterbury Archaeological Trust
92a Broad Street
Canterbury
Kent

DR MIKE CRESSEY
CFA Archaeology Ltd
The Old Engine House
Eskmills Park
Musselburgh
East Lothian

PROFESSOR GORDON COOK
SUERC Radiocarbon Dating Laboratory
SUERC
Scottish Enterprise Technology Park
East Kilbride

TREVOR COWIE
Department of Archaeology
National Museums Scotland
Chambers Street
Edinburgh

DR ANNE CRONE
AOC Archaeology Group
Edgefield Industrial Estate
Edgefield Road
Loanhead
Midlothian

DR SUE DAWSON
Geography
School of Social and Environmental Sciences
University of Dundee
Perth Road
Dundee

DR DAMIAN GOODBURN
The Cottage
Tonge Corner
Sittingbourne
Kent

MARK HALL
Perth Museum and Art Gallery
George Street
Perth

SEÁN McGRAIL
Professor Emeritus, University of Oxford
Bridge Cottage
Chilmark
Salisbury

DR PAULA MILBURN
Archaeology Scotland
c/o RCAHMS
John Sinclair House
16 Bernard Terrace
Edinburgh

ROBERT MOWAT
RCAHMS
John Sinclair House
16 Bernard Terrace
Edinburgh

DR ROB SANDS
School of Archaeology
University College Dublin
Belfield Campus
Dublin

DR THEO SKINNER
Conservator, Marine and Wetland Archaeology (now retired)
Department of Conservation and Analytical Research
National Museums Scotland
West Granton Road
Edinburgh

DAVID STRACHAN
Perth and Kinross Heritage Trust
4 York Place
Perth

DR STEVEN TIMONEY
Perth and Kinross Heritage Trust
4 York Place
Perth

DR RICHARD TIPPING
School of Biological and Environmental Sciences
University of Stirling
Stirling

SARAH WINLOW
Perth and Kinross Heritage Trust
4 York Place
Perth

# List of figures

## Chapter 13



## Chapter 14



## Appendix I

# List of tables

# Note

Perth and Kinross Council provided the Ordnance Survey-derived mapping included in this publication under licence from Ordnance Survey in order to fulfil its public function to interpret and promote the archaeology of the area. Persons viewing this mapping should contact Ordnance Survey copyright for advice where they wish to licence Ordnance Survey mapping for their own use.

# Chapter 1

# An introduction to logboats

SEÁN McGRAIL

## 1.1 Background

The serious study of logboats began over 80 years ago, in September 1925, when Sir Cyril Fox, then Director of the National Museum in Cardiff, examined a logboat recovered from Llyn Llangorse, Brecon. This led him to seek information about other similar boats, and three months later he was able to present a paper to the Society of Antiquaries of London on this Llangorse boat, together with 'notes on the chronology, typology & distribution of monoxylous craft in England and Wales'. 'Monoxylous' is the Greek-derived word for a boat made from one piece of wood. Another term Cyril Fox used in his paper was 'dugout canoe'. Rather than either of those terms, I prefer 'logboat', since to my mind that word more aptly describes a vessel made from a single tree: moreover, it is similar to the corresponding terms in the German and Scandinavian languages.

An expanded version of Fox's paper was subsequently published in *The Antiquaries Journal* (Fox 1926): it consisted of an account of the Llyn Llangorse boat; an inventory of 62 other finds from England and Wales; measured drawings of 25 of these boats; a typological classification with five main types identified; and a discussion of the spatial and chronological distribution of those types. Fifty years or so later, when I was Chief Archaeologist at the National Maritime Museum in Greenwich, I began a survey of the logboats of Britain and Ireland. After two seasons of fieldwork I realised that there were so many of these boats that I would have to limit my work to southern Britain, although I had already compiled notes on a number of Irish and Scottish examples. My research was published in 1978

as *Logboats of England and Wales: with comparative material from European and other countries* (McGrail 1978). A gazetteer of Scottish logboats was published in 1996 (Mowat 1996).

## 1.2 Early logboats

Logboats are one of the seven basic types of boat: the other six being boats made of bundles (reeds etc), hides, basketry, bark, pottery and planks. Of these types, only logboats and plank boats have ever been excavated, although vestigial evidence for bundle boats and hide boats has also been found; the other types are known from their recent use in pre-industrialised societies. Logboats have been built around the world, wherever trees of sufficient size grew, say a bole over three metres in length and commensurate breadth. Only in Europe have logboats been studied in any detail, but progress is now being made in Russia, China, Japan and northern America.

The earliest dated logboats – two of them are the world's earliest dated boats – are from Pesse in the Netherlands (Fig 1) and Noyen-sur-Seine in France (Arnold 1996, 30). These boats were fashioned from pine (*Pinus* sp) logs and are radiocarbon dated to the seventh to eighth millennium BC, as soon after the end of the last Ice Age as sizeable trees are believed to have grown in north-west Europe. Subsequently, during the later Mesolithic, European logboats were hewn from lime (*Tilia* sp), alder (*Alnus* sp) and poplar/aspen (*Populus* sp) logs, and, from the late fourth millennium BC onwards, oak (*Quercus* sp) trees were used almost exclusively. The earliest known logboat in Britain is the oak fragment from Catherinefield, Dumfries and

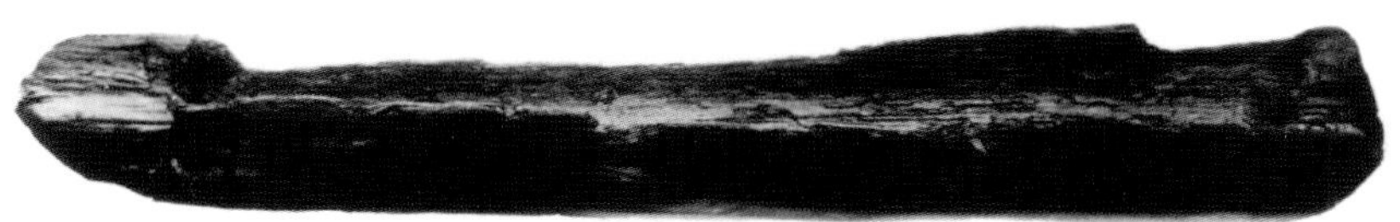

*Figure 1*
The Mesolithic pine logboat from Pesse, the Netherlands (photo: Paul Johnstone)

"

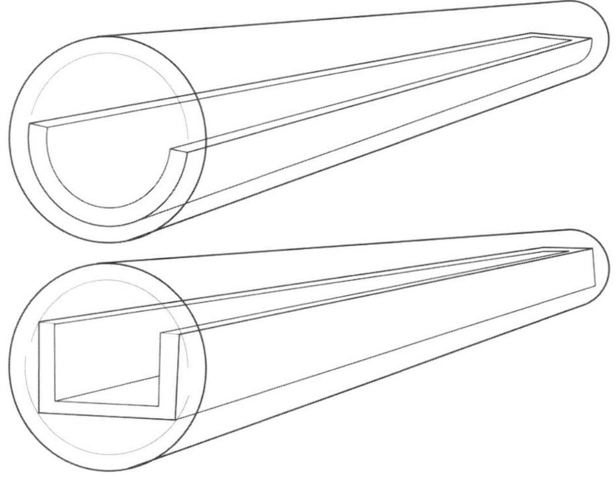

*Figure 2*
Diagram showing logboats within their parent logs: the upper one made from a half-log; the lower, from a whole log (redrawn from an original by the Institute of Archaeology, Oxford)

Galloway, of around 2000 cal BC (SRR-326) (Mowat 1996, 18–20). The latest are late medieval in date, but there are 18th-century Scottish documentary references to their use. In Fox's day, all British logboats were assumed to be prehistoric, ie pre-Roman. Now that a number of logboats from this country have been dated scientifically, we realise that most are of Roman or of medieval date, so a prehistoric logboat such as Carpow is both unusual and most welcome.

### 1.3  Simple logboats

Simple logboats are made by removing bark and sapwood from a log, then hollowing out that log and shaping the ends and the outside. They are thus similar in shape to wooden troughs, coffins, mill-chutes and the like, and when excavated remains are fragmentary it can be difficult to recognise whether they were once a boat or some other hollowed-out artefact.

Stability and freeboard are some measure of a logboat's fitness for purpose. A boat with adequate transverse stability will return to an upright position after being disturbed from the vertical, and the greater a boat's waterline beam (or breadth), the greater her transverse stability. Freeboard is the height of a boat's sides above the waterline and is a measure of reserve of buoyancy. A boat hewn from a log is inevitably narrow and shallow in relation to her length: she is limited in her breadth and depth of hull by the diameter of her

parent log (Fig 2) and thus constrained in her stability and in her freeboard. Such constraints can restrict operational performance unless the parent trees are of exceptional diameter, as are some trees in such regions as the Americas.

### 1.4  Complex logboats

Simple logboats may be turned into complex logboats by adding fittings and using advanced woodworking techniques. For example, freeboard may be increased by adding a plank, or wash-strake, to each side, thus allowing the boat to carry a greater load and to be used in rougher waters. Transverse stability can be improved by increasing a boat's effective waterline breadth in one of three ways:

1. after heat treatment the sides are forced apart (expanded), and ribs added to hold the new shape (Fig 3);
2. by pairing two boats side-by-side (Fig 4);

*Figure 3*
Inserting temporary framing into a hollowed log made malleable by heat: an early stage in the expansion of an aspen (*Populus tremulens*) logboat in Satakunta, Finland. The photograph was taken by Eino Nikkilä in 1935 (© National Museum of Finland)

Figure 4
Paired logboats from Sumuinmäki, Pieksämäki, Finland, fitted with stabilising timbers at the waterline (after Itkonen, T I, 1941.
'Suomen Ruuhet' Kansatieteellinen Arkisto, 5.1)

3. by adding stabilising timbers at the waterline, either alongside the boat (Fig 4) or boomed out on outriggers.

Each of these modifications has been used somewhere in the world during recent centuries. In north-west Europe, although pairing two logboats may have been undertaken in later prehistory, early evidence for stabilising timbers has not yet been excavated, and there is no evidence for log expansion until medieval times. Furthermore, outriggers are known only in the Indian and South Pacific Oceans.

## 1.5 Hasholme and Carpow

When logboats are excavated it is usually found that the fittings added to the hull to improve the boat's performance are no longer there. What do survive, however, are holes bored into the hull through which these fittings had formerly been fastened. The post-excavation work on the Carpow boat has included a search for such holes, followed by attempts to deduce what fittings had been fastened there when she was a working boat. Some of this speculation may be answered by examining complex logboats in use today in India, South East Asia and South America.

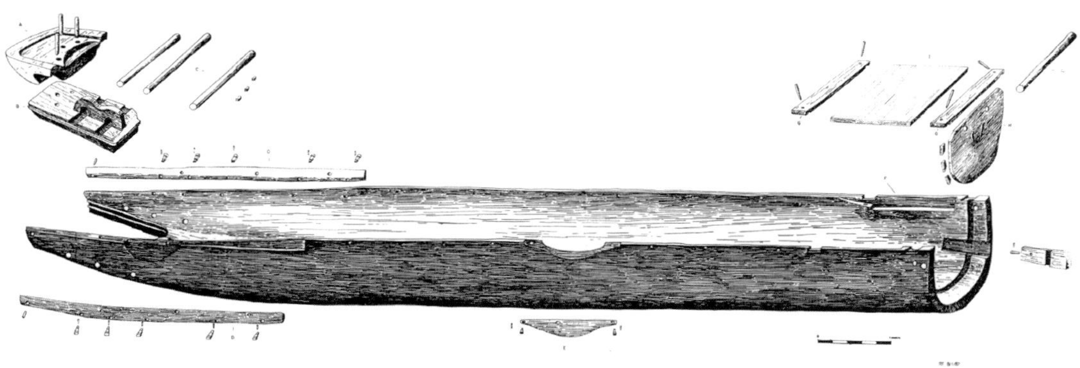

Figure 5
Exploded reconstruction drawing of the Hasholme logboat (drawing: Institute of Archaeology, Oxford)

*Figure 6*
View of the Hasholme logboat during excavation: loose timbers, including the two-part bow, have been lifted but the transom board remains within its groove (© Seán McGrail)

But we are fortunate here in Britain that we also have the Iron Age logboat from Hasholme in eastern Yorkshire (Millett & McGrail 1987). This large boat was excavated in 1984 from a field, now below sea level, that had formerly been a creek of the Humber Estuary. She measures 12.78m in length, with a 1.4m maximum beam and 1.25m maximum height, so she is somewhat larger than the Carpow boat, but she is much younger, being dated by dendrochronology to around 300 BC. As you can see on Fig 5, almost the entire length, breadth and depth of the Hasholme boat survived, as did several of the fittings that had been added to the main hull.

Like the Carpow boat, the Hasholme boat had a fitted transom at the stern (Fig 6). Her parent oak was at least 300 years old when felled, and, by that age, such old trees have developed heart rot at their butt (lower) end. Thus a watertight stern could not be hewn out of the parent log of either of these boats.

Instead, a groove was worked around the inside of the log and a transom board inserted and wedged within that groove, then caulked with moss. The Hasholme transom was further held in position by a beam-tie aft and a capping tie above: these ties forced the transom down into its groove.

Fortunately for the Carpow folk, heart rot had not yet reached the upper end of their log when it was felled, so that boat has an integral bow. The Hasholme logboat, on the other hand, had to have a two-part bow fastened to the main hull. These two bow elements were excavated some distance from the hull: they had probably become detached whilst the boat was underway and that could be why she sank.

Grooves to take inserted transoms have been found at the stern of several other British logboats, but the Carpow and Hasholme boats are the only two from which the transom board itself survives. The oldest known British logboat fitted for a transom was until recently the Appleby boat from northern Lincolnshire (McGrail 1978, 147–9), dated *c* 1320 cal BC (Q-80), only two or three centuries earlier than the Carpow boat, however, the Croft-na-Caber vessel, from Loch Tay, would appear to predate Appleby by a similar amount (Chapter 9, p 130). The youngest transom logboat is Errol 2, about to be redisplayed in the McManus Galleries and Museum, Dundee: she is dated *c* 550 cal AD (Q-3121 and Q-3141) (Mowat 1996, 28–30). From that time onwards few large logboats appear to have been built in Britain. This change may have been because no more large oaks survived, or it may have been because, by that time, plank boats had become more widely used on inland waters. The shorter, therefore younger, trees that continued to be used for logboats did not have heart rot and therefore logboats made from them did not need transoms.

A notable feature of the Carpow boat is that she appears to have been fitted with a 'dwarf' transom aft of her main transom. This may have been inserted to stem the flow of water that could have swept through the main transom when this boat had, on occasions, to be paddled stern-first: for example, while manoeuvring within a narrow river (Chapter 8, p 122). Boats of this length (*c* 9–10m) would not have been the most convenient to use in narrow estuary creeks and tributary rivers. Tall oak trees may have been chosen, however, so that boats built from them would become a symbol of the status of some important person. The oculi on the bow of the Hasholme boat and the decorative, possibly anthropomorphic, embellishment of her transom stern give support to this possibility (Fig 6).

Possibly inspired by a sixth-century BC model logboat with warrior crew from Roos Carr in the Humber region (Fig 7), some people have argued that large prehistoric logboats such as the one from Carpow were 'boats of war'. Possibly they were so used at times, but they also had great potential as cargo carriers, and surely this was their major role. It is relevant in this context to note that, on her last

*Figure 7*

A wooden model from Roos Carr, East Yorkshire, recently reassembled for display in the Hull and East Riding Museum. It is believed to represent a logboat with warrior crew. The bow, to the right of the model, resembles the 'animal-head' bow of the Loch Arthur 1 logboat, now in the National Museum of Scotland, Edinburgh and dated 75 cal BC (SRR–403) (Mowat 1996, 52–4). The Roos Carr model boat's bow was originally fitted with quartz 'eyes' (© Hull and East Riding Museum, Hull Museums)

voyage, the Hasholme boat carried beef joints and baulks of timber.

Other features of the Hasholme boat include:

1. thickness-gauges: before the Hasholme log was hollowed, eight 25mm-diameter holes had been bored into what was to be the lower part of the hull, to a depth equivalent to the required bottom thickness. The log was then rolled over through 180 degrees for hollowing. When the boat-builders encountered these holes they stopped work with their axes and adzes. Each hole was then filled with a wooden plug to make the boat watertight;

2. wash-strakes: a wash-strake was found on the starboard bow of the Hasholme boat; the corresponding port wash-strake had not survived. Wash-strakes were needed at the bow of this boat to level off the sheerline (upper edge of sides) where the taper of the parent log resulted in inadequate freeboard. Tree-nails that fastened the wash-strakes to the hull were each locked by a wooden key or 'cotter' (Fig 8). These keys did not survive but they left pressure marks around fastening holes through the hull. Marks on the Carpow boat, associated with holes through the boat's sides (Chapter 5, pp 65–9), are similar to these Hasholme marks. If these are indeed evidence for cotters, this will be the earliest known use of this technique.

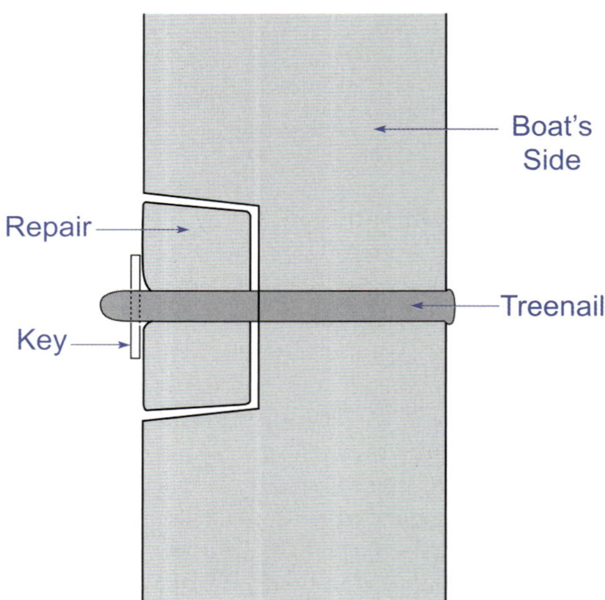



*Figure 8*
The tree-nail fastening a repair to the Hasholme logboat was locked in position by a wooden key or cotter through a hole near the inboard end of the nail. Similar key-locked tree-nails were used to fasten wash-strakes to the boat's port and starboard bows (redrawn from an original by the Institute of Archaeology, Oxford)

Other fittings did not survive on the Hasholme boat, but left vestigial traces.

1. The fitting that had formerly rested across the two ledges near the stern. We deduced that this had been a steering platform from which the helmsmen could see over the paddlers' heads or over the cargo;

2. A series of 40mm-diameter holes bored through the sides *c* 80mm down from the top edge of the hull, with no associated fittings. These holes were *c* 1m apart, and were paired, port and starboard. These proved difficult to interpret. They were too high on the hull to have been for stabilising timbers at the waterline, and unlikely to have been for wash-strakes (the boat has short wash-strakes further forward) or for pairing this boat with another, as such a pair would be very unwieldy. It may be, however, that they were used during construction. Since Hasholme's parent log had heart rot throughout its length, it would have tended to open out as it was being hollowed. Ropes laced through these holes could have held the sides of the boat together until the transom stern and the two bow elements had been fastened in position. An alternative possibility is that these holes were where covers were fastened to the boat to keep cargo dry; or it may be the boat could have been manhandled on the strand using wooden poles passed transversely across the boat, through opposing holes. As frequently happens in archaeology, there is no definitive answer to this question, rather a number of possibilities.

You will now appreciate that David Strachan's team has had much to do since the Carpow boat was excavated, including the interpretation of enigmatic features and vestigial remains on that boat. Were thickness-gauges used in her construction? Were transverse timbers fitted to hold her transom in place? Did she have wash-strakes to compensate for low freeboard? Or would such wash-strakes have made paddling difficult? It is unlikely that she had been expanded because of the thickness of the wood, but could she have been fitted with stabilisers or been paired with another boat? Or did she have sufficient stability not to need these modifications? These are some of the questions that the Carpow team has been tackling over the last two years, and the answers are to be found in the succeeding chapters of this volume.

## 1.6 Further research

### The boat's performance

It has proved possible to reconstruct the full shape and structure of the Carpow logboat, allowing some

*Figure 9*
A 1:10 scale reconstruction model of the Hasholme logboat (© the Institute of Archaeology, Oxford)

aspects of the performance of the original boat to be estimated (Appendix II). For the Hasholme boat we built a small-scale model of such a reconstruction (Fig 9), and this helped us to produce performance figures. In one of her roles, when carrying *c* 3.5 tonnes of cargo, she would have been afloat in *c* 600mm of water so that, in addition to voyages within the Humber Estuary, the Hasholme boat could have been paddled inland up the Humber's several tributary rivers. In another role, with two steersmen and a crew of two paddlers at each of nine stations, she would probably have achieved three knots, possibly five knots in a short burst.

### Comparative studies

Lanting (2000, 628 and 630) has noted that, up to 1998, of the 650 to 700 logboat finds that have been noted in British and Irish journals and newspapers, only 135 have been scientifically dated: 125 by radiocarbon; and ten by dendrochronology. Of the 154 logboats listed in Mowat's catalogue of Scottish logboats, only seven have been dated by radiocarbon (1996, 129), and none has a dendrochronological date. We shall not be able to appreciate the full importance of the Carpow boat until many other logboats have been dated scientifically. Furthermore, until such dates are available, it will not be possible to investigate regional groupings, recognise changes in logboat building over time, or establish links with contemporary plank boats.

It is important for all of us to remember that logboats are not just any old piece of wood: their parent tree was chosen by an experienced woodsman; they were built by skilled craftsmen; and they were used by specialist boatmen (Chapters 7 and 13 *passim*). Nor are logboats in some sense inferior to planked boats. Bangladesh boat-builders build both logboats and plank boats:

the job the boat is to undertake, and the environment in which it will be used, determine which is built (Greenhill 1971). Logboats had an important role in British economic and social life from Mesolithic times until the 18th century AD. They were used to catch fish, to hunt fowl and to gather reeds. Furthermore, goods, animals and people would have been ferried along and across lakes, rivers and estuaries, and within natural harbours and sheltered archipelagos, in paddle-propelled logboats, using the ebb and flow of the tides to advantage wherever possible.

## 1.7 Conservation, publication and display

Of the 14 Tayside logboats noted by Mowat (1996), only one, Errol 2, was on display during his survey. Two were in museum reserve collections, and three were still underwater. Of the other eight, there was no trace. During my logboat survey in the mid-1970s I found that only eight out of 179 logboats were on display in museums in southern Britain. A further 72 were in reserve collections, but no trace could be found of the other 99 (McGrail 1978). Clearly logboats have proved to be a problem for some museums: they are large, heavy and an awkward shape, and are easily fragmented if mishandled. They require special environmental conditions even after they have been conserved. If not conserved, they may simply disintegrate or, at best, droop until it becomes impossible for the visitor to recognise the handsome shape of the original boat. In the past, some museum logboats have become unwanted, in contrast to the care formerly expended on them while they were being built and during their working lives.

In comparison with earlier finds, the Carpow boat has had, and continues to have, numerous advantages. This boat was carefully assessed and documented from the time she was discovered. She was left, as found, where she had been deposited 3,000 years earlier, until it became clear that, if left any longer in that high energy environment she would rapidly deteriorate or be swept away. Perth and Kinross Heritage Trust, with assistance from several other bodies, excavated her from that difficult inter-tidal site that could only be worked during daylight at very low water. Much of her length had to be cleared of estuarine deposits before she could be cleaned and documented. After being freed from her estuarine matrix, she was floated in the Tay and towed to a safe berth among reeds where she was moored overnight. Subsequently she was housed in the National Museum's conservation laboratories at Granton, Edinburgh, where she was further cleaned and recorded in great detail: her array of boat-building features are now fully documented.

The signs are now favourable for this boat. Deposited 3,000 years ago in the Tay Estuary after a lifetime of use within that river's catchment area, she has now found a new berth. After conservation by the National Museums of Scotland and publication by Perth and Kinross Heritage Trust she will be brought to Perth Museum and Art Gallery to be seen and admired by countless people. In this way the principle aims of the project will be achieved: excavation, documentation, conservation, publication and public display.

# Chapter 2

# Glossary

*aftmost*
farthest aft; near the stern of a boat.

*amidships*
in or towards the middle part of a boat.

*beam-tie*
a length of wood used to fasten or secure; in terms of logboats, to hold together the two sides of the vessel and prevent them opening out or drooping in.

*bilge*
that part of a boat's hull between the sides and the bottom; also bilge water, used to describe water collecting in bottom of boat.

*bole*
the trunk of a tree.

*bow*
foremost part of a boat.

*buttresses*
above ground swelling of a tree bole; the beginning of the root system.

*caulking*
material inserted between two timbers in order to make the joint watertight.

*diatom*
microscopic unicellular algae which live in water and are characterised by their outer silica shell.

*displacement*
the weight or volume of water a boat displaces when afloat.

*facet*
the general shape, size and form of a surface impression caused by a blow with an edged tool such as an axe, adze or chisel.

*freeboard*
the vertical distance between the top of the hull sides (sheerline) and the water line; usually measured near amidships.

*grain*
the general direction of the timber fibres relative to the main axis of the tree.

*grommets*
loops of withy, sinew or other organic material that secure an oar to the sheerline of a vessel.

*hull*
the body of the boat, independent of fittings.

*knot*
a) circular whorl of wood grain showing a section through a tree branch embedded in the bole due to natural growth; b) a measure of boat's speed: one nautical mile per hour.

*lacustrine*
of, or inhabiting on, a lake.

*medullary rays*
linear strands of cells running out from the centre of a tree to the circumference (see Fig 11).

*monoxylous*
a Greek-derived word for a boat made from one piece of wood.

*oar ports*
aperture through the side of a boat through which an oar is used.

*oculus*
a structure or marking resembling an eye, usually on each side of a boat's bow (plural oculi).

*parent log or parent tree*
the log (or tree) from which a logboat, or other object, was made.

*pedunculate oak*
a species of oak (*Quercus robur*) that supports its acorns on small stalks, native to Britain and north-west Europe.

*PEG*
polyethylene glycol; a water-soluble wax used to strengthen ancient timbers by replacing lost cellulose.

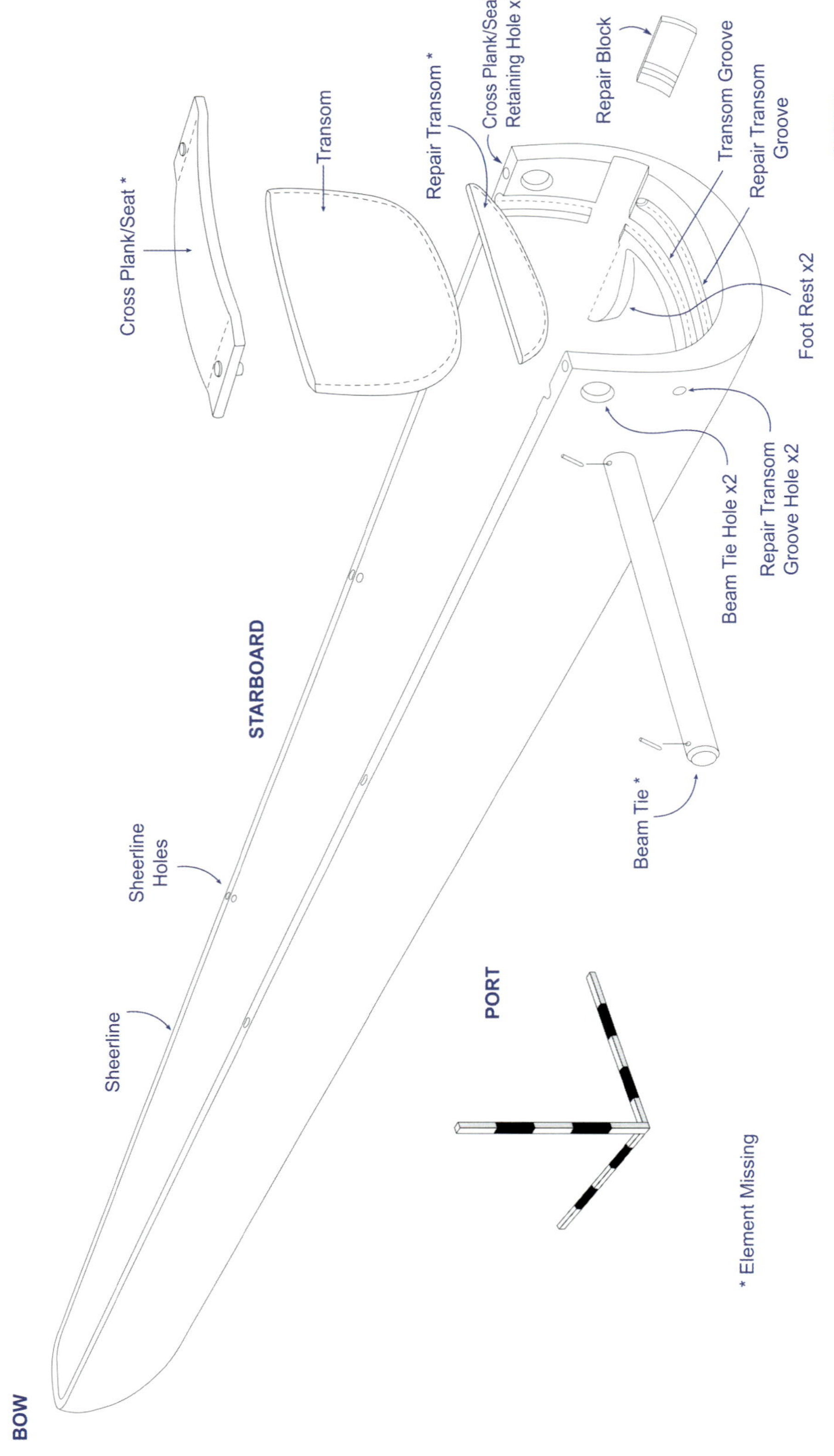


*Figure 10*

An exploded reconstruction of the Carpow logboat, illustrated as complete, showing the main elements referred to in the text

*port*
the left hand side of a boat when facing forward.

*poling or punting*
to propel a boat by use of a pole from a standing position within the vessel.

*prow*
see bow.

*quanting*
use of a pole to propel with the pole user walking aft along the boat.

*radial splitting*
splitting a log along its medullary rays, producing a timber with a wedge-shaped cross-section (Fig 11).

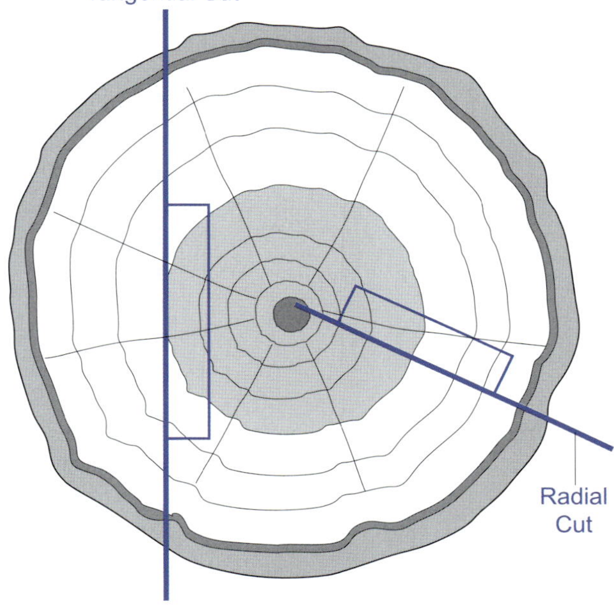


*Figure 11*
A schematic section of a log showing both radial and tangential cut planks. Tree-rings and medullary rays are also depicted

*resin*
a hard, sticky substance secreted by trees and other plants.

*riparian*
of, or inhabiting, the banks of a river.

*round-wood*
generally small stems of wood with a complete cross-section of stem or branch.

*sapwood*
the outer part of a tree bole, just beneath the bark, that consists of living tissue.

*sessile oak*
a species of oak (*Quercus petraea*) that supports its acorns attached directly to the stem. It is native to Britain and north-west Europe.

*sheer*
in the profile of a logboat, the upward curve of the upper edge of the hull towards the bow.

*sheerline*
upper edges of a boat's hull.

*signature of a woodworking tool*
a distinctive pattern of small ridges or striations on a worked surface, created by nicks or dull areas in the blade of a tool (Fig 12).

*starboard*
the right hand side of a boat when facing forwards.

*stern*
after end of a boat.

*strake*
a single plank or course of planks that stretches from bow to stern of a vessel.

*taphonomy*
a term used by archaeologists to describe the processes by which artefacts or materials are deposited into their final position.

*tangential splitting*
splitting a log at right angles to its medullary rays, tangential to its annual growth rings (Fig 11).

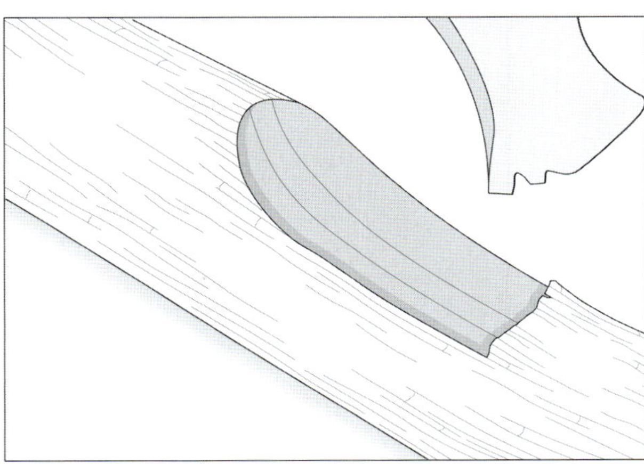

*Figure 12*
An illustration of the signature left by an axe blade on a round-wood

*thickness-gauge holes*
    holes bored to a preset depth into a debarked log which is to be hollowed. The preset depth is the required thickness of the boat's hull.

*thole(pin)*
    a pin projecting upwards from the sheerline of a boat to provide a pivot for an oar. Other pivots are known as: crutch, oarlock/rowlock, and oarport.

*toolmark(s)*
    any mark or group of marks made by a tool used on the surface of a timber.

*transom*
    a transverse board or plank fitted and made watertight, at the end of a logboat, usually at the stern.

*transverse stability*
    measurement of a vessel's ability to right itself when displaced from vertical.

*tree-nail*
    a wooden peg or through fastening, made watertight, used to join two members in boat-building.

*tree-rings/ring pattern*
    the sequence of layers of new wood laid down between the bark and old wood of a tree during each growing season.

*wash-strake*
    a plank fitted to the upper edge of a logboat to keep out spray and water.

*wedge*
    a tapered piece of wood to give gradually increasing pressure when used as a fixing.

*withy*
    tough, thin flexible branches of a tree used, after twisting, to stitch together planks.

**Chapter 3**

# Waterways, geology and the historic landscape

DAVID STRACHAN

with contributions from Michael Browne and Sarah Winlow

## 3.1 The Tay, the Earn and the Firth of Tay

Carpow Bank is a small inter-tidal shelf of sands, gravels and peats on the south bank of the Firth of Tay, where the River Tay and the River Earn flow into the head of the estuary (Fig 13). While the Tay dominates the region, both as a river and an estuary, it is the importance of this confluence that makes the find-spot an appropriate focus for discussion of one aspect of prehistoric transport and communication.

The place-name Tay, as used for the river, strath and loch, was noted by Tacitus as *Taus* in AD 98 and by Ptolemy as *Tava* around AD 150. The name may derive from either a pre-Celtic or Celtic root, such as *ta-* or similar, and may be related to the names Thames and Tyne. It is thought to mean 'silent one' or 'strong one', perhaps aspects of a controlling deity associated with the river, or simply 'flowing' (Watson 1926, 51; Nicolaisen 1976, 244). At 193km in length it is the longest river in Scotland and the sixth longest in the UK, and drains much of the lower region of the Highlands.

The Tay's source is located high on the slopes of Binn Laoigh, which is only *c* 32km from the west coast town of Oban in Argyll and Bute. The river has a variety of names in its upper catchment: for the first few miles the river is known as the River Cononish; then the River Fillan; then the River Dochart until it flows into Loch Tay at Killin. The River Tay proper emerges from Loch Tay at Kenmore in Highland Perthshire and flows through Strathtay and Strathmore to Perth and on to the Firth of Tay and the North Sea, some 190km to the east of its source. The main tributaries of the Tay before Perth are the Tummel, the Isla and the Almond. The latter confluence is the point to which the Tay is tidal, and was undoubtedly a consideration in the location of the Roman fort at Bertha (Woolliscroft & Hoffmann 2006, 147).

The Tay has the largest catchment in Scotland at approximately 6,200km² (followed by the Tweed and the Spey at 5,000km² and 3,000km² respectively). In addition, and arguably most importantly in terms of the Firth of Tay, it has the largest freshwater discharge

of all rivers in the UK with an average of 170m³/s. The maximum recorded flow of 2,269m³/s was recorded on 17 January 1993, when the river rose 6.48m above its usual level at Perth, and caused extensive flooding in the city. The highest recorded flood at Perth occurred in 1814, when the river rose 7m above the usual level, partly caused by a blockage of ice under Smeaton's Bridge. Other severe flood events occurred in 1210 and 1648 when earlier bridges over the Tay at Perth were destroyed (Bowler 2004).

The River Earn leaves Loch Earn at St Fillans and runs east through Strathearn, then east and south, meandering through lower Strathearn with large oxbows before joining the River Tay at Carpow. The place-name Earn, as used for the river, strath and loch, is first recorded as *Eirenn* in *c* AD 889, *Sradeern* in 1164 x 1184, *Eryn* in 1219–20, and as *Stratherne* in 1317. The traditional source is *Erin*, an ancient name linking a mythical goddess-queen with the land itself, and the name *Eireann* (Old Gaelic) 'of Erin' in this context has been taken as evidence of an eastwards expansion by the Scots from Dalriada in the sixth and seventh centuries AD (Watson 1926, 228; Watson 2002, 183; Nicolaisen 1976, 241). The source is more likely to be a pre-Celtic or Celtic river name, from a root form *ar-* indicating flowing water, as found in other river names, such as Deveron, and common in parts of France (McNiven pers comm).

The River Earn is commonly, though erroneously, called a tributary of the Tay. In fact the confluence occurs at the head of the Tay Estuary, well below the high tide limit of the River Tay. The Earn is tidal to Kirkton of Mailer, to the west of Bridge of Earn, a distance of 15km from the confluence as the river flows or 10km as the crow flies. In total, the river is 74km long and today is relatively fast flowing with numerous shoals, navigable by only the smallest of vessels. Comparison between the current course of the river and its route on the Ordnance Survey (OS) first edition maps (*c* 1860) reveals the dynamic nature of this stretch of river through the frequency of large meanders, oxbow lakes and islands, only some of which are visible today (Fig 15). In the section

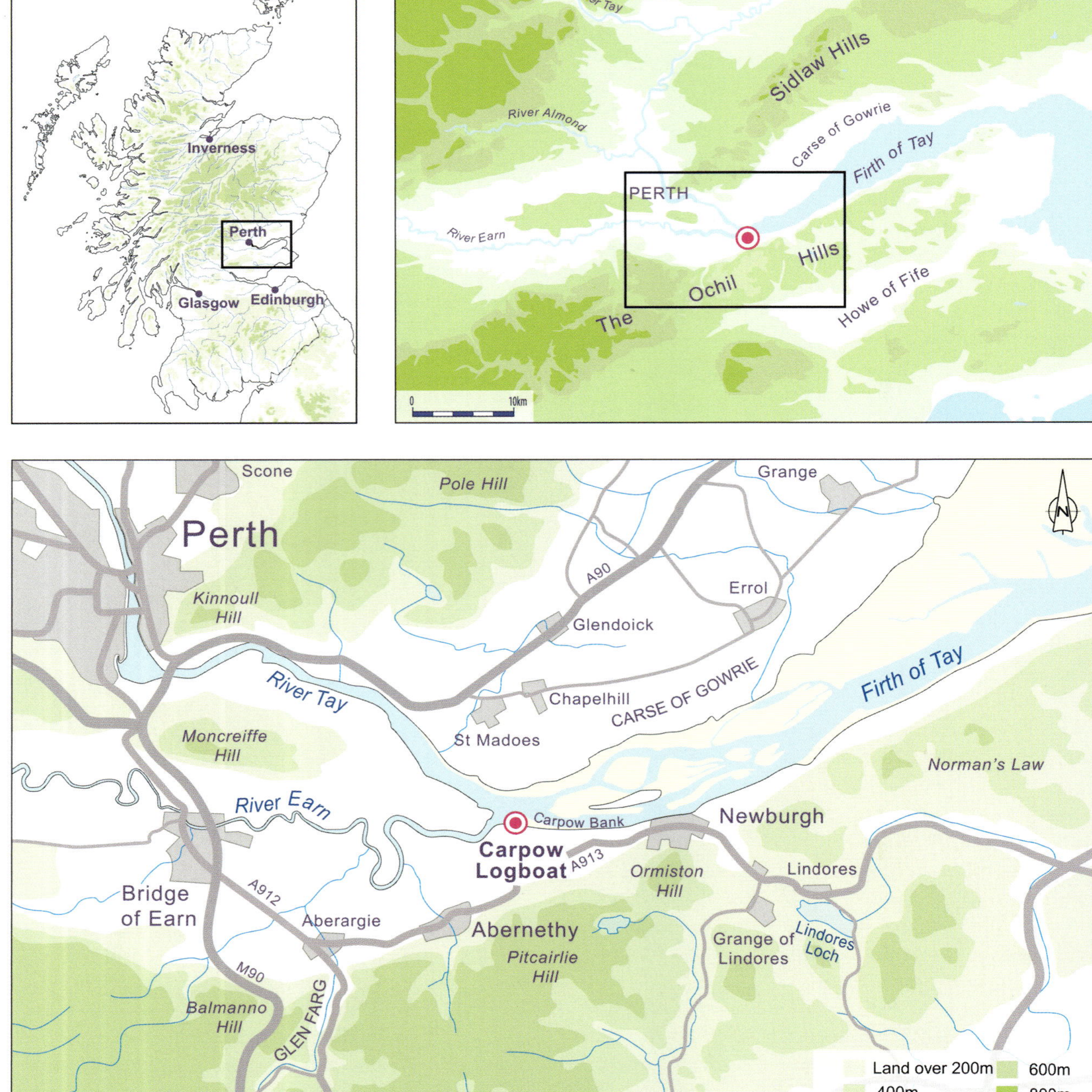


*Figure 13*

Location maps for Carpow Bank on the Tay Estuary (© Crown copyright and database right (2009). All rights reserved. Ordnance Survey Licence number 100016971)

between Forteviot Bridge and Kirkton of Mailer, for example, the river has changed course in four places since the mid-19th century alone, losing named features such as Upper Island and Middle Island through the improvement of pasture by embankment and drainage. The Earn is still prone to flooding and the riverbanks are regularly breeched after periods of heavy rainfall, allowing a glimpse of the extent of

*Figure 14*
An aerial view of the estuary taken at low tide with the north Fife coast on the right and the Carse of Gowrie on the left.
Mugdrum Island and numerous inter-tidal banks are visible in the foreground with the larger flats of Carthagena Bank beyond
(photo: David Strachan © Perth and Kinross Heritage Trust)

*Figure 15*
An aerial view of lower Strathearn and the confluence with the Tay. In the foreground is Fittie Haugh, a meander of the Earn, with
the River Tay and the Carse of Gowrie beyond (photo: David Strachan © Perth and Kinross Heritage Trust)

former flood plains. In general terms, however, it is a smaller lowland river in comparison with the broad and shallow, fast-flowing Tay.

The Firth of Tay flows 35km from Carpow to the mouth of the estuary into the North Sea between Buddon Ness, Angus and Tentsmuir Point in north-east Fife. From the head of the estuary at Carpow Bank, the estuary gradually broadens to incorporate Mugdrum Island and its related sandbanks, at this point measuring a uniform width of around 1.6km. Beyond Errol, the Firth broadens significantly, incorporating Carthagena Bank and Dog Bank, to a maximum internal width of $c$ 5km between Kingoodie, to the west of Dundee, and Balmerino on the north Fife coast (Fig 14). At the Tayport Narrows, to the south of Dundee, the estuary closes to a minimum width of 1.3km between Broughty Ferry and Tayport. The total area of the estuary is 122km²; of which around 57km² (or 47%) is inter-tidal (Buck 1993). There is one significant island in the estuary, Mugdrum Island, opposite Newburgh, Fife, with the North Deep and South Deep channels

running around its marshy banks. Mugdrum has a number of inter-tidal banks attached to it: Abernethy Bank, Wonder Bank and Reckit Lady Bank to the north-west, west and south respectively, and The Turk, to the east. In addition, Kerewhip Bank to the north is separated by another small channel (Fig 14). To the east of Mugdrum are a number of mud and sandbanks, regularly revealed at low tide, with intriguing and often enigmatic names including Gilderoy Bank, Peesweep Bank, Dispute Bank, McInne's Bank and the dramatic Sure as Death Bank. Beyond this is the extensive Carthagena Bank, off the foreshore to the east of Errol, and the largest of all, Dog Bank, which covers an area of around 17km² and runs from Errol to Dundee. The maximum depth of the estuary is $c$ 30m at the Tayport Narrows. The waters of the Rivers Tay and Earn provide the highest freshwater inflow into an estuary in the UK (Pontin & Reid 1975) and the mean daily discharge of freshwater is 205m³/s, with a recorded maximum of 2,350m³/s (Anderson *et al* 1997). The Firth of Tay was designated a Ramsar site, indicating a wetland of

16

international importance, in 2000, and has a number of other environmental designations, including Site of Special Scientific Interest (SSSI) and Special Protection Area (SPA).

## 3.2 Geology

MICHAEL BROWNE

The bedrock geology of the area is summarised on Fig 16. The logboat site is overshadowed to the south by the Ochil Hills and to the north, across the Tay, by the Sidlaw Hills formed from Early Devonian andesitic lavas. The estuary sits within a rift valley, the result of ancient movements of the North and South Tay faults.

To the north-west, in Highland Perthshire, the Dalradian rocks are deeply trenched by the River Tay. Below Dunkeld the river traverses lower ground of Lower Devonian sedimentary rocks at the western end of Strathmore. The north-east orientation of Strathmore is bounded in the south by the Sidlaw Hills, which are made of both volcanic and sedimentary rocks of the Lower Devonian. To the south-west of the narrow valley transversed by the River Tay at Perth, the Sidlaws are continued by volcanic rocks forming the ridge of Moncreiffe Hill, which overlooks the broader valley of lower Strathearn to the south. The confluence of the River Earn with the Tay occurs at the head of the Firth of Tay north of Abernethy, at Carpow. The low ground of Strathearn is continued north of the Firth of Tay by the extensive lowland known as the Carse of Gowrie. Both areas are underlain by down-faulted Upper Devonian and Carboniferous rocks which are largely concealed by thick Quaternary deposits. North of the Carse of Gowrie is the steep southern fault-face of the Braes of the Carse. South of Strathearn and the Firth of Tay, the ground rises abruptly across a north-facing fault scarp which delimits the Lower Devonian volcanic rocks of the Ochil Hills. The most prominent summit in this

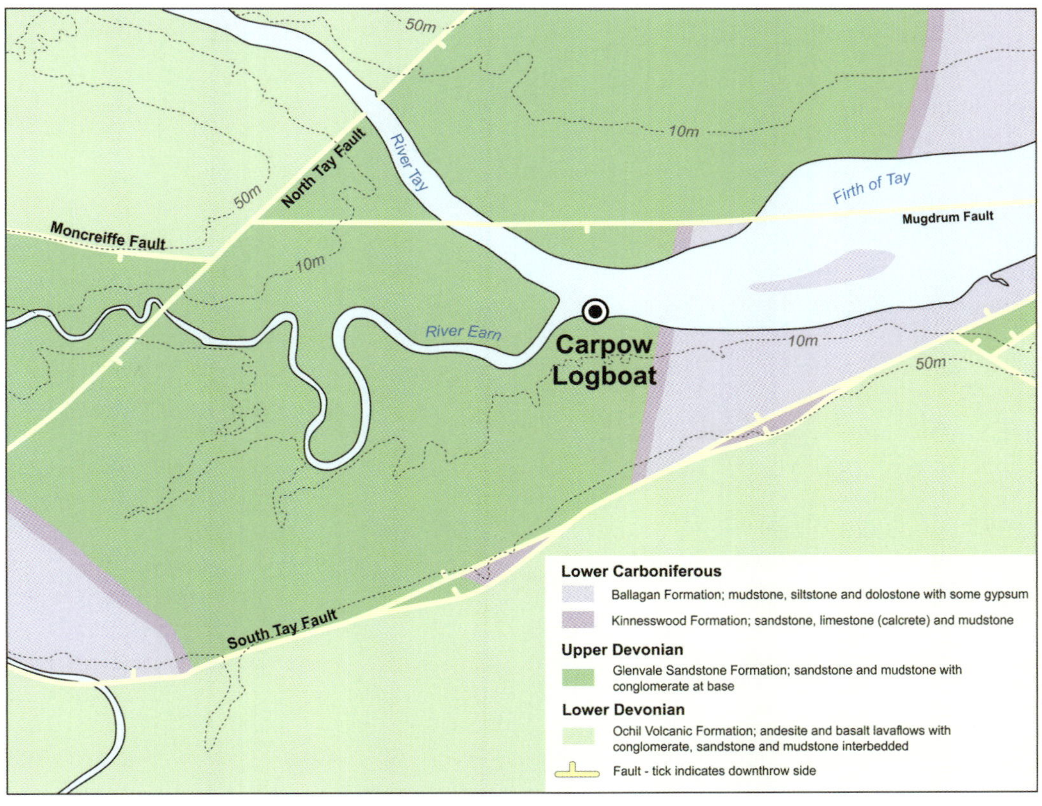


*Figure 16*
Solid geology of the Carpow area (© Crown copyright and database right (2009). All rights reserved. Ordnance Survey Licence number 100016971; Geology copyright: BGS, NERC)

area is Norman's Law in North Fife (285m OD). To the south and east the Ochil Hills are succeeded by the low ground of the Howe of Fife, Stratheden, and the coastal area of Tentsmuir.

Although the Carpow area must have been glaciated many times during the Quaternary, the unconsolidated (drift) deposits preserved locally were formed during and since the last ice age. The main Late Devensian ice sheet advanced from the Highlands and occupied the Earn and Tay valleys about 30,000 years ago forming widespread deposits of glacial till that is commonly found covering the local bedrock. The till (a melange of clay, silt, sand and stone) formed as 'ground moraine' at the sole of the local ice mass. About 20,000 years ago the ice started to retreat, pulling back westwards from its most easterly extent in the North Sea. Glacial melt-waters released by the wasting glacier in the Tay valley laid down the sand and gravel deposits which form the sub-soils in the higher fields around Newburgh (Fig 17) and also laid down the Lindores esker in the Newburgh Gap. They were formed either beside or within stagnant ice. These deposits usually rest on the glacial till.

Final clearance of ice from the Tay and Earn valleys was achieved about 15,000 years ago. At this time, local sea level was over 40m higher than present so that the farms like Jamesfield and Culfargie were largely or wholly submerged. The Tay and Earn valleys were fjords initially with icebergs and then later, as the glaciers withered, only with winter ice. Evidence of these arctic waters is reflected in the presence of red plastic clay in some of the fields which was deposited by melt-water plumes in the fjord. The clay is generally buried by pink sand and silt, and occasionally gravel. These deposits form the subsoil across the middle of Jamesfield farm. They were formed when the local climate was sub-arctic or at least colder than today.

From 15,000 to about 11,000 years ago, local sea level fell from over 40m to about present level. This change in level is marked in places on the valley side by

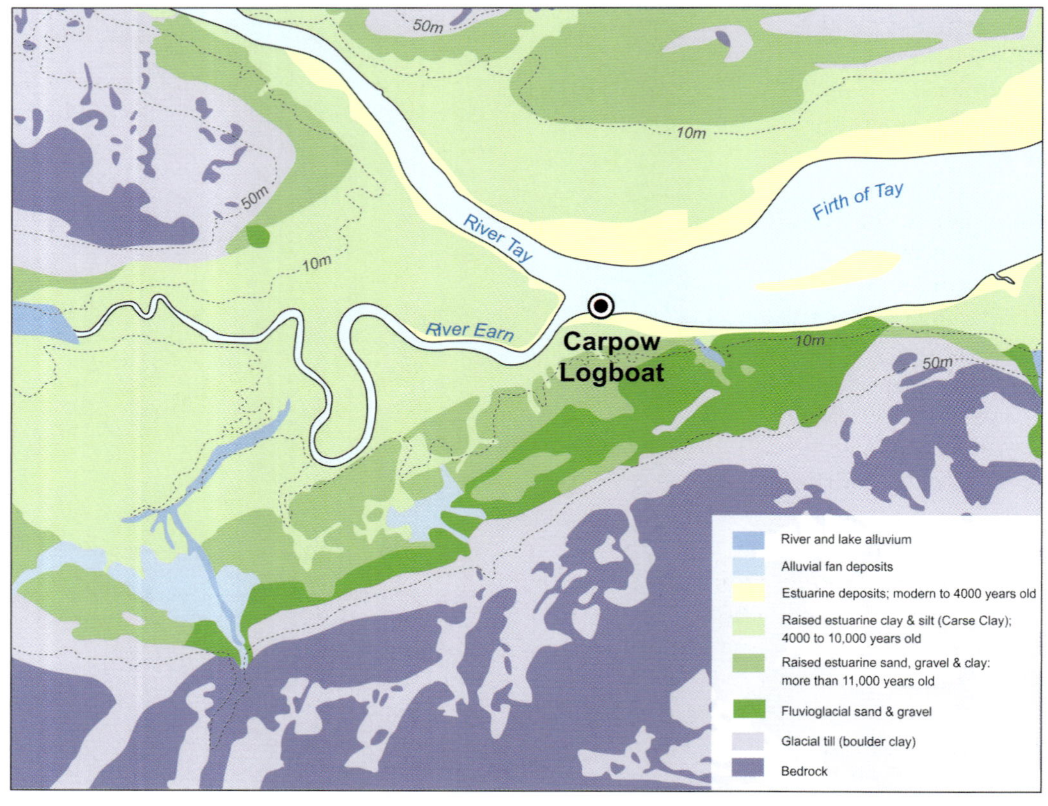



*Figure 17*
Drift Geology of the Carpow area (© Crown copyright and database right (2009). All rights reserved. Ordnance Survey
Licence number 100016971; Geology copyright: BGS, NERC)

the presence of breaks in hill-slope which indicate the positions of former coastlines. For evidence of sea levels lower than present in the general area it is necessary to look a little farther west to Bridge of Earn. This period of lowered levels partly pre-dated another period of fully arctic climatic conditions in Scotland, known as the Loch Lomond Stadial, from about 12,800 to 11,600 years ago. Glaciers again returned to the highlands and parts of the lowlands north of Glasgow and west and north-west of Stirling, but did not reach this area.

Around 12,800 years ago the local sea level was possibly at least 3m below OD, reflected in a sand and gravel filled channel now buried under younger deposits, discovered during the drilling of site investigation boreholes for the M90 road bridge over the River Earn. The estuarine sediments which conceal the channel were deposited during a period of generally rising but also fluctuating sea level. They are usually silts and clays which are split into two units by an intervening bed of peat, the well-known Sub-Carse Peat. Much of the lower ground around Jamesfield and other farms are on the Carse, ancient inter-tidal mudflats that were deposited more than 6,000 years ago. The Carse Clay is seen in an exposure west of Ferryfield of Carpow where the Sub-Carse Peat can be exposed at the base of the sequence only with minimal excavation. The local sea level reached a maximum of about 9m above OD when the Carse Clay was laid down (Chapter 10).

In the last 6,000 years, sea level has fallen to that of present times. There are, however, fields where a lower Carse terrace is preserved above the level of the present, partly reclaimed, inter-tidal flats of the Earn and the Tay. This intermediate level was formed by about 4,000 years ago.

The Soil Survey's mapping of the area recognises several soil types: Alluvium Association (Marine Saltings Series); Stirling Association (Stirling Series of estuarine silts and clays of the 'low raised beach'); and Carpow Association (Carpow Series of the upper terrace deposits mainly of sand and gravel; Carey Series of the upper terrace deposits but mainly of sand and silt). The Stirling Series is the soil type developed on the Carse Clay, and the Carey Series is developed on the raised estuarine sediments which are more than 11,000 years old. The Carpow Series is developed on the glacial melt-water sand and gravel deposits.

### Geological summary

The area was glaciated on a number of occasions in the Quaternary, resulting in significant landscaping in the process. Glacial deposits appear to relate exclusively to the last (Devensian) glaciation when till was laid down extensively. During the retreat of the ice, melt-waters deposited spreads of sands and gravels, mainly near the ice-margins. Marine deposits laid down during the glacial retreat now occur well above present sea level as a consequence of the recovery of the land from glacio-isostatic recovery imposed by the weight of the ice-sheet. A series of shorelines (notably visible along the southern edge of the Strathearn up slope of Aberargie and Abernethy) mark the stages of this recovery. The sea fell below its present level during the period of the re-advance of glaciers in the west of Scotland between 12,800 and 11,600 years ago. Subsequently the sea rose, but a later fall is recorded by a peat layer formed approximately 8,000 years ago (Chapter 10, p 135). A later marine transgression culminated about 6,000 years ago, and the deposits of this episode form the widespread carselands of lower Strathearn and the Carse of Gowrie. Subsequently the sea gradually withdrew to its present level.

The glacial features and deposits of the area are attributed to the last major Devensian ice-sheet, although some of the ice-moulded features probably owe their form to the accumulated effects of more than one glaciation. All of the evidence of glacial striae, erratics and drumlins shows that late-Devensian ice, advancing from the west Highlands, fanned out over east central Scotland, moving eastward across this area, depositing extensive deposits of till. During the subsequent recession, the emergence of high ground confined active glaciers to the major valleys for a further period. In addition, various sediments were deposited during the numerous fluctuations of sea level in late- and post-Glacial times, making the distribution of deposits in the area highly complex (Armstrong *et al* 1985).

### 3.3 Topography and present land use

The general topographic nature of the lower reaches of the Rivers Tay and Earn and the Firth of Tay is one of rolling lowland farmland between 5–50m OD, bounded by the Ochil range to the south and the Gask Ridge and Sidlaws to the north (Fig 18). Whilst these hills are not part of the Highland massif, and are to the south of the Highland Boundary Fault, at 200–300m OD they form solid and occasionally dramatic boundaries to Strathearn and the estuary. Land use in the Carse and lower Strathearn is primarily agricultural with some light industry, while recent decades have seen a slight increase in settlement.

The inter-tidal Carpow Bank is a flat and low lying bank with a ground surface at *c* 0.75m OD and an area of some 24 hectares. Much of the bank is covered with reeds; however, 7.5 hectares are exposed as mud, sands, gravels and peats at low tide. Directly north of the bank, on the opposite side of the estuary, lies the western edge of the Carse of Gowrie, an extensive low-lying area with the Sidlaw Hills some 5km to the north. To the west, a key feature of the landscape is the 'island' of Rhynd, bounded by the Earn to the south and the Tay to the north and topped by Moncreiffe Hill, which rises from around 50m OD to a height of 223m OD (Fig 18). To the immediate south of Carpow Bank, an apron of land rises gently for about 2km to the bottom of the slope of the Ochil range. The overall character of the landscape at the head of the estuary is one of a funnel, opening and stretching to the east with flat expanses of the estuary itself and the Carse of Gowrie contained on the horizon by the Ochils to the south and the Sidlaw Hills to the north. Westwards, the landscape is dominated by Moncreiffe Hill, with the river cliffs of Kinnoull Hill blocking the horizon to the north-west and the Ochil range drawing the eye along rolling landscape towards upper Strathearn.

The immediate land use beyond Carpow Bank was, until recently, for commercial reed beds. The reed beds give way to rich agricultural land, used for arable crops, soft fruits and vegetables. Settlement patterns reflect the agricultural improvements of the 18th and 19th centuries with farmsteads regularly spaced throughout the landscape. The historic settlements of Abernethy and Newburgh, both locations of important medieval religious houses, are situated on the south side of the estuary with the smaller historic settlements of St Madoes and Cottown to the north. Above 50m OD, land use changes swiftly to hill pasture for sheep and cattle and commercial forestry. Again, the pattern of upland settlement, made up of farmsteads and small settlements, is little changed since the 19th century.

### 3.4  Historic land use and river crossings

Prior to canalisation, land reclamation through embankment and drainage, much of the Carse of Gowrie and Strathearn would have been prone to flooding. The estuary fringes would have been characterised by extensive areas of inter-tidal mudflats, reeds, salt marsh and coastal grasses, reminiscent of the estuaries of East Anglia, the Fens and the Humber (Strachan 2004, 61–2). The reclamation of

*Figure 18*
Lower Strathearn taken from the high ground above Newburgh. The River Earn on the left meets with River Tay at the head of the estuary. Moncreiffe Hill (centre), Kinnoull Hill (right) and the Gask Ridge (left) are clearly visible with the snow-covered Highland Boundary Fault line beyond (photo © David Strachan)

*Figure 19*
Pont (extract of Sheet 21) showing the River Earn and Strathearn between Kinkell and Dupplin (reproduced by permission of the National Library of Scotland)

land is thought to have begun in the Carse of Gowrie by medieval monks at Grange (RCAHMS 1994, 2) with, no doubt, other landowners following suit. Improvements have clearly taken place along the lower reaches of the Earn with much of the course of the river embanked and canalised. Prior to these improvements the Earn would have been a wider, shallower river, meandering through and frequently spilling over into meadow floodplains. While insight into the prehistoric character of the estuary and its hinterland can be gathered from palaeoenvironmental studies (Chapters 10 and 11, pp 141–2), and through comparison with similar environments elsewhere, echoes of the prehistoric nature of the area also survive on early maps and charts and in historical accounts.

### Historic cartography and accounts

Historic maps reveal the later histories of the Tay and the Earn and illustrate the degree of 'taming',

through reclamation, formalisation of flood plains and embankment that has taken place over the past 300 to 400 years. They also give insight to the changes that had occurred in the few hundred years before the maps were made, offering a glimpse into the medieval landscape. The earliest detailed maps are by Timothy Pont and date from the late 16th century. The first Pont map covers lower Angus and Perthshire east of the River Tay and the second covers Strathearn. Whilst the estuary is clearly not the subject of the former (Sheet 26), it does indicate some differentiation between the river and the estuary, with the banks of the Tay depicted using parallel straight lines from Perth until 'Rybre' where the depiction changes to horizontal strokes, perhaps suggesting inter-tidal mudflats of a more estuarine character. 'Rybre', which is now known as Tofthill (*c* 900m upstream from Inchyra), is over 3km upstream of where the estuary now begins.

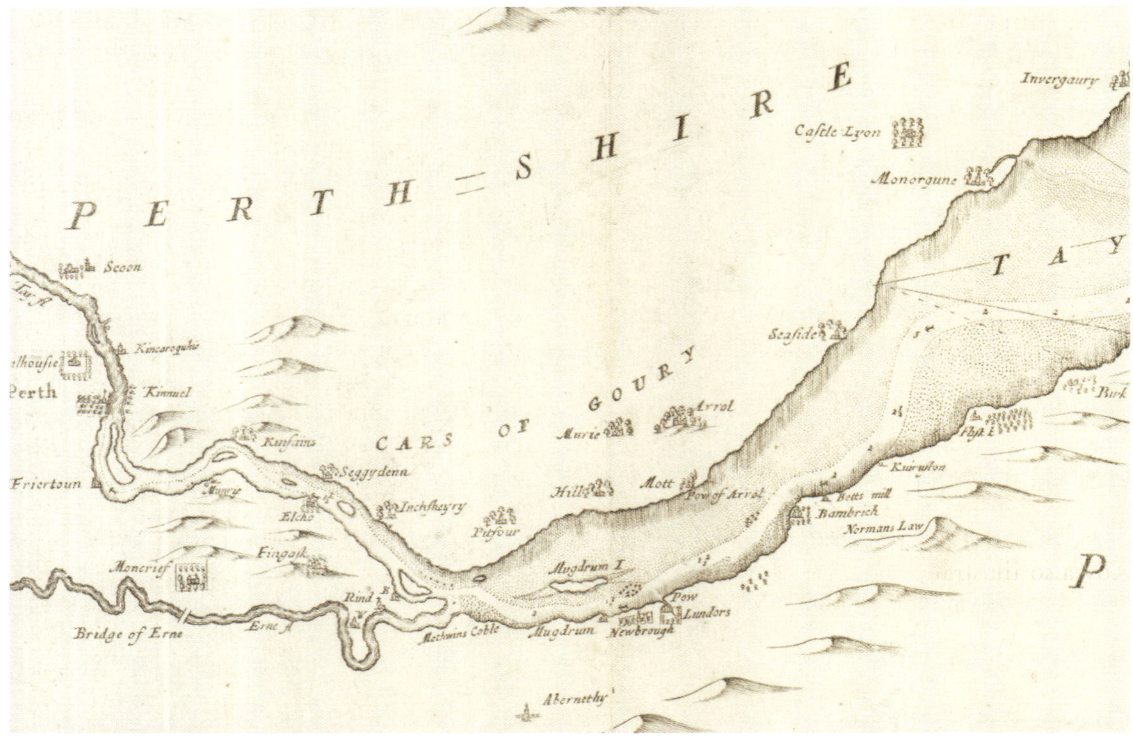

*Figure 20*
An extract of 'The Frith and River of Tay with all the Rocks, Sands, Shoals, &c.' by John Adair (reproduced by permission of the
National Library of Scotland)

The second Pont map (Sheet 21) includes the lower reaches of Strathearn (Fig 19). Though the map does not depict the confluence with the Tay, it does provide useful insight into the past character of the Earn, now a managed embanked river, canalised in places. Pont depicts a wide river of three parts: the first, between Loch Earn and the Meanie Burn to the west of Aberuthven, has no shading. In the second section, between the Meanie Burn and Dupplin, Pont uses sketchy linear strokes and shading; and, for the third stretch, beyond the confluence with the Water of May he uses bolder lines. The middle section is of interest as in comparison with other rivers mapped by Pont, particular attention appears to have been paid to the banks of the Earn, perhaps representing meanders and oxbows, for example, above 'Dalreoch'. Further, the sketchy strokes used on this section are similar to those used on other parts of this map to depict rocky, fast-flowing watercourses; of interest as the Earn is certainly not a tumbling river in this section today. This crude annotation could be interpreted as representing an unpredictable meandering river, whose levels were affected both by the tide and volume of water flowing downstream.

A useful source for both the rivers and the inter-tidal estuary is *The Frith and River of Tay with all the Rocks, Sands, Shoals, &c.* by John Adair (Fig 20). This early bathymetric chart, imprinted in 1703, includes detail of the inter-tidal environment, perhaps differentiating between reeds and salt marsh (indicated by vertical strokes) and inter-tidal mudflats (depicted in faint stipple). Further, Adair differentiates between inter-tidal deposits, clearly marking, for example, the raised mudflat around Mugdrum Island, perhaps indicating the extent of spring tides. Significantly, in addition to Mugdrum Island and Moncreiffe Island (at Perth), Adair shows five substantial islands on the river between Friarton and Newburgh, the largest one of which is at Easter Rhynd upstream from the confluence of the Earn and Tay, capturing the survival of a braided river channel that existed until the improvements of relatively recent times.

Roy's mid-18th-century map also shows the confluence of the Tay and Earn in some detail, as well as illustrating the extent of improved lands under cultivation and unimproved marsh along the water's edge (Fig 21). While it is unfortunate that the mapping of the Carpow Bank is broken by the fold of the map-sheet, an additional island can be seen at the confluence, but on the north side of the Earn. It is possible that the reclamation of this island, as well as other parts of Rhynd, may have had the effect of pushing the debouchment of the Earn eastwards, causing the exposure and erosion of Carpow Bank. The Roy map is also valuable as it depicts land use; by the mid-18th century, arable strip field cultivation is shown along the River Earn and along the River Tay close up to the riverbank, indicating earlier, medieval agricultural improvements. Marsh is depicted on the fringes of the estuary and in notable pockets along the courses of the Pow of Errol and the Cairnie Burn. Roy also illustrates the scale of post-medieval improvements, for example, the course of the Cairnie

Burn has been altered so that it flows west and joins the Tay at Inchyra rather than Cairnie, as on the Roy map.

Prior to the agricultural improvements of the 18th century, lower Strathearn and the Carse of Gowrie would have supported much more diverse flora and fauna than is now apparent. The successive Statistical Accounts for the parishes bordering the Tay contain valuable information for how the river and estuarine environments were exploited in the relatively recent past. They present a consistent picture of the use of the river as a fishery resource, specifically of salmon, as well as an access route for shipping. The Statistical Accounts also note the deliberate development of the extensive reed beds that line the estuary shoreline. To cite one account, the author for the parish of Invergowrie (OSA 1797 xix, 467) notes that a 'species of the *arundo*, called *phragmites*, or common marsh-reed, and which grows by the sides of rivers, or in standing waters, is

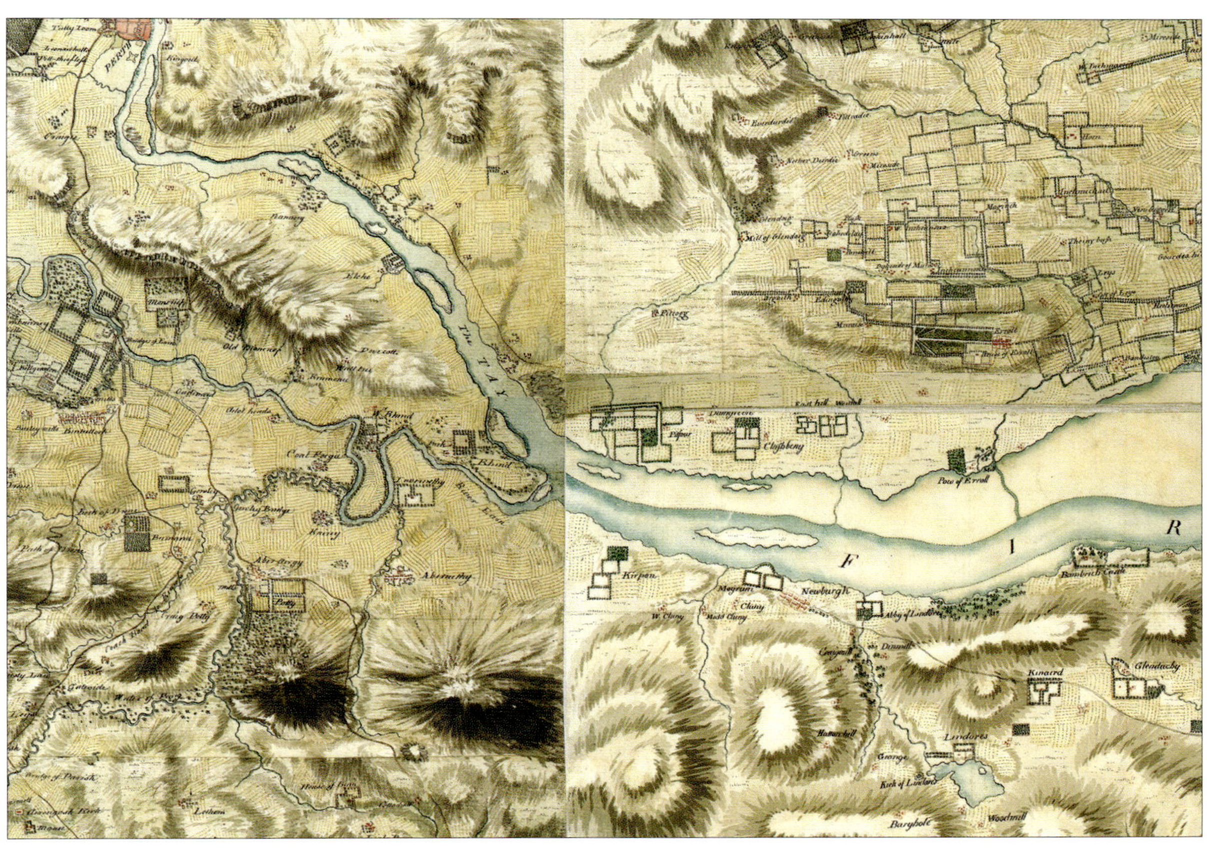

*Figure 21*
Roy's mid-18th-century map showing the confluence of the Tay and Earn (© British Library Board C.9.b 18/2d, C.9.b 17/4f, C.9.b 18/2a,C.9.b 17/4c)

*Figure 22*
The Kinnoull Ferryman, Perth (© Perth and Kinross Heritage Trust)

found in great abundance here. Of late years it has been propagated upon the banks of the river Tay with great success'. Significantly, this species was apparently native to the estuary before being developed as a specific industry in the Improvement period.

As the cartographic sources clearly illustrate, the nature of the Tay between Perth and Newburgh has changed significantly as salt marsh and riverine islands were reclaimed and the course of the Tay straightened. Much of the work was begun in the mid-1830s by the Harbour Commission of Perth to facilitate access for larger vessels (Baxter 1930, 192–3). A detailed account of this work was presented to the Royal Society of Edinburgh by David Stevenson in 1845, who outlined the process as consisting of the removal of a large number of 'fords' (defined as stretches of shallow water), shoals, rocks and fishing cairns. By blocking off watercourses between the riverine islands and excavating shallow, sloping banks to provide unrestricted flows of water, the Harbour Commission created an unimpeded flow of water along a single, dredged channel. Stevenson's 'before and after' comparisons of river statistics demonstrate the remarkable effectiveness of the scheme. One example is of the increase in speed of the tidal flow; in 1833 prior to the commencing of the works the 'tidal wave' of a flood tide took 2 hours 30 minutes from Newburgh to reach Perth, however, by 1845 this had been reduced to 1 hour 40 minutes (Stevenson 1845, 21–9).

### Historic crossing points: fords, bridges and ferries

By land, the River Tay and its wide firth presented serious barriers to transport and communication, and so crossing points and, eventually, bridges developed in key places. Conversely, by boat the watercourses offered conduits for access; linking places which by land were separated by days of travel on foot or by horse. Geography has dictated the easiest points to cross both the river and estuary, and it is very likely that many of the fords, bridge sites and ferry crossing points in use during the post-medieval period and into the 19th century were also used in prehistory.

Ferry routes, harbours, bridges and fords on waterways within the range of the Carpow logboat are shown on Fig 23. The two key crossing points are at Perth and at Bridge of Earn. At Perth, a succession of wooden bridges spanned the Tay from the foot of the High Street between the 12th and 17th centuries AD, replaced by a short-lived stone bridge in 1617 which was washed away in 1621. As a result, Perth was served by two ferries for much of the 17th and 18th centuries until the opening of Smeaton's Bridge in 1771 (Bowler 2004, 3). The gravestones of the ferrymen in Kinnoull Old Parish Church graveyard are a reminder of this era (Fig 22). At Bridge of Earn, the medieval stone bridge remained in use until the early 19th century (Gifford 2007, 243), with the surviving ruins demolished in 1976. The grant of stone for the construction of the bridge is mentioned in a record dated AD 1329 (Inglis

1912–13, 20–1) probably to replace an earlier timber bridge. The stone bridge was repaired and rebuilt from generation to generation following successive flood damage. At both Perth and Bridge of Earn, it is likely that the medieval bridges would have been preceded by a ferry and/or ford. One further, intriguing instance of a crossing point local to Carpow Bank is the mooted Roman boat-bridge, suggested on the basis of such a bridge depicted on an early third-century AD coin, perhaps connecting Carpow fortress to the north shore of the Tay above the Channelhead Bank (Reed 1975–6, 92–3).

The mouth of the River Earn is known as 'Ferryfield of Carpow', and *c* 700m to the south-west of Carpow Bank is the pier of Ferryfield of Carpow for the Heughhead Ferry. Ferries from this pier ran to the opposite bank of the River Earn (a distance of 150m) to the pier at Easter Rhynd, or journeyed the kilometre or more around the point of Rhynd to Cairnie Pier, Inchyra or Seggieden on the north bank of the Tay:

There are two passage boats on the Earn: one at Carey, which is seldom employed; another at Ferryfield, upon the estate of Carpow: this place being near the junction of the Earn and the Tay, the boat belonging to it is often employed carrying passengers over the Tay to the Carse of Gowrie (OSA 1791–9 xi, 443).

A second ferry ran from Muirhead on the south bank of the Tay to Inchyra, a crossing of *c* 500m. Both these ferries connected the historic route from Fife and Kinross-shire via Glenfarg or the Den of Lindores to Perth and the Carse of Gowrie, and farther afield Strathtay and Strathmore.

There are many legends and historical accounts relating to the Heughhead Ferry illustrating its significance. These include the story of the 'Ferry of the Loaf', so called owing to Macduff's payment-in-kind for the crossing when fleeing from the scene of Macbeth's murder (Weir 1988, 99). King Charles II used the Heughhead Ferry and the 'ancient route' of previous Scottish monarchs along the Coronation Road

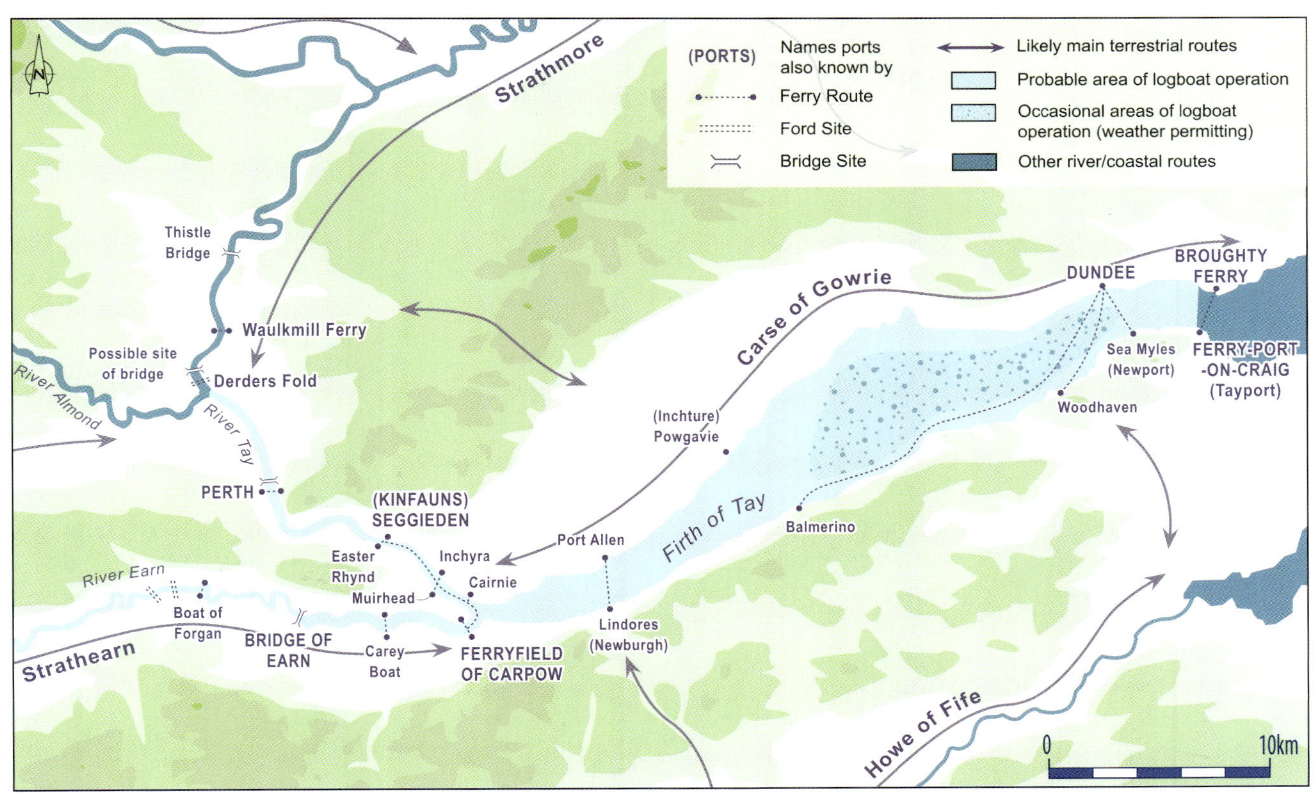


*Figure 23*

A map showing the main historic crossing points of the rivers and estuary, along with main terrestrial routes and the probable extent of operation of the Carpow logboat (© Crown copyright and database right (2009). All rights reserved. Ordnance Survey Licence number 100016971)

between Scone and Falkland following his coronation in 1651 (Melville 1986, 26–7; McLaren 1944).

Other significant ferries and fords include Boat of Forgan, farther inland on the River Earn and, upstream of Perth on the Tay, a ford and bridge at Bertha, the Waulkmill Ferry and Thistle Bridge. The Boat of Forgan linked the settlements of Forgandenny, Forteviot and Dunning to Kirkton of Mailer en route for Perth. It is likely that the Boat of Forgan ferry became redundant following the construction of the Forteviot Bridge (Gifford 2007, 93–4) in the late 1760s. Both a bridge and a ford are recorded above the confluence of the Almond and the Tay. The foundations of an old bridge were visible in 1795: 'large oak planks from 6" to 8" in diameter, fastened together with long skairs, but coarsely jointed and surrounded with clasps of iron, frequently twisted" (OSA 1791–7 xxv, 528). The ford, known as Derders Ford, lies closer to the confluence and has been suggested to be a weir (Crawford 1949, 61), though this has not been substantiated by underwater survey. The Waulkmill Ferry *c* 700m downstream from Luncarty operated until 1964 (Duncan 1997, 218) however, it is unknown as to when the ferry was established. Similarly, little is known of the Thistle Bridge, the site of which is marked on the OS first edition map (*c* 1860). This bridge is situated downstream of the huge meander at Stanley and, as with the Waulkmill Ferry, would have linked West Stormont (the area between the Almond and the Tay) with Strathmore.

On the Firth of Tay, the primary medieval crossing point was between Ferry-Port-on-Craig (now Tayport) and Broughty Ferry, crossing the estuary mouth at its narrowest. The first reference to this ferry dates to AD 1425 though it is thought the ferry dates back at least to the 13th century AD (Weir 1988, 99). The amount of trade on this ferry route was only surpassed following the development of Woodhaven and Newport in the early 19th centuries and by 1845 only a single passenger boat plied the crossing. Part of the success of the Ferry-Port-on-Craig ferry appears to have been that the route bypassed urban Dundee and so provided ample grazing for cattle en route to market. A second significant medieval ferry route is known to have run between Sea Myles (now Newport) and Dundee and other passages included Balmerino to Dundee and Lindores to Port Allen (*ibid*, 99–109).

Medieval and post-medieval harbours around the estuary (Fig 23) include Perth, Friarton, Cairnie Pier, Port Allen, Powgavie, Kingoodie, Dundee, Tayport, Newport, Woodhaven, Balmerino and Newburgh. The significance and scale of trade from the ports of Perth and Dundee with the eastern coast of Britain and Lowland and Baltic Countries between the medieval period and late 19th century is well documented (Bowler 2004, 21; Perry 2005, 15–22). The late 19th century and early 20th century saw the development of a number of passenger steamers between Perth and Dundee and the use of the firth for leisure. The last of these was the diminutive paddler *Cleopatra* which provided a summer service until 1931 from Dundee up to Perth via Newburgh, with irregular stops at Broughty Ferry, Balmerino and Bridge of Earn (Aitken 1986, 28).

### 3.5 Conclusions

The topography of the area is a result of the underlying geology and the effects of the last ice age in particular, and is dominated by the influence of the River Tay, the Earn and the estuary. However, the character of both the rivers and estuary has been changed significantly since prehistory. Agricultural improvements of land drainage and reclamation, beginning in the medieval period, accelerated in the 18th and 19th centuries AD and continuing to the present day have altered and compartmentalised lower Strathearn and the Carse of Gowrie. Navigational improvements have drastically affected the bathymetry of the River Tay between Perth and Newburgh; straightening, smoothing and speeding the flow of both rivers and estuary. Historical sources offer a glimpse of these previous environments, as do less altered fragments of the estuary, and parallels can be drawn with other areas of wetland along the east coast of Britain where similar processes have occurred (eg Gardiner 1993). In prehistory, at a time when arable agriculture was still in its infancy and hunting, gathering and fishing would have formed an important part of human economy, the Firth of Tay would have been one of the richest ecotones on the east coast of Scotland. The available natural resources, and their implications for this study, are discussed in greater detail below (Chapter 13, pp 172–5). Finally, the survival of ferries and shipping in the estuary until recent centuries has also provided insight into the earlier waterways of the Tay and the Earn and what would have formed an integral transport network. These abundant and diverse environments, and the tidal power of the estuary itself, provide us with a backdrop for our consideration of the Carpow logboat.

# Chapter 4

# Discovery, excavation and recovery

DAVID STRACHAN

with contributions from Mike Cressey and Mark Hall

## 4.1 Discovery, evaluation and monitoring

### *Discovery*

The discovery of a logboat, partially buried in intertidal mudflats at Carpow Bank was initially reported to the McManus Museum, Dundee, in August 2001 by metal-detectorist Scott McGuckin (Strachan 2001). He and his two metal-detecting colleagues, Martin Brooks and Robert Fotheringham (all three of them members of a Dundee-based metal-detecting club), were searching the mudflats during low-tide, when Mr McGuckin's keen eye first spotted what proved to be the boat. Once the news broke, widespread local, regional and national press coverage captured something of the excitement of the three companions at their discovery. The *Daily Telegraph* of 11 September 2001 quoted Mr Fotheringham as saying: 'The most important artefact we had found to date was a couple of Roman medallions, so this is much more exciting.' Meanwhile, on the same day the *Scotsman* quoted Mr McGuckin as saying: 'I have only been doing this for a few months and can't believe this find.'

Mr McGuckin has subsequently reported:

> I went out detecting with a couple of friends onto the sandbanks near the Roman fort at Carpow. The sandbanks are fairly inaccessible so we thought they'd be worth searching. We all split up and made off into different directions searching quite a big area at low tide. I had only begun searching really, when I came upon the bow of the logboat sticking out of the sand. I knew … it was a logboat, having seen them in publications and also viewing the example in Dundee Museum. It felt excellent to make such a discovery (pers comm).

The curator of archaeology at the McManus Museum relayed the news of the discovery to the Fife Council Archaeologist, who reported the find to Perth and Kinross Heritage Trust (PKHT) once it had been established that the site of the find was upstream of the Fife border and so within the Perth and Kinross local authority area. In September of that year a site visit was made by archaeologists from PKHT (David Strachan), Historic Scotland (HS) (Ian Oxley); the National Museums of Scotland (NMS) (Trevor Cowie); Perth Museum and Art Gallery (PMAG) (Mark Hall) and The Royal Commission on the Ancient and Historical Monuments of Scotland (RCAHMS) (Robert Mowat). The aim of the meeting was to confirm, or otherwise, that the remains were of a boat, and to attempt to assess its potential importance and condition.

The result of this meeting was that the find was confirmed to be a logboat, partially buried in the sands and gravels with *c* 5m of the vessel exposed from the estuarine mud (Figs 24 and 25). The exposed end, tentatively assumed to be the bow of the craft, was found pointing upstream, with the stern remaining buried (Strachan 2004). While the surface of the exposed portion of the boat was much abraded through the scouring effect of sands and gravels carried by tidal currents, it was clear that the overall condition of the logboat was good. It appeared to be in one piece and, exceptionally, its overall shape was not gnarled and contorted, suggesting comparatively little exposure to the elements.

Credit is duly acknowledged to Mr McGuckin and his colleagues for recognising the find for what it is. The majority of people coming across the boat as it appeared in 2001 would simply have assumed it to be an old eroded tree, of which there are many surviving amongst the peat deposits on Carpow Bank (Chapter 10). It is interesting to note that it was familiarity with the Errol 2 vessel, which has been on display in Dundee since shortly after its discovery in 1895, that contributed to the initial recognition of the boat.

It is also interesting to note that, further to the initial media coverage of the discovery in local and national press, a number of other individuals, living around the estuary, contacted the Trust to explain that they had either previously 'discovered' the vessel (though had not reported it) or had always known about it and thought it unnecessary to report the 'discovery' of something that was fairly widely known within the local community. While there is no reason to doubt many of these claims, as even the inaccessible parts of the estuary are widely used by wildfowlers, fishermen and canoeists amongst others, the pertinent point is that Mr McGuckin was the first to report it to a professional archaeologist who could at the very least add it to the local Historic Environment Record and to the National Monuments Record of Scotland. Prior to this, the boat was completely unknown to the archaeological community and so absent from both of these records, and the definitive gazetteer of Scottish logboats (Mowat 1996).

Further, under Scottish Treasure Trove law, Mr McGuckin is legally recognised as the discoverer of the logboat because he reported it to the proper authorities. Scotland is not covered by the 1996 Treasure Act, which applies to the rest of the UK (and only covers objects of gold and silver and any associated materials) but by its own laws of bona vacantia, which enable the Crown (on behalf of the nation) to claim any object found in Scotland. Scottish Treasure Trove law applies to all newly found artefacts and to all old finds which have not been reported, whether they have

been found by metal-detecting, by field-walking or by archaeological excavation. Finders or landowners have no ownership rights to anything they find in Scotland and, with the exception of Victorian or 20th-century coins, all finds must be reported to the Treasure Trove Unit for assessment (Scottish Executive Education Department 1999). In order to exercise its legal rights over archaeological finds the Crown Office relies on the recommendations of a panel of experts, the Scottish Archaeological Finds Allocation Panel (SAFAP), appointed by the Scottish Ministers. Although SAFAP was notified of the discovery it could only record the fact whilst the logboat remained *in situ*, and like other parties it awaited with interest the results of the initial archaeological investigations and the radiocarbon determination. For SAFAP it became an active case once the decision to fully excavate and uplift the logboat was made in 2006. Initially the Panel had to consider

*Figures 24 and 25*
The Carpow logboat as first recorded after being 'discovered' in 2001

whether it was even appropriate for the logboat to be considered Treasure Trove as opposed to being a case for the Receiver of Wreck, based in Southampton and with a UK-wide remit to administer cases of voluntary salvage wreck (Merchant Shipping Act 1995). Having established that its inter-tidal location, with effectively 'dryland' exposure at low tide, did qualify the logboat as Treasure Trove, Perth Museum and Art Gallery was formally notified that the logboat would be claimed by the Crown. The bidding and allocation process took place over 2006 and 2007, with Perth Museum informed that the boat had been allocated to it in August 2007. A reward value of £1,000 was set on the boat, which Perth Museum paid (with 50% grant aid from the National Fund for Acquisitions), to the HM Paymaster General, who then paid the finder.

### Evaluation strategy

Further to the initial site meeting in September 2001, a strategy was developed by PKHT, incorporating the recommendations of colleagues from HS, RCAHMS and the NMS, for initial recording, evaluation and interim *in situ* management of the boat. The overall aim of the strategy was to assess the cultural significance of the vessel both in terms of logboat studies and to gauge the level of threat posed by tidal action. The criteria agreed to assess whether the boat could be described as being of local, regional or national importance were primarily date and condition. The peak in numbers of the British series of logboats occurs between around AD 1000–1300, with the survival of prehistoric logboats being relatively rare (Lanting 2000, 630). The condition of logboats, of any date, is often poor, usually as a result of the fact that they have been exposed for long periods of time before they are deposited, or that they have suffered deterioration through a variety of processes after deposition. While the truncated hulls of logboats often survive, to varying degrees, the survival of what can be described as fixtures and fittings is rare (Mowat 1996, 122). It was therefore recognised that a medieval logboat of poor condition would not score as highly as one in similar condition of prehistoric date.

In order to assess cultural significance, a programme of evaluation was developed which had four main objectives:

- to establish the date of the vessel;
- to establish the condition of the buried portion of the vessel;
- to establish the full length of the vessel;
- to protect the vessel *in situ* while long-term management options were considered.

A staged approach to this process was adopted, with an initial sample of timber taken from the exposed bow for radiocarbon dating. It was agreed that a prehistoric or medieval date would warrant limited excavation to establish the condition of the buried portion of boat. The results of this evaluation would then be used to consider the long-term management options for the vessel, which would range from basic on-site recording and occasional (probably annual) monitoring; through regular monitoring and proactive on site protection (involving sandbagging and the promotion of marine vegetation); to full excavation and recovery of the vessel. A boat of prehistoric date and in good condition would require the latter option.

### Inter-tidal archaeology: access and logistics

From the outset of the evaluation process, the implications of the inter-tidal nature of the site were clear: very limited access during only low tide windows, and additional inconveniences and challenges not usually encountered in terrestrial archaeology. Primarily these resulted from the effects of regular submergence of the site under fast-flowing tidal water; namely re-covering of any excavation by tidal deposits and floodwater. The site was also considerably more isolated than its location initially suggested, and the team, and much of the equipment, had to access the site through the thick reed-beds and thigh-deep mud which border the inter-tidal in this part of the estuary, although water pumps were on occasion delivered by boat during the recovery phase.

The process of inter-tidal archaeological excavation can vary considerably from site to site according to a number of factors, including the nature of the surviving archaeology, available tidal windows, and the type of deposit in which these occur. In England, notable excavations from similar estuarine environments include The Stumble, Essex, discovered in 1985 as part of the Hullbridge Survey (Wilkinson & Murphy 1995, 76–81) and excavated in 1986 (Wilkinson *et al* forthcoming). Also in the late 1980s, the study of various archaeological deposits in the Severn Estuary resulted in a prolonged and systematic programme of work (Bell 1993; 1994; and Bell & Neumann 1999). Further, the significant long-term inter-tidal survey at Wootton-Quarr on the Isle of Wight (Loader 2007 and

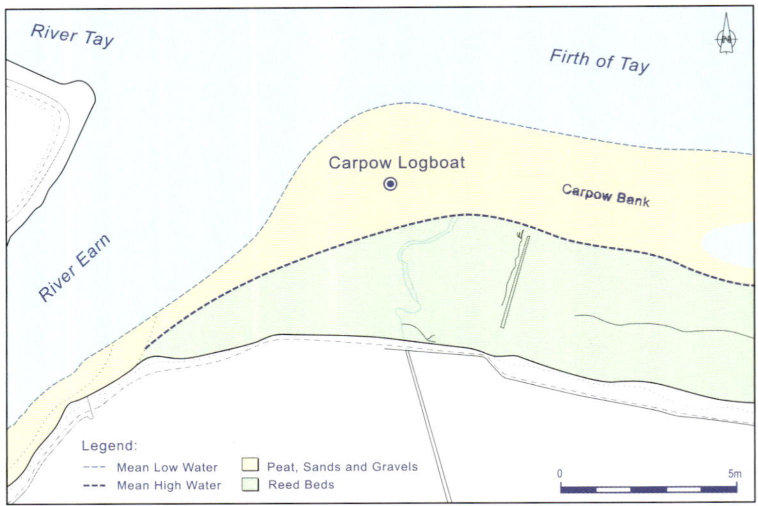


*Figure 26*

The location of the logboat in the lower inter-tidal zone of Carpow Bank (© Crown copyright and database right (2009). All rights reserved. Ordnance Survey Licence number 100016971)

Tomalin *et al* forthcoming) also dating back to the late 1980s, was indicative of the increasing awareness of the potential of the inter-tidal for wetland archaeology at both a local and national level. The 1990s saw both The Humber Wetlands Project, the fourth large scale survey of wetlands in England funded by English Heritage (eg Van de Noort & Ellis 1995) and the multi-disciplinary study at Langstone Harbour (Allen & Gardiner 2000). However, it was perhaps the excavation in 1998–9 of the Bronze Age timber circle, dubbed 'Seahenge', at Holme-next-the-Sea, Norfolk (Brennand & Taylor 2003), that most appreciably raised the profile of inter-tidal archaeology both within the profession and with the public.

In Scotland, inter-tidal excavations have been carried out in sandy deposits (Owen & Dalland 1999), in more gravel/cobble deposits (Parker-Pearson & Sharples 1999) and, as a result of coastal erosion on dune/cliff faces, on the edge of the inter-tidal zone (Armit 2006). More recently, excavations at Baile Sear, North Uist included the use of spoil to create a temporary sea wall on the edge of the inter-tidal zone (Dawson pers comm). The excavations at Carpow were therefore, the first to take place in the lower reaches of the inter-tidal in Scotland, with similar problems as those faced by the Stumble team in Essex, largely based around the twice daily submersion of the site under metres of water.

The tidal amplitude of the inter-tidal zone at Carpow Bank (Fig 26) is significantly affected by the volume of water flowing downstream as a result of rainfall and/or snow-melt carried by both the River Tay and River Earn. Familiarisation with the site-specific tidal regimes on this particular part of the estuary included some gauging of wind direction and strength: as this was also found to affect the extent of tidal fluctuation. This 'local knowledge' was developed through occasionally aborted trips where one, or many, of these factors had a significant enough effect to result in the boat remaining submerged, or partially submerged, at the lowest point of the low tide. Experience gained from regular monitoring visits over 2001 and 2002 indicated that only low spring tides (with a predicted height of less than 1m OD at Dundee) preceded by a dry period of around one week, ensured a workable tidal window of around 3–4 hours. By 2003 it became clear that Carpow Bank was only exposed with a workable tidal window during the roughly twice-monthly spring-tides between June and August, and on each of these occasions the bank was revealed at each low tide for 4–5 days. These are the parameters around which access to this site had to be scheduled.

In addition to the problems of physical access to inter-tidal sites, there are a number of common logistical problems not encountered during terrestrial excavation. The re-covering by water and inter-tidal deposits (whether sand, mud or gravel) have a combined effect of delaying progress, requiring not only the removal of water flooding excavations carried out during the previous tidal window, but also re-excavation of new deposits carried by the tide (Figs 32, 33, 35 and 36). Water removal was required, in the form of between one and three motorised pumps, however, the time involved in this process, along with the time to partially re-excavate the site after each flood tide, had a significant impact on the already very limited time available within each tidal window. As a result of this compound effect, the excavations were extremely challenging and required a flexible and pragmatic approach which developed as the project progressed, with work on site involving short bursts of rapid, well-planned activity.

As far as possible, concessions on the usual methods of excavation and recording were kept to a minimum; however, compromise was often required as result of

*Figures 27 and 28*
Carpow Bank at high and low tide showing the confluence of the River Tay and River Earn on the left and the estuary, to the east, on the right

*Figure 29*
The site as it became gradually exposed during the ebb tide (27 July 2006)

*Figure 30*
In order to maximise working time within each tidal window, the team walked onto site with the falling tide to begin work
(27 July 2006)

*Figure 31*
Early stages of excavation showing inter-tidal environment (26 July 2006)

*Figure 32*
At the beginning of each working window, the site was gradually exposed with a fresh deposit of estuarine silt (28 July 2006)

*Figure 33*
As the flood tide arrived the excavation was once again submerged (27 July 2006)

*Figure 34*
During the excavation the interior of the boat was sandbagged during low tide to protect it from objects
carried by the tide, and to avoid its untimely transportation (27 July 2006)

*Figure 35*
At the end of each working window, the site was rapidly submerged during the flood tide. The stepped shoring is visible to the right of the frame (9 August 2006)

*Figure 36*
The flat nature of the inter-tidal bank resulted in the flooding within around 20 minutes, once the water-level was above the exposed flat. The excavation trench itself became covered in around 4–5 minutes (9 August 2006)

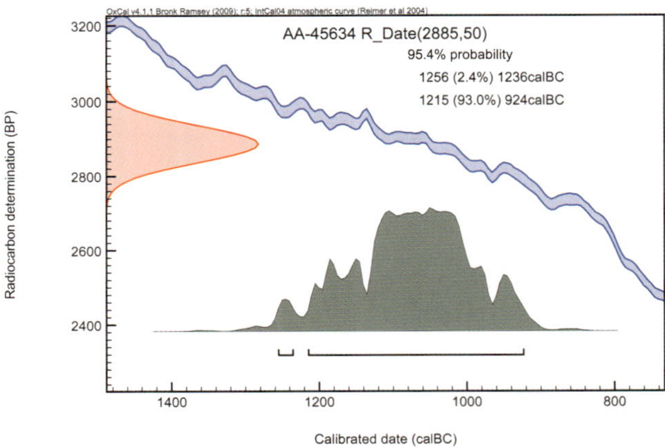

*Figure 37*
The first radiocarbon date from the boat, which confirmed a prehistoric date

The methodology employed involved exposing 3m of the bow and the sheerline on the port side to *c* 4m from the bow, and the starboard side to a length of around 6m (Fig 38). In addition, the starboard sheerline was identified by touch only, through the water, sand and gravels, to a length of *c* 7m. The evaluation showed that the buried portion of the bow was considerably better preserved than the exposed section, and indicated that the vessel was at least 7m in length and probably in one piece. It also indicated that the vessel was buried, to a depth of at least 0.75m, in relatively fine estuarine gravels, and highlighted the extent to which flooding was likely to occur during excavation, as the water table beneath the exposed ground surface fluctuated over the tide. In addition, the evaluation clearly illustrated that the vessel lay at a considerable angle within the inter-tidal deposits, with the bow much higher than the stern. This suggested that excavation to *c* 1m in depth would

the very difficult working conditions. The specific health and safety requirements of the site, including the regular monitoring of the incoming tide in particular, were an additional concern.

### *Evaluation Phase 1 (2001): initial dating*

In November 2001 the radiocarbon age of the initial sample was confirmed as 2885 ± 50 BP (AA-45634 – GU-9597), producing calibrated dates of 1260–910 cal BC at 2-sigma (95.4% probability) (Chapter 6, pp 93–4), placing the vessel within the local Late Bronze Age. On the basis of this information, a strategy to assess the condition of the buried stern of the vessel was developed.

### *Evaluation Phase 2 (2002): assessing the condition of the bow*

The second phase of evaluation was carried out in October 2002 (Strachan & Glendinning 2002) and aimed to assess the condition of the partially buried section of the vessel at what was assumed to be the bow (Fig 38). The exposed bow was clearly physically abraded by the sands and gravels carried by tidal action in recent decades. The degree to which the buried bow was eroded, however, would indicate whether the hull had been completely exposed over significant periods in the past, resulting in erosion across the entire vessel, or whether the vessel had become buried prior to significant exposure. The latter would clearly indicate the potential for much better preservation of associated fixtures and fittings, small finds and other deposits.

*Figure 38*
Evaluation excavation exposes the bow for the first time in 2002

be required to expose the stern, with considerable implications in terms of water-removal. Following evaluation of the bow, the vessel was sandbagged for protection and monitored on a roughly monthly basis. Monitoring confirmed that the high-energy inter-tidal environment continued to scour and erode both the peat deposits and the vessel. Hessian sandbagging was found to provide temporary protection for the vessel, however, it was estimated that these would require replacement on a quarterly basis to provide ongoing protection of any value.

### Evaluation Phase 3 (2003): assessing length and the condition of stern

In July 2003, a third phase of evaluation was undertaken (Strachan & Glendinning 2003) with the aim of establishing the full length of the vessel and assessing the depth and condition of the buried stern. The depth of the stern, as outlined above, placed serious limits on the extent of information recovered. A trench, *c* 2m by 3m, was extended across the projected line of the vessel *c* 9m from the bow. Despite the use of a motorised water-pump and timber shoring, the excavation was hampered by persistent flooding. The sheerline of the stern was, however, eventually revealed for only a few minutes to allow photography and basic measurements to be taken.

At the time of evaluation, the full length of the vessel was estimated to be *c* 9.25m and the top of the buried stern was found to be *c* 0.75m below the ground surface. The width of the vessel was shown to be between *c* 0.9–1m. The evaluation, however, revealed the excellent condition of the stern, which appeared to have suffered little erosion from either tidal action or regular exposure to the air. Of particular importance was the identification of an *in situ* transom (*ibid*; Strachan 2004), the only other known example of which being from the Iron Age Hasholme vessel (Chapter 1, pp 3–6). The presence of the transom also indicated the potential for the survival of other fixtures and fittings.

The evaluation was restricted by the adoption of a minimal intervention policy involving only key-hole excavation at the stern of the vessel. This was employed to reduce the possibility of the boat working free from the inter-tidal deposits and being lost through transportation by the tide. As a result, the central section of the hull was not investigated during the evaluations. The resulting plans and sections from the evaluations, however, suggested the possibility that central section of the hull may have been broken in some way. Specifically, the interim plan the vessel appeared to have a kink in the projected line from bow to stern. During the full excavation, however, it became clear that this 'kink' was a result of the angle at which the boat lay and the fact that it was also sat at an angle longitudinally, with the port side lower than the starboard side (Fig 43). This, along with compression of the starboard sheerline gave the impression that the central section of the boat was twisted or even broken.

The regular exposure of the highly abraded upper third of the vessel to the air during low tides was found to have resulted in some rotting of the wood, particularly on the tops of the sides, which had increased the scouring effects of the tidal waters. As a result, abrasion had removed any traces of toolmarks or faceting on the bow, and some splitting of the timber had occurred at the exposed end. In contrast, the condition of the wood stern was much better, having a leeched mineral conglomerate deposited over the timber which served to protect the surface.

*Figure 39*
The key-hole excavations in 2003 revealed the well-preserved stern for only a few minutes, although the significance of the *in situ* transom was immediately clear

*Figure 40*
Sandbagging of the evaluation excavation in 2003

An initial national grid reference of NO 2001 1859 was collected with a hand-held Global Positioning System (GPS) during the evaluation work of 2003, giving an accurate location to within *c* 10m, which was verified by the use of Differential GPS in 2006.

***Interim management and publication***

Further to the excavations in 2002 and 2003, the vessel was sandbagged as an interim measure of protection against further erosion, transportation or damage from objects carried by the tide (Fig 40 and Strachan 2004). In addition, the use of sandbags as a protective layer also minimised the negative effects of exposure of the waterlogged timber to air and sunlight at low tide. As the site was a Site of Special Scientific Interest (SSSI), permission was obtained for excavation work by Scottish Natural Heritage and only biodegradable hessian sandbags were used to protect the vessel, and for site reinstatement subsequent to excavation. Monitoring of the site was continued on a quarterly

basis after the 2003 excavations. This work confirmed that while deposits would occasionally accrue around areas of sandbagging during periods of minimal river flow from the Tay and the Earn, the deposits were later removed during periods of scouring resulting from heavier river flow. As a result, it was considered that long-term preservation *in situ* would be impracticable to achieve, as it would require re-sandbagging of the site on at least a quarterly basis.

An interim account of the evaluation work in 2002 and 2003 was published (*ibid*) along with a short discussion on the significance of the vessel, both in terms of other logboats from the area, and the Late Bronze Age archaeology of the area. The drawing together of this paper highlighted the importance of the vessel and indicated its national, rather than regional, significance. The paper concluded with a statement that various options for preservation were being considered, including both *in situ* preservation and full excavation and recovery, followed by conservation and display.

*Management options and project planning*

By the time of interim publication in late 2004, however, the results of monitoring made it clear that *in situ* preservation was not a viable long-term option, and plans were developed for excavation and recovery. A strategy for conservation was agreed with the National Museums of Scotland, and an in-principle agreement to display the boat in Perth was made with Perth Museum and Art Gallery. While an initial bid to Historic Scotland for 50% grant aid, submitted in 2004, was unsuccessful, a subsequent bid to Historic Scotland in 2005, with Perth and Kinross Heritage Trust funding the remaining costs, was successful and initiated project planning for the summer of 2006.

### 4.2 Excavation methodology

*Project aims and objectives*

The aims and objectives of the 2006 project were to:

- Excavate the logboat and recover/record any artefacts associated with it;
- Record and study the archaeological/palaeo-environmental context of the logboat;
- Recover the logboat from its location and transport it to the National Museums of Scotland, Granton, Edinburgh;
- Conserve the vessel;
- Consider the vessel both in terms of the contemporary archaeology of the area, and its importance in relation to logboat studies.

*Project timetable (July–August 2006)*

The project was carried out over seven days in the two tidal windows as outlined in Table 1. The latter included some of the lowest predicted tides of the year, occurring in summer when water flow from the rivers was at a minimum, thus maximising the available low tide working windows.

*Logistics of excavation and recovery*

The inter-tidal nature of the excavation and the logistical challenges involved in the recovery and transportation of the vessel, as outlined above, required a pragmatic approach to project planning (Strachan 2006). The most significant modification concerned transportation of the vessel from the site to the quay at Newburgh. The original plan involved inserting the logboat into a lifting frame on site, with the frame subsequently being floated and towed to Newburgh. This was founded on the possibility that there was a break, or partial break, in the vessel as had been suggested by the 2003 evaluation, which would require support along the hull while lifting. Early in the excavations, in July 2006, however, it became apparent that the boat was fully intact and robust enough to float, with the aid of air barrels, and as a result the recovery was modified to involve towing the floating boat to meet the lifting frame at Newburgh. In summary, the operation involved four stages:

- Excavation and securing of the logboat *in situ* at low tide windows;
- Floating the vessel at high tide to a suitable lifting location;
- Lifting the logboat from the water to suitable transport;
- Site reinstatement.

*Low tide excavation methodology*

The aim of the excavation was to loosen deposits around the vessel prior to floating/lifting while allowing any associated deposits and finds within the vessel to be recorded and recovered archaeologically in the best conditions available. The excavation was carried out in two stages: the excavation of the interior and exterior of the upper (bow) half of the boat; and subsequently of the lower (stern) half of the vessel.

*Upper (bow) section*: Excavation was carried out on the 26 and 27 July 2006, with hand excavation to a depth of *c* 0.5m over an area *c* 1m around the vessel, along with excavation of the interior of the vessel. The upper section was well above the water table and so did not require water removal. Once the vessel had been undercut, and following recording of the deposits, the boat was underpinned with sandbags to provide additional support.

*Lower (stern) section*: Excavation of the stern area of the vessel began early in the project, commencing on 26 July 2006, and continued until the excavation was complete on 10 August 2006. Stepped shoring, using plastic scaffold planks and sandbags, was employed to prevent the sides of the trench slumping and filling with estuarine sands/gravels. Combinations of water-pumps were employed to remove water, as the bottom of the stern lay *c* 1.75m below the ground surface and low tide water table. The fully excavated logboat (Fig 46) lay supported on a layer of sandbags, allowing final on site recording by photography, scale drawing and survey.

*Table 1*
The project timetable indicating the dates of the two main tidal windows,
predicted tides and available working time

| Window | Date | Predicted tide Metres OD (Dundee) | Predicted tidal window (BST) | Project Event | Event time (BST) |
|---|---|---|---|---|---|
| 1 | 26/07/06 | 1.00 | 1025–1300 | Excavation | 1100–1300 |
| 1 | 27/07/06 | 0.92 | 1100–1350 | Excavation | 1050–1340 |
| 1 | 28/07/06 | 0.90 | 1140–1420 | Excavation | 1120–1420 |
| 1 | 29/07/06 | 0.96 | 1210–1440 | Excavation | 1210–1440 |
| 2 | 09/08/06 | 0.69 | 0930–1220 | Excavation | 0910–1220 |
| 2 | 10/08/06 | 0.36 | 1010–1330 | Excavation | 1030–1220 |
| | | | | Excavation complete | 1220 |
| | | | | Rigged to float | 1230–1315 |
| | | | | Float | 1325 |
| | | | | Move | 1330–1430 |
| | | | | Reed-bed location | *c* 1430 |
| 2 | 11/08/06 | 0.18 | 1050–1420 | Vessel exposed at Reed-bed location | 0830–1100 |
| | | | | Photography | 1100–1115 |
| | | | | Site reinstatement | 1100–1400 |
| | | | | Mud-pack applied | 1115–1130 |
| | | | | Re-rigged to float | 1200–1430 |
| | | | | Float | 1620 |
| | | | | Tow to Newburgh | 1700–1810 |
| | | | | Rigged within frame | 1810–1930 |
| | | | | Lift | 1940–1943 |
| | | | | Leave Newburgh | 2010 |
| | | | | Arrive Granton | 2240 |
| 2 | 12/08/06 | 0.17 | 1140–1450 | Unused | – |
| 2 | 13/08/06 | 0.33 | 1230–1530 | Unused | – |
| 2 | 14/08/06 | 0.64 | 1310–1600 | Unused | – |

### On site recording strategy

A temporary benchmark (TBM) was established on site *c* 10m NNW of the logboat, to which all survey work, including the environmental studies (Chapter 10) and on-site recording were referenced. The position of the TBM was located with Differential Global Positioning System (DGPS), using Real Time Kinematic features to provide centimetre precision in three dimensions. The value of DGPS technology on this inter-tidal site, where no control was available for conventional survey, cannot be over-emphasised, particularly given the time pressures placed on the conventional recording team as a result of the short tidal windows.

Plans and sections were made of the vessel and its context *in situ*, at a scale of 1:20 (Fig 43) and verified by a total of 14 three-dimensional points recorded across the vessel (while *in situ*) with DGPS. The entire excavation process was fully recorded using high-resolution digital photography and high-resolution digital video with a view to using the material in future displays (Fig 41).

### 4.3 Excavation results

### The stratigraphic sequence

The sequence recorded was simple (table 2 and Fig 43), however, it should be considered in the light of the highly dynamic inter-tidal environment, where sediments are continually eroded and accrued through a variety of processes, and the logistical problems of excavation outlined. As a result, while it was possible to photograph and draw sections as per a 'dry' site on

*Figure 41*
The excavation process was filmed, both as a record of the excavation, and in order to provide exhibition material (27 July 2006)

to a point upstream beneath the bow of the vessel may suggest that the deposit has been eroded away, and gradually replaced by shifting sands and gravels on ebb tides (Figs 43 and 44). As a result of continual flooding, the extent of Context 106 could not be adequately recorded at the stern, so it is not possible to suggest a similar process during flood tides. Context 107, provisionally identified as a lower peat deposit during excavation, was later confirmed as being comparable to the tabulated peat found on the surface of the bank (Context 101; Chapter 10). This fact is significant; it indicates that the boat was originally deposited on the peat (Context 101), possibly when it was already much truncated and tabulated, and that the weight of the stern, and probably the additional weight of the water and organic debris later to become Context 106, caused the stern to sink much farther down than the bow. This force has gradually pushed the tabulated block of peat (Context 107) down to its final position, *c* 1.75m into the estuarine sands and gravels.

the upper section of the vessel, this was not possible on the lower section where excavation below the inter-tidal water table continually flooded the trench. It was therefore not possible to recognise and record stratigraphic changes in the sands and gravels below *c* 0.75m in depth.

### *The logboat in relation to the sequence*

The orientation of the logboat was such that the bow of the vessel pointed upstream towards the River Earn (Figs 26 and 35). The stern of the boat was found to be considerably lower than the bow (Figs 46 and 47), however, with the base of the stern being *c* 1.75m below ground surface while the bow of the vessel was truncated above ground level. This could be explained by the fact that the stern of the boat, being heavier than the bow, gradually sank deeper into a soft deposit, such as a river or estuarine mud. The good level of preservation of the stern might suggest that this process occurred over a relatively short period of time, certainly before rotting of the timber had begun.

It is suggested that the logboat was originally deposited in an alluvial silt which survives as Context 106. This black/grey organic-rich deposit was found to survive both under the vessel and inside the vessel. Further from the vessel however, it appears to have been replaced by the ubiquitous inter-tidal sands and gravels. The survival of Context 106 as a lens shaped

### *Small finds and grab samples*

A total of 15 small finds, all waterlogged wood, were recovered (Fig 49) on the basis that they appeared to have been worked, however, on subsequent closer examination, the vast majority of these were considered as only possibly worked (Appendix II). Only three were clearly worked: SF001 (probably part of a small barrel lid), SF002 (a wooden peg) and SF015. The former two of these could not be securely associated with the logboat, coming from the upper estuarine sands and gravels (Contexts 102 and 103 respectively), and it is likely that both are relatively modern. The only small find which was confidently associated with the vessel is SF015, a rectangular block of worked wood, found in two pieces fitted into the transom area of the boat. A full description and discussion of this find follows (Chapter 5, pp 85–7). In addition to the small finds, a total of 11 grab samples were taken in order to assess the nature and make-up of each identified context (Fig 49 and Appendix IV).

*Figure 42*
Differential Global Positioning System (DGPS) survey of the boat and
environs provided accurate position in three dimensions

### *Wood assemblage from grab samples*

MIKE CRESSEY

*Introduction*

A small assemblage of waterlogged wood, recovered from various parts of the logboat as it was being excavated, either as individual fragments or part of larger grab samples (Fig 49 and Appendices III and IV) was examined as part of the palaeoenvironmental assessment. The objective was to establish how much of the material was contemporary with the logboat, notwithstanding the highly dynamic environment in which the finds were made, and the potential taphonomic changes following deposition of the assemblage. At an early stage it was recognised that only radiocarbon dating would resolve which samples were contemporary with the logboat. Cost implications prohibited the possibility of dating every sample of wood recovered and so a critical appraisal on the relative antiquity and the selection of suitable material was made during the preliminary analysis of the assemblage.

Among the samples assessed were twigs from small brushwood; miscellaneous fragments of amorphous wood that had been affected by erosion or had clearly been redeposited and were considered intrusive. Other fragments were clearly archaeological in nature and these include a stake with two oblique

*Table 2*
The stratigraphic sequence at Carpow Bank, with contexts as shown on Fig 43, reflected the highly dynamic
inter-tidal environment. Appendix IV provides details of the grab samples

| No | Context | Description |
|---|---|---|
| 101 | Peat | tabulated peat truncated in depth to *c* 100–300mm (Chapter 10) |
| 102 | Recent tidal deposits | *c* 50–100mm deep, consisting of mixed sands, gravels and mud |
| 103 | Sand/gravel | orange sand/gravel (Grab Sample 3) |
| 104 | Grey alluvial silt and sand/gravel | a gravel-rich grey alluvial silt (Grab Sample 4) |
| 105 | Alluvial sand and gravel | alluvial sands and gravels (Grab Sample 5) |
| 106 | Alluvial silt | a black organic-rich deposit containing large quantities of small round-woods (hazel and birch), fragments of peat and hazelnut shells (Grab Sample 1; 2; 6; 7 and 11) |
| 107 | Peat | a block of peat beneath the boat |

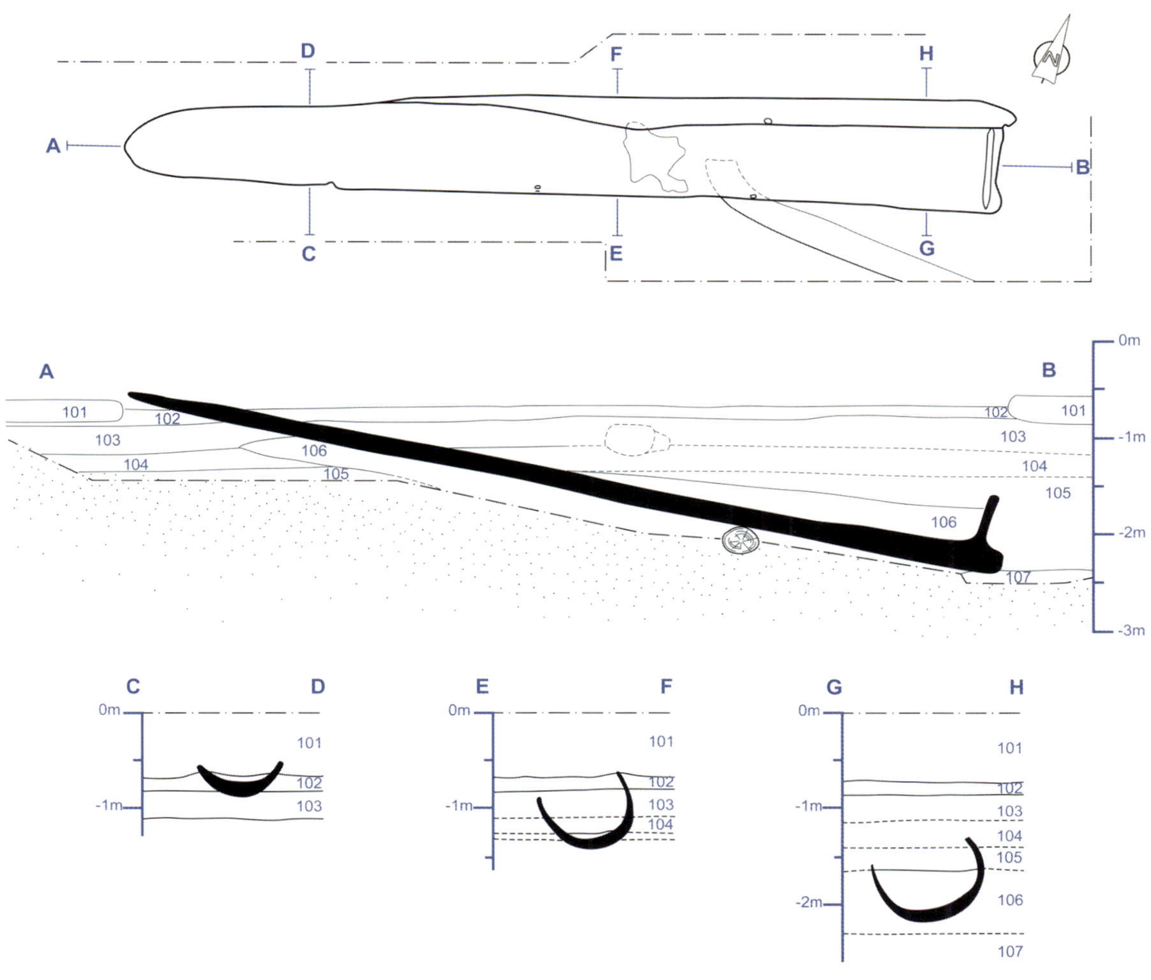

*Figure 43*
Plan and sections of the *in situ* logboat showing contexts (101–7). Section A–B illustrates the considerable longitudinal angle at which
the vessel lay with the base of the stern 1.75m below the ground surface. The plan and sections C–D, E–F and G–H also indicate the
lateral angle at which the vessel was pivoted, with the starboard (north) side of the vessel much higher than the port (south) side. C–D
also illustrates how the exposed bow has been truncated by erosion

facets present and a possible toggle-shaped piece that may be related to a cover-fastener. Of significance from samples within the boat were ten hazelnut shells which are considered to have been securely sealed below the basal sediment within the logboat (Context 106).

*Wood identification methods*

Individual sub-samples of wood were placed in a freezer at −10° Celsius for 12 hours prior to sectioning in order to facilitate clean fractures and where necessary to allow thin sections to be taken from the frozen wood. When required, reference was made to the keys listed in Schweingruber (1990). The majority of the wood was identified using a binocular microscope at between $\times 10 + 20$ magnification on transverse sections. When required cross-checks using thin-sections were obtained and compared to type slides. Observations on the morphology of the material included age and diameter measurements, along with other information such as side-shoot trimming and toolmarks. Fragments of wood considered as carpentry waste were compared to the wood conversion keys provided in Crone and Barber (1981). This method allows comparisons of primary and secondary tooling events as well as the methods used.

*Figure 44*
The sequence of deposits beneath the bow of the vessel, looking north (27 July 2006)

*Figure 45*
Detail of the trunk, identified as hazel, which the stern of the boat lay upon (10 August 2006)

*Figure 46*
The excavated logboat, still partially supported by sandbags, showing both the angle of deposition of the boat and the truncated bow which had protruded above the sands and gravels (28 July 2006)

*Figure 47*
The fully excavated boat, in preparation for the initial floating stage (10 August 2006)

*Figure 48*
The excavated boat showing the angle at which the vessel sat within the sands and gravels with the port (south side) considerably lower than the starboard (north side) (10 August 2006)

### Tree-ring identification

Wood sub-samples, obtained from the SP1–3 stumps found *in situ* around Carpow Bank were frozen prior to thin sectioning for species identification and species types are listed in Appendix IV. Two species of tree are represented and include oak (*Quercus* sp) and birch (*Betula* sp). Both are native to Scotland and well represented at waterlogged sites throughout the prehistoric (Brunning 2000 and Rackham 1977). Birch is a light demanding pioneer that can tolerate acidic damp ground and normally lives no longer than 150–200 years. Oak is tolerant of a wider type of soil and is at the apex of woodland species and has a slow rate of growth living up to and beyond 500 years (Cressey 2007). During the tree-ring study, grab samples of branch wood were identified from samples

obtained from below the boat (Appendix IV). Ten hazelnut shells (Sample 2) along with a tooled piece of straight branch wood were recovered between *c* 1–2m from the bow.

### Significance of the finds

#### Tooled wooden objects

Seven fragments of probably worked wood were identified from Context 106. Of the assemblage the most interesting was a birch stake SF016 (table 3 below) and SF017, a fragment of worked alder that may have functioned as a toggle (Appendix III). The rest of the pieces fall into a non-descript category of what perhaps appears to be carpentry waste. The stake has two oblique facets chopped on one end. These appear to have been done with a sharp blade and with single strokes. The archaeological record is rich in similar material and stakes are synonymous with hurdle manufacture (Rackham 1977) but can also have been used for a multitude of tasks, ranging from uprights in wattle fish-traps to hurdle and brushwood structures interpreted as walkways across inter-tidal creeks, contemporary examples of which have been recorded on the Essex estuaries (Wilkinson & Murphy 1995 *passim*).

#### Hazelnut shells

Four hazelnut shells were radiocarbon dated. One returned a date considerably earlier than the others and this was rejected on the grounds that it was anomalous. The three acceptable dates are shown in table 3 along with a radiocarbon date on a fragment of tooled wood (SF016).

The hazelnut shells represent a food source that was gathered from mature hazel woodland in the autumn, however, it is impossible to say whether or not the hazelnut assemblage was part of a larger collection which have not survived. It seems likely that if such foodstuffs were bountiful then larger numbers would have been collected.

It is clear, however, that the cache of hazelnuts were predated on by a rodent, as four of the shells had distinct concentric tooth-marks attributed to a dormouse. The common, or hazel dormouse (*Muscardinus avellanarius* L), is a small rodent found in woodlands (Fig 51). It is an excellent climber and capable of leaping from branch to branch or reaching fruit and nuts at the ends of the thinnest twigs. In fact it rarely comes down to the ground, where it would be vulnerable to predators. Dormice eat a variety of flowers, fruit, seeds

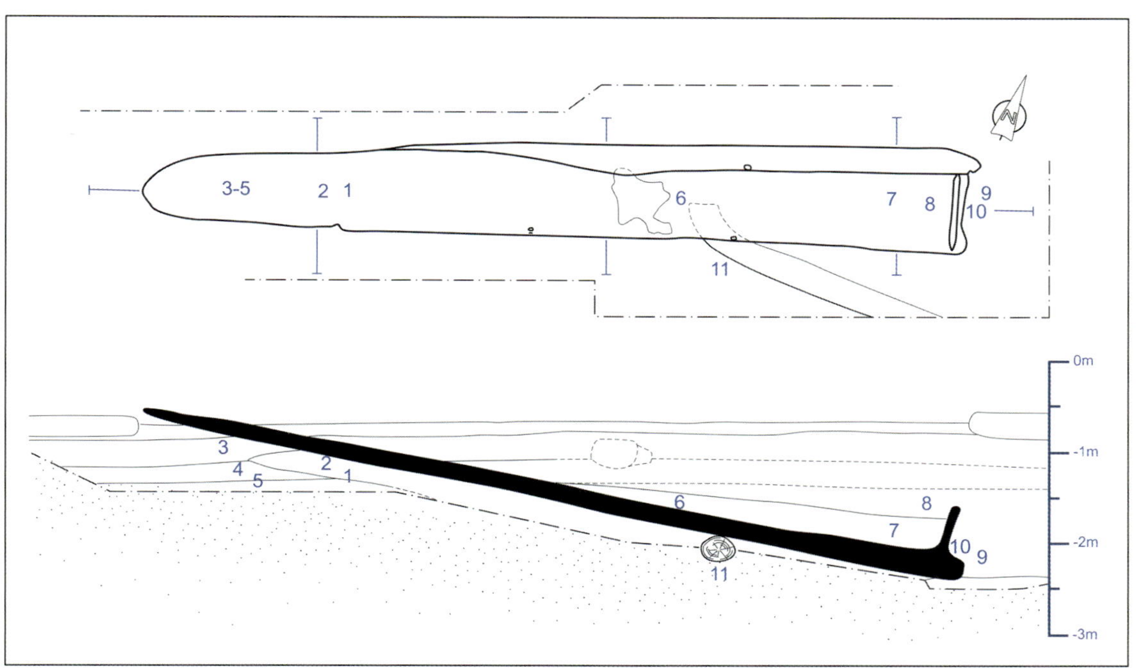

Plan & Section of the logboat showing samples taken during excavation

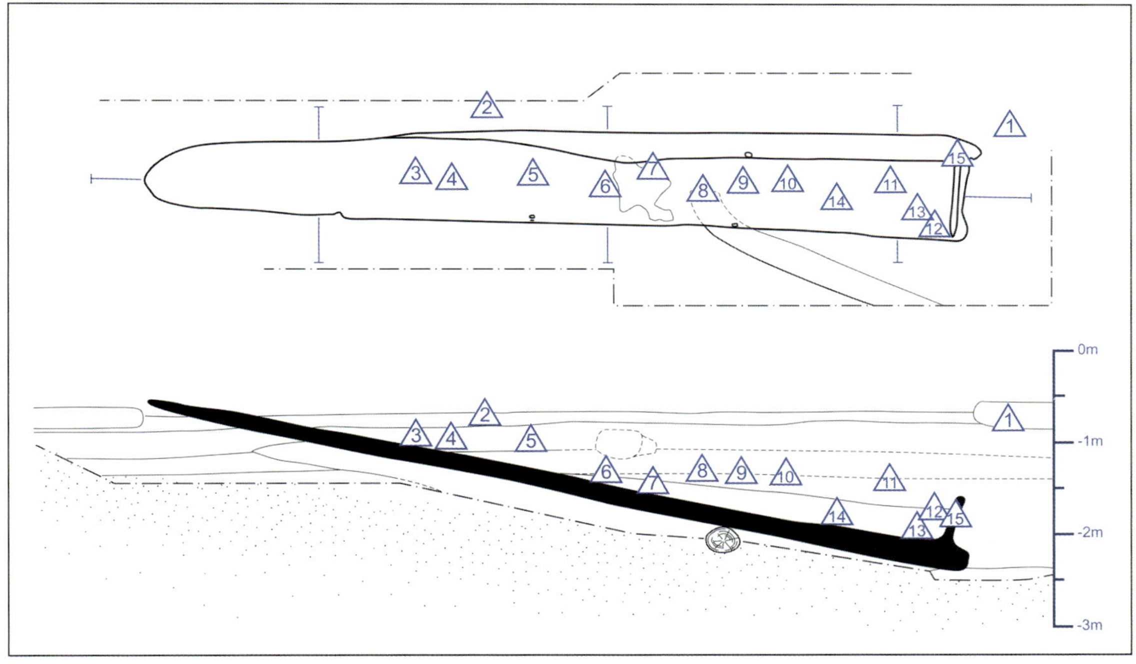

Plan & Section of the logboat showing small finds recovered during excavation

*Figure 49*
Location of grab samples and small finds recovered during the excavation

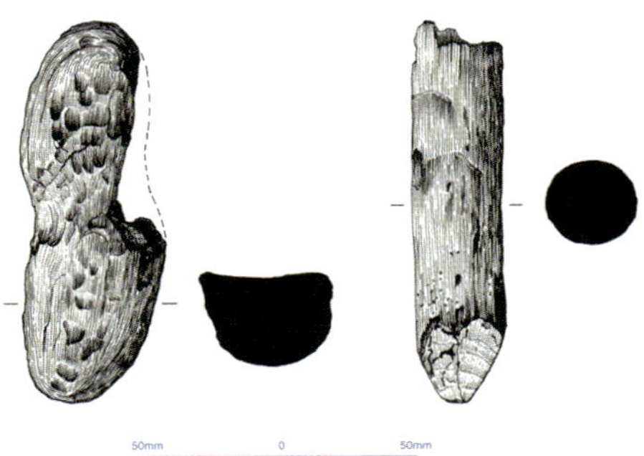

*Figure 50*
Small Finds SF016 and SF017

*Figure 51*
The common or hazel dormouse (*Muscardinus avellanarius* L)

and nuts and are particularly fond of hazelnuts and blackberries. They will also eat aphids and caterpillars when fruit and nuts are in short supply. At present it is found in England and Wales but not in Scotland and Ireland. The northern limit of dormouse distribution in Britain at the beginning of this century was stated to be the county boundary between Durham and Northumberland. Modern day farming practices and diminishing woodland have led to a reduction in populations.

### Grab samples: conclusions

From this small assemblage of wood the following conclusions are drawn:

- Some of the wood recovered from the interior of the logboat is clearly archaeological in nature and contemporary with the logboat

- The hazelnut finds may represent the remains of a larger cache of food gathered by the boatmen during the autumn
- The hazelnuts were predated on by a dormouse, a species that is no longer living in Scotland but would have been common in Bronze Age woodland.

The study also indicates that Context 106 is broadly contemporary with the logboat, through dating of material in Grab Sample 2 and 6, although it is not possible to ascertain whether the material below the logboat was part of the contemporary river or estuary bank.

*Table 3*
Radiocarbon dates for the wood and hazelnut shells found within the logboat

| Lab code | Sample no/small find no, location and context | Species type | Age BP | Cal BC 2 sigma |
|---|---|---|---|---|
| GU-15133 | SF016: within the logboat Context 106 | *Betula undiff* | 2845 ± 35 | 1120–910 BC |
| GU-15135 | Grab Sample 6 Context 106 | *Corylus avellana* | 2825 ± 35 | 1120–890 BC |
| GU-15136 | Grab Sample 2 Context 106 | *Corylus avellana* | 3175 ± 35 | 1520–1390 BC |
| GU-15137 | Grab Sample 2 Context 106 | *Corylus avallana* | 2860 ± 35 | 1130–910 BC |

### 4.4 Recovery

*Tidal recovery, lift, transportation to Granton and site reinstatement*

Following full excavation, the vessel was rigged to float by inserting three 200 litre plastic barrels within the hull. These were supported by foam blocks to protect the surface of the boat and secured within the vessel by load-bearing ratchet straps, which were isolated from the surface of the boat by a layer of plywood (Fig 52). This operation was overseen by conservation staff from the National Museums of Scotland, who confirmed that the condition of the hull was robust enough to undergo the operation, and who aided in the rigging. Once in position, the air barrels could be partially filled with water to decrease buoyancy, allowing control over the upward lift.

The schematic diagram (Fig 53) shows the method of lifting the vessel from its *in situ* location. Following full excavation (Fig 53B), the vessel was supported almost entirely on sandbags and had been completely undercut. During the rigging process (Fig 53C) the air barrels were secured within the vessel, while the deposits beneath the bow were further undercut to allow a downward motion of the bow as the stern lifted during the incoming flood tide (Fig 53D). Once the tide had risen farther and the vessel was clear of the excavation trench, it was guided to its new temporary location on a nearby mud bank (Fig 53E). This operation was carried out by a team of ten people. The vessel was anchored at this temporary location overnight, during the high tide, resting on the soft mud to minimise the risk of damage to the base of the vessel. At the falling tide the following morning the boat was gradually revealed completely for the first time. The vessel was then de-rigged to allow a full photographic record to be made and a mud-pack to be applied by the conservation team to prevent it from drying out over the next seven hours in the hot summer sun.

By late afternoon on 11 August 2006, the vessel had been re-rigged to float for the second time (Fig 71) this time with a mesh net designed to collect any items dislodged during the tow from Carpow Bank to Newburgh quay. At the next flood tide the vessel was once again floated and then towed by a small powerboat the *c* 3km journey. During the tow a diver accompanied the floating logboat to protect the stern (from which the tow was made) against the force of the oncoming water (Figs 72 and 73). The tow was done at a slow speed in order to minimise this effect, and

care was taken to wait until slack water to ensure that no additional tidal force was added. After a journey of around 30 minutes the vessel arrived at Newburgh quay, where a bespoke 9.3m long steel box lifting-frame and flatbed lorry with lifting crane awaited (Figs 74–81). On arrival, the dive team guided the floating vessel into the lifting frame, and secured it using closely spaced load-bearing straps secured to the top of the frame, suspending the logboat within the frame. This provided equal support along the structure of the vessel and minimised stress-loading during the lift. The lifting frame and vessel were then craned onto the flatbed lorry, an operation which took around three minutes from water level to lorry.

Once the lifting frame had been secured onto the flatbed lorry, the logboat was lowered onto the base of the frame, though still secured by the load-bearing straps, and further cushioned with padding to minimise shock to the vessel by vibration. In addition, a jacket of polythene sheeting covered the boat within the frame to minimise drying during transportation. The logboat was transported to the Department of Conservation and Analytical Research at the National Museums of Scotland facility at Granton, Edinburgh. The vessel was then lifted into the Granton laboratory within the lifting frame, again with the suspension time being kept to a minimum. Further to recovery of the logboat, all lifting materials and aids were removed from the site and the excavation was back-filled with hessian sandbags. At the end of a very hot, long and busy day the Carpow logboat was once again on the move, probably for the first time in 3,000 years.

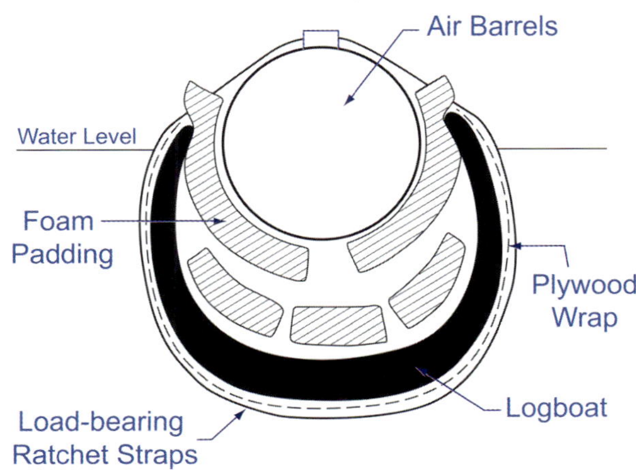


*Figure 52*
Schematic section showing the floating rig employed during recovery

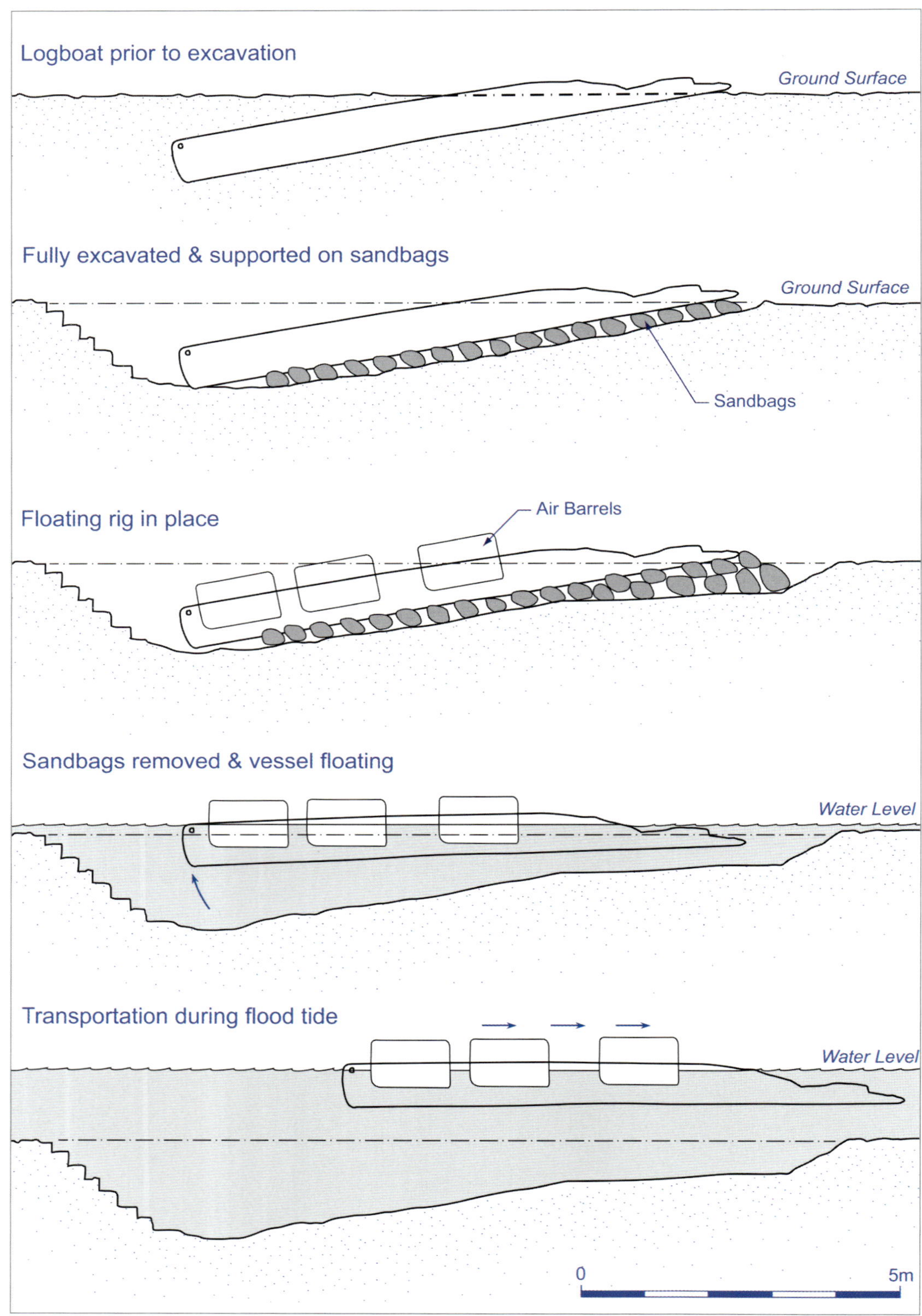



*Figure 53*
Schematic stages of excavation and recovery

*Figure 54*
The first load-bearing straps are inserted underneath the hull of the boat in preparation for the insertion of the air barrels (10 August 2006)

*Figure 56*
A view of the boat, looking north, during the rigging process (10 August 2006)

*Figure 55*
The fully excavated vessel prior to being rigged to float (10 August 2006)

*Figure 57*
Removal of the supporting sandbags from underneath the bow and the insertion of load-bearing straps to retain the air barrels (10 August 2006)

*Figure 58*
The first of the air barrels are inserted into the hull (10 August 2006)

*Figure 59*
The rigged boat awaiting the incoming tide (10 August 2006)

*Figure 62*
With the stern now free, the team await the rising tide to lift the bow of the boat (10 August 2006)

*Figure 60*
The team prepare for the initial floating of the boat in the rapidly rising tide (10 August 2006)

*Figure 63*
Free and floating, the vessel is walked by the team, through the considerable force of the incoming tide, to the mudflats in front of the reed-beds where it is anchored overnight (10 August 2006)

*Figure 61*
The stern of the vessel gently rises for the first time on the flood tide (10 August 2006)

*Figure 64*
The following morning the boat is revealed again at its temporary location (11 August 2006)

*Figure 66*
The entire vessel is revealed for the first time (11 August 2006)

*Figure 65*
As the tide drops the boat is gradually revealed
(11 August 2006)

*Figure 67*
The boat at its interim location on the soft mud of the estuary bank (11 August 2006)

Figure 68
The stern of the vessel (11 August 2006)

Figure 70
National Museums of Scotland staff apply the mud-pack prior to
re-rigging of the boat (11 August 2006)

Figure 69
The stern of the vessel (11 August 2006)

Figure 71
The boat being rigged for refloating under the supervision of
Dr Theo Skinner of the National Museums of Scotland
(11 August 2006)

Figure 72
The re-rigged vessel is refloated on the flood tide prior to being towed
to Newburgh quay (11 August 2006)

Figure 74
Arrival at Newburgh quay where the lifting frame, crane and flatbed
lorry awaits (11 August 2006)

Figure 75
The floating vessel is gently inserted into the lifting frame (11 August
2006)

Figure 73
The final journey of the Carpow vessel as it is towed downstream to
Newburgh (11 August 2006)

Figure 76
The vessel is suspended within the lifting frame using closely spaced
load-bearing straps secured to the top of the frame (11 August 2006)

*Figure 77*
The lift from the water begins (11 August 2006)

*Figure 79*
The vessel within its frame being lifted onto the flatbed lorry
(11 August 2006)

*Figure 78*
At the highest point in the lift, the vessel was around 6m above the
mudflats at the quay (11 August 2006)

*Figure 80*
The frame is finally lowered onto the flatbed lorry (11 August 2006)

*Figure 81*
Protective plastic sheeting is wrapped around the vessel within its
frame prior to transportation to Edinburgh (11 August 2006)

# Chapter 5

# A description of the boat

DAVID STRACHAN

with contributions from Theo Skinner, Rob Sands, Anne Crone and Damian Goodburn

As with other prehistoric boat projects, such as Hasholme (Millett & McGrail 1987) and Dover (Clark 2004a), a three-stage approach was adopted for Carpow: recording the remains of the vessel *in situ*; further detailed study of the vessel once the boat had been recovered; and finally interpreting this information to reconstruct the boat, and establish how it was manufactured.

## 5.1 Post-excavation cleaning and recording

The process of *in situ* recording of the vessel, in the challenging inter-tidal environment, is described in Chapter 4. The second stage of recording took place rapidly following arrival of the boat at the National Museums of Scotland Waterlogged Organics Laboratory at Granton, Edinburgh. This was carried out in conjunction with initial task of removing the mud, sand and gravel which covered the stern and bottom of the vessel. The process was carried out by both archaeologists and conservators in order to record as much information as possible while minimising damage to fragile features, such as toolmarks and caulking. The detailed recording of features on the boat was carried out in this stable environment during which time the vessel was kept wet through the use of pierced pipes (Appendix I), and carried out prior to conservation treatment so that distortion due to conservation was prevented. A Leica Reflectorless Total Station, linked to PENMAP surveying software, was used to produce a highly accurate three-dimensional wire-frame computer model of the vessel that can be viewed from all angles, elevations and scales (Figs 82 and 83). In addition, high-resolution digital photography was taken to capture the logboat in its entirety and then rectified using the metric survey wire-frames (Fig 87). Selected views were then extracted in order to form the basis of ink drawings (Fig 86). The ability to rotate the metric survey data in three-dimensional space allowed the illustration team to obtain scaled three-dimensional isometric views of the boat, in particular the detail of the transom grooves,

*Figure 82*
Recording of the hull in three dimensions with a Total Station further to initial cleaning and prior to conservation

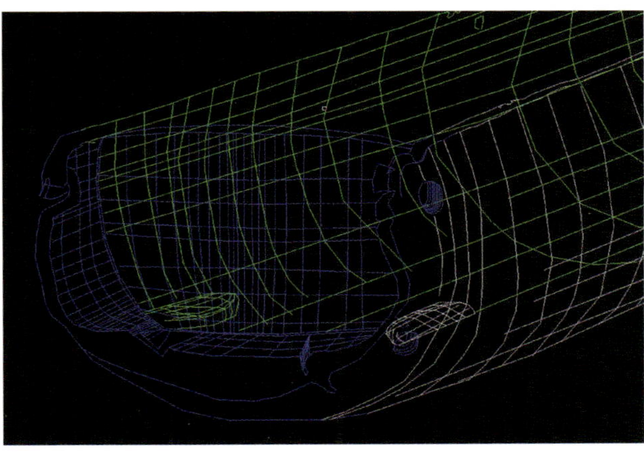

*Figure 83*
The 3-D CAD model of the logboat created by survey of the vessel in the Granton laboratory

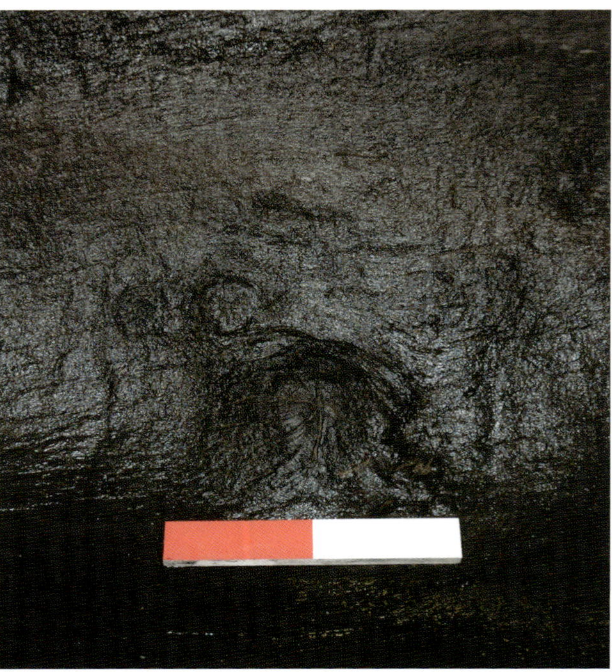

*Figure 84*
The large knot (F4) at the bow

perspectives that traditional drawing techniques would have found difficult to capture in a short amount of time (Figs 98 and 100).

## 5.2 The parent log of the hull

The logboat as excavated measured 8.9m in length and this suggests that the hull was fashioned from an oak tree with a straight trunk of at least 10m in length, possibly much more (Fig 87). As no sign of the curve of the bow survived, it is not possible to say how much of the bow has been lost, though it is possible to estimate the maximum total length of the boat, by extrapolating the sides of the hull in plan until the bow becomes too narrow to be functional. This process indicates that the boat was originally no more than *c* 11m in length, as the hull would be too narrow if any longer. For the purposes of this study it is assumed that the boat, when complete, was in the region of *c* 10m in length. It is possible that the full length of the bole of the parent tree was in the region of 12–15m (Fig 129). There are two knots at

| Code | STERN | | | BODY | | | BOW | | |
|---|---|---|---|---|---|---|---|---|---|
| | Plan | Elevation | Transverse Section | Plan | Elevation | Transverse Section | Plan | Elevation | Transverse Section |
| 1 | Rectangular | Rectangular | Rectangular | Parallel Sided | Parallel | Rectangular | Rectangular | Rectangular | Rectangular |
| 2 | Rounded | Rounded | Rounded | Tapered | Tapered | Rounded | Rounded | Rounded | Rounded |
| 3 | Rounded point | Inclined | Flared | Boat shaped | Sheer | Flared | Rounded point | Inclined | Flared |
| 4 | Transom | Transom G | Sub-rectangular | | | Sub-rectangular | | | Sub-rectangular |
| 4A | | Transom A | | | | | | | |
| 4B | | Transom B | | | | | | | |
| 4C | | Transom C | | | | | | | |
| 5 | Sub-rectangular | Duck-billed | V-Shaped | | | | Sub-rectangular | Duck-billed | V-Shaped |

*Figure 85*
McGrail's morphology chart with the Carpow form in red (after McGrail 1978)

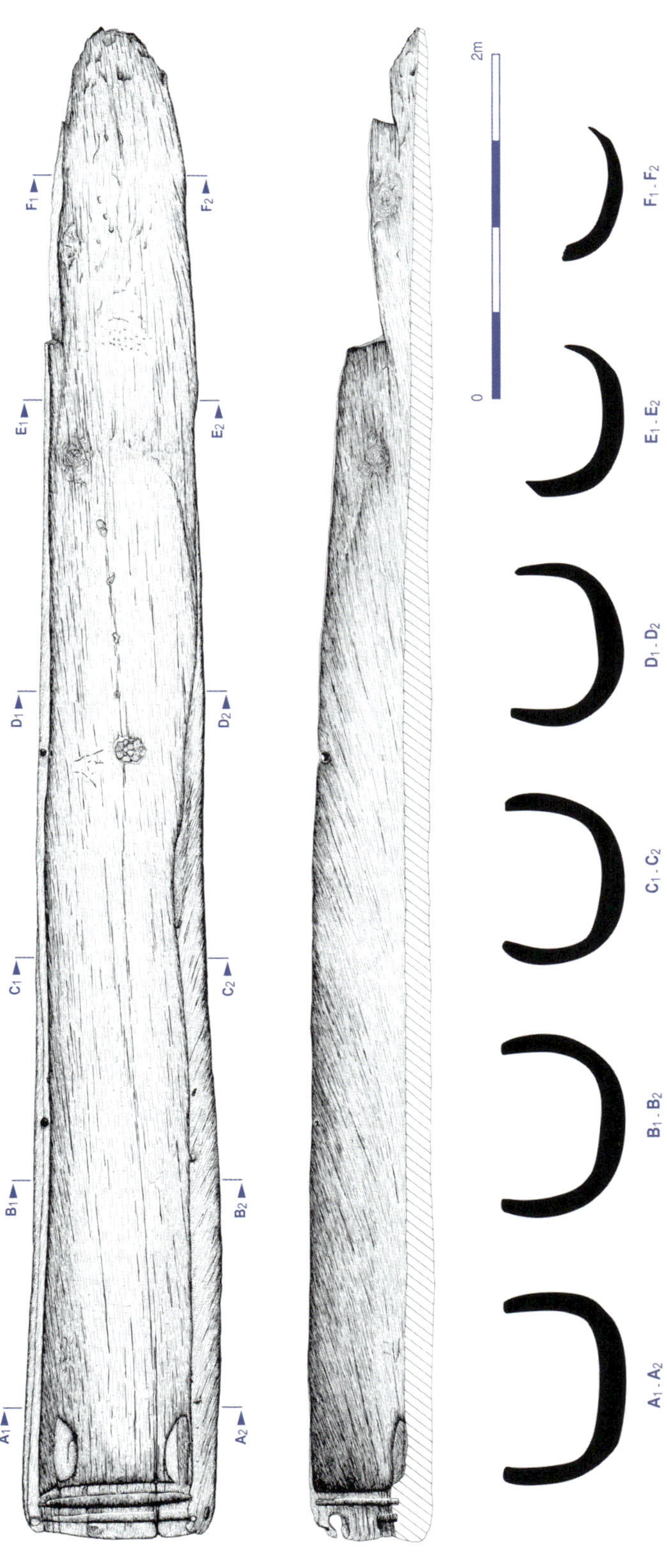

*Figure 86*
A plan and sections of the logboat

*Figure 87*
A photomosaic of the logboat. The composite image is made
up of over 20 photographs

the bow, F2 and F4, the latter being a fairly large branch insertion which has rotted on the outside of the vessel to produce a fairly significant hole (Fig 84). No sapwood was evident on the outside of the vessel, although most other early logboats and plank boats have proved to have some sapwood present (McGrail pers comm). Finally, oak trees the age and size of the Carpow logboat's parent tree would probably have suffered from 'brittle heart' rot (Jane 1970, 228). This rotting of the heart wood starts low down at the base of the tree, which almost always becomes the stern of the vessel and spreads upwards into the bole. This is the primary reason that separate transoms were fitted, and in the Hasholme example, why the elaborate extended bow was also constructed (Millett & McGrail 1987, 112).

### Spiral grain

Characteristics such as large size and lack of knots are often taken as indicators of high quality, but in this case the parent tree had a serious flaw that would have rendered it virtually useless for many other purposes: that of a strongly spiral grain creating an anti-clockwise helix when viewed from the butt (stern) end (Figs 86 and 87, and Chapter 7, pp 100–1). It would appear that some distortion or twisting inward of the starboard side of the Carpow boat may have happened as a result of this feature of the parent tree. As this defect can usually be seen in the fissures of the bark of a mature oak, the Carpow boat-builders almost certainly would have known what lay in store for them. The use of a tree with this feature might be read as the result of a restricted choice in the region.

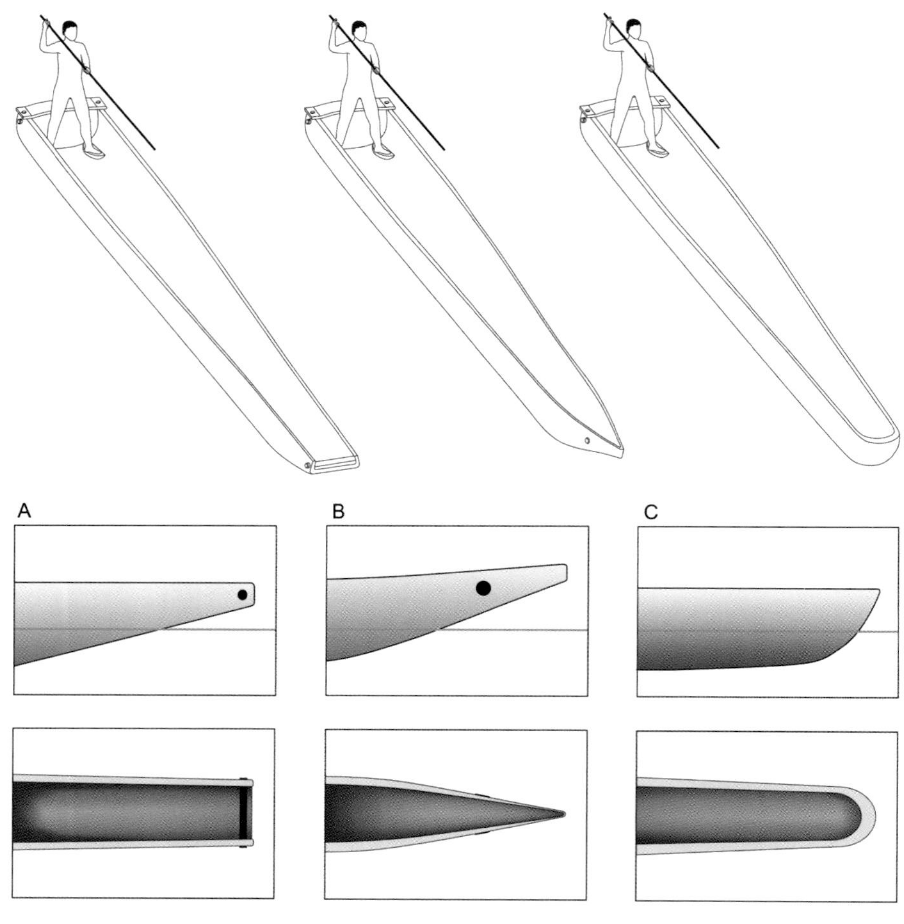

*Figure 88*
The reconstructed options for the Carpow bow: a Hasholme-style expanded bow (A); a pointed bow with 'oculi' (B); and simple rounded form (C). Option C is considered the most probable

## 5.3 Shape of the boat

The vessel is overall log-shaped and tapers towards the bow. The boat was made from a whole log, rather than a half log split longitudinally (Chapter 1, p 2 and Chapter 7, pp 107–9). The bow of the vessel has been lost to tidal erosion and there is no indication, such as an upturn in the base of the bow, to suggest either where the bow began, or what form it took. The form of the boat can be described using the McGrail morphology code (Fig 85; McGrail 1978, 129–30, fig 205) which describes the morphological characteristics of the stern, body and bow in terms of plan, elevation and transverse section. The Carpow boat can be described as 44B2:212:??2, and most likely to be 44B2:212:222 or 44B2:212:322. The code works from left to right describing the morphological characteristics as outlined in Fig 85.

## 5.4 The bow

A number of possible reconstructions for the missing bow were considered. McGrail's morphological chart for logboats (Fig 85) describes four main types of bow when viewed in plan: rectangular; rounded; rounded point and sub-rectangular, with variations of these when viewed in elevation and transverse section (McGrail 1978, 129 and fig 205). The main body of evidence for consideration is from broadly comparable contemporary logboats.

### Comparanda

The usefulness of comparison with other contemporary logboats is restricted, largely as result of a lack of dating evidence, and the fact that the survival of the bow of logboats is often poor. A number of examples, however, can be used in discussing the above options with respect to Carpow.

Firstly, there are the four oak logboats of Late Bronze Age date from Lincolnshire are worthy of consideration. The Appleby 3 vessel, which is *c* 7.5m in length and has produced a date of *c* 1320 cal BC (Q-80), has a pointed bow when viewed in plan, but as much of the hull is truncated, detail of the shape of the bow has been lost (*ibid*, 147–9 and fig 2).

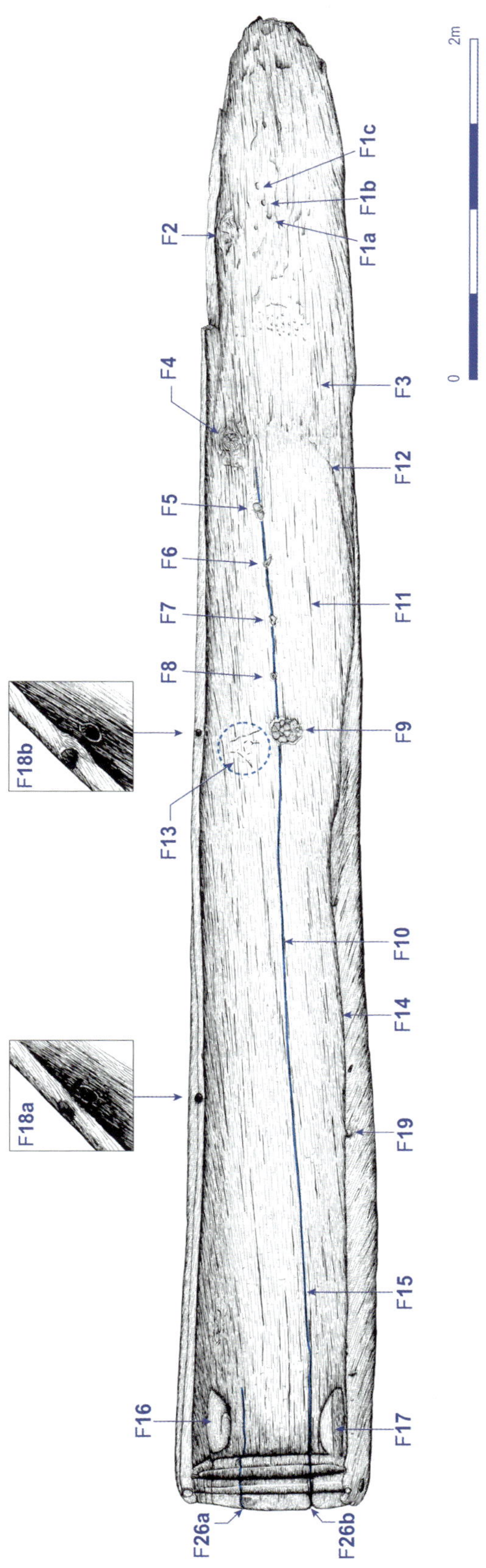

*Figure 89*
Plan of the logboat indicating features mentioned in the text, F1–19 and F26

The Short Ferry boat, which is 7.35m in length and calibrated to *c* 950 cal BC (Q-79), has again suffered erosion across the sheerline of the vessel, but is clearly of a more rounded canoe end form (*ibid*, 271–2). While the value of the radiocarbon date of 834 ± 100 BC (Q-78) for the massive (14.78m) Brigg boat, has been questioned (Chapter 9, p 127 and 131), a Late Bronze Age date is still probable. Again, despite truncation of the sheerline, a canoe end bow is clear (McGrail pers comm; McGrail 1978, 166–72, and fig 9). Unfortunately the Catherinefield boat, from Dumfries and Galloway, dated to the beginning of the Bronze Age (Chapter 9, p 127) was so truncated that no information could be gleamed as to the nature of the bow (Mowat 1996, 18). Similarly, only fragments of the two Late Bronze Age alder logboats from Lough Neely, Co Fermanagh, survive (Fry 2000, 110–11).

From the Iron Age, two boats, again of roughly similar scale to Carpow, Poole Harbour, 10m in length and from the middle of the local Iron Age (McGrail 1978, 254–7) and Shapwick, from Somerset, at just under 6m and from the middle part of the local Iron Age (*ibid*, 254–7), have similar canoe end forms. A well-preserved pointed canoe end form was also found at the Fiskerton vessel, from Lincolnshire, dated to the Iron Age (Field & Parker-Pearson 2004).

Two notable examples of more unusual bows exist and are also worth consideration. The first is the remarkable Hasholme bow, dating to the later Iron Age, which has a bow of almost unparalleled composite form, described as 'end-extended' (Millet & McGrail 1987). This involved two vertically superimposed transverse bow-timbers, retained by tree-nails, and with wash-strakes on both sides. The reason for this approach is probably that the heart rot of the parent oak had travelled so far up the bole as to require the closing of both ends of the boat, and being faced with this necessity, the builders decided to take advantage and increase internal volume (*ibid*, 107). It is almost certain that the Carpow vessel did not have a Hasholme-type bow with extended end boards, as the size of the Carpow parent oak would not have had such extensive heart rot. Secondly, a group of logboats display a type of bow interpreted as incorporating zoomorphic figureheads.

### *Zoomorphic figureheads*

The second type of unusual bow documented involves elongated bows with figureheads, which are widely known in the ethnographic record (McGrail 1978,

67) and in the British archaeological record, primarily through four Scottish logboats. The 13.7m long oak logboat known as Loch Arthur 1 from Dumfries and Galloway is dated to between 150 BC and AD 200 (Mowat 1996, 50–2; Close-Brooks 1975). The bow of Loch Arthur 1 was described thus:

> The boat gradually tapers from the stern to the prow, which ends in a remarkable prolongation resembling the outstretched neck and head of an animal. When excavated this portion of the canoe was entire. At the neck of the figurehead there is a circular hole about 5 inches in diameter from side to side. At the prow a small flight of steps has been carved in the solid oak from the top to the bottom of the canoe (Gillespie 1876, 22).

As outlined below, the horizontal hole, of *c* 130mm in diameter, cut through the bow has been suggested to represent the eye of an animal head, but has also been more mundanely interpreted as for receiving a painter or boat rope (Mowat 1996, 51).

From Loch of Kinnordy, in Angus, another oak vessel, *c* 4.6m in length has been suggested as having a zoomorphic element to the bow. According to the geologist Lyell, who recorded the Loch of Kinnordy vessel in the 1820s, this 'had evidently been carved into an ornamental shape, representing, apparently, the head of some animal' (Lyell 1829, 87–8). It was originally thought to be prehistoric but subsequently produced a date of *c* 800 cal AD (Q-3142). A publication drawing by Lyell for the Transactions of the Geological Society of London for 1829 and reproduced by Mowat (1996, 66, plate 19) clearly shows what appears to be a mouth carved at the end of the head, or equally likely a horizontal hole, similar to that on the Loch Arthur 1 bow, which has been opened by erosion. Indeed, Mowat again suggests that the figurehead is 'probably to be explained as fortuitous, although the hole may have served to retain a boat-rope' (*ibid*, 66).

Another possible figurehead is from North Ayrshire and known as Buston 1, another oak logboat of 6.7m length, with a rounded bow and a projecting stem which was pierced horizontally with a large hole (Munro 1882, 208; Mowat 1996, 13–5). The description sounds uncannily like Loch Arthur and Loch of Kinnordy. Unfortunately the boat was destroyed by fire at the Dick Institute, Kilmarnock, in 1909.

Finally, while McGrail notes a less convincing case for the claim by Hutcheson (1897) that the Errol 2 vessel has a pointed bow with a 'rude but forcible resemblance to the head of an animal' (McGrail 1978, 67), Mowat suggests that the bow had probably been pointed externally in both the horizontal and vertical plains but that this has been foreshortened by splitting and breakage (Mowat 1996, 30). This 8.9m long oak logboat dates to the sixth century AD and is also from the Tay Estuary, remarkably indicating a 2,500 years tradition of very similar large oak logboats on the same body of water.

### *Oculi*

While the appearance of eyes in figureheads is one form of zoomorphic representation on the bows of vessels, a perhaps related phenomenon is when boats themselves were given eyes. In addition to the archaeological record outlined below, there is much ethnographic evidence for logboats, of various dates, with what can be described as decorative bows incorporating 'oculi', or the 'eyes' of the boat (McGrail pers comm). The Hasholme vessel was interpreted as having a pair of 'oculi' carved into the upper bow (Millet & McGrail 1987, 108). The Brigg vessel had two protruding plugs, or bosses, on the port and starboard sides of the bow which served two purposes: to fill knot holes and to act as oculi (McGrail 1978, 167). As outlined above, the idea of 'eyes' on the animal head of Loch Arthur 1 may have a more direct symbolic meaning, but could be related to this more widespread phenomenon. While it has been suggested that the Loch Arthur 1 hole could have served to receive a painter or boat rope (Mowat 1996, 51) it shows little sign of the erosion that might be expected with such use and may have contained a wooden plug inset to represent an eye as in the Brigg example. Similar arguments can be made for the horizontal holes cut into the bows of the Loch of Kinnordy and Buston vessels.

Finally, the Roos Carr model from Holderness (Chapter 1, Fig 7), on the Humber Estuary is thought to represent a Late Bronze Age logboat. It was found in 1836 and has at one end a representation of an animal head with sockets for quartz eyes (Sheppard 1901). Sheppard's original interpretation was of a warrior crew of four, including one carrying a shield. A fifth figure was apparently found within a box, however, which was given to the finder's daughter as a toy and wasn't accessioned by the Hull Museum until 1902. Following conservation treatment in the late 1990s a reinterpretation of the artefacts was made addressing the issue of the additional figure (there are only four pairs of foot sockets in the hull of the model). Indeed, what had previously been interpreted as curving arms fitted much better into the holes in the pubic region as phalluses. The reinterpretation

shows a crew of only two, although there are sockets for four, with the paddle and 'shield', along with the two other figures now on display separately. It is suggested that there may originally have been two boats since there appears to be one figure too many (Gentil pers comm).

Of the two knots (F2 and F4) evident on the port side near the bow of Carpow, one (F4) takes the form of a noticeable hole outboard, and it is likely that this would have been patched when in use. They are both low on the hull, however, the centre of both being around 0.5m below the projected sheerline of the boat. As result, when the boat was in use, both would have been underwater, and therefore unlikely to have been decorated as oculi. Given that these knots occur at 6.55m and 8.05m from the stern of the vessel, there remains the likelihood that additional knots could have existed above these, which have subsequently been lost through the erosion of the bow.

### *Bow conclusions*

While caution has been exercised in reconstructing the bow, given that the sheerline is truncated, the general nature of the vessel, which is unlikely to have been built for speed, and the surviving plan, would suggest a simple form. And so, of the three possible options considered: a Hasholme-type bow with an end board; a pointed bow; and a relatively rounded bow; the simple, rounded canoe end bow would appear the most probable (Fig 88C). This would be 44B2:212:222 or 44B2:212:322, or what McGrail refers to as a Canoe End or Spoon End (McGrail 1978, fig 206). It is almost certain that the Carpow vessel did not have an extended Hasholme-type bow, and while it may be tempting to envisage an elongated decorative bow for Carpow, perhaps in the form of a Tay salmon, or perhaps 'oculi' to guide the boat on its journeys, there is no evidence to support this, and it will have to remain speculation. It is, however, pertinent to recall here the adage 'absence of evidence is not evidence of absence'.

## 5.5 The hull body

As outlined above, the hull is tapered towards the bow, however, in elevation, the sheerline and bottom of the hull are parallel (Fig 87). The bottom of the hull varies little in thickness from stern to bow (Fig 86: A1–A2 = *c* 152mm; C1–C2 = *c* 133mm and E1–E2 = *c* 126mm). A number of significant features on the body of the hull (Fig 89) are outlined below.

*Figure 90*
The evenly spaced repair features F5 to F8 along basal split F26b

### Basal splits and evidence of repairs

There are two significant basal splits in the hull (Fig 89 F26a and F26b and Appendix III) both of which originated at the stern and worked along the hull towards the bow. Both splits run roughly parallel and follow the anti-clockwise spiral grain of the parent log. Basal split F26B has a total of seven features (F5–10 and F15), interpreted as patch-type repairs and taking the form of small daubs of tar-like material, which have been applied to the split in roughly circular patches. A sample of the repair compound was studied by Professor Carl Heron, at the University of Bradford, who reported that it appeared to be fat- or oil-saturated plant matter and not the expected birch or pine resin. The distribution of repairs along split F26b is also worthy of consideration. There are only two evident repairs (F10 and F15) between the stern and F9, roughly halfway along the hull, then four (F8–5) are then found, regularly spaced, further towards the bow. With the probable main concern of leakage at the stern being addressed through a number of repairs and refittings (below, pp 85–8), it is possible that the crew would have watched the split develop over time, and may have used other materials (mosses, bark, hide) to caulk the split between the stern and F9. Notably F5 to F8 are all roughly equally spaced (Fig 89) which may suggest that they were a carried out as a single event, for example, a rapid repair carried out when afloat and perhaps when a cargo prohibited similar repair in the stern area.

The large composite patch F9 is noticeably different from the other patches, being made up of numerous smaller sub-circular daubs, of which around 20 are visible. It is also of interest that F9 is positioned approximately halfway along the hull of the reconstructed length of *c* 10m, and that the centre of the feature is slightly offset from the basal split itself, and its excessive size would appear unnecessary compared with the others. It is therefore a possibility that the patch served a different function, for example, a thickness-gauge hole. These are fairly common features on logboats from many areas, and are holes bored to a preset depth into the partly worked log before it is hollowed, to aid the boat makers in achieving the

*Figure 91*
The enigmatic large composite patch F9

unusual. Feature F29 remains enigmatic, therefore, and is unlikely to be full explained until after the conservation process is complete (Appendix I). The central position of the feature is significant, as it would, for example, make it an ideal location for a mast socket which has subsequently been plugged.

The basal splits F26a and F26b appear to have been a continuing cause of concern for the Carpow boatmen, as indicated by these repairs and the probability that the outer transom groove (below) was a repair in response to leakage through them. Indeed, it is possible that this continuing problem was instrumental in the decision to abandon or deliberately sink the boat (Chapter 13, pp 163–5).

### Sheerline holes

Holes carved through or around the sheerline are common features of many of the logboats in which the upper parts of the hull survive. Though not uncommon, it is usually not possible to ascribe a function as a result of erosion and lack of associated fixtures (Millett & McGrail 1987, 110). As outlined by Millett and McGrail, such holes are usually related to one of three functions:

> Constructional: either pushing the sides of the parent log apart following heat treatment, or holding them together, during the construction stage.

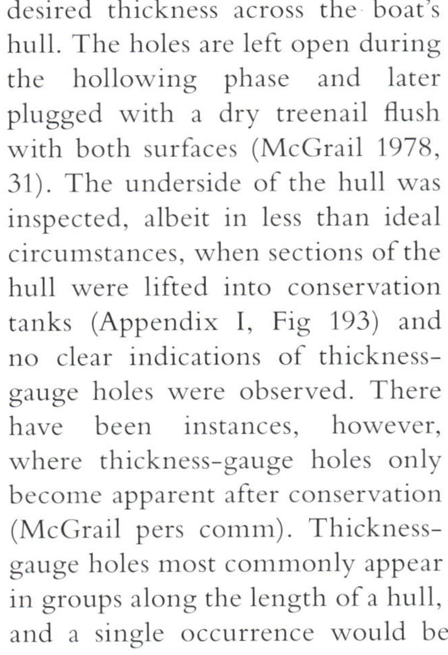

desired thickness across the boat's hull. The holes are left open during the hollowing phase and later plugged with a dry treenail flush with both surfaces (McGrail 1978, 31). The underside of the hull was inspected, albeit in less than ideal circumstances, when sections of the hull were lifted into conservation tanks (Appendix I, Fig 193) and no clear indications of thickness-gauge holes were observed. There have been instances, however, where thickness-gauge holes only become apparent after conservation (McGrail pers comm). Thickness-gauge holes most commonly appear in groups along the length of a hull, and a single occurrence would be

*Figure 92*
Sheerline hole F19 viewed from the outside of the hull

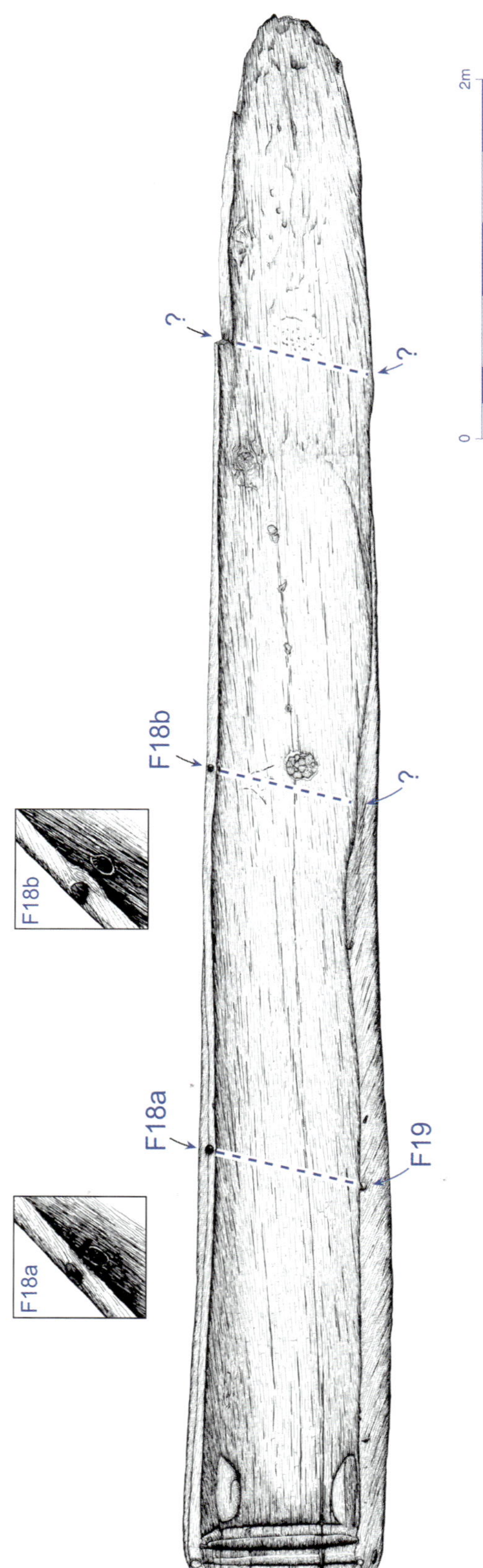

*Figure 94*
Sheerline hole F18a with the faint imprint of a toggle, pin or wooden key

*Figure 95*
A proposed fastening for a 'loose toggle' or 'cotter', possibly the earliest example on such craft

Structural: relating to fittings such as wash-strakes, stabilisers or ribs.

Operational: for example, paired oar-ports through which oars would be passed to allow the vessel to be lifted and carried, or as fastening points for hides to cover perishable goods (effectively a 'spray deck').

A series of 17 sheerline holes in the Hasholme vessel were fairly regularly spaced and positioned *c* 80mm down from the top of the sheerline. They were also

*Figure 93*
The surviving sheerline holes were not positioned opposite each other, but staggered slightly fore and aft. If the pattern was maintained, the hull could have accommodated a total of at least six

*Figure 96*
The stern of the vessel with transom *in situ*

positioned directly opposite one another (*ibid*, 110). While a number of possible functions were considered in the Hasholme example, it was suggested to be most likely that they were either temporary beam lashings to hold together the parent log during construction, or operational by way of a spray deck (*ibid*, 122–4). The Brigg vessel had a combination of horizontally cut holes below the sheerline and cut notches on the sheerline itself, and some suggested interpretations, including fittings for wash-strakes and spray defectors, being mutually incompatible (McGrail 1978, 170), might suggest modifications over a period of time. One suggestion for the three equally spaced surviving holes cut just beneath the starboard sheerline on the Loch Arthur 1 boat, is as handholds for portage (Mowat 1996, 52), and this suggestion is more plausible as a drawing made shortly after its discovery shows that these were part of a series of at least six (*ibid*, plate 10). A series of holes bored diagonally into the bow and stern of a small logboat from Lower Glassaneeran/ Carnbore Townlands, near Moss Side in Co Antrim, have been interpreted as a method of attaching ropes

*Figure 97*
The stern of the vessel with transom removed

67

to allow portage across land (Fry 2000, 63). While this may be plausible with a boat of this size, it is unlikely to explain the diagonally cut holes at the Carpow stern or the sheerline holes. The Carpow vessel would have been large and heavy to manhandle, and there is limited potential for portage out with the estuary and river system in which it operated.

The Carpow holes (Fig 93) share none of the characteristics outlined above, and consist of L-shaped holes (F18a, F18b and F19) cut vertically into the top and outboard of the sheerline itself, and then horizontally out through the inboard of the hull just below the sheerline. They are fashioned in such a way as to leave a thin rod of timber, carved in the solid, surviving *c* 10mm in diameter, in place across the top of the hole (Fig 92). Allowing for the affects of erosion, however, it is possible that when in use, these delicate features could have had withy ties attached. Significantly, one of the holes, F18a has an imprint on the inboard face on either side of the hole (Fig 94). This could indicate a 'loose toggle' fitting, straddled across the hole on the inboard of the hull, as a fastening for an external lashing (Fig 95; McGrail pers comm). It is possible that both forms of fastening were employed at different times.

Only three holes survive, F18a and F18b on the port side and F19 on starboard. It would be reasonable to assume that there were at least two pairs of holes, with the opposite companion to F19 missing due to erosion of that part of the sheerline. Indeed, if the pattern was maintained, a total of six, or possibly even eight, may have originally existed, all lost through erosion of the sheerline towards the bow (Fig 93). Another noticeable and intriguing feature is that F18a and F19 are slightly offset, a fact that requires consideration when discussing possible function.

### Sheerline holes: function

A number of functions can be considered for the sheerline holes. In terms of construction, it is possible that the holes relate to the hollowing-out phase of manufacture, although the manner in which they are fashioned would appear over-elaborate for this function, and the advantage of offsetting the holes is unexplainable.

Similarly, structural explanations, such as fastening for wash-strakes, stabilisers or ribs must remain a possibility, although again it is difficult to envisage how the configuration of the holes, or their spatial relationship would work in this scenario (McGrail pers comm).

A range of operational functions exist, including ties related to net-fishing, or if feature F9 did prove to be a socket for a mast, fastenings for a sail. More probable however, is the model whereby the holes, with the 'loose toggle' fastenings, served as fastening points for either a spray deck or net to cover the open boat, or perhaps for wet hides to cover the hull in order to keep the vessel wet at low tide. A spray deck of skin covers lashed down onto the fastenings would have proved very useful in a fairly unstable vessel with a low freeboard, both protecting any cargo and minimising incoming bilge water. Covers of wet hides would be useful to keep the vessel wet in hot weather. Once again, while the advantage of offsetting the holes is obscure, the function sits comfortably with the scale and configuration of the holes, and the probable 'loose toggle' fastenings. This may have been of particular value with the rounded hull of Carpow, which in comparison with other British Bronze Age logboats, with wide flat bottoms and a hard turn of the bilge, would have resulted in low stability and a propensity to have drawn in more water.

A final operational function, tentatively proposed, is that the holes could have held loop-like lashings, or grommets, for oar pivots, offset so as to allow overhand rowing. A withy fastening such as this could have held oars for occasional use, for example, in the open estuary where punting was not possible. The gap between F19 and F18a holes in fore and aft distance is *c* 110mm and the centre of those holes for'ad to the next hole F18b is *c* 2.2m. The first pair of holes is also about this distance from the transom. The internal diameters of 40mm are exceeded outboard where the holes were cut to emerge upward rather than truly horizontally. Although unknown in recent British vernacular craft, they have been documented as oar pivots in recent logboats in Austria and vernacular craft elsewhere (Salemke 1972, 5), and were known in traditional Shetland rowing vessels in conjunction with a single tholepin (Osler 1983, 42). Historically they are associated with the earliest oars on images of ancient Egyptian craft from *c* 2500 BC (Rudolph 1974, 59; Vinson 1994, 35). The earliest evidence from the British Isles comes in the form of the Late Iron Age Broighter boat model from Ireland which shows oar pivots of twisted gold wire set through holes just below the sheer (McGrail 1987, 214). If grommets were used they would probably have been made of twisted withy at this period, though the raw hide often used in Shetland would also have been a viable material. Either material would have been rather stiff pivots rising a little above the sheerline. These may have appeared very similar to the Broighter configuration. The grommets could have been attached via wooden toggles, as outlined above, or by forming a loop round the sheerline, and seizing it together to form a stiff loop above the sheerline. The type of bulge in the handle of the Late Bronze Age Canewdon 'oar' (Chapter 8, pp 118–19) could then have a function of stopping the oar slipping through the pivot loop. This loop would have to have been formed by lashing each time the oar was used, but they could have remained attached and pivoted inboard when not needed. Grommets in some traditional northern boats allow the user to release oars in moderate conditions without risk of loss, a positive feature not exhibited by most other forms of oar fulcrum. If such an arrangement was used with the Carpow logboat the modest wear on the sheer, in the vicinity of the holes, could perhaps be accounted for. The implications are considerable at the level of boat technology as oars are far more powerful than paddles, and if this tentative interpretation for Carpow is correct, it is important, as it would be the earliest evidence for the use of oars in north-west Europe by several hundred years. However, there are some problems with this interpretation. As outlined below, there are numerous Irish examples of later logboats with fittings and fixtures for rowing (Fry 2000 *passim*), notably seats and footrests promoting grip within the hull and allowing 'leg-work'. The lack of such features within the Carpow vessel would result in crew kneeling or standing on the curved floor of the hull and only effectively using arm power.

### 5.6 The stern

The stern of the Carpow vessel is well preserved, retaining as it did, an *in situ* transom. Both the hull and transom show little sign of erosion resulting from exposure to the elements for elongated periods of time, as commonly witnessed on coastal hulks exposed for one or two centuries. In plan the stern is at right angles to the overall run of the boat and can be described as four in McGrail morphology code (Fig 85), which is usual for boats with separately fitted transoms. A feature unique to British prehistoric logboats, however, are the footrests which survive carved in the solid at the stern. Some elements of the fixtures and fittings at the stern, such as the beam-tie and cross plank, were not recovered, but are inferred from features on the hull and through comparison with other logboats. Consideration regarding their loss is given later

(Chapter 13, pp 164–5). From the configuration of features at the stern, it is clear that there was one, if not two, major repairs made to the stern in at least two separate phases. This following will document the features recorded, and inferred, and attempt to outline probable phasing in modifications of the stern over time, from original design to full development.

### Stern hull form

The boat has a raised transom ridge at stern (F29 and Fig 99) left to receive the transom in a cut groove. This is a fairly common feature and the elevation and transverse section is described in the McGrail morphology code as 4B2: a fitted transom slotted into a raised ridge at the stern, with a rounded transverse section. This form is also found on Brigg (McGrail 1978, 167); Short Ferry (*ibid*, 271); Garmouth (Mowat 1996, 35–6); Glasgow Springfield 2 (*ibid*, 41–2); and River Clyde (*ibid*, 76–7) boats, with slight variants including Clifton 2 (McGrail 1978, 181–2); Poole (*ibid*, 255); and Orkney (Mowat 1996, 74–5).

### Footrests

At a position just forward from the transom ridge (F29) a matching pair of shelves have been fashioned in the solid from the parent log on both internal sides of the hull (Fig 89, F16 and F17 Appendix III), and as such they are clearly part of the original design of the vessel. While these resemble features described as seat blocks on other logboats, they are much lower down in Carpow, being as much part of the floor of the hull as of the sides. While it is possible that these shelves supported a short raised deck, or plank platform, on which a helmsman may have stood, it is more probable that the shelves themselves are footrests on which a helmsman would have stood directly, with one foot on each footrest, while punting, steering or directing the craft. As outlined above, this slight additional height would have afforded the helmsman a view over the heads of the crew and a commanding position from which to steer.

As noted above, the floor of the hull of Carpow is noticeably curved transversely; this would have made it uncomfortable to stand on for long periods of time, and potentially more difficult to achieve grip and stability. The footrests, however, would offer a flat surface on which to stand when inside the logboat, and being raised from the floor of the hull would have kept the user's feet out of any bilge water. In fact, the surface of the footrests decline

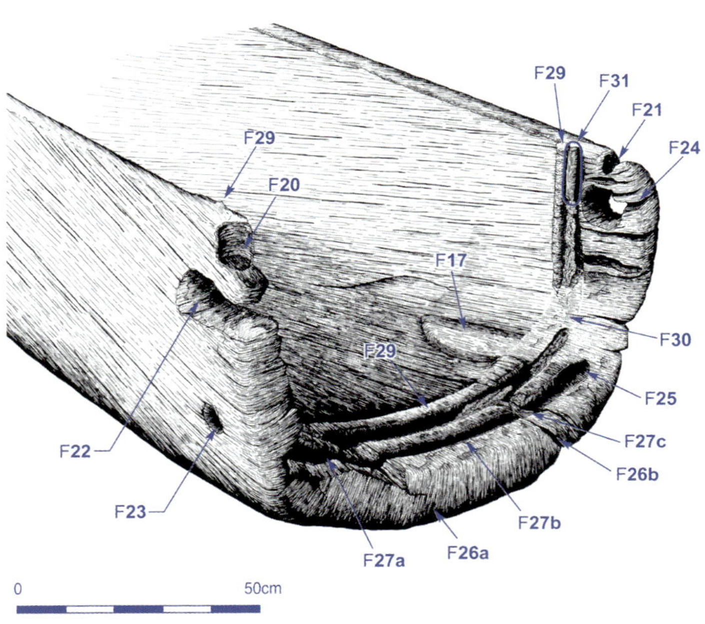



*Figure 98*
An annotated drawing of the stern showing features F17 (starboard footrest); F20 and F21 (cross plank/seat retaining holes); F22 and F24 (beam tie holes); F23 and F25 (repair transom groove holes); F30 (repair block slot); F27a–c (repair transom groove where letters a–e indicate dimensions recorded in Appendix III); F26a and b (basal splits in hull); and F29 (transom 'ridge')

*Figure 99*
A general view of the stern with the transom removed: starboard detail

slightly from the inside of the vessel down to where they meet the internal hull face. This may have offered slight additional grip over a completely level surface, and when bending the knees to, for example, use a punt (Chapter 8, pp 120–1) would have allowed the weight of the helmsman to be used against the inside face of the hull. Finally, the firm foot grip offered by the footrests would have provided a sound platform from which to balance the logboat, which would have had poor transverse

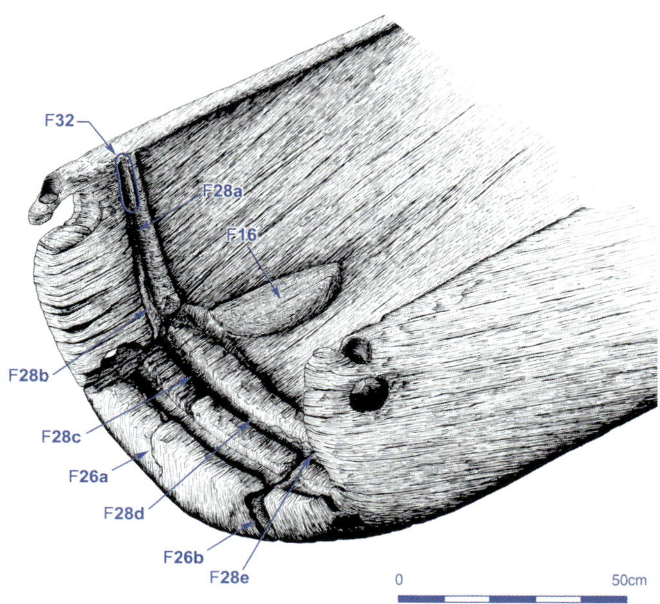



*Figure 100*
An annotated drawing of the stern showing features F16 (port footrest);
F28a–e (transom groove where letters a–e indicate dimensions recorded in
Appendix III)

*Figure 101*
A general view of the stern with the transom removed: port detail

stability, have a tendency to roll starboard to port side, as result of the rounded hull (Goodburn pers comm). By applying weight on either footrest, the helmsman could make very minor adjustments to counter-balance this movement.

There are no exact parallels known from logboats in Britain and Ireland, however, an undated boat, probably from Loch Aughlish, near Castlecaulfield in Co Tyrone had two D-shaped depressions cut into the floor of the boat *c* 60mm from the stern which

*Figure 102*
The footrests with the transom *in situ*

*Figure 103*
The starboard footrest F17, with transom *in situ*, showing wear on the
partially lost section

*Figure 104*
The port side footrest F16 and its relationship to the transom
grooves

were 'almost certainly used as footrests' (Fry 2000, 54). While the position of these features is similar to the footrests in Carpow, there the similarities end. The boat itself is only *c* 2.23m in length and clearly a different scale of craft, however, the D-shaped features do show an attempt to provide internal positions, and also presumably, in this instance, grip for the feet.

Indeed, most of the references to footrests and grips come from a series of rowing logboats from Ireland, where they are often clearly associated with features such as seat supports and rowlocks. An example is the substantial oak rowing logboat from Bartin's Bay, Lough Neagh, Co Antrim, which was left *in situ* and is now believed destroyed. Fragmentary remains survived to a length 13.72m and it has been suggested that the original craft could have been in the region of 15m in length. Pairs of regularly spaced crescent-shaped footrests, carved in relief onto the base of the floor, along with rowlock fulcrums and seat-fittings, indicate that at least 11 oarsmen were accommodated. Indeed, it has been suggested that the crew could have comprised double this number if each only worked a single oar apiece. Unfortunately the boat is undated (*ibid*, 61). Similar features are recorded in the much smaller 5.1m long rowing logboat, from Upper Glassaneeran Townland, near Moss Side, Co Antrim (*ibid*, 64). Here two pairs of seat supports were carved in relief into the interior of the hull with corresponding D-shaped raised heelrests on the floor of the boat. Blisters in the upper parts of the sides with apertures to accommodate tholepins for four oars were also found. Interestingly in this example the seat supports have a similar profile in section as the footrests on Carpow. Again, this boat has not been dated. Finally, records of a substantial oak logboat, also undated, from a crannog lough, *c* 7.62m long from Lisnagonnell Townland, south-west of Lough Brickland, Co Down, suggest two pairs of seat supports with foot grips in the floor. While the boat was published without illustration (Lett 1895), a reconstruction drawing, based on the field notes, was later made by Seaby. Perhaps most interesting in this example is that the seats were confined to the rear half of the vessel suggesting that the front half of the boat had been reserved for cargo, perhaps to ferry building materials or trussed animals to the crannog (Fry 2000, 71). While unfortunately none of the above examples are dated, the evidence is that these footrests clearly relate to rowing, through the use of seats, foot grips and rowlocks, which is very different to the type of function that the Carpow features suggest.

As discussed above, the sheerline holes may suggest the possibility of rowing for Carpow, however, the absence of internal features in the floor and sides of the body of the hull would suggest that this area was restricted for another use: namely retaining cargo.

### The transom

As outlined above (p 60 and 69), separate fitted transoms are relatively common in larger prehistoric logboats, over *c* 7m in length, where the parent logs were older and more likely to have suffered from 'brittle heart' rot (McGrail 1978, 64–5). While this rotting of the wood could make the process of hollowing out the interior of the vessel at the stern, the thickest part of the log, easier, it was the primary reason that the stern in such vessels is not fashioned, in the solid, from the parent log (Millett & McGrail 1987, 107). In such instances, the separate transom is usually fitted into a retaining slot or groove, which is often caulked to make the seal watertight. While numerous references are made to the survival of separate transoms from logboats in the past, many were subsequently lost or only briefly recorded prior to reburial, and few have undergone any detailed study. The Hasholme vessel produced a separate transom, excavated *in situ*, which is one of only a few prehistoric transoms to survive in an almost complete state. It is a single-piece board cut from one half of a log, which had been split longitudinally, and measures 0.99m in height by 1.08m at its maximum width, and, in cross-section, is lens-shaped, varying in thickness from *c* 25mm at the edges to *c* 90mm near the centre. Two unusual features were recorded on the Hasholme transom: a pair of horizontal holes at the top of the transom; and, underneath these, a U-shaped projection carved in the solid on the outboard side. While a possible anthropomorphic design (two eyes and a mouth) was noted for these features when viewed from astern, the protruding U-shaped feature was found to be in contact with the beam-ties above, effectively transferring downward pressure to push the transom down and into its retaining groove, securing the transom. Further, as this boat was 1m high at the stern, it was suggested that the two holes were used with ropes or spars to lower the transom (estimated at 60–75kg) into the groove during construction. Finally, the transom was held firm within its retaining groove with small wedges, and watertightness was promoted through caulking with a variety of materials including moss (*ibid*, 112–13).

The Carpow transom is a substantial piece of oak, measuring 0.6m in height and 0.85m in width, and

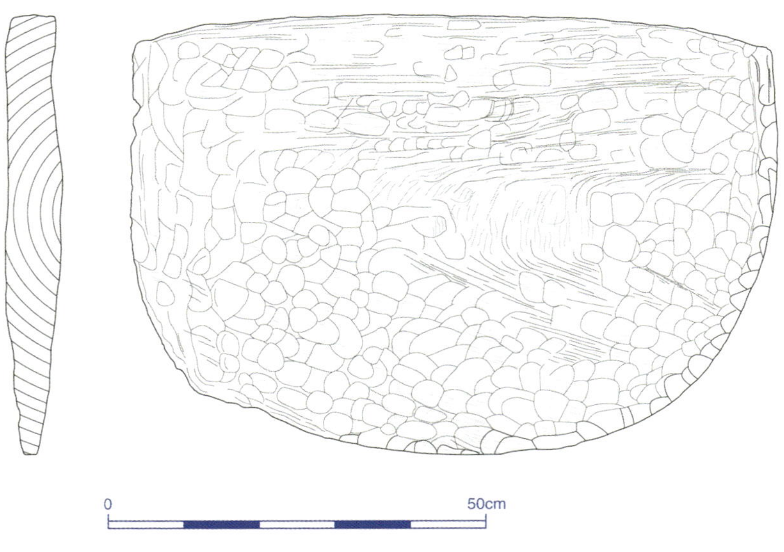



*Figure 105*
The transom showing wood-working detail

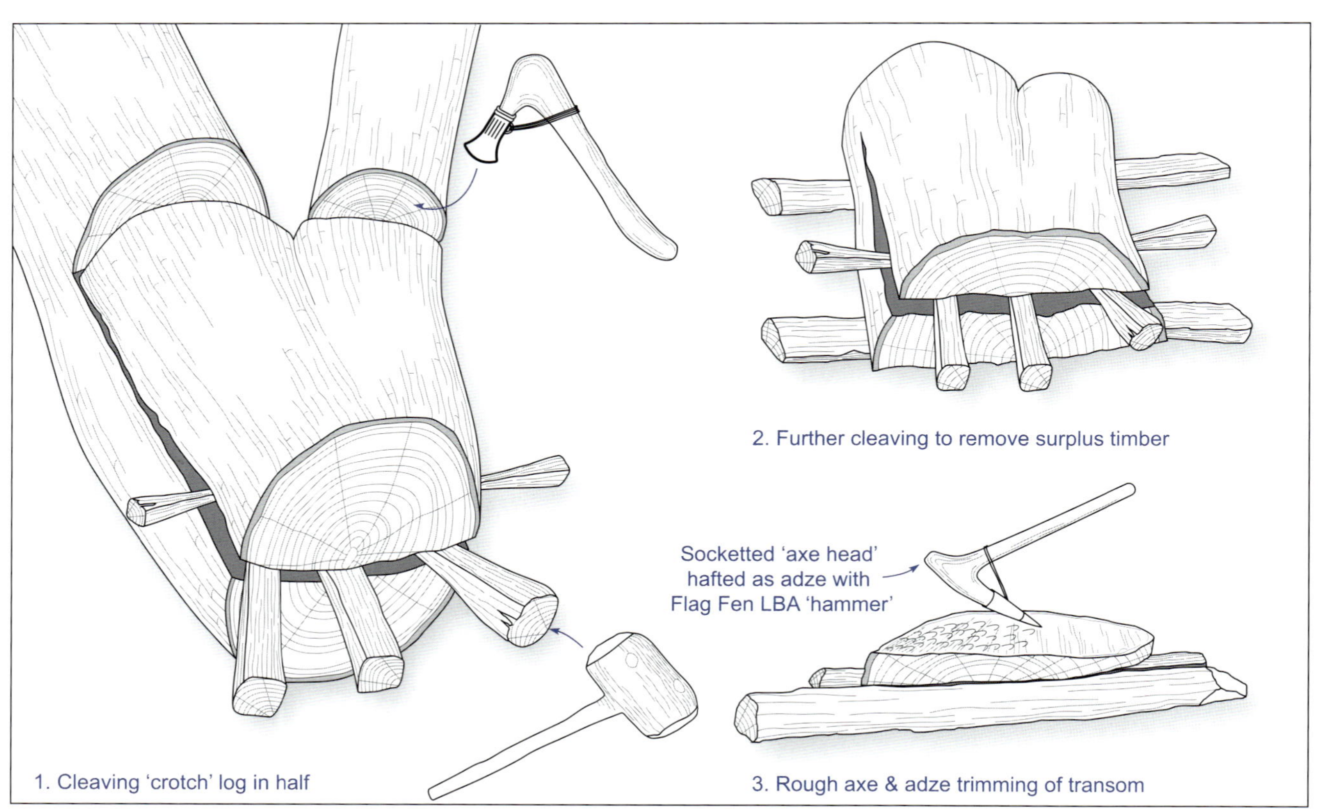



*Figure 106*
The process of cleaving the tangential plank from the top of the parent log, or another log, where the trunk begins to branch, to create the transom

*c* 75mm at its thickest part (Figs 105 and 106). It is slightly convex on the inboard side and flatter on the outboard. The tree-ring study (Chapter 6, pp 91–3) has shown that it was fashioned by cleaving a plank tangentially from part of the crown of a large tree, high up where the tree bole forked into the two main branches of the trunk (Figs 127 and 129). The tree bole at this point must have been at least 0.8m in diameter, allowing for sapwood and bark. The tree-fork often has a wider diameter, and therefore the ability to provide a wider-sectioned log, than the area below it, however, its convoluted grain can make it more difficult to cleave and trim. Figure 106 shows how the transom was made by splitting a large forked oak log in half and then cleaving and hewing off the surplus timber to end up with a D-shaped plank. The transom was then cut to fit the internal section of the boat with its edges trimmed to form a regular bevel to fit the original transom groove. This trimming and bevelling results in a lens-shaped cross-section, like Hasholme (Fig 105). Thin oak wedge packing and moss caulking were used to secure the transom within the transom groove (see below, pp 81–4). Once cleaned, fairly well-preserved toolmarks were revealed over the inboard face of the transom.

### *Characterisation of the transom toolmarks*

ROB SANDS

The entire inboard face of the transom has toolmarks present, which vary in preservation from good to poor, with no facet having a complete set of facet features (Sands 1997). The registrations of the sides of the blade used are non–existent or at least ephemeral. In a limited number of cases there are jam features, where the strike has been unsuccessful and the blade has had to be removed, however, in all cases these are small and partial. The lack of these features makes exact reconstruction of the blade edge impossible. Despite not being able to make exact blade reconstructions some approximate suggestions can be made (Fig 109).

The widest observable facet is 53mm and general observations suggest that this could be close to the full size of the blade used; the longest continual single facet is around 58mm. The facets are also dished in cross-section, which results in the overall impression of the transom surface as scooped or pockmarked. The deepest facet represented being approximately 3mm from the horizontal. The scooped nature of the faceted surface is characteristic of the use of a Bronze

Age tool and the presence of the neat jam feature combined with the facet length indicates a metal edge (O'Sullivan 1996, 293; Sands 1997). There is no surviving evidence, or any reason to assume, that more than one tool produced at least the bulk of the facets observed. If this tool was close to 53mm or slightly larger this fits well with the average size of Late Bronze Age finds from Scotland and northern Britain (Fig 110). It also fits well with other surviving marks of a similar date (eg Nayling and Caseldine 1997, 177–88 and fig 101).

Without full facet features, especially jam registration, direction of cut can be difficult to determine and Fig 111 is intended only to give a general sense of possibilities. Although the general flow of working in any given instance is probably correct, the direction of working might be reversed. The parallel nature of some facet groups might suggest that the tool used was mounted as an adze but this needs some further experimentation. In the Bronze Age it is likely that at least some blades could be used in both ways depending on the manner of hafting. The use of bronze tools hafted in different ways is also suggested on timbers from the Dover Bronze Age boat (Goodburn 2004, 129).

On rare occasions tool signatures survive, in Fig 112 labels A and B mark two ridges, which are the product of damage in the tool edge. Small indentations in the blade edge cause these ridges and the resultant pattern of ridges is unique to the tool that produced them. In addition to the more prominent ridges shown in Fig 112 there are other smaller far less distinct ridges also apparent but not clearly visible in the photograph. However, such signature traces were only positively observed in two locations. The survival shown in Fig 112 is probably a by-product of a slightly deeper cut, which resulted in the tool jamming into the wood surface. This left a proportion of the facet at a lower level than the surrounding wood, effectively protecting it from abrasion. Similarly, the slightly better survival of delicate detail at the edges of the transom are probably the result of the piece being protected within the transom groove (Fig 113).

Signatures can be extremely useful in determining when the same tool has been used. This can be particularly important when toolmarks are found on more than one item or on different elements in a structure, allowing those items or elements to be associated through the tool that was used to work them. Exact matches are also likely to represent almost exactly the same time of working because tools would continually be resharpened. Unfortunately, the surviving signatures on the Carpow transom are too small to make positive matches and as the only part of the boat that seems to have decent mark survival is the transom, they have limited immediate value other than to indicate the general level of preservation.

In some areas the woodworker clearly had more difficulty in cutting the surface. Toward the centre of the concave side of the transom a series of shorter less distinct facets are present, demonstrating numerous small cuts, this part of the wood surface has a generally more 'confused' grain pattern and was probably somewhat harder to work (Fig 115).

In conclusion, the marks on the transom board fit nicely with currently understood characterisation of Late Bronze Age toolmarks, both in terms of general size and the shape of the facet. Full facet definition is absent and consequently blade shape reconstruction can only be done at a basic level. It is likely, however, that a single tool was used and this was close to the size of the largest facet observed (53mm). The edge of the tool was gently curving

*Figure 107*
Side view of the Carpow transom showing tangential conversion (photo: R Sands)

and the straight, parallel areas of faceting suggest that the tool itself may have been mounted and used as an adze.

The Dover boat experiment showed that with such facets, the whole scoop-shaped removal can often be a little wider than the blade that made them, as blades are often wielded at a slight angle to the grain with a slight slicing action that makes tools cut better. It is therefore likely that the tool used to trim the transom was a maximum of 53mm wide and possibly a little narrower (Goodburn pers comm). It is difficult to tell whether the blade used was hafted as an axe or adze though the width of the transom timber would have made it very difficult to use an axe. The depth of the facets suggests that the blade was rather thick

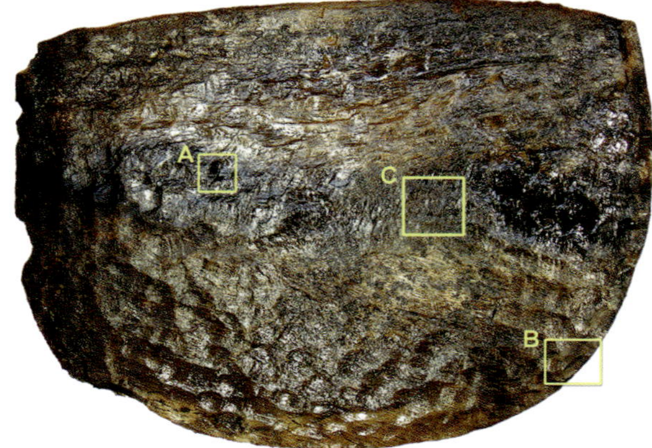



*Figure 108*
The faceted transom surface showing positions of detailed photographs
(photo: R Sands)

*Figure 109*
Tentative blade shape reconstruction. The curve indicated by the dark line is reasonably good, the right hand registration of the blade side is reasonable but not 100% definite, the left hand side is more ephemeral

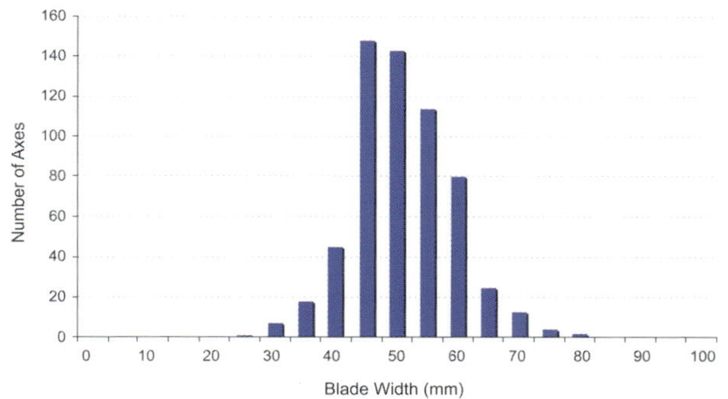

*Figure 110*
Frequency distribution of Late Bronze Age axe widths based on known axe finds from Scotland and Northern Britain. Data derived from Schmidt and Burgess (1981)

with a steep bevel. The size and form is typical of socketed axeheads of the Late Bronze Age (Fig 110 and Goodburn 2003). No attempt was made to finish the timber by hewing across the grain of the transom as in most of the inside of the hull.

***Transom conclusions***

The transom is a well-preserved example found *in situ* within the boat, however, while radiocarbon dating has shown that it is broadly contemporary with the hull, it was not possible to verify, from the tree-ring study, whether it came from the same tree as the hull, or whether it came from a different tree at a later date (Chapter 6, pp 91–5). In addition there are a number of factors that could suggest that the surviving transom may be a replacement.

Firstly, the surviving transom was fitted over what appears to be an inserted block repair (F15) (see below, pp 85–8). It is possible that F15 was a 'repair' to the hull in the first phase of development, inserted to replace rotted wood, resulting from brittle heart rot, on the inside of the hull on the starboard side. It is equally possible, however, that the repair is secondary, and a response to spreading of the hull over time. Basal splits (F26A and F26B) are drying fissures that would have led to an eventual spreading of the hull, with the knock-on effects of an increasingly

*Figure 111*
General directions of strike. Grey arrows are approximate, yellow arrow based on multiple facet features (photo: R Sands)

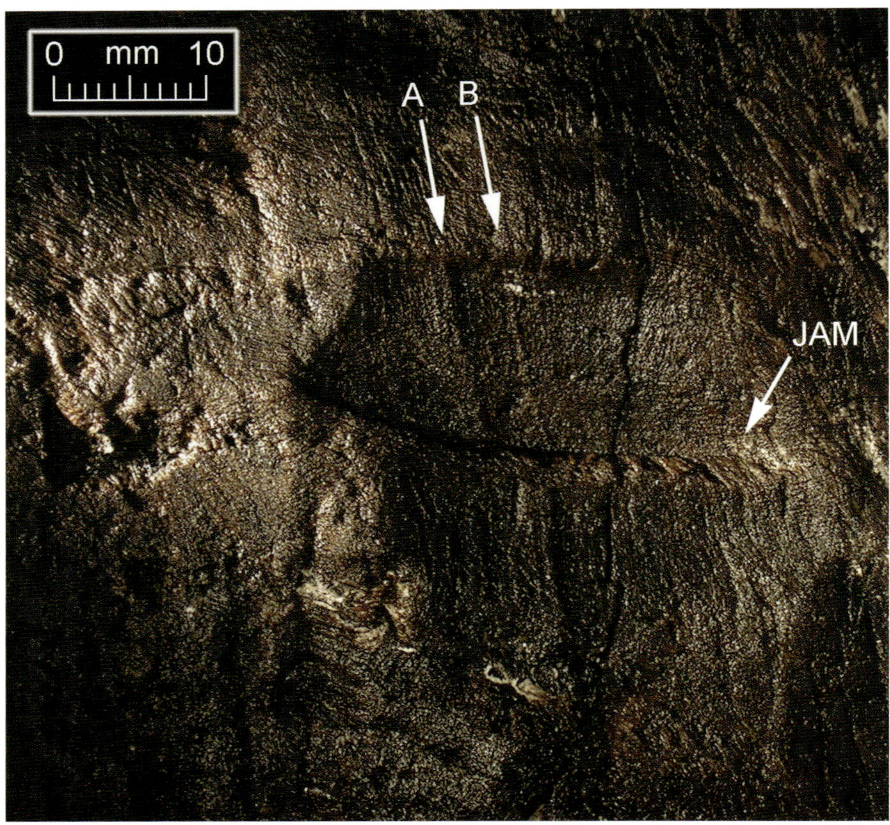



*Figure 112*
Area A (photo: R Sands)

*Figure 113*
Area B: rays are viewed end on, see also Fig 107
(photo: R Sands)

loose-fit for the original transom and leakage. The fissures may have resulted from a period of neglect when the stern of the vessel was left exposed to the elements. Oak is particularly susceptible to end grain splitting and this process has been observed in reconstructed logboats, for example, the Poole Iron Age boat. Built in 1990, this boat had to be made river-worthy some ten years later by fitting a new transom and significantly, the replacement transom needed to be 100mm wider than the original to fit the expanded vessel (Goodburn 2002, 51). If this was the case, then it would suggest that the repair block, and the surviving transom, replaced an original, smaller, transom. Secondly, the preservation of toolmarks on the transom only (see below, pp 87–9), may indicate that this timber had less time to be weathered and worn in use. Finally, and perhaps more subtly, is the rougher nature of the workmanship and finishing of the transom, which is distinct from the finishing of the timber surfaces of the rest of

*Figure 114*
Area B in context (photo: R Sands)

*Figure 115*
Area C: an area of shorter strokes coping with a tighter grain pattern
(photo: R Sands)

the boat, suggesting that either the work was done at a different time, perhaps by different people with different aesthetic standard or in circumstances where time was limited.

### *Transom grooves*

Transom grooves are transverse features cut into the bottom and sides of a hull at the stern, to house separately fitted transoms. During the excavation, it became evident that the stern of Carpow was unusual in that there was a second groove outboard of the main transom groove in which the surviving transom was fixed (Figs 89, 98 and 100; F27 and F28 Appendix III). The existence of two transom grooves on the Carpow boat is very rare, though not unparalleled (see Loch Eskragh, below).

The transom groove (F28), which housed the surviving *in situ* transom is considered to be the main and original transom groove for a variety of reasons.

Firstly, F28 is cut around 220mm from the stern, the usual sort of distance at which transom grooves are cut in logboats (McGrail pers comm). Secondly, unlike the aftmost groove (F27), it is cut from the base of the boat to the top of the sheerline, allowing a full-sized transom board to be fitted. The outer transom groove (F27) is cut *c* 120mm from the stern, and is unusual in that it does not run up the internal sides of the boat, but stops short at the lower pair of holes (F23 port side; F25 starboard) (Figs 98 and 100). It is clear therefore, that the outer, smaller transom F27 could not have functioned alone, as it would have been underwater when the boat was in use.

Indeed, the much smaller outboard transom groove F26 (covering less than 25% of the area offered by F27) would in effect only reseal the watertightness of the floor of the hull at the stern, and it is that function that has been interpreted for its use. It is more probable that the outer groove is a repair, probably responding

*Figure 116*
Basal split (F26b) across both transom grooves at the starboard stern

*Figure 117*
The transom grooves showing *in situ* caulking materials

*Figure 118*
The transom grooves and basal split F26a

to leakage through basal splits (F26a and F26b), and designed to restrain differential vertical movement of the two sides of the split rather than lateral separation (Figs 89 and 98).

Finally, it is important to note that F26 is not symmetrically positioned across the stern, and continues noticeably higher on the port side than on the starboard side: illustrated by the relative heights of through-holes F23 (port) and F25 (starboard) which terminate the groove. This is explained by F30, the longitudinal retaining slot cut to house the repair block SF0015 (below, pp 85–6). Through-hole F25 (starboard) is cut directly below F30 and therefore must either post-date it, or be contemporary with it. This is an important piece of phasing which is critical to understanding the evolution of the stern to its fully developed state considered below.

The exact function of F23 and F25 is, however, less clear: it is noticeable that they are cut at slightly different angles, which means that it is very unlikely that a single cross-piece (ie a beam-tie function), could have been inserted from one hole to the other, across the top of the smaller transom. It is therefore probable that the holes housed retaining pegs or tree-nails which held the smaller transom in place, and applied downward pressure to keep the base of this transom tightly in contact with its retaining groove.

Given that the entire outer transom, which was not recovered, would have been submerged when the boat was in use, it is very probable that in order for this to function properly as a seal, the space in between both transoms must also have been caulked,

as otherwise water would have simply flowed over the top and reached the base of the inner transom where the basal splits were allowing water in. This important space between the transoms could have held caulking, such as moss or perhaps clay, mixed with other organic materials, as have been found in other boats (see below). Unfortunately none of this material was recovered.

The only other logboat found with twin transom grooves is one of the Early Iron Age examples from Lough Eskragh, near Dungannon in Co Tyrone (Collins & Seaby 1960; Fry 2000, 56). While the Lough Eskragh 1 vessel was found to have a stern fashioned from the parent log, Lough Eskragh 2 had a similar series of fixtures to Carpow, including double transom grooves and beam-ties. The excavators suggested that Lough Eskragh 2 had been originally designed in the same way as Lough Eskragh 1, but that 'by reason of some accident, probably the continual damping and drying of the heart-wood of the oak which composed the solid end' a large part of the stern had become displaced. Further, it was argued that the outer transom was added first, and held in place by a cross-piece at the very stern of the vessel, and then a second transom was added further inside the vessel, held in position by pegs at the base of the hull and a further cross-piece (Collins & Seaby 1960, 30).

It is equally possible, however, that the parent log of Eskragh 2, with a minimum length of *c* 7.3m already suffered heart-rot and was constructed with a fitted transom from first design; indeed, the usual place for the main transom is the position of what has been interpreted as the replacement (inboard) transom. It is therefore perhaps more likely that the development of Eskragh 2 was similar to that proposed for Carpow, rather than as interpreted by Collins and Seaby, with the outer transom being later.

### *Transom caulking*

The transom and transom groove was found to have been caulked with both moss and carpentry waste with two fashioned wedges (F31 and F32) on the inboard face of the transom groove at the sheerline. The *in situ* moss caulking recovered from the inner transom groove (F28) has been identified by Dr David G. Long, Bryology Section of the Royal Botanic Garden, Edinburgh, as *Rhytidiadelphus squarrosus (Hedw.) Warnst*, or 'Springy Turf-moss' (Figs 119 and 121). It is a very common moss of disturbed grassland,

*Figure 119*
The transom grooves showing *in situ* caulking materials at basal split F26a

heathland and upland woods, usually with an acid soil. In addition to the moss, numerous small woodchips were found, ranging in size from *c* 10–15mm in length. Only the two main wedges (F31 and F32; Figs 122 and 123) from the sheerline were fashioned into any shape, and it is probable that the other woodcuttings were waste from faceting of the transom itself. It is likely that both forms of caulking on Carpow were applied at the same time during the fitting of transom, irrespective of whether the surviving transom was the original, or a replacement.

Moss caulking of a fitted transom is recorded on the Brigg logboat (McGrail 1978, 317, 320); the Clifton 1 and 2 logboats (*ibid*, 317–18, 320); and the Holme Pierrepoint 2 boat, where moss was combined with flowering plants to caulk a split emanating from a knot near the sheerline (*ibid*, 320). The transom groove of the Hasholme boat was found to be caulked in parts by a mixture of clay and wood debris, and in some parts with a matt of caulking mosses, *Hylocomium splendens* and *Rhytidiadelphus triquetris* along with small organic remains of twigs and other material (Millet & McGrail 1987, 113). Other reported forms of caulking include the use of bark on the fitted transom of Preston 1 (McGrail 1978, 332); seaweed from a knot hole in the Brigg boat; and animal hide from the Poole boat (*ibid*, 320). Experiment has shown that the insertion

*Figure 120*
The transom grooves showing *in situ* caulking materials at basal split F26b

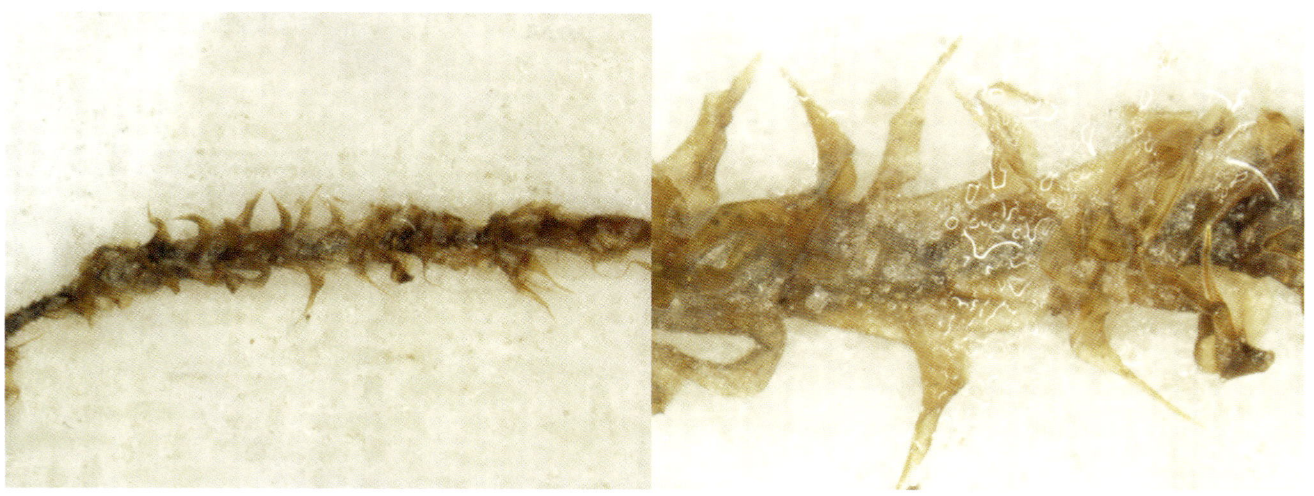

*Figure 121*
Detail of the moss caulking (*Rhytidiadelphus squarrosus (Hedw.) Warnst*) from the transom grove

*Figure 122*
The port side main wedge (F32) at the sheerline of the
transom groove

*Figure 123*
The starboard main wedge (F31) at the sheerline of the
transom groove

of dry moss into a transom groove provides effective caulking once the moss saturates and expands when the boat is in use.

### Beam-ties

While fitted transoms are caulked and wedged within a groove, their structural integrity and watertightness are generally further enhanced by two types of beam-tie: one on top of the transom that forces the transom down onto the groove; and/or one aft of the transom primarily designed to pull the sides of the vessel together (McGrail pers comm). Both beam-ties would also, importantly, serve to hold the sides of the boat together against the transom, thus stabilising the structure and also decreasing leakage. The two sets of symmetrically positioned cut features F20 and F21 and F22 and F24 are interpreted as having this function.

### Aft beam-tie holes

Originally identified in the evaluation excavation of 2003, were a pair of circular features (F22 and F24), cut horizontally through the sides of the vessel at the sheerline aft side of the transom (Fig 98). A good parallel for these can be found in the Hasholme vessel, where similar features were identified as retaining holes for a beam-tie. Beam-ties are timbers fitted athwartships and high-up in a boat with the function of pulling together the two sides of the craft. These are particularly important for logboats with fitted transoms where there could be a tendency for the sides of the parent log to splay out at the stern, releasing the transom board.

In the Hasholme boat, two types of beam-tie were employed, one of these also held the transom board in place by contacting from above with a U-shaped projection from the transom (Millet & McGrail 1987, 113). The position of the beam-tie holes on the Carpow vessel is similar to those on Hasholme, being on the aft of the transom. The beam-tie probably protruded from the outside of the hull and was possibly secured with a tapered cotter peg, as used in the Hasholme boat (*ibid*; Chapter 1, p 6).

While the beam-tie itself was missing from Carpow, we can infer from the retaining holes that it would have been a simple timber spar of circular, or sub-circular, cross-section. The diameter of the surviving beam-tie holes F22 and F24 are between 80–100mm and so given visible erosion around the features, it is likely that the beam-tie would have been in the region of 60–80mm in diameter.

It is very probable that the beam-tie was part of the original design, as suggested by the configuration of the transom in relation to the beam-tie holes, with the function of providing additional security in retaining the transom by pulling together the sides of the hull. While there are no projections on the Carpow transom itself, it is possible that, p 77–8), the original transom had a Hasholme-style protrusion designed to contact with the beam-tie with the additional function of bearing downward pressure on the transom.

### A reconstructed seat

The pair sheerline features F20 and F21 consist of relatively deep, circular sockets, *c* 60mm in diameter and *c* 70mm deep, cut vertically into the top of the vessel aft side of the transom board (Fig 98). While there are few exact parallels known from previously recorded examples, as a result of the rarity of surviving sheerlines in prehistoric logboats, it is suggested that these relate to the fitting of a horizontal board over the stern, which would have both acted to push the transom down into its retaining groove, hence promoting watertightness, and acted as a seat (Fig 126).

The suggested reconstruction of the Hasholme vessel included a raised deck or platform at the stern, based on the survival of shelves fashioned in the solid on the hull at the stern and a rectangular cross-piece which apparently also supported this (Millet & McGrail 1987, 122 and figs 24 and 25). Millet and McGrail also note that the stern is the obvious place from which to steer and command a logboat, and this is best achieved from a raised position where the helmsman can see over crew or cargo. In addition, the platform would have assisted in the strengthening of the stern, both holding down the transom and pulling together the sides of the hull; and would also have provided storage space protected from spray (*ibid*, 122). While the position of the footrests F16 and F17, preclude a full deck as in Hasholme, the proposed seat in the Carpow reconstruction (Fig 126) would certainly have fulfilled the latter two of these functions, and may also have been used as a deck for standing on, in a similar fashion to Hasholme, when needs arose.

A similar arrangement to Hasholme is suggested for the Brigg vessel, unfortunately no longer available for inspection, again on the basis of shelves or brackets fashioned in the solid on the inside faces of the hull (McGrail 1978, 168–9). Perhaps a better comparison for Carpow can be found in the Holme Pierrepont 3 vessel, which included fragments of a horizontal board, with dovetailed ends fitting into the hull. While this was interpreted primarily as a transverse strengthening fitting designed to hold the sides of the boat together (MacCormick *et al* 1968; McGrail 1978, 212) it may also have been used as a seat/standing deck as in the Carpow model.

### *The repair block*

McGrail notes two main types of repair: those pulling a split together, often using tar, clamps or stitching; and patching, where a tingle, or small wooden block, is fitted over a more serious split or hole (McGrail 1978, 37). The Carpow vessel appears to have both these types of repair. In addition to the repairs to the basal splits on the bottom of the hull (above, pp 64–5) a timber block (SF015) was found *in situ* in two pieces, one inboard and the other outboard, of the transom on the starboard side of the hull (Fig 124). This is significant in that it is the only fitting, apart from the transom itself that can be positively associated with the logboat with certainty. Notwithstanding the difficulties of excavating the stern, which remained partially water-covered for periods, familiarity with a very similar feature on the Hasholme boat (Chapter 1, Fig 5) had alerted the team to the potential survival of such features. When initially located, by touch only,

the parallel with the Hasholme boat was recognised and it became clear that while the block survived *in situ*, it was in two separate pieces, one found inboard of the transom, the other outboard. Numerous patches of grey clay were also noted, possibly another caulking material. The wood has been identified as oak (*Quercus* sp), and although the poor condition of the object prohibits an exact description of its shape, it appears roughly rectangular, and possibly slightly trapezoidal. It also had a roughly flat inner face, while the outer face curved corresponding with the curve of the hull to fit tightly, curved in section to fit against the inside of the slot in the hull (Fig 124). While much eroded (for individual dimensions on discovery see Appendix III), it is estimated that its minimum dimensions would have been *c* 0.3m in length by 0.2m in height, and *c* 40–50mm in section. The block was found slotted into cut feature F30; a groove cut longitudinally along the inside of the hull, across the transom grooves (Figs 98, 124 and 125).

The addition of a separate timber block, fitted between the transom and the inside of the hull, is recorded on a number of vessels. Hasholme provides the best documented and closest comparison, however, where a very similar feature was interpreted as a repair to damage of the starboard inner face of

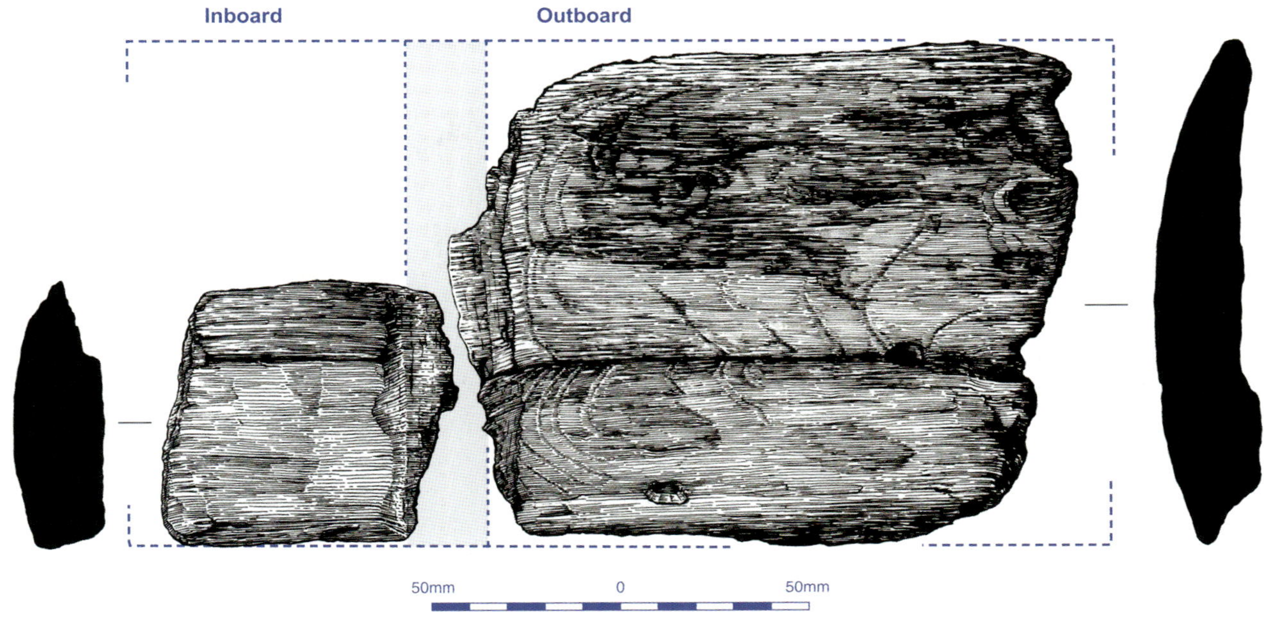


*Figure 124*
Detail of the Repair block (SF015) found *in situ*, but in two pieces, annotated to show its position relative to the transom (shaded grey)

the hull at the stern (Millett & McGrail 1987, 119–20). The roughly rectangular block (T15), measured *c* 0.72m in length and was trapezoidal in shape: 0.19m in breadth and 80mm in thickness at its forward end; 0.25m and 110mm at the after end, and was inserted into a cut horizontal slot, approximately half of the original thickness of the boats side. The Hasholme block slot was also cut across the transom groove, and in this instance, the block was fastened in place by a horizontal treenail *c* 45mm in diameter driven from outboard, and locked inboard with a vertical key. Two species of moss: *Hylocomium splendens* and *Rhytidiadelphus triquetris* were found mixed with small twigs between the block and the retaining groove (Millett & McGrail 1987, 119–20).

The Holme Pierrepont 3 vessel, which was found in 1968 during gravel extraction to the south-east of Nottingham (MacCormack 1968, McGrail 1978, 210–11), was *c* 10m in length and made of oak with a separate, fitted transom. The bottom of the boat, across the transom groove, had been repaired by a wooden block, *c* 0.3m × 0.13m × 60mm, which itself contained a groove designed to line up with the main transom groove. Unfortunately the boat was reburied under sand following basic recording, though the photographic archive suggests that the block was slightly raised above the flow of the hull, which would provide the wedging function as described above. The Holme Pierrepont 3 block is roughly comparable in size with the Carpow example.

Another parallel can be found in one of the five logboats found by Lord Lovaine at the drained Dowalton Loch, Dumfries and Galloway in 1863–4 (Mowat 1996, 24–5). The undated Dowalton Loch 3 boat measures *c* 5.7m in length and 0.8m in beam, and it was found that a 'block of wood cut to fill a hole, left probably by a rotten branch, was inserted in the side, 2ft long, 7 inches wide, and 5½ inches thick, and was secured by pegs driven through the side' (Stuart 1866, 120). The block, which was inserted into the port side of the hull, has reasonably been interpreted as a repair feature adjacent to an area of splitting (Mowat 1996, 25). The Dowalton block dimensions of *c* 0.6m long by 178mm in width by 140mm thick are more comparable in size with Hasholme than with Carpow. Unfortunately, all three of the Dowalton logboats were donated to the then museum of the Society of Antiquaries of Scotland, but cannot now be identified among the collections of the present Royal Museum for Scotland (*ibid*, 24).

The similarity of the Hasholme and Dowalton blocks to the Carpow example is striking: a block, albeit of smaller scale, inserted into a specially cut horizontal slot itself cut at right angles across the transom groove. While there are no indications of the use of treenails to secure the Carpow block, as on the larger Hasholme and Dowalton examples, it is possible that all traces of such features have been lost to erosion.

Such blocks were probably repairs made to address defects in the parent logs, most likely areas of softer, partly rotted wood that were the outer limits of the brittle heart rot. While it is possible that such a 'repair' was carried out to the hull in the first phase of development, it is equally possible it was secondary response to spreading of the hull over time (Fig 145). The block would have provided a wedging function, pushing the transom more tightly into its groove and thus promoting increased watertightness. The survival of similar 'repairs' on other vessels, in the same part of the hull (midway between the hull bottom and sheerline starboard side) might suggest a third possibility: that the features were in effect a design feature, a wedging technique, as outlined above, employed during the original fitting of the transom to promote tightness.

### Stern phasing

On the basis of the above, a likely development of the stern over time can be outlined thus (Fig 126):

1. A single, full-sized transom fitted into the inner groove (F28), with a circular beam-tie through holes F22 and F24, capped with the stern seat.

2. Possibly in response to leakage and spreading as a result of the basal splits, retaining cut F30 and repair block (SF 015) were added. A replacement transom may have been added at this time.

3. As a result of leakage under the main transom, through the basal splits, the outer transom groove

(F27) was cut and a miniature transom was added with caulking between both transoms.

It is possible that there could be some expansion or contraction of this series of events, for example, the replacement transom, if there was one, could have been added after stage 2 or even as part of stage 3. The basic phasing of events, however, must have occurred in this order.

### 5.7 Conclusions

Having outlined the shape and features of Carpow, it is worth initially considering a few of the features common on logboats of this period, which do not appear on Carpow. For example, there would appear to be no thickness-gauge holes on the Carpow vessel, a fairly common feature on logboats from many areas; these holes are bored into the future bottom of the parent log to allow an even thickness of hull to be achieved during hollowing. The absence of these may be explained simply by the thickness of hull which is sufficient to allow for acceptable error during the hollowing process. Other fixtures and fittings include the extension of logboats, where wash-strakes are added to heighten the sheerline and increase freeboard, and this remains a possible for Carpow, although it is difficult to explain how the sheerline holes would adequately support such planks. Finally, the poor stability of the Carpow vessel, resulting from its rounded hull, could be have been partially resolved by the addition of outriggers, stability timbers, longitudinal timbers or floats attached to the sides of the boat to increase buoyancy. These are known only in the Indian and South Pacific Oceans (Chapter 1, p 3), however, and so while this technique can remain a possibility for Carpow, it is only a slight one.

It is also worth addressing the widely held belief that logboats were frequently expanded: the process of opening out of the hollowed hull to create a wider waterline breadth (and therefore increased stability) and a greater internal volume. While in Europe, the process is known from, for example, Finland (Chapter 1, p 2), it is not known in any prehistoric British oak logboats. Indeed, oak logs are seldom, if ever, expanded successfully (McGrail pers comm).

In summary, therefore, Carpow is a basic, but well-crafted, logboat of good size. It is likely to have had a simple canoe-end bow, though decoration with 'oculi' or a zoomorphic head may have existed. The splitting of the hull, presumably during use, resulted

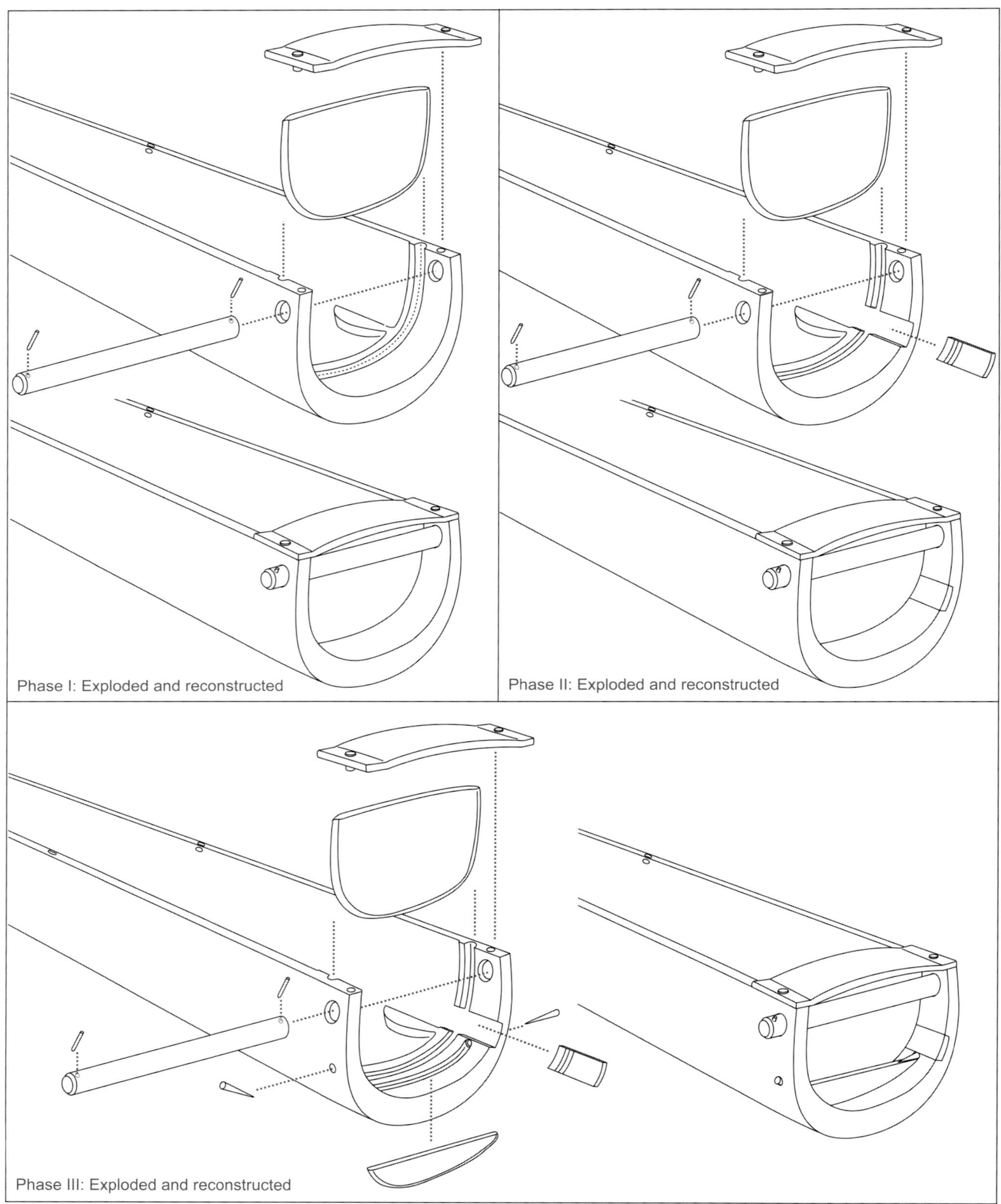


*Figure 126*
Schematic reconstructions of the development of the stern from initial construction to full development

in a series of attempts, both within the hull and at the stern, to maintain watertightness. This resulted in the probable replacement of the transom, a block repair of this transom and, at its full development, the addition of a very unusual outer miniature transom. The good survival of the hull bottom at the stern indicates that this is an unusual step to take, and may reflect the seriousness of the leakage, and the value assigned to the boat by its users. It has also been suggested that a miniature transom could have proved operationally useful in a boat of this size, where 'three point turns' may have been required in river use. In such circumstances the boat would have to 'make a sternboard' (ie be propelled stern-first) which would result in water flowing into the open stern aft of the transom and the second transom would have stemmed the force of such a flow and minimised leakage into the main hull (McGrail pers comm). In either case, the extensive repairs to Carpow indicate the seriousness the leakages and may well indicate the boats ultimate demise, whether through accidental loss or deliberate abandonment. Many of the additional features of Carpow, such as the inclusion of footrests and the possible stern seat, indicate a good understanding of how the boat was to be used and for what purpose. The good design and skilful manufacture of the logboat is indicative of a long-established boat-building tradition in the area, but also of skilled craftsmen who have become experienced with the newly expanded toolkit available in the Late Bronze Age. In the next two chapters we will explore exactly when, and how, this was done.

**Chapter 6**

# Dating the boat

DAVID STRACHAN, GORDON COOK and ANNE CRONE

## 6.1 Background

Upon verification in September 2001 that the find on Carpow Bank was indeed a logboat, one of the three initial questions asked (in addition to how long was it and how well preserved was the buried portion) was: how old is it?

It is likely that logboats, with an almost world-wide distribution, were invented and developed, from floating logs, in different places at different times. In Europe, the oldest logboats are found in Germany, the Netherlands and northern France, and it has been suggested that they spread to the rest of Europe from this core area (Lanting 2000). There was a popular misconception, common in the 19th century, that logboats are predominantly prehistoric in date (Mowat 1996, 129). In fact, the peak in the British series of logboats occurs between around AD 1000–1300, with prehistoric logboats being relatively rare. It is clear, however, that only a small sample of British and Irish logboats have been dated, with Scottish logboats being particularly under-represented (Lanting 2000, 630). Including Carpow, only eight out of the 155 recorded have been dated, and of these, seven are dated from the first century BC to the 11th century AD (Mowat 1996, 129; Lanting & Brindley 1996). Indeed, the only proposed logboat of Mesolithic date, from the Tay Estuary at Perth, must be considered suspect as it was recorded by Geikie in 1878 or 1879, a year after it had been found, and was assigned a date only on the basis of a second-hand description of its context (Mowat 1996, 35). Given the above, from the outset of the project in 2000 the confirmation of a prehistoric date for the Carpow vessel, in any condition, would be considered an important factor in weighing up the cultural importance of the boat and informing consideration of subsequent management options.

As it is inadvisable to try to assign a date to a logboat on the basis of morphology alone (McGrail 1978, 105; Lanting 2000, 627), and given that logboats are often recovered from undated contexts and without associated finds, dating must be based on either radiocarbon assay or tree-ring analysis (dendrochronology) of the log itself. While radiocarbon dating provides a broad time bracket, dendrochronology can provide a more precise calendar date, even after allowance is made for missing outer rings. There are pros and cons to both of these methods when applied to logboats (Fry 2000, 8–9). The reductive nature of logboat manufacture, removing both the outer sapwood and internal heartwood, both limits the number of tree-rings available for study and makes it difficult to say, with certainty, how the surviving timber relates to the parent log. This is part of what is referred to as the 'old wood effect', which can make the radiocarbon age of a specimen appear older than it should be, as the sample submitted does not represent the immediate pre-felling phase in the life of the tree. Both methods of dating were applied to the logboat.

## 6.2 Tree-ring studies

Logboats are notoriously difficult to sample for dendrochronological purposes, and consequently relatively few have been successfully dendro-dated (Baillie 1982, 241; Hillam 1987b; Tyers 1989), but not for the want of trying. One of the problems is that, after hollowing out the parent log, the points at which a relatively long and complete tree-ring sequence can be obtained are restricted to the stern or the bow, or more rarely, the bulkhead, if one has been left in, as in the late Saxon logboat from Clapton (Marsden *et al* 1989). The bow of the Carpow logboat had not survived, there was no bulkhead, and the stern of the boat had not been carved out of the log but had been constructed by inserting a separate transom into a prepared slot (Chapter 5, pp 73–84). Thus, the candidate locations for sampling were through the hull itself and on the transom.

### The hull

The thickest part of the hull lay just in front of the innermost transom slot; it was 250mm thick at this point. An attempt was made to core the logboat from interior to exterior at this point using a Swedish incremental corer, but this was unsuccessful. The upper, ie inner facing, 150mm of the wood was very soft, presumably as a result of decay, and consequently the core broke up on removal from the corer. The lower, ie outer facing, 100mm was much more solid but was still fragmented and contained insufficient rings for dendrochronological analysis. However, as these fragments contained the outermost surviving growth rings of the parent log they provided an ideal sample for the second radiocarbon date (below pp 93–4). Small horizontal cracks had developed along the inner surface of the hull as coring progressed so it was considered too damaging to make a second attempt to retrieve a core.

Despite the failure to obtain an intact core for analysis, the fragmentary cores have enabled us to make some useful calculations about the age of the parent tree. An average growth rate of *c* 6–7 rings per 10mm was measured and the diameter of the parent tree (Chapter 7, p 100) at around shoulder height is estimated to be *c* 1.3m (excluding sapwood); if we simply multiply the growth rate observed at this point with the estimated radius of the heartwood there will have been between 390 and 455 heartwood rings present (65 × 6; 65 × 7). However, the growth rate of a tree slows down with age and so the outermost rings, which are what we have measured, are usually the narrowest present in the tree. Thus some allowance must be made for the faster early growth of the tree. Very crudely, if we allow a growth rate of 4–5 rings for the inner 0.4m of the radius and a growth rate of 6–7 rings for the outer 0.25m we arrive at a rough age of between 310 to 375 years of age. To this must be added a calculation for the sapwood which was probably deliberately removed, although there is no evidence of tool marks on the external surface of the hull (Chapter 5, p 60). The curved outer surface of the hull probably lies on, or very near, the heartwood/sapwood boundary, give or take a few growth rings that may have been trimmed off. The number of sapwood rings on oak varies with age and longitude (Hillam *et al* 1987). Studies have shown that a range of 15 to 60 years is applicable for mature oak (ie over 100 years) in the British Isles; given that the Carpow tree was very mature, the maximum estimate of 60 sapwood rings should be applied. Thus, the tree could have been between 370 and 435 years of age.

There are very few examples of oak timbers of Bronze Age date in Scotland with which to compare the Carpow tree. Three squared planks from Buiston crannog, in Ayrshire, one of which was radiocarbon-dated to the Late Bronze Age at 915–795 cal BC (GU-2999), had ring-sequences of 150, 196 and 202 years (Crone 2000, 57–8), but these are minimum ages as the planks had been fully squared and an unknown number of rings would have been trimmed off. Large oak trunks lying under a wooden platform of Neolithic date at Parks of Garden, on the edge of the Carse of Stirling, were comparable in age to the Carpow tree, with ring-sequences of up to 403 years (Crone 2002).

### The transom

The transom was too thin for coring so the edges of the transom were pared using a razor blade to reveal the ring pattern. However, it became clear that the growth characteristics of the tree from which the transom had been converted made it unsuitable for dendrochronological analysis. The transom had been fashioned by cleaving a plank tangentially from the tree at the point at which the bole divides into two minor trunks or branches (Fig 126A). On one edge of the transom there were two 'centres' visible and between them the ring-pattern was wavy and distorted (Fig 126B). On the opposing edge the growth rings displayed a more regular pattern but because they lay parallel with the surface of the transom (Fig 126C) there were too few rings present to be of use for dendrochronological analysis.

Fig 126D shows the likely position of the plank within the parent tree. The plank had been trimmed on either edge to make the transom and consequently the relationship between the outermost measurable ring on each radius and the outer growth rings of the parent tree is unknown.

The growth rate on the transom was the same as that observed on the hull of the logboat, *c* 6–7 rings per 10mm. Beyond this similarity there is no way of demonstrating that the transom was carved from the same parent tree. However, it is possible that the section of the trunk from which the transom was cleft is that from the upper reaches of the tree from which the logboat itself was fashioned (though see discussion in Chapter 5, pp 77–8 and Fig 106). This would have saved the need to fell another large tree and the savings in energy might explain why the logboat-builders chose to use what must have been a difficult piece of timber to cleave, with the grain running in several different directions (Fig 108).

### 6.3 Radiocarbon dating

As outlined above, confirmation of date was a priority of the initial evaluation and so, in October 2001, a sample was recovered from the exposed bow of the *in situ* vessel. The reason behind this was to assess the cultural importance of the vessel from the outset, the consideration of further work being dependant on the vessel's age and condition.

The initial sample was measured by accelerator mass spectrometry at the University of Arizona AMS Facility on behalf of the Scottish Universities Environmental Research Centre at East Kilbride. This produced a single radiocarbon measurement with a radiocarbon age of $2885 \pm 50$ BP (AA–45634 (GU–9597)), producing calibrated age ranges of 1130–970 cal BC (62.3% probability at 1 sigma) and 1220–920 cal BC (93.1% probability at 2 sigma). Although the outermost surviving rings on the exposed section of timber were used for dating, it was recognised that, coming from the eroded bow of the vessel this was not an ideal sample; not only would many outer rings have been removed during shaping of the bow but there would inevitably have been additional loss of rings through erosion. Further to the evaluation work carried out in 2003, when good preservation of the stern was confirmed, it was recognised that a better sample could be recovered at a later date.

In April 2007, during post-excavation study at the Granton laboratory, a second sample for radiocarbon dating was taken from the hull, this time from the outermost rings on a core which had been extracted for dendrochronological study. As described above, the curved outer surface of the hull probably lies on or near the heartwood/sapwood boundary, allowing for a few heartwood rings that may have been trimmed off, so this sample came from the outermost surviving heartwood rings. This produced a single radiocarbon measure-ment with a radiocarbon age of $2910 \pm 35$ BP (SUERC–13984 (GU–15238)) producing calibrated age ranges of 1160–1020 cal BC (63.0% probability at 1 sigma) and 1220–1000 cal BC

(92.1% probability at 2 sigma). The addition of the missing sapwood rings, estimated as *c* 60 rings (see above) would not materially affect the accuracy of this date. As would be expected, these two dates are not statistically significantly different.

A third sample was also taken in April 2007 from the transom. It had been hoped that the dendro-chronological study would help to determine whether the transom had been formed from the same parent log as the hull, and was thus original, or whether it was a later replacement. As this proved unsuccessful, a sample for radiocarbon dating was taken in order to inform this discussion. A sample from the outside edge of the transom, representing the youngest rings present, was taken and produced a single radiocarbon date with a radiocarbon age of $2965 \pm 35$ BP (SUERC–14610 (GU–15325)) producing calibrated dates of 1260–1120 cal BC (68.2% probability at 1

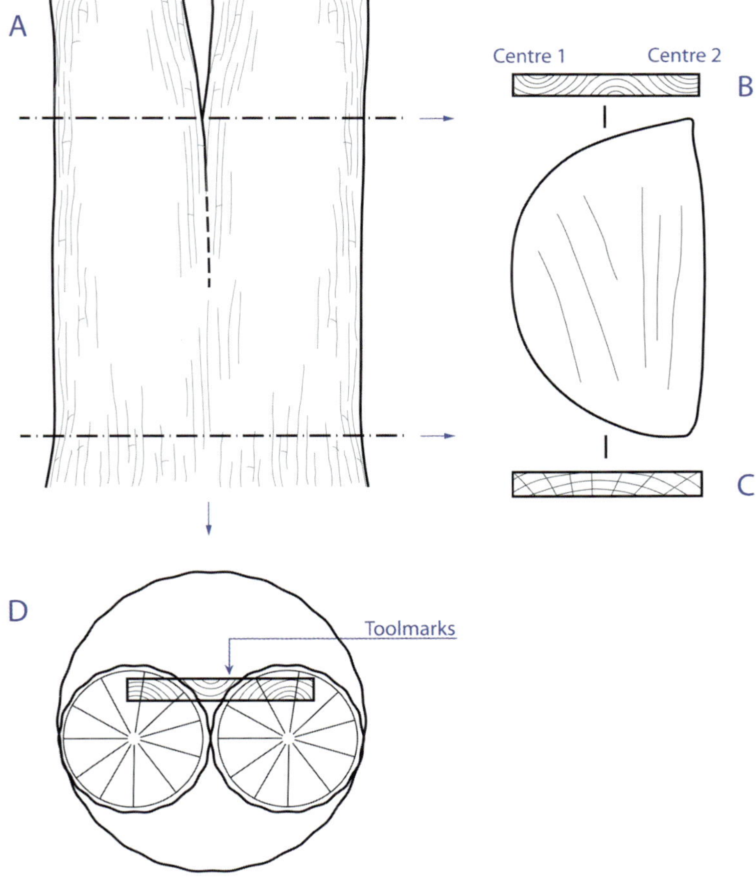



*Figure 127*
The tree-ring studies show that the transom came from high in the tree where the trunk began to fork

Table 4

The three radiocarbon dates from the logboat

| Laboratory no | Material dated | Radiocarbon age (years BP ± 1 sigma) | Calibrated age range (95% confidence) |
| --- | --- | --- | --- |
| AA-45634 (GU-9597) | hull at bow | 2885 ± 50 | 1260–1230 BC (2.4%) 1220–920 BC (93.0%) |
| SUERC-13984 (GU-15238) | hull at stern | 2910 ± 35 | 1260–1230 BC (3.3%) 1220–1000 BC (92.1%) |
| SUERC-14610 (GU-15325) | transom | 2965 ± 35 | 1310–1050 BC (95.4%) |

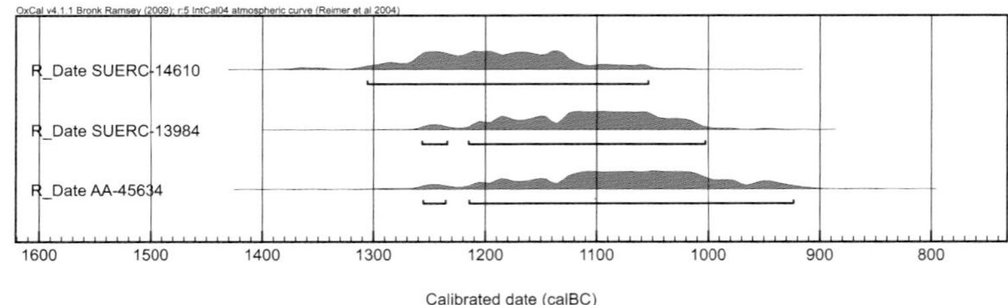


Figure 128

The radiocarbon plots for Table 4

sigma) and 1310–1050 cal BC (95.4% probability at 2 sigma). A Chi-squared test was carried out on the three measurements which indicated that all three were statistically indistinguishable as a group of measurements (T statistic for the group was 2.12 ($\chi^2_{:0.05} = 5.99$).

Given the way in which the transom has been fashioned from the parent oak (see above), it is clear that significant numbers of growth rings have been removed and these must be taken into account in assessing the radiocarbon date. However, as we cannot determine the relationship between the outermost rings present on the transom and the outer growth rings of the parent tree (see above) it is difficult to estimate how many rings, or rather years, have been lost. It is possible that, in a tree of this size, as many as 200 rings need to be added.

## 6.4 Conclusions

A study of the tree-rings has produced vital information about the manner in which the timber used to make the logboat was converted from the parent tree, and has allowed us to estimate, if very crudely, the age of the tree. The condition of the wood and its irregular growth combined to deter dendrochronological analysis and consequently, the boat has been dated by radiocarbon assay. As there are currently no tree-ring chronologies for Scotland which cover the Bronze Age (Crone & Mills 2002) a precise calendar date for the logboat could never be guaranteed. In some ways the value of an exact calendar date for the logboat is moot; many years ago Baillie (1982, 209) pointed out that our understanding of certain objects and sites does not necessarily improve with precise dating, primarily because there are often few other precisely dated objects with which to compare them; the usefulness of a site or object dated by dendrochronology can be limited when all other related chronologies are based on radiocarbon. While this is no longer the situation in many parts of the British Isles, where there are now many tree-ring dated sites, it unfortunately remains true in Scotland. That said, the only way to develop a prehistoric tree-ring chronology for Scotland, is to take every available opportunity to acquire tree-ring data, even if successful dating cannot currently be guaranteed.

The radiocarbon dates from the hull and transom are statistically indistinguishable. Furthermore, the tree-ring studies make it clear that we need to add in the order of 60 years to the date of the hull, to account for lost sapwood, and in the order of 200 years for lost rings from the transom. The breadth of the calibrated date range combined with the uncertain, but probably large number of missing rings means, that the chronological relationship between the two components of the logboat cannot be disentangled. Consequently, neither the radiocarbon dates nor the tree-ring studies can confirm whether the transom came from the same parent log as the hull, and was thus original, or whether it was a replacement. As a result the discussion of whether the transom is a replacement rests on the stylistic argument that the transom appears relatively crude in comparison with the rest of the hull (see Chapter 5, p 78 and 80).

Equally, while it could be argued that the fact that the transom has been formed from the top of an oak, where branching has begun, indicates that the main part of the parent log was used for the hull of the logboat, it is as likely that a replacement transom, from a different tree, would be taken from the same position, allowing the main parent log to be used for either another boat, or long planks for a different function.

Chapter 7

# Reconstructing manufacture: tools, techniques and logistics

DAMIAN GOODBURN

## 7.1 Background

The vessel is best described as a 'basic' logboat, with an inserted transom: 'basic' in that it was neither expanded nor extended (Chapter 1, pp 2–3). As previously outlined, the stern was unusually well preserved and included an *in situ* transom. For many years the study of 'logboat canoes' was dealt with in a rather cursory way by archaeologists drawn to the study of larger plank-built vessels. However, the importance of logboat finds has been increasingly recognised and the study of the Carpow boat is a thorough, multi-disciplinary addition to the slowly accruing corpus on such vessels.

While space does not permit a detailed account of the development of this specific field, certain key references are extensively used below and are put in context here. A comprehensive gazetteer of logboats in England and Wales was produced by McGrail (1978). In this work there is some discussion of varied approaches to logboat building recorded ethnographically, but caution is expressed as the accounts do not deal with building the craft of oak as was used for the vast majority of British finds, including Carpow. In 1987 a detailed multi-disciplinary study of the large Iron Age Hasholme logboat was published which provides a number of parallels for this study, including evidence for the same hull finishing method (Millett & McGrail 1987). In 1989 a study of a small early medieval logboat from London was published which included a detailed study of the surviving toolmarks and evidence for building processes, later experimentally tested during the building of a replica (Marsden *et al* 1989; Goodburn & Redknap 1988). A more recent gazetteer and synthesis on logboat finds in Europe was produced by Arnold (1996), which covers some British material and includes many detailed studies of Bronze Age toolmark evidence and other features discussed here, and has provided many parallels. Finally, the provision of a gazetteer of Scottish logboats collated by Mowat provides parallels for aspects of the Carpow find, but does not contain detailed investigations of building

processes (Mowat 1996). In 1992 the well-preserved remains of a planked boat, with logboat features, was found at Dover (Chapter 14), and dated to *c* 1550 cal BC (Clark 2004a). The project included a detailed multi-disciplinary study of the processes, toolkits and raw materials used in building the craft (Goodburn 2004; Darrah 2004a), and has also provided much parallel information for this part of the Carpow investigation.

Much Bronze Age woodwork has been excavated over the last 20 years in several regions of Britain, and it provides some general parallels for some aspects of the Carpow woodworking study. These include the increasingly closely dated use of particular types of bronze tool forms (Coles & Orme 1985; Taylor 1992; Sands 1997; O'Sullivan 1996; and Goodburn 2003). While some of this work remains as yet unpublished, it contains much relevant information, such as the nature of wooden tools like splitting wedges (Goodburn & Minkin 1999); key equipment used in logboat manufacture in the Bronze Age.

## 7.2 Indirect sources of evidence

This contribution draws on information and experience of many types of logboats and Bronze Age woodworking from Britain. This includes both some of the published material listed above, such as the Dover boat, and many other assemblages from England currently at the pre-publication stage (eg Bronze Age woodwork from Ebbsfleet, Kent, in Goodburn forthcoming).

In addition, the following two types of sources have been used with considerable caution, but both can provide invaluable insights into the varied approaches and procedures that can be used to build logboats. Firstly, the ethnographic record can sometimes provide potential explanations for recorded details of the Carpow boat which are possibly inexplicable otherwise, such as the use of blades hafted as adzes for finishing the inside of the vessel (as documented in Petersen 2000). Space does not permit a summary of the ethnography of logboat building, but particular works will be cited where they are directly relevant to particular stages in construction discussed below. One of the many problems of directly using information from ethnographic sources first recognised by McGrail (1978, 27) is that they are accounts of making craft in materials other than oak. An even greater problem with most ethnographic accounts of logboat building is that they were written by people who were not woodworkers themselves and who rarely had the patience to stay at the work-site for the weeks, or more, required.

Although women have been involved in many experimental projects to build replica logboat vessels this writer is not aware of any ethnographic accounts in which this was the case. Indeed, in some areas women were strictly prohibited from visiting the building site, for example, in Maori New Zealand (Best 1976, 97). In this account the term men is used to mean men.

Secondly, targeted experimental work in logboat building can provide many practical and often subtle insights into the use of tools, logistics and materials, not known in the ethnographic records and extremely difficult to obtain from the study of artefacts themselves. Here projects using replica bronze and wooden tools to work large oak timbers for boat building is essential. The Dover boat project involved carefully documented experimental woodworking to throw light on many aspects of the archaeological record, as well as logistical considerations such as roughly how many people could have worked on different aspects of manufacture at once (Darrah 2004c, 163–88). Another relevant experimental project was the reconstruction of the Late Bronze Age Short Ferry boat. This vessel was a little smaller than the Carpow vessel, and much more flat bottomed, but otherwise similar, with a D-shaped inserted transom. In total, this author has taken part in the building of 13 logboats to date, of many styles and using many types of tools, seven of which were archaeology-led and involved largely or entirely period tools and materials.

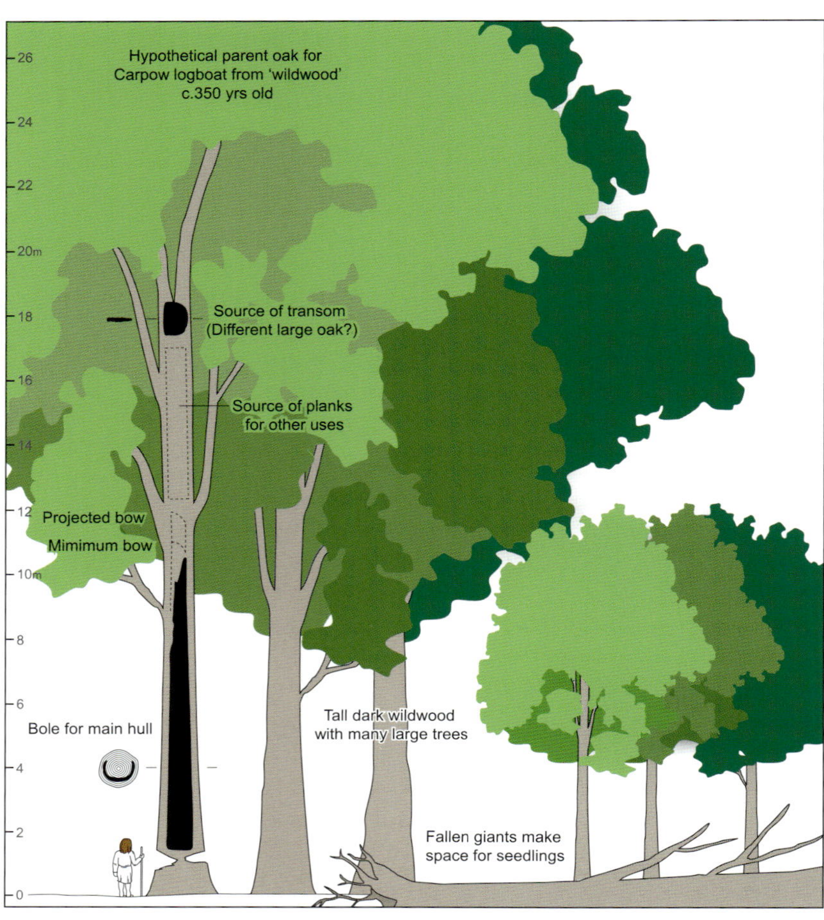


*Figure 129*
A hypothetical parent oak, *c* 400 years old, showing the position of the logboat to be

## 7.3 Stages of manufacture

### *An important proviso*

It must be noted that although the main wood-working operations are reconstructed below, the precise order of the stages may have varied from that proposed. Ethnography has shown that, for example, the stage at which the hollowing out is begun can vary from region to region. It is also possible that some of the nominal stages distinguished here, in reality may have run concurrently. The general order of work proposed here has been tried and tested on several reconstruction projects with native oaks, however, and concords with the evidence recorded for this boat. The intention is to present a summary of the evidence and develop inferences that will take the Carpow vessel from the natural wild living plants she was made of, to a product of the Bronze

Age community that made her: 'from the tree to the sea'.

### Stage 1: selecting the parent tree

Although some logboats were made from half logs, Carpow, like most British prehistoric logboats, was made from a whole log with small additional timbers at the stern end. Superficially we might suggest that searching for a suitable large oak was the first stage in the process of building this boat. However, this is only true if we take the boat out of its social, economic, cultural and environmental context. A logboat is as much a social product as are pottery or house forms. The community that built the vessel also operated in an established cultural milieu that may have impacted on boat building through rituals and 'rules of thumb'. The ritual aspect of logboat building is often a serious issue in ethnographic accounts (McGrail 1978, 34) but may be difficult to throw light on here. In some cultures the boat building team is led by a high status priest-like master builder, while in others simply an older man with experience. It is possible that archaeological synthesis and environmental evidence in the region may provide some useful information. Questions that might be asked include: what was the typical size of Late Bronze Age settlements regionally?; and was there a lot of high dense woodland with a likely supply of suitable large oaks, or would they have been scarce? Functional considerations, such as intended loading with bulky or light materials, may also bear on the size of tree selected.

A 'parent tree' had to be found, however, and Fig 129 is an attempt to graphically reconstruct the parent tree used for the main hull of the Carpow boat. It should be noted here that British native 'oak' is actually two species (*Quercus robur* and *Quercus petraea*) and their hybrids. Although this is not a factor to consider for recent boat-builders in Britain, it may have been in the Late Bronze Age. Clearly we also have to consider that she may have been built elsewhere, though probably not outside the River Tay drainage. The parent tree

*Figure 130*
Prospecting for trees in the wildwood (artist: David Hogg, after sketches by Goodburn)

used for Carpow had to have been large enough to make the whole hull as it survives without leaving any sapwood. Allowing an additional *c* 60mm for mature oak bark and sapwood (Chapter 6, p 92), the diameter at chest height (level with the wider stern end of the boat) would have been *c* 1.3m; a very large tree. Towards the bow end of the tree, the equivalent untrimmed diameter would have been *c* 1m. Reading the grain patterns shown clearly on the drawings of the boat, the first substantial knot can be seen on the port side *c* 6.5m from the stern end allowing *c* 1m (probably more) for the felling height. The first branches would therefore have been at *c* 7.5m. An oak of this size and form must have grown in tall dark woodland. If we look at the average annual ring width of the timber it is *c* 6–7 rings/10mm or well under 2mm per ring. Given that old oaks tend to develop narrower rings from middle age onward we would suggest an age for the parent tree of *c* 370 to 435 years (Chapter 6, p 92). So the parent oak was large even by the standards of many prehistoric oaks, with a high branching point and fairly narrow annual rings. These are classic characteristics of a temperate wildwood oak (Goodburn 1992, 118; Peterken 1996, 149). Oaks with these characteristics are very rare in Britain today, where no wildwood exists, but can still be glimpsed in forest reserves in eastern Poland. This is a particularly dramatic image to place in a Scottish landscape which now has very few really large native trees, though many of North American origin in early plantations.

### Spiral grain

As described above (Chapter 5, p 60), the parent log had a noticeable spiral grain which meant that the timber could not be split into long regular pieces, an important issue when removing the large quantities of 'waste' timber in logboat building (below). Indeed, it is tempting to suggest that straighter grained oak of large diameter, such as could be split into regular boards may have been reserved for other purposes. This problem was experienced, on a smaller scale, when building a copy of the Late-Saxon Clapton boat, in which the original also had a spiral grain. The tree for the replica was similar to the original in grain quality, and spiral

*Figure 131*
Felling the parent oak (artist: David Hogg, after sketches by Goodburn)

grain slowed down the hollowing process greatly. It also caused both the replica and original vessel to twist after hollowing considerably, and in the replica this process occurred after approximately three years.

### Stage 2: Felling the parent tree

While it is often assumed that later phases of work generally remove evidence of the felling methods used, felled ends can often be found on excavated early wood-work even in nautical finds. In modern forestry work in Britain, trees are felled very low down with chain saws using a lower V-shaped 'gob' or 'drop' cut first, to help direct the fall of the tree. When axes were the sole tools used for felling, it was carried out higher up to avoid the worst of the buttress and allow the development of a swing. An estimate of cutting at *c* 1m up for a large stem appears appropriate. Gob cuts with slightly higher back cuts have been recorded on some large Bronze Age posts such as those on the bases of massive oak posts from the recently excavated timber circle at Old Hall, Essex (Goodburn 2007). It may also be the case that the lopsidedness of the stern of the Iron Age Hasholme logboat boat is a result of leaving part of the 'back cut' made for felling the parent tree (Millett & McGrail 1987, 133).

Axe-type tools cross cut timber most effectively at angles of *c* 40–60 degrees rather than straight across like a saw, so felling cuts must be V-shaped. If a stem is very large and tools small, such as those of Late Bronze Age Britain, then a wide V cut may be started with two smaller cuts and the timber split out between them (Fig 131). While this author has not felled a large oak with Late Bronze Age type socketed axes, an oak of *c* 0.7m diameter was felled with larger, Early Bronze Age axes by inexperienced workers in three hours, with several stoppages to repair axe helves (for the *Time Team* Seahenge television programme). It is likely that felling large oaks with small, light, Late Bronze Age axes would have been a communal activity, with the fellers taking turns and two or three people working at the same time. While there is no surviving evidence from the Carpow boat, two different axes have been distinguished on each of the large Early Bronze Age post bases found recently at Old Hall Essex (Goodburn 2007). With ancillary tasks such as clearing undergrowth, small trees in the way of the fall, possibly erecting a shelter, and possibly ritual practices, one could suggest that between two and four people would have spent about one day on these initial tasks. Indirectly, from experience of cross cutting deep notches in large green oak timbers during the Dover

boat experimental work, albeit with slightly heavier, broader bladed Middle Bronze Age axe replicas (Darrah 2004c, 180), an estimate of around one day, for two or more people for the felling process might be broadly correct. In practice, hard and usually dust-impregnated old oak bark, or 'krap', dulls tools quickly. Regular tool sharpening must have been carried out in the early stages, though it would have been required less frequently later, when only fresh green timber was being worked. Bronze tools generally require resharpening roughly two to three times more often than modern steel edged hand tools, though, there are many variables to consider such as the hardness of particular alloys, the degree of work hardening (edges of bronze tools have to be hammered before rubbing on a whetstone) and the precise condition of the timber being worked.

### Stage 3: lopping the side branches and 'bucking' the parent log

Once the great parent tree had crashed to the ground, the next stage of work, that of cutting the log to length, or 'bucking', and the removal of side branches, or 'lopping' (often called 'snedding' today), could begin. The parent oak was from tall dark 'wildwood', which tends to produce trees with tall boles free of large branches for many metres. Reading the grain patterns (Fig 86) the first major knot left by a medium sized branch occurred at 6.3m from the stern, or *c* 7.3m from the ground, with some other small knots apparent at the bow. As a result, there would have been few branches to remove before the full form of the parent log could be assessed and the bucking cut begun. If the hull was initially shaped upside down, as proposed here, then the very process of making a V-shaped cut for bucking would also be forming the up curving bow, whatever precise form it originally took. As only the lowest branches of the parent tree had been removed, it is likely that it extended much further up with a top at around 30m or so.

The stern end would have been rather ragged at this stage, with the rough felling bevels and torn hinge fibres requiring cutting back. Experience has shown that cross cutting such a large log to form a flat, 90 degree end would have taken considerable effort. Cutting such log ends with heavy steel axes is difficult enough, but with much lighter Late Bronze Age tools the labour would have been very much slower and heavier. Based on the experience of cross

*Figure 132*
Lopping (artist: David Hogg, after sketches by Goodburn)

cutting large sections of green oak for the Dover boat project experiment (*ibid*) it is probable that two to four people could have worked at this job for a day or more at the stern end, and longer at the bow end, to start roughing it out. It is also possible that the next phase of work may have begun in the middle of the log, a safe distance from sharp flying oak chips at each end. We can not reconstruct the time period the original builders had in mind for their project, but a practical consideration is that the surfaces of the green oak would dry and begin to split if they are left exposed and thick. In practice, the latter problem can be acute in warm, sunny and windy weather occurring in March or early April before the leaves are on the trees and woodland humidity rises.

### Moving the log?

At this stage the parent log would have weighed *c* 9.5tonnes, based on an average green oak density of *c* 1.073 tonnes/m$^3$ (Millett & McGrail 1987, 106). Today, logs are moved when snedded and bucked, as suggested for the Hasholme Boat, but without good

roads, or water access, this is unlikely in the Late Bronze Age. Further, the practical difficulties of handling such a large and heavy log around the other trees of the dense wildwood make this very unlikely. It is probable that most of the following stages of work took place in the wood where the parent tree was felled (eg Petersen 2000; Leshikar 1975). The general pattern in the ethnographic record, before modern transport existed, is that logboat vessels were roughed out where the parent trees were felled, with only the final trimming being done close to the shore, usually near the builders' home (eg *ibid*; Best 1976, 101; and Petersen 2000).

### Stage 4: Removing the bark, sapwood and 'waste' timber from the developing hull

The suggested order of carving the main hull, starting with the bottom and outside, allows defects in the final hull skin to be found and avoided, or dealt with early on, before the investment of significant labour. This approach also provides a surface to work to from the inside, during the hollowing. These assumptions are made cautiously, however, as Bronze Age attitudes to labour could well have differed to those of today.

All the bark and perishable sapwood was removed from the hull, and it is clear that some heartwood was also removed to fair out bulges in the natural tree, particularly towards the stern where the bottom is flatter than elsewhere (compare Fig 86 A1–A2 with D1–D2). Although the details of toolkits differ, the basic, world-wide process of bulk removal of unwanted timber in hewing logboat hulls is to cut grooves and then split off timber between them, as evidenced in the Dover boat (Goodburn 2004, 132) or in recent central Europe (Arnold 1996, 175). The principal is to use controlled splitting rather than removing timber chip by chip. The split out chunks of timber would have provided high quality firewood, rather than waste, and it is likely that the whole community took part in gathering this material, including women and children. By the end of the project the firewood produced would have been in the region of six tonnes,

even allowing for the retention of selected pieces for making objects under *c* 1m long, the spiral grain preventing the production of long split sections as useful by-products.

The length of the emerging hull of *c* 10m provided plenty of space for many workers to cut splitting scores at the same time. With a distance of *c* 1.5m between workers on either side of the log, there would have been space for a team of up to ten people at some periods. Once the scores were cut, the larger lumps of unwanted bark and sapwood would have been split off using seasoned hardwood wedges driven by clubs or mauls (hammer-like one piece mallets). The wedges were probably similar to a pair of fast grown oak heartwood wedges found in London on a Later Bronze Age site, abandoned close to where alder logs had been split in half (Goodburn & Minkin 1999). Carefully fashioning and repairing wooden wedges, and possibly wedges of bone and antler, would have been a key part of the daily work from this point on.

*Figure 133*
Splitting off bark, sapwood and surplus heartwood from what will become the bottom of the boat to be
(artist: David Hogg, after sketches by Goodburn)

*Figure 134*
Finishing the bottom and lower sides: trimming and smoothing with adzes and axes
(artist: David Hogg, after sketches by Goodburn)

*Figure 135*
Rolling the developing logboat onto bearer logs using poles and wedges (artist: David Hogg, after sketches by Goodburn)

### The human dimension of the work

At a human level, experience of building logboats with bronze and wooden tools has shown the heavy nature of the work, and regular rest days, would have been required. Modern concerns of repetitive strain injury to muscles and joints pale into insignificance against the repeated jarring actions required for this very heavy woodwork. Particularly good supplies of nutritious food and drinking water would also be required by the team.

### Stage 5: Smoothing and fairing down lower external hull

Experience of using a number of replica oak logboats has shown that the external surfaces are subject to much wear, even with only irregular summer use, over roughly three to five years. The wear is created by rubbing over abrasive shallows and dirty timber skids, and rubbing against the banks of watercourses or wooden structures such as jetties. This, along with the added abrasion from weathering and cleaning,

explains why clear toolmarks have not survived on the outboard faces of the hull. In the case of the Carpow boat, the development, and subsequent removal of the concretion that covered the better preserved parts of the hull, may also have acted to remove toolmarks, despite the great care taken by conservators in the cleaning process. It is likely, however, that the builders attempted to make the outer hull relatively smooth and fair, probably executed through gentle paring blows with socketed bronze blades hafted as adzes and axes. Again practical experience would suggest that materials such as animal fat or fish oil would have been smeared on the hull at this point, to slow down drying and reduce splitting. It is also likely that they would use brushwood to protect it from strong sunlight and winds.

### Stage 6: rolling the partly shaped hull on to its base

At this stage, with the shape of the bottom, and the lower parts of the sides, either finalised or nearly complete, the weight of the hull would have still be

*Figure 136*
Splitting off surplus to near the sheerline using maul and wedges (artist: David Hogg, after sketches by Goodburn)

*Figure 137*
Marking out the shape (artist: David Hogg, after sketches by Goodburn)

in the region of *c* 8tonnes. The process of rolling it onto its bottom, to complete the rest of the carving work, therefore required the co-ordinated effort of many people. From experience of rolling vessels of about half that weight, it is suggested that around ten people, equipped with stout poles over 4m long and timber debris to act as chocks and fulcrums, could have rolled the timber over. Indeed, the rounded hull cross-section of the Carpow boat would have been an advantage here, and the team required may have been smaller. It is likely that the part-shaped log was rolled on to bearer logs, to raise it just off the ground and make it easier to move and level up for the next phase of work.

### Stage 7: splitting off unwanted timber to the sheerline

At this stage the unwanted timber above the intended sheerline of the finished boat had to be removed. No doubt the more experienced men, or master builder if such existed, would be involved with marking out reference points to work down to. Here again the natural spiral grain of the parent tree would have been

a problem, with a tendency to split into the sheerline at this point. We have no direct evidence of how this considerable amount of timber was removed, but cutting grooves and splitting out blocks of timber along the grain with wedges is again the most likely method.

### Stage 8: marking out the hull shape in plan ready for hollowing and trimming

Once the unwanted timber was split and hewn down very close to the intended sheerline, the shape of the part trimmed log would be clearly apparent and it is likely that experienced eyes were cast over the log, and marks made to indicate the finished line of the hull sides and both bow and stern shapes. Experience with green oak shows that soft charcoal works well on the damp timber, but other pigments could have been used. A string line was used to mark out the central seam of the Dover boat's plank bottom (Goodburn 2004, 136) and such a simple aid was probably used in the Carpow boat to check symmetry. It is likely that any culturally derived 'rules of thumb and proportion' might now be applied.

106

### *Stage 9: hollowing out the interior of the hull*

The methods used to hollow out a logboat often seem to be the prime focus of attention for the lay audience and there are many myths, the most pervasive of all being that fire was always used in the process. More widely fire has been used in logboat building to singe away splinters, to soften and expand thin hulls, to colour surfaces, and for ritual purposes. There is as yet, however, no clearly documented evidence for the use of fire for hollowing a logboat from Britain. One of the key problems here is that fresh oak in a large mass is virtually fire retardant, so that fire shaping is very much slower than in most timbers. Allowing drying into the heart of a log would have taken many years and also rendered it unusable as the timber would become very hard, and hence difficult to shape with hand tools, and developed drying shakes and splits. Finally, oak stains black in the vast majority of deposits, and given superficial decay or rapid drying out, the surfaces can look charred to those not used to dried-out ancient waterlogged wood. The early European explorers, who described the practice of hollowing out

logs with fire in America, were observing stone and shell tool using peoples, not those with more effective metal tools. Having noted all these provisos, however, there is now some archaeological documentation of the use of fire to hollow Neolithic and Mesolithic logboats on the continent and this is currently the subject of serious experiment (Arnold 1996, 33).

In the case of Carpow, there is no evidence for the use of fire in the hollowing process. Due to the smooth final finishing of the inboard faces of the hull, however, there is no clear direct evidence of how this work was done at all. Very faint possible vertical 'in cuts', left from cutting V-shaped grooves, for groove and splinter hollowing, have been noted, however, not as clearly as in, for example, the hollowed side planks of the Dover boat (Goodburn 2004, 132). It is probable, however, that the bulk of the hollowing was executed by cutting deep grooves with axes across, and possibly along the grain, followed by the use of wedges that may have been slightly curved, so their butt ends were raised off the timber surfaces and they could be cleanly hit with mauls. Where the grain was particularly tough, bronze

*Figure 138*
Hollowing by groove and splinter technique (artist: David Hogg, after sketches by Goodburn)

*Figure 139*
Thinning out the hull (artist: David Hogg, after sketches by Goodburn)

blades hafted as adzes, or possibly even large chisels, could have been used to start the split, as was found useful during the Dover boat experimental work.

### Hauling out the part-finished vessel

It may well have been at this roughed-out stage that the part-finished and much lighter hull was hauled to the waterside, probably close to the home settlement of the builders, so they could keep an eye on the valuable hull. The green roughed out hull – *c* 10m long – would have weighed in the region of *c* 1.5–1.8tonnes, and therefore a more realistic proposition to drag, on skids, out of the wood to a finishing-off site.

### Stage 10: trimming down the hull and the upper parts of the sides

The final stage of thinning out the hull would have involved carefully cutting shallow scores, or incuts, close to the final thickness of hull desired, a more delicately applied version of the technique used above. Down inside the hollow of the hull such

grooves were probably cut with an adze or possibly chisel-type tool, as an axe would have been difficult to manipulate in the enclosed space. In the Dover boat the builders judged this groove and splinter technique very finely, so that in some areas small patches of torn grain were found next to the shallow incut lines. The incut lines were the very bases of the last scores cut inside the hull timbers. The torn grain was left from the splitting out of surplus timber along the grain, while hollowing the half round, logboat-like planks that joined the sides to the flat bottom. It was found that splits could be made to follow the annual rings if started with sharp adze blows (Goodburn 2004, 132; Darrah 2004c, 176). In the case of the Carpow boat the builders were even more careful than those of the earlier Dover boat not to cut the last scores too deep and no really clear examples have been identified.

Ethnographic records for logboats with very rounded cross-sections, like Carpow, document various forms of short-handle adzes, used in finishing internal surfaces. Excellent examples can be found in detailed descriptions of logboat manufacture in Borneo (Petersen 2000, 105). Using a blade, hafted as an adze, across the grain in this way produces wave-like slight ridges and dips running across the width of the boat, which can be seen in raking light on cleaned wet surfaces. Faint traces of such ridges can be seen in places on the inside of the hull, and on the bottom of the aftermost section of the hull, in the Carpow vessel. This patterning of marks was regular and it is clear that attention was given to make the finish smooth and even. In green oak this cross-grain hewing (often termed 'dubbing' when an adze is used) works well with metal blades, but represents a break with the earlier practice of hewing along the grain, producing longitudinal furrows as found on the Dover boat timbers and some other large Bronze Age timbers (Goodburn 2004, 129). The longitudinal adze finishing method for large timbers seemed to follow earlier Neolithic practice, were it was very difficult to dub smoothly across the grain with stone blades, but easier along the grain where the tool worked also as a wedge. Experimentation has shown, however, that it is easy to hew across the grain with fine edged bronze blades, so the woodworkers of the Bronze Age could finish the timber in both directions creating patterns they desired. This patterning of marks may indicate a culturally derived aesthetic sense of the builders to some extent. The Buiston Crannog logboat 3 provides the clearest evidence for finishing by this technique (Crone 2000, 31) although it can also be seen in some photographs of the Hasholme boat (Millett & McGrail 1987, plate XVIII).

Nearer the upper edges of the sides, it is likely that blades hafted as axes were used, as the line of the edge of the vessel can best be seen from above, although in the Carpow example toolmarks were not preserved at this level. Arnold, however, presents photographs of an unfinished Swiss prehistoric logboat with a pattern of shallow scores in the base, and an axe-hewn step on the upper sides, similar to the work situation shown in Fig 139 (Arnold 1996, 91). In the centre of the bottom of the Carpow boat inboard, very faint undulations were noted that could suggest the use of an adze swung along the grain. Due to wear in use and subsequent erosion, these marks were not clear enough to discern the tool blade edge dimensions.

### A lack of thickness-gauge holes

It is useful at this point to discuss the apparent lack of thickness-gauge holes, cut through the hull to gauge the thickness of the lower parts, a technique documented in many logboat boat finds and living traditions. For example, the bottom of the Late Bronze Age Short Ferry boat had three holes in it which were found useful in judging the thickness of the base of the replica. The cross-sections shown in the main hull of Carpow show only slight variation in thickness (Fig 86) so it is likely that the builders had another way of gauging the thickness of the hull as they were reducing the timber. McGrail notes several simple methods such as feeling down both sides with opposed digits and also gently tapping and listening to the pitch of the sound (McGrail 1978, 33). Other simple aids include the use of stick laid across the finished sheerline from which measurements could be made downwards with other sticks. However, relating the internal distances to external surfaces of the hull would have been very difficult in the case of a very rounded hull form like that of the Carpow Boat. The reasonably even bottom of the vessel is a testament to the builders' skill and much more regular than in some finds. The Carpow boats bottom thickness (Fig 86) varies from $c$ 150mm to $c$ 130mm, except in the raised transom fitting groove where the hull was left thicker to allow for the cutting of the joint. The top edges of the sides are rounded and at the point where that rounding stopped they measure $c$ 60mm thick.

### Moving the boat when it was finished

If the bottom was $c$ 110mm thick and the upper sides $c$ 60mm then the boat would weigh, with the inserted transom, $c$ 1.3tonnes in green condition, decreasing

*Figure 140*
Detail of transom grooves showing toolmarks. Note the differences in size and shape between inner and outer transom grooves. The inner transom groove is the upmost in the picture

*Figure 141*
Detail of toolmarks in the outer transom groove

*Figure 142*
An incut from an axe or adze visible as a faint line running
concentrically below the footrest

to perhaps a tonne in regular use, where the bottom would remain fairly wet but the sides dry out somewhat. On wetted or greased skids, it would be possible for a group of around ten strong adults to drag her along, except up a steep incline. Indeed, based on experience of moving the Short Ferry boat short distances on land, an experienced crew of five using stout poles as levers could move her short distances up and down a shore, or over short portages.

### Stage 11: carving the fittings in the stern section and sheerline

The stern of the boat required the most complex workmanship with the forming of the original

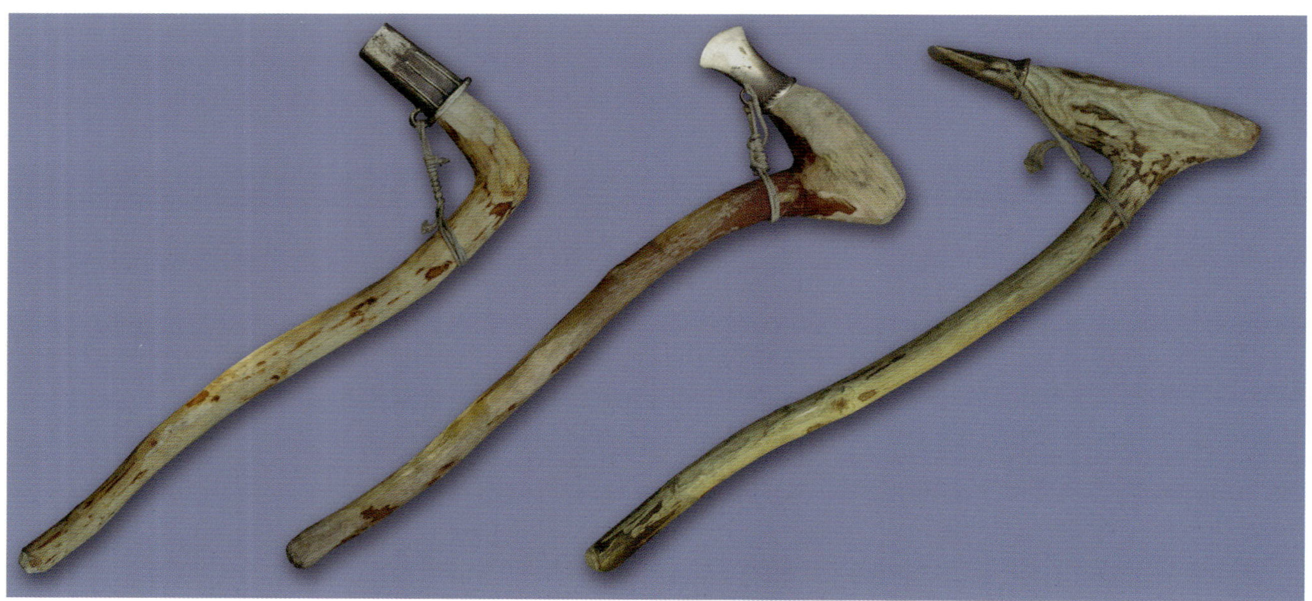

*Figure 143*
A replica bronze hammer (left) and socketed axes, hafted as an axe (centre) and adze (right). Part of the Late Bronze Age toolkit probably used for
Carpow

*Figure 144*
Replica small edge tools: a chisel (above) and socketed gouge (below)

transom groove, the beam-tie, the retaining holes and the two footrests (Chapter 5, pp 69–86). The initial stage, Phase 1 (Chapter 5, pp 87–8) involved cutting the original transom groove, beam-tie holes and the retaining holes for the proposed cross plank, or seat (Chapter 5, Fig 126).

Inside the outer transom groove, clear toolmarks survive, in cuts *c* 30mm wide left by a rounded metal blade. They were probably left from chopping out the groove using an adze or short handled axe with a blade probably not more than 40mm wide, typical of the Late Bronze Age (Chapter 5, pp 76–7) and Goodburn 2003). A gouge may have been used to tidy up the grain at the bottom of the groove, but no clear marks left by its use could be seen. Around the footrests, a number of axe or adze incuts were noted in good raking light, and even a few faint 'stop marks' on the starboard side (Fig 142). These marks were a little wider at *c* 40mm but may have been made by the same kind of tool, with a blade not much wider than 40–45mm.

The holes for the missing beam tie were probably cut with a gouge type tool, but no marks survived the extensive erosion in this area. Also interpreted as being part of the original design, the vertically cut retaining features, to secure the proposed seat (Fig 126) were *c* 60mm in diameter by 70mm deep and almost certainly cut with a gouge, though again extensive erosion has removed any marks. There is no evidence of auger

bits for drilling holes in wood from Late Bronze Age Britain, but in other Bronze Age woodwork, such as the Dover boat, clear marks of small gouges and chisels have been recorded (Goodburn 2004, 133).

### Sheerline holes

The three surviving, very similar holes cut just below the sheerline (Fig 93) appear to have been cut with a gouge and chisel type blades, with the neater, oval holes, *c* 40mm in diameter, on the inboard face of the hull.

### Stage 12: subsequent transom repairs

The boat clearly underwent at least one major phase of repair of the transom, after wear damage had taken its toll and the two basal splits appeared running along the bottom of the hull. It was apparent to the excavation team that the transom found *in situ*, the repair block and the low, outer transom, were probably not original features, but evidence of repair (Chapter 5, pp 85–8).

### The repair transom groove

Perhaps the most unusual feature of the Carpow boat was the existence of the second, outer transom groove (F27). This groove was relatively fresh and crisp in appearance, with a square cross-section, and must have been cut with a square ended chisel while the boat was

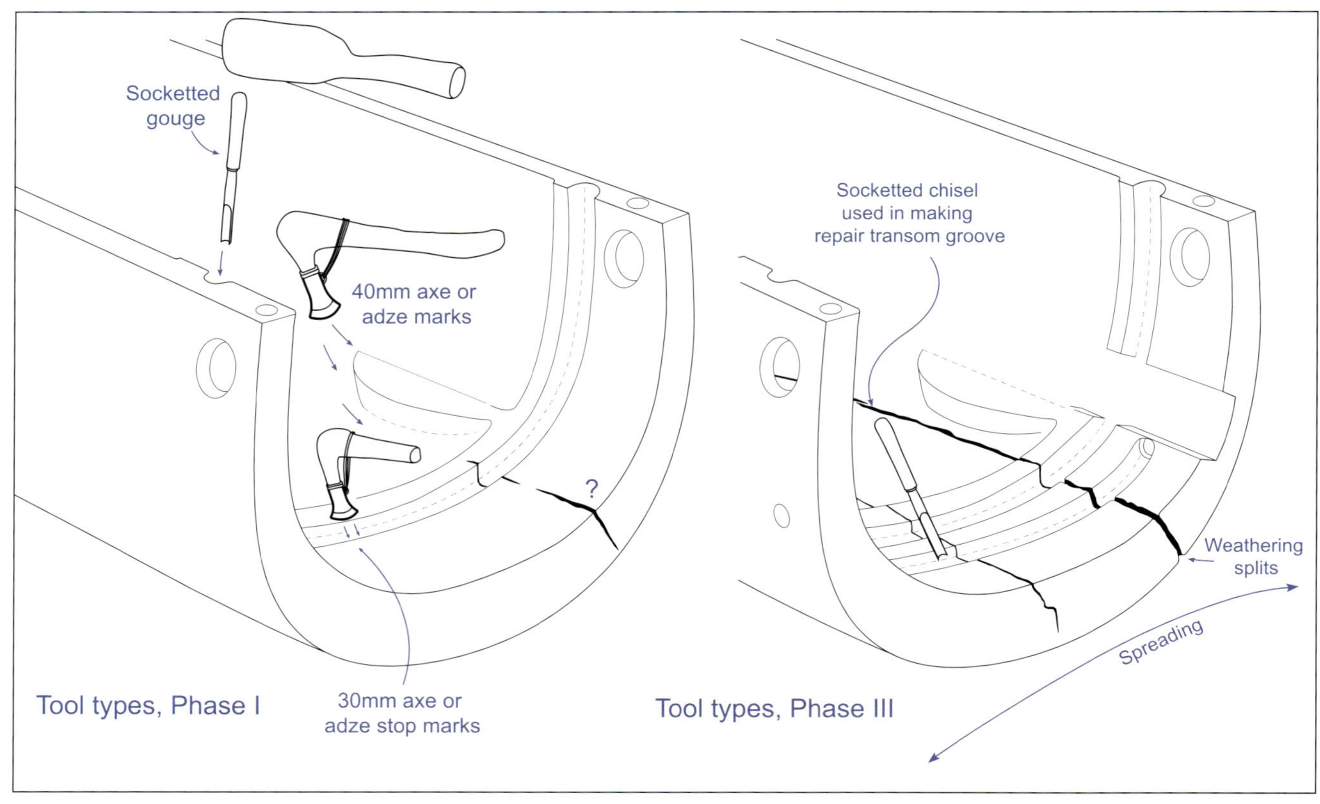


*Figure 145*
A schematic drawing showing the type of tool used in both the original manufacture and repair of the stern

out of water. An explanation that might take account of the fairly fresh nature of this groove, and the fresh toolmarks on the transom together with the absence of the repair transom, would be that it represented an intermediate phase of repair. That is, it is relic of an earlier repair, by fitting a second repair transom, while the original transom was still *in situ*.

## 7.4 The toolkit for building and repair

The variety of tools used by the builders is clearly small, the most important of which would have been their true eyes, experience and muscle. The edge tools evidenced by their toolmarks are axes and adzes with narrow rounded edges between *c* 40–50mm in width. These would have been typical socketed axe heads, hafted in line with the handle as axes, and transversely as adzes (Figs 143–5). These tools were smaller than those that both preceded and followed

them. From a modern efficiency perspective the decrease in blade size of the larger tools during the Bronze Age is difficult to explain. For a woodsman of *c* AD 1900, the small, light Late Bronze Age tools would look laughably small and impractical, but finds like the Carpow boat show how very heavy, large-scale woodworking was quite possible with such tools. How many of these larger edge tools the boat-builders had remains uncertain. Smaller metal edge tools would have included a gouge and a chisel. To maintain and sharpen the tools a hardening hammer, possibly a socketed bronze example, would have been needed in addition to whetstones. As important as the metal edge tools were the numerous wooden tools, principally dry, seasoned wedges, for cleaving surplus wood away, and mauls and clubs to drive them. Poles, log bearers, fatty lubricants (animal fats) and skid logs would have been needed to handle the log and roughed out boat and aids such as a string line

112

and pigments for marking, such as charcoal, would also have been required.

### 7.5 Conclusions

It is clear that the building of a logboat the size of the Carpow example was beyond the resources of one family, and must be seen as a communal effort, at least at the level of an extended family with additional support. Although classed as a 'basic' logboat with inserted transom, it is clear that her builders invested not only considerable effort and time in her manufacture, but also skilled extra work of an aesthetic nature. This is evidenced by the smoothness of the original hull finish and the fairly even thickness attained, apparently without the use of thickness-gauge holes. While it is possible to suggest that a maximum of about ten people could have worked at the same time on the early stages of shaping her hull, we cannot be precise, as the toolmark preserva-

tion did not enable the identification of individual tools. Indeed, trying to estimate how many man-days it would have taken to build her is problematic given the number of variables to consider. We know little of how the people of the period in the region organised their time, but it is likely that the building of such a vessel would have been spread over several weeks in the cooler months of the year. If the labour force was around ten for the early stages, however, then it may have taken somewhere in the region of three weeks, with a smaller team doing the finishing.

The nature of the wear and weathering of the hull shows that the Carpow boat was used for several years at least, during which an impromptu repair was carried out and eventually a new transom was fitted. The condition of this new, rather roughly made transom suggest the boat was not used a great deal more, after its fitting, before her last voyage to her final resting place.

# Chapter 8

# Considering propulsion and performance

DAVID STRACHAN and DAMIAN GOODBURN

## 8.1 Propulsion

### Methods of propulsion

While logboats can be powered by sail and more recently by outboard motor, the most common form of propulsion is human-power, delivered through paddling, rowing, punting and quanting. In general terms, paddling and rowing involve the use of paddles and oars, respectively, which contact only the water, while punting and quanting both involve the use of poles which contact and push against the river or estuary bed to propel the vessel forward. With the use of paddles, the number of paddlers is dependent on the size of the canoe or logboat, but is commonly two. Paddlers face the direction of travel, and either kneel or stand directly on the hull, or are seated on supports in the hull. Paddles can be single- or double-bladed. With rowing, the rowers are seated, usually facing the stern using mounted oars. The difference between paddling and rowing is that rowing requires a mechanical connection between the oar and boat, while with paddling the paddles are hand-held. In punting, the punter generally propels the vessel by pushing against the bed of the river or estuary with a pole from a stationary position, while in quanting, the operator drives a pole into the river bed near the bow, and then walks down the side of the boat, braced against the quant pole, the boat being propelled forward at the speed he walks. The quant is then pulled out of the water by placing hand over hand on it and pulling upwards and the process is repeated.

The nature of the Carpow boat would make it very suitable for both paddling and punting, and while there is little evidence for rowing, it remains a possibility (below p 122 and Chapter 5, pp 68–9). While quanting is known ethnographically on logboats, it is unlikely on Carpow because the U-shaped, rather than flat-bottomed, nature of the hull would have made the balance of the vessel, from port to starboard side, very delicate. In addition, the thinness of the hull along the sheerline would have made walking along the hull, even with the additional stability of a pole, extremely difficult. Whatever the function of the Carpow vessel, it is likely that it was propelled by a combination of paddling in deeper waters and poling or punting in shallow water. Of the implements used for water-borne propulsion: paddles, oars and poles, as archaeological artefacts, the former two are usually indistinguishable and the latter very difficult to recognise.

### Early Scottish paddles and oars

There is no known archaeological evidence for punting and quanting, and reliably distinguishing oars from paddles, and both of these from spades, bakers peels, and other implements, is difficult, but can be attempted perhaps most easily on the basis of size as below (Mowat 1996, 136).

The archaeological evidence of prehistoric paddles from Scotland can be summarised in three groups: early discoveries of definite or probable paddles, which often do not survive; artefacts which are possibly paddles, though may have another function; and surviving examples identified with certainty and either dated or recovered from contexts that reliably suggest a prehistoric date.

Within the first category, the quality of records varies enormously, from merely passing references to full descriptions. For example, there is a reference to the discovery of a 'Canoe Paddle' at Kirkbog, Dumfries and Galloway, in 1862, but no further detail, and the artefact does not survive (*ibid*, 90). While slightly more detail, in the form of dimensions, is recorded about the paddle found at Buiston Crannog, Ayrshire, during Munro's excavations of 1880–1, it unfortunately did not include information on the form. Recorded as 175mm broad, 30mm thick and handle 125mm in circumference, the find was recovered from 'on the crannog' and so a prehistoric date is likely. It is worth noting that the sheerline of the Buiston 1 boat had 'short pieces of wood fastened to it with vertical pins, as if intended for the use of oars' (*ibid*, 14).

Perhaps the most useful account is of the paddle discovered near the Loch Coille-Bharr crannog, Argyll and Bute in 1887. A prehistoric date is again suggested from its proximity to the crannog, where it was found under *c* 1.8m of mud. It was described as being 'very well, even elegantly made, like a barbed arrow – rather convex on one side, and concave on the other' (Mapleton 1868, 323). While again lost, the paddle was identified as being of oak, and a detailed account of its dimensions indicate that the handle was about 1.2m long and 51mm in diameter and the blade was 216mm in length, 203mm at the greatest width and 51mm thick. While the paddle broke on discovery, the account also notes two holes measuring 51mm in diameter and 76mm apart 'as if pegs had been inserted' (Mowat 1996, 91).

The second category of artefacts includes a wide variety of objects with other possible functions often with vague references, such as the recovery of a 'wooden shovel or paddle' from a burnt mound at Staura Cottage, Shetland in 1972 (Hedges 1975, 75–6). Other references might suggest a different interpretation, such as the record of five or six paddles found near a 'mass of timbers' in 1866 at Ravenstone Moss, Dumfries and Galloway (Fig 146J). Amongst the contradictory accounts of the finds, Munro notes that they were all of a similar size (Munro 1885, 82–4), and while Stuart suggests they were part of a crannog (Stuart 1866, 122–3), Mowat notes that the eccentric shape of the sole survivor suggests that it could in fact be a rudder (Mowat 1996, 104). It may equally be possible that the group represent the remains of a small waterwheel. At Rubh' an Dunain, Skye a cave site, apparently occupied from the Bronze Age to the Early Historic period, was excavated in 1932 and produced a wooden 'paddle' near an Iron Age furnace (Fig 146M). The excavator suggested that it was related to iron-smelting (Scott 1934) and Mowat questions whether it was a paddle (Mowat 1996, 105). The 1980s excavations at Buiston (Fig 146F) also produced an unconvincing paddle or oar of oak fashioned from a radially split plank (Crone 2000, 126 and 262), which has a rectangular handle which, if the interpretation is correct, would make it very unusual in form.

The final group in this category comes from the unpublished 1960 excavation of Loch Glashan Crannog, Argyll and Bute. A study of the wooden artefacts (Earwood 1990) lists containers, pegs, pins, spatulae, handles, and tools as well as parts of other unidentified structures, and these suggested occupation between the sixth and eighth centuries AD. It is widely recognised that crannogs are often multi-period, however (Guido 1974), and as the excavations did not penetrate the (then) water table, it is very probable that the crannog was occupied for considerably longer than

this. Close to the Loch Glashan 1 logboat in Argyll and Bute, a 'possible wooden paddle or oar' (Fig 146E) was found and suggested to be associated with it. Only part of it survives, measuring 410mm length, 68mm breadth and 15mm thick, and as a result the form is not clear (Mowat 1996, 92). From the crannog itself, proposed paddles include an 'oar-shaped implement' suggested as being a structural member (*ibid*, 92); and two spatulae that are leaf-shaped (Earwood 1990, 86–7); domestic functions have been proposed for both, one as a possible platter (Mowat 1996, 94) and the other, a 'miniature paddle', as a possible toy or model paddle (*ibid*, 96). This is a reminder that artefacts of broadly similar form performed a range of domestic and industrial functions, from weaver's beaters to implements for winnowing grain (Lerche & Steensberg 1973, 87–104). High concentrations of cereal pollen from the site point to the cultivation of crops but the use of canoes is also a certainty (Dixon 2004, 151–2).

Finally there are a number of surviving examples of paddles identified with certainty and recovered from contexts that suggest a prehistoric date. Two of these were found at the Loch Glashan crannog, the first measured 1.1m in length and 0.1m transversely with a handle roughly circular and 40mm in diameter. The blade becomes more pointed towards the end, where it appears to have been cut square across, though possibly may have simply broken as can be seen in a number of the other examples (Mowat 1996, 93; Fig 146G). The second, less well-preserved example, was described as a 'paddle-like object', though confirmed as a paddle by Mowat (*ibid*, 93). Much damaged, the length is similar to the former example and the blade is recorded as 90mm in breadth and 25mm thickness, roughly rectangular with rounded corners (Fig 146H).

Less certain are the paddle and double-bladed paddle from the Lochlea Crannog in Ayrshire. Munro noted discovery of a 'large oar, together with the blade portion of another' during the excavation of the crannog, and it has been suggested that either of these is possibly the example on display at the Dick Institute, Kilmarnock (Mowat 1996, 99–100). It measures 1.04m in overall length and consists of an elongated straight-sided blade, 0.86m in length by 80mm breadth and 30mm thickness. The stump of the handle is irregularly rounded and *c* 40mm in diameter (Fig 146D). A proposed double-bladed paddle was also recovered from Munro's crannog excavations in the late 1870s (*ibid*). When reconstructed it was 1.37m long with two roughly oval blades, about 0.5m by 0.95m by 30mm thick. The shaft was roughly circular and about 30mm in thickness. Mowat (*ibid*) questions this interpretation, arguing that it is too short for practical use, and notes the similarity with double paddle-spades, used in peat cutting, from the Danish Iron Age (Lerche 1977) (Fig 146C).

A paddle blade from Loch Kinord in Aberdeenshire can probably be associated with a crannog on the loch.

It has an overall length of 0.52m, the near rectangular blade is 0.22m long with an approximate thickness of *c* 12mm, and the handle is slightly oval and *c* 20mm in diameter (Mowat 1996, 97–8) (Fig 146L). Finally, two paddles have been recovered in recent years from Oakbank Crannog on the north bank of Loch Tay. The crannog has been dated to the Late Bronze Age and Early Iron Age, with a date range identified

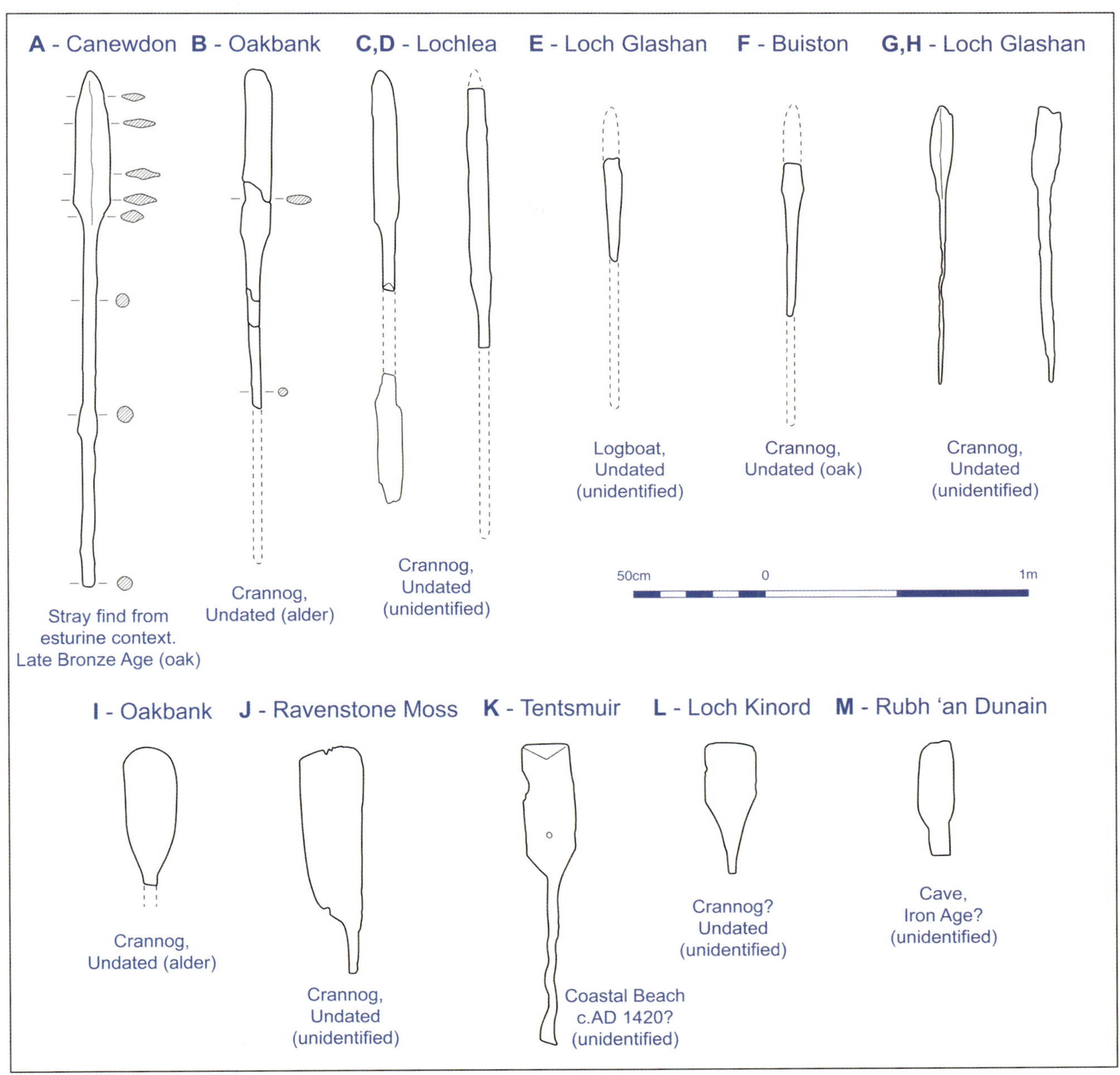


*Figure 146*
A comparative illustration showing selected paddles/oars mentioned in the text

from around 800 to 300 cal BC (Dixon 2004, 178). Both paddles were made of alder, and the first, found in 1981 amongst the crannog material, was found to measure 1.35m in overall length (Mowat 1996, 101; Dixon 2004, 151–2), although clearly much of the handle is missing and when complete would have been at least 2m long. The blade is roughly rectangular and elongated in form, bearing numerous tool-marks, with a convex back to the blade and a relatively flat face (Fig 146B). The second was later recovered from the same area and is quite different in form, being much wider and rounded (Fig 146I). It has been suggested that the varying form of these two paddles may represent different functions, with the former being a steering oar, with a notch in the blade near the handle possibly the result of friction with the sheerline of a boat, and the latter a paddle for powering a logboat (Dixon 2004, 152). While no logboat has so far been found at Oakbank Crannog, a large oak logboat 11.5m long, dating to *c* 1500 cal BC (GU-10558), was discovered at the crannog reconstruction near Kenmore (Chapter 9, p 125 and 130; Dixon pers comm), and logboats would almost certainly have been in use at Oakbank.

In addition, two paddles were found in estuarine clay close to the three mid-Bronze Age sewn boats at North Ferriby (Wright 1978, 193–5). The first was incomplete when discovered in 1939, and was lost in the wartime fire that destroyed Hull Museum, however, a replica had been made which showed that the blade measured 0.85m in length and was of elongated spade-shape with curving, convex shoulders. The second, surviving only as a small fragment, has been identified as being ash, and it is likely that this was also the material of the first one. Wright suggests that the North Ferriby paddle was similar to Maori paddles used to propel large logboats, though not suitable for steering (as it is too small) or as an oar (as the shaft was too light).

One of the few dated paddles is worth consideration at this point. The Tentsmuir paddle (Fig 146K) was recovered from the inter-tidal sandy beach on the north-east Fife coast. It measures *c* 1.2m in length with the blade measuring 0.53m in length and is roughly rectangular with a slightly raised centreline and was dated to *c* 1411 cal AD (GU-1076) (Mowat 1996, 106). Its rectangular form is noticeably different from the elongated curved lines displayed by the paddles from crannog sites, which by association, can reasonably be assumed to be prehistoric.

### *The Canewdon paddle*

While the Scottish examples are useful in indicating the types of paddle that are likely to be used, none have been dated other than through association with crannogs or logboats of prehistoric date. In 1983, however, a paddle recovered during an inter-tidal survey on the Essex coast at Canewdon has been shown to be broadly contemporary with the Carpow logboat (Wilkinson & Murphy 1995, 152–7; Wright 1990, 153). It was found complete and recovered from an excellent stratigraphic context, though without any associated archaeology. It has been dated to the Late Bronze Age at *c* 1255–998 cal BC (BM-2339) and comes from the Crouch Estuary which has, and would have had, very similar landscape characteristics to the Tay. It was made from split oak (*Quercus* sp) well away from the pith and bark, suggesting that the blank would have been between a quarter and a half of the circumference of the original round-wood (Wilkinson & Murphy 1995, 157). The paddle is notable for its length (2.08m) and quality of workmanship, having a blade 630mm long and 140mm wide with a central carination along either face. In section, the blade is diamond-shaped. The shaft is roughly circular in section and *c* 0.5m in diameter with a noticeable swelling around 60% along the shaft, away from the blade (Fig 146A). The proportions are very large for a paddle; for example, in comparison with 17 other recent and ancient examples tabulated by McGrail it is *c* 0.5m longer (McGrail 1987, 208, table 12.1). The paddle shows no signs of having been used in a rowlock or grommet, or of having been permanently fixed to a vessel by any other means, and it has been noted that when held, the swelling on the shaft falls naturally to the lower hand, with the upper hand holding the slightly expanded end (Wilkinson & Murphy 1995, 157). As a result, the massive Canewdon paddle is probably the best evidence for the sort of paddle employed on the Carpow vessel.

The possibility remains, however, that the Canewdon find was some form of small steering oar, rather than a large paddle. It is similar in size and shape to the Oakbank example (Fig 146B), suggested as having that function, indeed, the sort of size to be found on a modern yachts dinghy used as an oar. At least five reasonably accurate replicas of this paddle have been made in oak and experimented with or displayed in conjunction with reconstructions of British Bronze Age boats. The paddle is simply too long to use as a paddle sitting down, but can be used as one

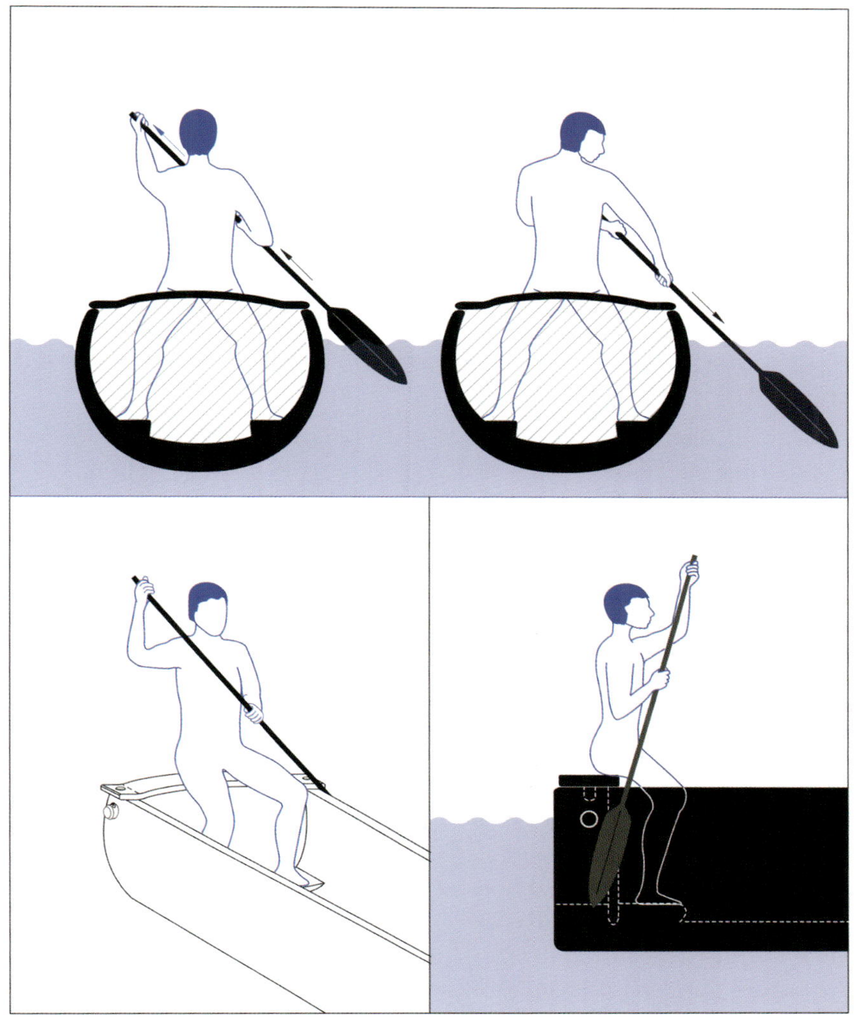

*Figure 147*
The use of the footrests and seat on Carpow, a Canewdon type paddle could have been used mainly as a steering oar in this instance. The human figure shown is reconstructed at 1.65m in height

standing up, as in the Short Ferry boat replica. Gifford and Gifford have even found that the reconstructed Canewdon 'paddle' works well as an oar in their half scale reconstruction of the early Bronze Age lashed plank boat Ferriby 1 (Gifford *et al* 2006, 610). In the latter case there might have been problems of scale as the original vessel was very much larger, but at least in terms of the Canewdon oar and human ergonomics they are shown to work well. The proportions of the Carpow logboat would suggest that a paddle of this size could have been used when standing on the footrests, or resting against the seat, either as oars used sitting or paddles used standing (Fig 147).

## 8.2  Performance

### Reconstructing the possible performance of logboats through calculation

McGrail's systematic survey and analysis of English and Welsh logboats (McGrail 1978) included methodical attempts to reconstruct the possible performance of some of the more intact vessels. Issues such as cargo and crew capacity, speed stability and sea-worthiness were considered. One problem with this approach is that some of the assumed variables used for standard comparisons may be significantly different to those operating in the Late Bronze Age. For example, a nominal crew weight of 60kg was assumed for '… a short, lean, wiry, person' (*ibid*, 131), as a basis for standardised calculations based on modern naval architects formulae. It is suggested that this figure may be somewhat low for adult males, and so an average 70kg has been used in the Carpow calculations, the results of which are summarised in table 5, with the detail of the formulae, and the criteria used, documented in Appendix II.

### Practical testing theoretical performance

While the introduction of theoretical calculations was a significant development in reconstructing possible parameters of performance in early boats, it was not generally tested experimentally with replicas or models. One instance where experimental tests were carried out was with the small Clapton Boat reconstruction, an accurately built replica of a tenth-century AD logboat (Goodburn & Redknap 1988; Marsden *et al* 1989). In the case of this small but heavy craft, 3.75m long 0.68m wide by 0.39m deep, the theoretically calculated performance and that actually experienced by the crew were quite close in some areas (McGrail 1990). The calculations showed that the practical crew of the boat was two nominal adults and up to 60kg of light cargo, such as dry peat. More likely with such a vessel, a nominal crew of one paddler could carry up to 133kg of the same light cargo with a freeboard of 100mm, the minimum acceptable in very sheltered water (*ibid*, 131). Thus, the calculated maximum weight capacity of the vessel with adequate freeboard, one crew and cargo at 133kg equates to some 200kg in fresh water. A maximum speed of 2.5 knots was calculated, given the presence of enough paddle power, which broadly tallies with what was possible for any distance with paddles. In practice the vessel could carry a few kilograms more than calculated, but not significantly more, though four light adults were actually accommodated. In general the standardised calculations were a fairly close match with practical results within perhaps rather narrow limits. Clearly there remains a need to subject the existing fleet of oak logboat reconstructions in Britain to systematic performance trials, providing 'control data' against which to compare the theoretical results derived through calculation.

### The key role of poles in shallow water propulsion of logboats

The findspot of the Clapton Boat was the lower River Lee in east London, a short way above the then tidal limits. This variable river flows over a gentle incline through what must have been braided and often reedy shallows. Practical considerations suggest that the most likely method of propulsion for such a craft at that time, in that locality, was using a pole for 'punting'. However, the standard calculations did not consider what the environment of use was. In practice, in skilled hands, in a shallow river environment, it was possible to punt the replica vessel at just under three knots for several miles with a crew of one and modest 30kg cargo. A skilled and athletic punt-racer at Taplow on the upper Thames was in fact able to punt the boat at jogging speed (*c* 5 knots) with a full cargo for around half a mile even though he had no familiarity with the boat. It must also be borne in mind that poles can aid the stability of the crew and boat unit; steering; short bouts of paddling over deep patches; and mooring and slewing the vessel around using currents or wind. Essentially the use of a pole, or direct hauling from a bank, maximises

*Table 5*

A summary of capacity and performance as calculated in Appendix II

| | Mass of boat | Unladen freeboard | Safe loading capacity | Max. crew | Max. cargo | Max. speed |
|---|---|---|---|---|---|---|
| Green oak | 1755kg | 337mm | 1046.7kg @ 150mm freeboard | 14 | 907kg | 7.5 knots |
| Green oak | 1755kg | 337mm | 1325.2kg @ 100mm freeboard | 14 | 1185kg | 7.5 knots |
| Seasoned oak | 1288kg | 368mm | 895.5kg @ 150mm freeboard | 13 | 756kg | 7.5 knots |
| Seasoned oak | 1288kg | 368mm | 1100kg @ 100mm freeboard | 14 | 960kg | 7.5 knots |

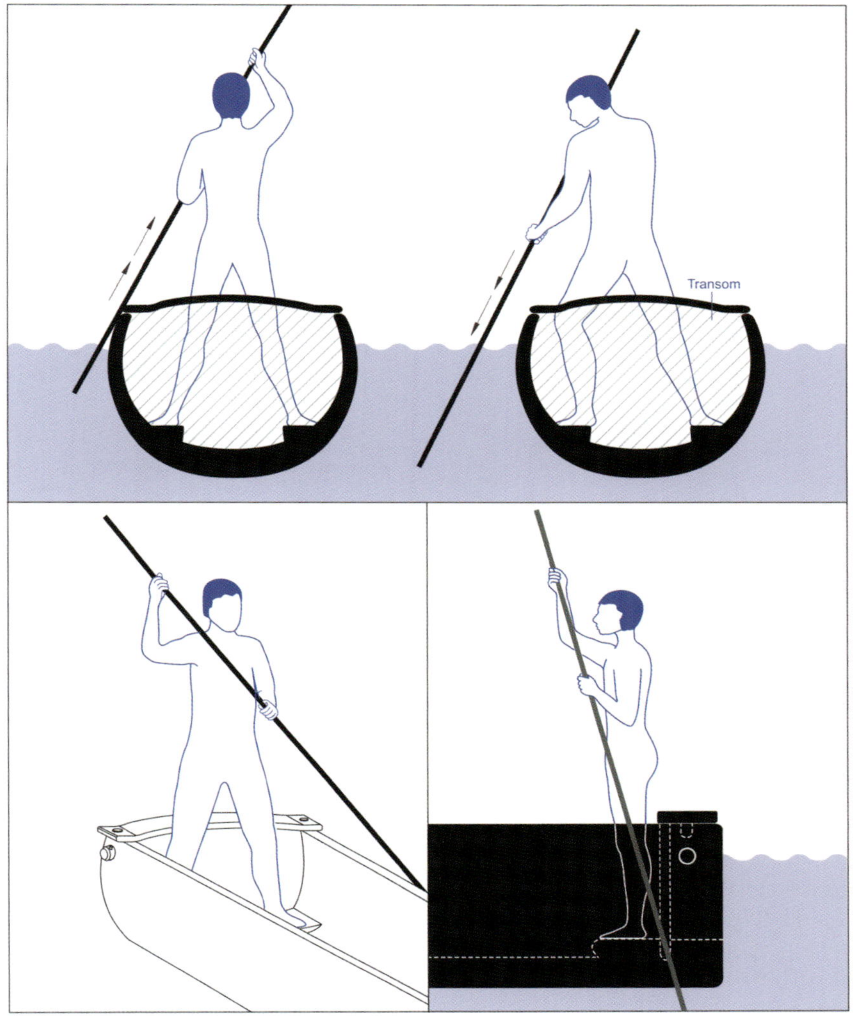


*Figure 148*
The footrests would have provided the ideal platform from which to punt the vessel, both for pushing the boat forward and allowing for minor balancing of lateral movement in the hull. The human figure shown is reconstructed at 1.65m in height

the power that a crewman can apply to move dugout vessels in sheltered waters far above what is possible by paddling or even rowing. In a vessel the size of the Carpow boat, at around 10m long, a pole used in the stern and one at the bow might have been useful in manoeuvring.

### *Problems of momentum in heavy 'basic' logboat hulls, and effects on handling*

Another important factor not highlighted by the standard calculations, but which practical experience makes immediately apparent, is that in the vast majority of cases, simple hewn logboats (un-expanded or extended) like Carpow, are much heavier than individual crew members. This means they build up enormous momentum, difficult to visualise from the modern 'western' experience of lightly built planked boats or canoes and kayaks of fibreglass, canvas or plywood. The consequence is that if the bow of a logboat starts to slew away from the desired course it takes great effort to bring back on to the correct course; and sudden stops are not possible. In practice, possibly partly due to the hull shape, this was a severe problem with the Clapton Boat reconstruction when paddled with maximum force. During a launch of the replica where the original boat was found on the River Lee, professional kayak instructors, used to ultra light glass fibre kayaks, tried to paddle the boat faster than the archaeologist crew did, but they were unable to control it. Subsequent experience of the longer, oak Short Ferry boat reconstruction, which is broadly similar to Carpow, has shown that directional stability was less of a problem. Momentum, however, still had to be considered carefully when manoeuvring.

### Methods of propulsion used in boats in Bronze Age northern Europe

McGrail has led the way in the systematic consideration of evidence for propulsion of early boats in north-west Europe (eg McGrail 1987, 204–16). The use of poles and paddles is recognised as far back as the Mesolithic, but the use of oars pivoted on a fulcrum of some type is not generally thought to have existed before the Iron Age. Even then the evidence is not very clear as it is based on the characteristics of two gold boat models. The small (65mm long) and crude Durrnberg model is made of gold sheet and appears to show a tapering vessel with up-sloping square ends (possibly a logboat), two crudely depicted oars and oar ports (Ellmers 1978, 2; McGrail 1987, 213). The model is from a grave dated to *c* fifth century BC by associated finds. The next dated evidence comes from Ireland; the gold Broighter boat model of the first century BC, which shows a round hulled craft with oars and a sail. Again this is crudely depicted (McGrail 1987, 205). The general consensus of archaeological opinion suggests that the widespread use of oars and sails in western then northern Europe may have been a result of classical influence originating from Bronze Age Greece. Practically minded researchers into early craft have, however, sought to push the evidence further and consider the possibility of both rowing and sailing in British waters in the Bronze Age (Gifford *et al* 2006, 61). Rowing could be inferred from the contemporary find of the Canewdon paddle (Chapter 5, p 68 and above pp 118–19) and, as such, the possibility remains that the Carpow boat may have been propelled by oars.

### Probable propulsion methods used for Carpow

The crew of the Carpow boat would have made use of tides and river flow currents whenever possible. Indeed, the importance of tidal power for transporting the logboat both on the estuary, and up and down the tidal stretches of the rivers Tay and Earn, cannot be under emphasised, and this issue along with its implications for how the boat operated is developed later (Chapter 13, pp 167–9). In this mode, manual power may have been used to boost speed, or only sporadically for steerage. The footrests F16 and F17 strongly suggest that one of the crew would have stood feet apart and well braced, above any bilge water, at the stern (Fig 148). This crew member would have had the best view and most secure position of anyone aboard and would probably have been the head boatman in control of the vessel. It is likely that that person wielded a pole at least 5m long, but probably much longer. The same person may also have used a steering paddle or oar in deeper water. Although formal sailing can be ruled out as a propulsion force, it is possible that wind effects may have been used casually as has been documented ethnographically, with standing crew possibly holding out capes, similar clothing or bushes towards the bows of a vessel when the wind was fair (Roberts & Shackleton 1983, 87; Rudolph 1974, 45, Chapter 5, p 65).

The manual power options clearly include punting and paddling, with the possibly of rowing. If rowing was used the basic crew of the boat would have been one helmsman and three oarsmen in deep enough water. Should the vessel have travelled up into the faster fresh water reaches of the Tay or Earn, punting and possibly hauling against the stream is likely. Quanting was probably not used with the Carpow logboat due to her likely lack of transverse stability and passengers, crew or cargo being in the way, though we cannot rule it out.

### The rounded internal hull of Carpow: atypical in contemporary logboats

It is easily agreed that the bottom of the Carpow boat is very rounded, for most of its length little heartwood was removed to make the bottom flatter, which would have increased stability and reduced draft, light or laden. Other British dugout boat finds from the Bronze and Iron Ages excavated fairly recently have generally been given fairly flat bottoms eg the Short Ferry boat, the Witham finds (unpublished photos from Gifford) all from Lincolnshire, and the Hasholme boat from Humberside (Millett & McGrail 1987). It is suggested that either the Carpow builders were struggling to make the largest boat they could out of a given log, or possibly they were more interested in speed than stability and low draft. The rounded hull would have had less 'wetted surface area' and, given the same power applied, ought to have been slightly faster than one with a flatter bottom. However, the hull must have been more prone to rolling than the flatter-bottomed craft and have needed more water to float in. In the very flat-bottomed Short Ferry replica it is possible for a heavy adult to walk along the boat leaning against the side of the hull without capsizing, whilst it is unlikely that this would be possible in the Carpow boat.

### Crewing and maintaining the Carpow boat

These comments are not intended to supplant 'scientifically calculated figures' for maximum possible crew-passengers or possible cargo weight (Appendix II) but to provide some additional estimates as to probable performance, based on the practical experience of using broadly similar reconstructed oak dugout vessels in a variety of water bodies. As suggested above, the partly dried vessel, given a length of $c$ 10m, would have weighed very roughly 1 tonne (with an average heartwood weight somewhat less than the typical green oak value of just over 1 tonne/m$^3$). In use, it is likely that the bottom of the hull was never seasoned but the sides were. Experience with reconstructions has shown that on level ground around six adults would have been able to slide the boat on wet skids. That is, short portages would be possible around shallows but were probably avoided. It is likely that the boat was protected against winds and strong sun, that might cause excessive drying, both by coatings of fatty or oily materials and by covering with boughs or wet skins. Controlling the seasoning of an oak logboat is important both to slow and reduce natural splitting and warping which can affect its use.

# Chapter 9

# Selected comparanda for the Carpow vessel

ROBERT J C MOWAT

## 9.1 Introduction

As with any archaeological discovery, the significance of the Carpow discovery can be assessed as an example of its type through consideration with recognised comparanda, and within the context of similar discoveries from its regional group. This paper aims to cover both approaches and assess the significance of the Carpow vessel in terms of previous logboat studies.

## 9.2 Carpow and selected comparanda from Britain

The significance of the Carpow logboat can be determined through comparison with other vessels of putative prehistoric date, several of which have been found in recent years. Reworking of selected information from McGrail (1978) and Mowat (1996), with subsequent additions, has yielded a sample from England and Scotland of adequate yet manageable size (24 examples). This excludes the Irish examples and medieval examples, which are the most prevalent date for this class of artefact (*ibid*, 128–9). The selection is further justified by the topographical similarity of the Tay Estuary to the major English wetland areas of Humberside, Fenland and the Somerset Levels from which most of the better-recorded examples derive. Table 6 outlines the key points of the vessels considered, along with dates where available, and references. All of the boats considered from beyond the Tay estuary are apparently of oak.

## 9.3 Carpow and its regional group

The regional group, including the logboat discoveries known from the Tay Estuary prior to the Carpow discovery, along with two further logboats from within the upper basin of the River Tay, are summarised in order of date of discovery or initial record, in table 7. This outlines the key points of the vessels from the Tay estuary, river and loch, along with dates, where available, and National Grid References (NGRs). It

is assumed that all of the boats were of oak, with the possible exception of Friarton Island, which, if correctly identified, was made from softwood.

The group listed in table 7 constitutes a group only in the geographical sense, as the boats do not share evident commonality of date, manufacture or function. There is no Scottish equivalent to the chronological group identified by McGrail and Switsur (1979 *passim*) from around Warrington, on the River Mersey. The inherent weight of any logboat effectively precludes its use in *voyageur*-style travel along the length of the River Tay, with the necessity to portage around rapids. It is likely that the vessels from Loch Tay and Dalmarnock would have been used on these stretches of the watercourse, for example, the Croft-na-Caber boat serving one of the numerous crannogs that fringe the loch (Dixon 2007), even though none is situated in the vicinity of the find.

Within this group, the Friarton and Dalmarnock boats may represent early vessels apparently found deep in postglacial deposits. Of particular interest is the Friarton boat recorded by Geikie (1880) in the late 19th century. Although considerably damaged before examination this was said to have been 'resting on its bottom' on the surface of the peat and sand layers that lay beneath a 'brickearth' or clay deposit. The peat was laid down on the surface of former estuarine sediments during the period of low sea levels prior to the marine transgression when the clay was deposited (see Chapter 3, p 19). Marine transgression is dated regionally have occurred between 8,400 and 6,500 years ago, however, the reported location of the discovery at an altitude of *c* 6.6m OD suggests that the area was inundated at a relatively late stage probably around 7,000 years ago. If we assume the account of the logboat being found at the base of the clay layer to be correct, a date within the later sixth millennium BC may be attributed to the boat though the reliability of the account must be borne in mind. The other five boats apparently lay in the riverbed, from which they were dragged by force. As a result, no associated structures or artefacts were noted, while a degree of recovery damage must be considered probable before they were (in four

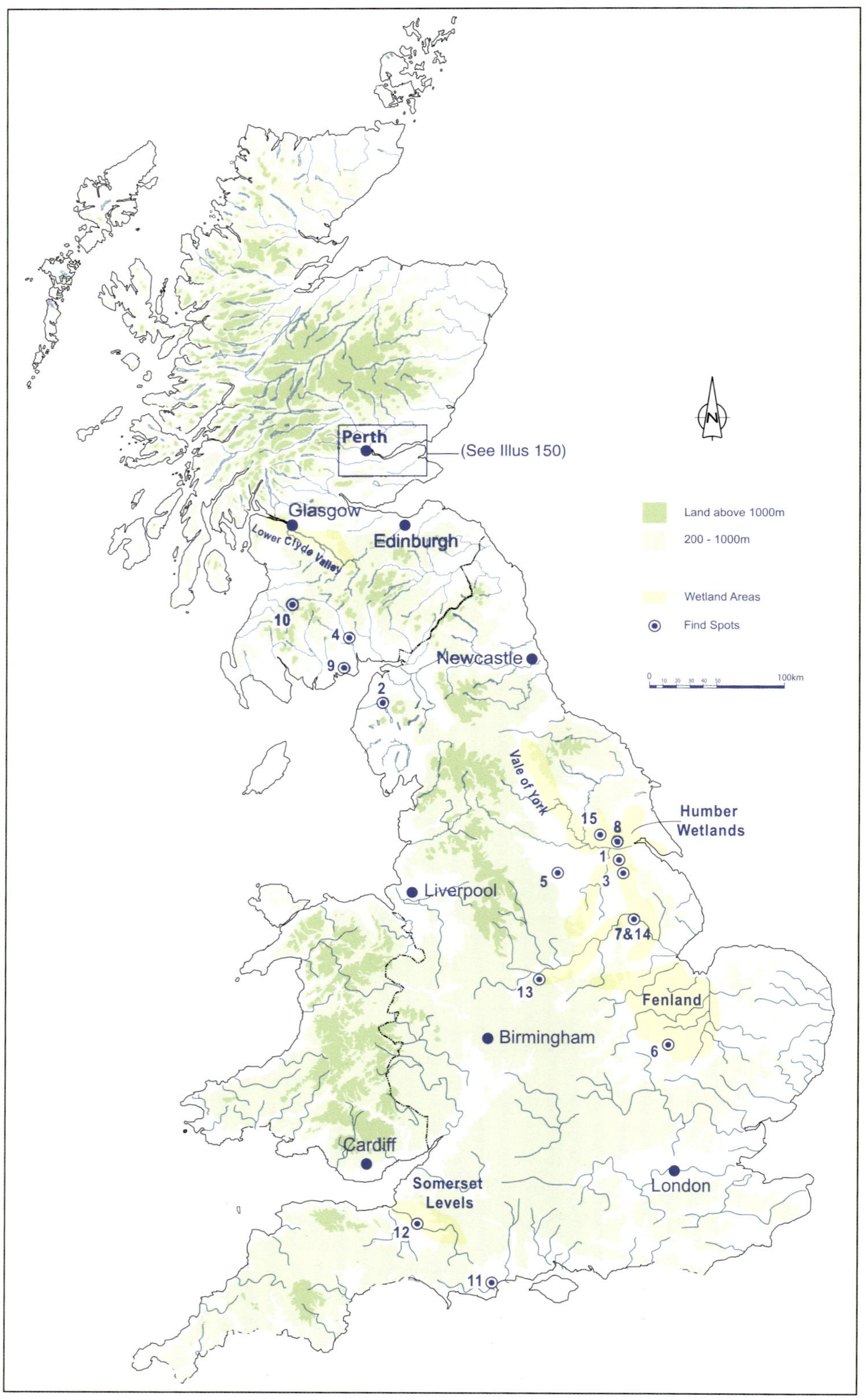


*Figure 149*
The distribution of logboats 1–15 mentioned in the text (© Crown copyright and database right (2009). All rights reserved. Ordnance Survey Licence number 100016971)

*Table 6*
Key points, dates and references for comparable logboats from the British Isles

| No | Name, county and date of find | Key points | Date, with Lab No, approx. calibrated date or range given when known | References |
|---|---|---|---|---|
| 1 | Appleby Lincolnshire 1943 | not recorded *in situ*; neither the complete length nor the sheerline survive; treenail- or thickness-gauge holes; birch (*Betula* sp) ropes were found in holes | 3050 ± 80 BP (Q-80) *c* 1320 cal BC | McGrail 1978, 147–9; Van de Noort 2004, 86 |
| 2 | Branthwaite Cumberland 1956 | only the tentative stern of a logboat – possibly re-used; two posts driven into the substrate on either side of the log; found beside an artificial platform | 1570 ± 100 BC (Q-288) *c* 1520 cal BC | Ward 1974, 19–22; McGrail 1978, 163–4 |
| 3 | Brigg Lincolnshire pre-1886 | exceptional length (14.78m); numerous and varied fittings; full height of the sheer in several places; birch (*Betula* sp) 'stretcher' was jammed transversely across the interior; repair-work splits included moss caulking and sewn or pegged oak patches | 834 ± 100 BC (Q-78) | McGrail 1978, 166–72; Van de Noort 2004, 86 |
| 4 | Catherinefield Dumfries and Galloway 1973 | small portion recovered (2.24m) with remainder left *in situ*; early date | 1804 ± 125 BC (SRR-326) *c* 2165 cal BC | Jardine & Masters 1977; Mowat 1996, 18, 20 |
| 5 | Chapel Flat Dyke Yorkshire 1963 | part of possible logboat (3.15m) | 1500 ± 150 BC (BM-213) *c* 1780 cal BC | McGrail 1978, 174 |
| 6 | Chatteris Cambridgeshire pre-1882 | early account of logboat with Middle Bronze Age rapier (Chatteris class Group II, *c* 12th century BC) – may suggest re-use as log-coffin? coffin? | – | Fox 1926, 127; Trump 1962, 95; McGrail 1978, 175 |
| 7 | Fiskerton 1 and 2 Lincolnshire 2001 | two logboats, one pegged between two posts and retained by a wooden wedge; fresh toolmarks on the underside suggest that the vessel was never used; found beside a possible timber causeway – provisional attribution to the Iron Age; late prehistoric ritual offerings including a metalwork assemblage (with six iron swords, an iron socketed axe, an axe-hammer head, and a spearhead), bone artefacts include a knife handle, 57 points (apparently gouges or spearheads) and various other finds. | Posts from causeway have been dated by dendrochronology to between 457 and 317 BC | *Current Archaeology*, no 176 (vol xv, no 8, October 2001), 327–9 |

*Table 6 (cont.)*
Key points, dates and references for comparable logboats from the British Isles

| No | Name, county and date of find | Key points | Date, with Lab No, approx. calibrated date or range given when known | References |
|---|---|---|---|---|
| 8 | Hasholme East Yorkshire 1984 | exceptional size (12.78m in length by up to 1.4m in beam); steering-platform at stern; thickness-gauge holes with oak plugs; two beam ties of different types; unparalleled composite bow; *in situ* transom with moss caulking; repair-work including an external patch and internal repair-block at the stern; animal bones and two timbers indicate cargo | Dendrochronology indicates parent log felled between 322 and 277 BC<br><br>Radiocarbon dates indicate parent log dates to 750–390 cal BC<br><br>Pottery found in association with boat 190 ± 270 AD (Dur TL44-IAS) | Millett & McGrail 1987; McGrail 1998, 81–3, 87; Van de Noort 2004, 86–7, 91 |
| 9 | Loch Arthur 1 Dumfries and Galloway 1874 | exceptional size (13.7m length recorded on discovery); described by two authors independently; damaged on discovery and stern discarded | 101 ± 80 BC (SRR-403) *c* 75 cal AD | Mowat 1996, 50–2, 129; McGrail 1998, 82, 84 |
| 10 | Loch Doon 1 Ayrshire 1823 | various artefacts and timbers found nearby probably came from the adjacent crannog; small (3.4m length); a vertically cut transom left in the solid | 509 ± 110 AD (SRR-501) *c* 619 cal AD | Mowat 1996, 55, 57 |
| 11 | Poole Harbour Dorset 1964 | measured *c* 10m in length; transom groove contained animal hair caulking | 295 ± 50 BC (Q-821) *c* 300 cal BC | Peers 1964; McGrail 1978, 254–7 |
| 12 | Shapwick Somerset 1906 | surviving length of just under 6m; probable thickness-gauge holes | 355 ± 120 BC (Q-357) *c* 400 cal BC | Dewar & Godwin 1963, 38–9; Godwin 1967; McGrail 1978 254–7 |
| 13 | Shardlow Derbyshire 1998 | length at least 10.5m; stern is lost and the bow detached and in three pieces; five large blocks of Bromsgrove sandstone and several smaller blocks of the same material indicate cargo; a nearby heavy timber structure possibly represents a causeway | 1440–1310 cal BC | Garton *et al* 2001, 196–200; *British Archaeology*, no 73 (September 2003), 5 |
| 14 | Short Ferry Lincolnshire 1952 | Full length of 7.35m; birch (*Betula* sp) twigs and branches were found within the vessel | 846 ± 100 BC (Q-79) *c* 950 cal BC | Smith 1958, 81–2; McGrail 1978, 271–2 |
| 15 | Welham Bridge Yorkshire 2003 | fragments of a logboat along with hurdles and wattlework which apparently formed a trackway | 530–569 cal AD (β-191780)<br><br>350–560 cal AD (β-191781) | *Yorkshire Post* (website entry, dated 20 March 2004) and York Archaeological Trust (website extract, taken 6 September 2004). |

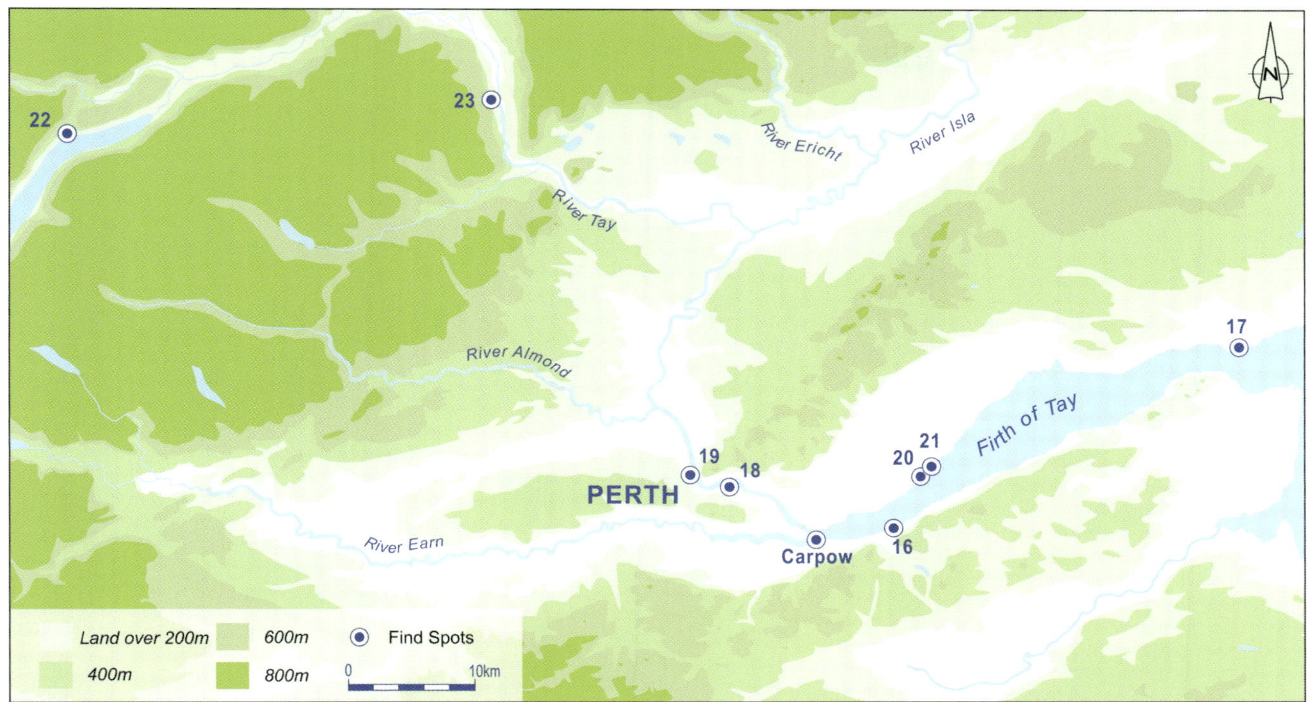


*Figure 150*

The distribution of logboats 16–23 mentioned in the text (© Crown copyright and database right (2009). All rights reserved. Ordnance Survey Licence number 100016971)

## 9.4 Carpow in context of comparanda

The primary parameter for comparison is the overall condition of the vessel on discovery, essentially dependent on completeness and state of preservation. Of the group studied, the following could be said to be in generally good condition when discovered: Catherinefield; Chapel Flat Dyke; Brigg; the Fiskertons; Friarton; Hasholme; Loch Doon 1; Loch Arthur 1; Shardlow; Poole Harbour (good although fragmentary) and Shapwick. Those which were slightly more truncated include Errol 2; Short Ferry (which suffered from flaking and splitting); and Welham Bridge (which was also fragmentary and split). Poor and fragmentary examples include Appleby and the example from Branthwaite, where only the possible stern survived. In comparison, Carpow scores well, being essentially complete with only the bow missing, along with three of the main fittings (beam tie, repair transom and cross plank/seat or similar).

A second indicator of condition is the survival of the sheerline (often truncated through erosion) and detailed fixtures and fittings, normally at the stern. The examples with this level of preservation, being essentially complete on discovery, include: Brigg, with numerous fittings and repair-work; Hasholme, with

*Figure 151*

The Errol 2 logboat on display in Dundee prior to renovation of the museum in 2009 (© Dundee Art Galleries and Museum)

*Table 7*
Key points, dates and references for comparable logboats from Tayside

| No | Name, date of find and NGR | Key points | Date, with Lab No, approx. calibrated date or range given when known | References |
|---|---|---|---|---|
| 16 | Lindores 1 and 2 *c* 1816 NO 24 19 | found 'in the bed of the Tay, opposite Lindores Abbey' in the area of Cruive Bank; both were subsequently cut up to serve as building-lintels in Newburgh; larger boat measured *c* 8.5m in length and was 'quite entire' | – | Mowat 1996, 49–50 |
| 17 | Barry Links *c* 1820 NO 53 32 | recovered during drainage operations to the east of Monifeith; described as a 'primitive canoe'; recovered embedded in peat moss; does not survive | – | Mowat 1996, 12 |
| 18 | Sleepless Inch 1848 cNO 146 220 | partial remains, *c* 6.7m in length; discovery was noted only as a newspaper account – no further details were taken; does not survive | – | Mowat 1996, 78 |
| 19 | Friarton, Perth pre-1879 cNO 117 219 | discovered during clay digging – recorded by antiquarian during 19th century; length at least 4.6m; wood identified as 'Scotch fir'; found in peat and sand layers that underlie brickearth – possible that boat dates to late sixth millennium BC; does not survive | later sixth millennium BC? | Mowat 1996, 34–5 |
| 20 | Errol 1 *c* 1889 NO 26 22 | found on Habbiebank sandbank; no detailed record was made at the time other than boat was not well-preserved; does not survive | – | Mowat 1996, 28 |
| 21 | Errol 2 1895 NO 26 22 | 8.9m in length and 1.3m in beam at the stern – starboard aftside lost; pointed bow possibly carried a 'rude but forcible resemblance to the head of an animal'; a 'roughly semi-circular hollow' at the bow interpreted as possible base of a figurehead; roughly formed of knotted timber – probably worked from a half-sectioned log; worn, distorted remains of the groove for the (lost) transom are visible; held at McManus Galleries and Museum, Dundee | 485 ± 40 AD (Q-3121) *c* 599 cal AD  430 ± 45 AD (Q-3141) *c* 548 cal AD | Mowat 1996, 28–30 |
| 22 | Croft-na-Caber, Loch Tay 1994 NN 769 448 | discovered during construction of replica crannog, this may be rediscovery of logboat reported by divers *c* 1977 at 'Portbane'; 11m in length by 0.85m in breadth; caulking material and toolmarks have been recognised within the transom groove | 1280 ± 50 BC (GU-10558) 1630 – 1400 cal BC (1 sigma) | Mowat 1996, 21 and 75 |
| 23 | Dalmarnock 1975 cNN 998 458 | discovered below gravel deposits on the haughland of Strathtay; much reduced by abrasion to near-flat bottom; 4.58m in length by 0.82m in beam; bow and stern are rounded; two possible thickness-gauge holes 'closed by reddish chert pebbles'; removed to a nearby loch for storage | – | Mowat 1996, 21–2 |

only the bow damaged in discovery; Loch Arthur 1; Loch Doon 1; Shapwick; and Poole Harbour, where both ends and some additional features survived although the sheerline was missing. The majority of examples provided limited or no information on the sheerline, or fixtures and fittings at the stern: Appleby, where the stern survived; Catherinefield, where only a portion was recovered; Errol 2, almost complete, although the sheerline was truncated; Shardlow, where the stern was missing; bow detached and fragmentary; and Short Ferry, where nearly all the sheerline was missing and no fittings noted. With these criteria Carpow fits in the former small group which provides information on the nature of the sheerline, and providing detailed information about the configuration of fixtures and fittings at the stern. Finally, condition is indicated by the survival of toolmarks on the surface of the vessel. From the available accounts, these have been recognised on only four of the group studied: Loch Arthur 1; Loch Doon 1; Poole Harbour, where possible examples were identified in a restricted area; and Hasholme, where their survival was recorded and studied in detail. Again, the tool marks preserved on the transom of the Carpow example indicate an excellent level of preservation.

In terms of associated structures, the Fiskerton examples were found with heavy timber (pile) structures and a metalwork (bronze and iron) depositional assemblage, apparently representing the tradition of votive deposition in later prehistory. Shardlow was found near a heavy timber structure, probably a causeway, and Loch Doon 1 can reasonably be associated with the nearby crannog. The Welham Bridge example appears to have been re-used: being incorporated into a timber trackway, following splitting. Associated artefacts are rare in logboat finds. The Middle Bronze Age rapier apparently recovered from inside the Chatteris example may suggest re-use as a log coffin, while possible paddles were recovered from, or near, the Loch Arthur 1 and Loch Doon 1 vessels, and Hasholme producing a single piece of pottery.

Recognised cargoes are also rare. Two lengths of split oak and an animal bone assemblage were interpreted as the cargo of the Hasholme boat. The Shardlow vessel was found to contain a cargo of several blocks of Bromsgrove sandstone, which occurs a few kilometres upstream from where the vessel was discovered, and it has been suggested that the cargo was ferried to the site to strengthen a causeway that crossed the ancient course of the River Trent. By contrast, Carpow has neither a secure archaeological context nor significant associated structures or finds.

The second parameter with which to assess significance is the quality of the archaeological record and our understanding of its wider archaeological context. This includes the circumstances surrounding the deposition of the vessels and their environmental context. Regrettably, many early British logboat discoveries have very limited records, particularly concerning the environmental context from which the artefacts were recovered. Of the 24 considered here, only seven have any record at all, and the quality of these is often very basic. Errol 2 was recorded only as coming from the estuarine sandbank; Fiskerton as from waterlogged peat; Poole Harbour as from unstratified estuarine deposits; Friarton lay in a suggested (though unverified) Holocene deposit, and Loch Arthur 1 within shallow lacustrine deposits which were not recorded in detail. From available accounts, details of context were not specified for Shapwick, Shardlow or Short Ferry. Only Hasholme, found in estuarine clay involved a detailed study of context, and Carpow scores highly in receiving a comparable assessment of the environmental context for the vessel.

In terms of dating, 16 of the boats considered in this text have been dated; 13 through a single radiocarbon determination: Appleby; Branthwaite; Brigg, of doubtful authenticity although verified by pollen evidence and stratigraphy; Catherinefield; Chapel Flat Dyke; Errol 2; Loch Arthur 1; Loch Doon 1; Poole Harbour; Shapwick; Shardlow; Short Ferry; and Welham Bridge. Of the group, only the Hasholme and Errol 2 vessels have been dated through multiple radiocarbon samples, and only Hasholme has received dendrochronological study. Tentative dating has been suggested for the possible Chatteris example through association with a Middle Bronze Age rapier, and at Friarton, where, as discussed above, inferred geomorphological dating, based on an unverified context, has been questioned.

Finally, a combination of the factors above result in the potential for the morphological description and reconstruction of logboats, and this has only been possible on a very few vessels. This is largely limited by the survival of the remains, and includes Branthwaite (outline record at time of discovery), Brigg (recorded, possibly inaccurately, at time of discovery though reconstructed by McGrail), and Errol 2 (of which a basic record was made on discovery, and a further record made in the museum). Only basic records survive for the others, the exception again being Hasholme where a comprehensive study of morphology and form was followed with theoretical reconstruction. Once again, Carpow scores well having received a detailed palaeoenvironmental study, multiple radiocarbon determinations of both the boat and its environmental context, and comprehensive morphological study and reconstruction.

### 9.5 Conclusions

The impression presented by this body of evidence is that of the increasingly frequent discovery of logboats in recent years. It is evident that in the case of logboats, as in other classes of artefact, increased survey activity under the stimulus of legislation has greatly increased the volume of evidence expected from chance discoveries alone. In consequence, the number of examples recorded in detail *in situ* and recovered for conservation, has also increased. This development is significant, both on its own account and as representing a shift from the common misconception of maritime and wetland archaeology as removed from the mainstream discipline. It is encouraging that ten of the 24 discoveries above have been made since 1950, three of these within the new millennium. The sensitive recovery and conservation to a high standard of the Carpow boat are both significant and consistent with this trend.

Nevertheless, the evidential limitations that are usual among artefacts of this class still apply. There is an inevitable bias in favour of the survival, recognition and recording of examples that are complete (or nearly so), of hardwood (oak) and of simple but recognisable form. Within these constraints, the Carpow discovery may be considered against the standard set by the other vessels within the sample, and against the normal criteria of association, chronology and typology. In summary, the Carpow discovery compares well with the group considered here which display, as might perhaps be expected, no clear pattern, but a significant range of variation. In terms of the immediate geographical comparanda and contemporary examples from farther afield, Carpow scores highly in terms of evidential value for both logboat and Late Bronze Age studies. It is significant because of not only its excellent level of preservation, but also as a result of the application of a suite of modern archaeological techniques to study both the vessel itself and its context. The Hasholme logboat, discovered and excavated during drainage works in the early 1980s, has acquired the status of *ne plus ultra* among British logboat discoveries by virtue of its recorded context, exemplary recovery, and detailed investigation. In Carpow, we now have a Scottish equivalent.

By comparison, it seems apt to echo the despairing comments of the then Dean of Wells (quoted Coles & Minnitt 1995, 10) regarding the state of the logboat that had been found at Crannel Farm in the Somerset Levels during the previous year (1892):

> The boat will crumble up if it continues in that very dry & very hot room with S.W. front: a conservatory needing no fire. It could be put in a tank, or even in a ditch, full of water; such a place as the barton behind Mr Bath's house could spare room for, it might, being wet always, last for years.

MIKE CRESSEY and SUE DAWSON

# Chapter 10

# A study of the inter-tidal peat at Carpow Bank

## 10.1 Introduction

In 2006 a large tract of eroding inter-tidal peat with *in situ* tree stumps was identified close to the site of the Carpow logboat. In order to understand the environmental potential of this material, and how it may or may not have related to local Bronze Age landforms, the peat was assessed for its environmental potential and to determine its age and significance. Diatoms (unicellular algae) contained within the silts at the base of the peat provide reliable evidence for the depositional environment and hydrological regimes in which they were laid. These results have been linked to what is currently known on relative sea level changes for the upper tidal reaches of the River Tay. The diatoms suggest an inter-tidal estuarine environment with *Paralia sulcata*, *Rhaphoneis surirella* and *Rhaphoneis amphiceros* diatoms in greatest abundance. This environment is in accord with the relative sea level model constructed for the Tay area by Cullingford *et al* (1980).

Inter-tidal organic deposits including peat and wood are very vulnerable and easily eroded due to the highly dynamic locations in which they are found. These deposits are a rare and valuable source of palaeoenvironmental information providing unique dating material to establish the timing of relative sea level change in Scotland. The majority of published field descriptions relate to deposits confined to the western seaboard and include the Inner and Outer Hebrides, including Islay and Coll (Dawson *et al* 1998 and Dawson *et al* 2001). In south-west Scotland, inter-tidal peats have been examined within the Solway Firth (Cressey *et al* 2001). More recently on the island of Raasay, inter-tidal peats have been found lying on top of a Mesolithic worked stone assemblage (Dawson 2009; Cressey *et al* forthcoming). In most cases these studies combine the use of pollen and diatom analysis to reconstruct the conditions in which the deposits were formed. Supported by radiocarbon dating, inter-tidal peat provides one of the most reliable indicators of relative sea level change during the early Holocene. This paper presents the results of diatom and fossil-wood analysis alongside a series of radiocarbon dating results in order to understand more clearly the origin and age of the peat in close proximity to the Carpow logboat. These results are then compared to an earlier model of sea level change for the upper River Tay.

## 10.2 Topographical setting and peat sampling

The peat is exposed for only a few hours at extreme low tidal conditions and is visible, over an area of *c* 100m, close to the confluence of the Rivers Tay and Earn (Figs 153 and 154). The surface of the peat is continually eroded by the scouring action of the main river channel. The peat survives as randomly distributed banks and hummocks, with depths ranging from shallow lenses several centimetres thick with deeper outcrops *c* 0.5m thick (Fig 155). Within the study area, four fossil tree-stumps were found situated in their original positions of growth (numbered SP1–4). SP4 was not sampled as it was too degraded. Prior to sub-sampling the mean High Watermark Spring Tide (MHWST) and the Low Watermark Spring Tide (LWST) marks were plotted using a Leica GS50 global positioning recorder.

A stratigraphic profile of the peat below SP1 was obtained using a series of Kubiana tins that were hammered into the peat below the tree-stump (Fig 156). The depth of peat below the stump was 0.35m. The SP1 peat was found to be much deeper than at the other two stump sites. A biostratigraphic profile of the peat below the SP1 stump sample was constructed and is summarised in Table 8.

## 10.3 Diatom analysis

A single sample of silt taken below the Unit 4 silt/gravel contact zone (levelled at −0.38m OD) was subject to preparation for diatom analysis. The aim of the analysis was to determine the provenance of the silt-clays and thus to determine the environmental context of the silts in relation to the logboat and to ascertain the former presence of marine and brackish estuarine waters in the vicinity of the site.

## 10.4 Laboratory methods

The wood sub-samples obtained from the SP1–3 stumps were frozen prior to thin sectioning for species identification. Identifications were carried out using a binocular microscope at × 10 and × 40 magnification using the anatomical keys in Schweingruber (1992) and in-house reference thin sections.

Diatom species were identified with reference to Hendey (1964) and Van der Werf and Huls (1957–74). Diatom nomenclature follows Hartley (1986) and salinity and lifeform classification is based upon Vos and de Wolf (1993) and Denys (1992). In general, *Polyhalobous* and *mesohalobous* diatom classes broadly reflect marine and brackish conditions whilst *oligohalobous* and *halophilics* classes reflect freshwater and terrestrial environments. It was not possible to determine 300 species per count for the sample as preservation was poor. However, an assessment of the environment of deposition of the silts from the species within the sample was possible and the species list and habitat preferences of the species present are shown in Appendix IV.

## 10.5 Results

Diatoms within the silts are present but limited in number and did not allow a full count to 300 to be undertaken. Nevertheless, the species present do allow an assessment of the environment of deposition of the silts in the vicinity of the Carpow logboat. Diatoms

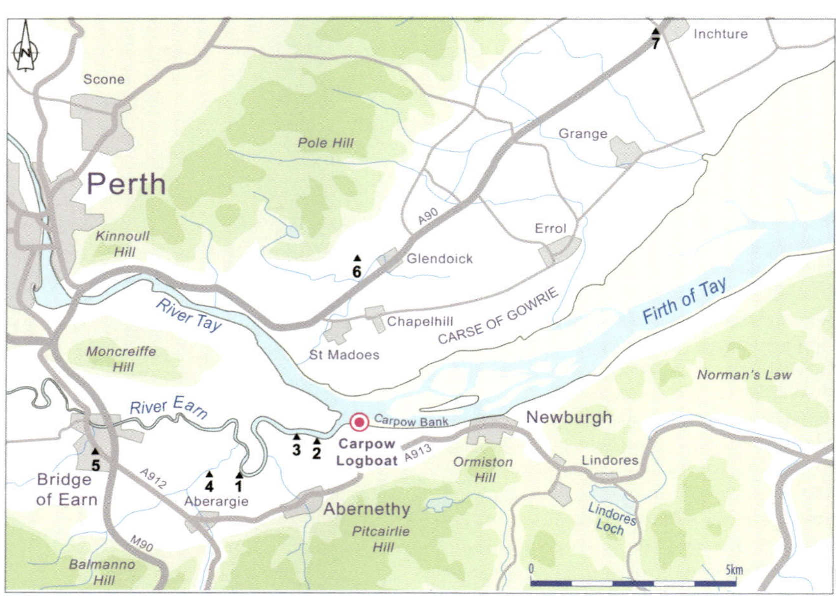


*Figure 152*

Location map showing the position of the logboat with nos 1–6 indicating the position of radiocarbon dating samples recovered by Cullingford *et al* (1980) (© Crown copyright and database right (2009). All rights reserved. Ordnance Survey Licence number 100016971)

*Table 8*
Biostratigraphic analysis of the inter-peat below the SP1 stump

| Biostratigraphic unit | Summary description |
| --- | --- |
| UNIT 1 | Munsell 10YR 2/1 Black, very fibrous peat, with 90% organic remains, marsh reeds (*Phragmites communis*) it is highly compacted. Boundary between Unit 1 and 2 is faint and merging. |
| UNIT 2 | Munsell 10YR 2/1 Black main colour, 10YR 2/2 very dark brown subsidiary colour. Very fibrous compacted peat, 90% organic remains, marsh reeds. Boundary between Units 2 and 3 is faint but identifiable. |
| UNIT 3 | Munsell 10YR 2/1 Black main colour, 10YR 2/2 very dark brown subsidiary colour. Very fibrous compacted peat, 90% organic remains, marsh reeds. Boundary with Unit 4 is sharp. |
| UNIT 4 | Munsell 10YR 3/1 Very dark grey marine fluvial deposit underlying the peat. There is no mottling or banding within the unit itself. Unit 4 rests directly on top of gravel. |

*Table 9*
Carpow Bank radiocarbon dating determinations, with calibrations carried out by the lab using Oxcal 3
and the 1998 calibration curve (Stuiver *et al* 1998)

| Lab code | Sample no | Species type | Feature/ altitude | Age BP | dC13 | Cal date 1 sigma | Cal date 2 sigma |
|---|---|---|---|---|---|---|---|
| GU–15125 | 2 | *Quercus* (SP2) | Trunkwood (–0.66m OD) | 2295 ± 35 | –26.1 | 410–250 BC | 410–200 BC |
| GU–15126 | 3 | *Quercus* (SP2) | Trunkwood (–0.66m OD) | 2210 ± 35 | –25.4 | 360–200 BC | 390–190 BC |
| GU–15127 | 4 | *Betula* (SP3) | Trunkwood | 3710 ± 35 | –30.2 | 2190–2030 BC | 2210–1970 BC |
| GU–15128 | 5 | *Betula* (SP3) | Trunkwood | 3765 ± 35 | –30.7 | 2280–2130 BC | 2290–2040 BC |
| GU–15129 | 6 | *Betula* (SP1) | Trunkwood (–0.61m OD) | 8865 ± 35 | –29.1 | 8200–7950 BC | 8220–7830 BC |
| GU–15130 | 7 | *Betula* (SP1) | Trunkwood (–0.61m OD) | 8830 ± 35 | –28.3 | 8170–7810 BC | 8210–7750 BC |
| GU–15131 | 8 | Peat | Peat (–0.61m OD) | 8200 ± 35 | –29.0 | 7300–7220 BC | 7320–7080 BC |
| GU–15132 | 9 | Peat | Peat (–0.61m OD) | 8120 ± 35 | –28.8 | 7145–7055 BC | 7190–7040 BC |

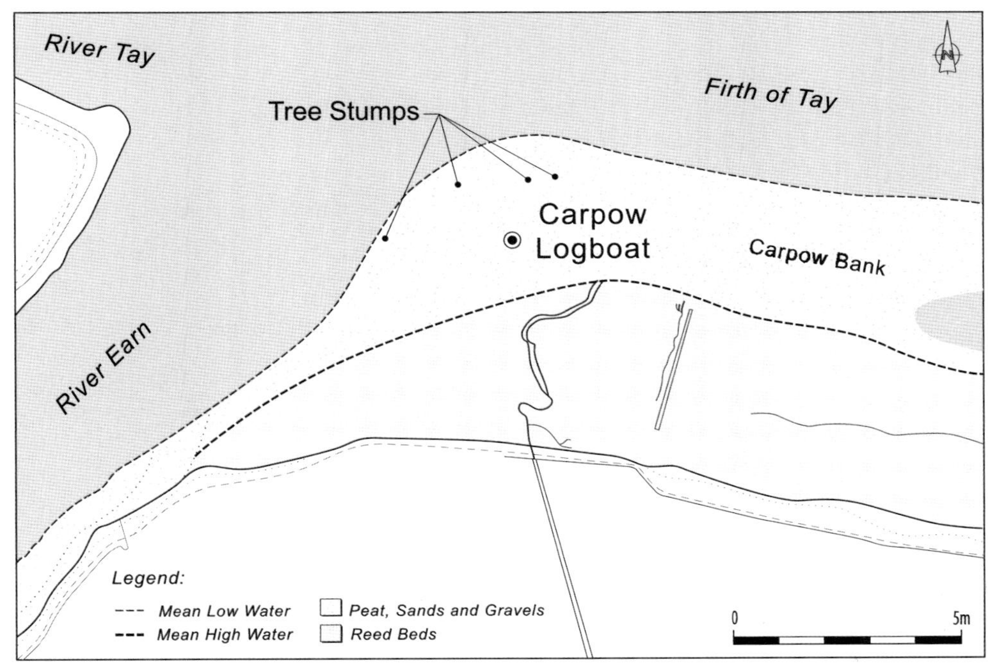


*Figure 153*
Location map showing the position of the logboat and the sampled tree stumps (© Crown copyright and database
right (2009). All rights reserved. Ordnance Survey Licence number 100016971)

*Figure 154*
An aerial view of Carpow Bank at low tide (photo: D. Strachan © Perth and Kinross Heritage Trust)

suggest an inter-tidal estuarine environment with *Paralia sulcata*, *Rhaphoneis surirella* and *Rhaphoneis amphiceros* in greatest abundance. Brackish species including *Diploneis interrupta*, *Navicula peregrina*, *Nitzschia punctata* and *Nitzschia sigma* are typical of inter-tidal mudflat areas and are in accord with the palaeoenvironmental analyses undertaken by Cullingford *et al* (1980).

### 10.6 Radiocarbon dates

The radiocarbon dates obtained from samples taken from three tree-trunks (SP1–3) and from the peat below SP1 using the humic acid fraction are listed in table 9.

### 10.7 Peat dates: potential problems

The humic acid dated samples (samples 8 and 9) are *c* 600 years younger than those samples obtained from SP1 trunkwood growing directly above. Radiocarbon dating of peat is known to be problematic (Shore *et al*

1995). The main problem arises from the possible deep penetration of roots (Nilsson *et al* 2001) that transfer current atmospheric $CO_2$-carbon to deeper layers, thus reducing the radiocarbon age of the affected peat. In addition, problems can arise due to the redistribution of dissolved organic matter, for example, by humic acids transported by ground water. Dates from individual plant fragments extracted from the peat minimize the problem of obtaining false ages. Thus, the dates of sample 6 and 7 are assessed to be more reliable than samples 8 and 9.

### 10.8 Discussion

If we accept that the dated stump samples 8865 and 8830 BP are more accurate than the two humic acid dates (which are *c* 400–600 years younger), the significance of the dates appear to be a tighter constraint on the early Holocene low stand of sea level. The relative sea level curve established by Cullingford

*Figure 155*
The tabulated peat found across Carpow Bank

*et al* (1980) suggests a fall in sea level from *c* 2.8m OD at *c* 8500 BP with a subsequent rise of sea level at *c* 7500 BP at *c* 3–3.5m OD. The new dates, obtained during the Carpow Bank investigation, place the low stand at least *c* 3m lower. The results obtained by Cullingford *et al* (1980) were taken at a time when conventional radiocarbon dates were obtained on bulk samples of peat which will invariably provide a wider age range in comparison to single entity dates which is the normal procedure today. Nevertheless, Cullingford's empirical model of relative sea level change for the upper Tay area is very reliable. This is also supported by a set of radiocarbon dates obtained from marine bivalve shell samples recovered from Inchture on the Carse of Gowrie (Site 7a–b, Fig 152) which provided a date of 7110 ± 60 BP (GU-9764) (Cressey *et al* 2003).

This date fits very comfortably on Cullingford's age-altitude plot.

*Figure 156*
An eroding tree stump and eroded tabulated peat on Carpow Bank

A single sample of silt located below the Unit 4 silt/gravel contact zone has a brackish-marine diatom assemblage. This is typical of shallow inter-tidal estuarine conditions at the site in the early Holocene. The new dates provide a tighter constraint on early Holocene relative sea level changes in the Tay Estuary.

The stumps of *Quercus* (oak) and *Betula* sp (birch) represent trees that were growing *in situ* along what was then one of several braided river channels. Both trees are native to Scotland and common throughout prehistory. Birch is a light demanding pioneer that can tolerate acidic damp ground and normally lives no longer than 150–200 years. Oak is tolerant of a wider type of soil and is at the apex of woodland species, with a slow rate of growth living up to and beyond 500 years.

During the lifetime of the trees, local conditions became wet enough for peat to form as a result of the decomposition of marsh plants, including *Phragmites communis* (common reed) and other plants tolerant to saline conditions. We cannot be certain on the true depth of the inter-tidal peat, but it is likely to have been significantly deeper than that which survives in the study area today. Scouring has led to the loss of the original surface of the peat. Compaction due to the weight of later Holocene marine clays (the carse clays) has depressed the peat, which in turn has been lost to erosion.

## 10.9 Conclusions

The research undertaken on the peat and stumps is timely as it is now very likely that much of the inter-tidal peat and inclusive plant macro-fossil remains will be lost to erosion. The results confirm that the peat dates to the early Holocene and that the *in situ* tree stumps are of a similar age. The radiocarbon dates provide evidence for a lower sea level which is estimated locally to be 3m lower than that proposed by Cullingford *et al* (1980). During the early Holocene, at the point where the Rivers Tay and Earn meet, this area was certainly dry enough for birch and oak to become established alongside or close to the main river channel. The rise in relative sea level led to the submergence of the peat below a thick deposit of carse clay which led to compression of the peat. These deposits were in turn eroded by the ever widening river channels. Since then the upper levels of the inter-tidal peat have been removed, leading to the present formations that are only visible at extreme low tidal conditions.

# Chapter 11

# Contemporary environment, sites and monuments

SARAH WINLOW

with contributions from Richard Tipping, Paula Milburn and Steven Timoney

## 11.1 Introduction

The evidence for Bronze Age activity in Tayside was last reviewed in the early 1970s by Coutts in two Dundee Museum and Art Gallery publications. In *Ancient Monuments of Tayside* ritual and funerary monuments (cairns, barrows, stone circles, standing stones and cup marked stones) and some settlement types (hillforts and hut circles) were presented in a gazetteer (Coutts 1970). The second publication *Tayside before History* concerns cist burials and cremation cemeteries; less visible site-types often only discovered by chance through agricultural improvements or development (Coutts 1971). Coutts wrote of the relative scarcity of settlement and burial monuments in comparison with the earlier Bronze Age, and noted that the prehistorian must rely on artefacts for the later Bronze Age to evidence human activity (*ibid*, 21). The scope for study of this period of prehistory through sites and monuments is much improved following nearly four decades of cumulative evidence.

The most significant contribution has been made by aerial photographic survey, filling out the record for previously blank lowland areas. The region is one of the most responsive areas in Scotland for cropmarks, particularly for settlement archaeology. Whilst some of this cropmark evidence has been published (RCAHMS 1994), little synthesis of this body of evidence has been made. Excavation prior to development and as a result of various research projects has also contributed to our understanding of the Late Bronze Age. However, for certain site-types discussed, examples must be sought from beyond the Tay Estuary. This situation is not unique to Tayside; interpretations of the Late Bronze Age tend to be fragmentary due to differential survival and recovery of archaeological information, with evidence used in the creation of narratives selected from different parts of the country (Cowie & Shepherd 2003, 168). The recent review of the archaeology of Angus (Dunwell & Ralston 2008) provides a useful update for that county. By setting the Carpow logboat in context, this paper will begin to collate evidence for

the hinterland of the Tay Estuary, outline potential avenues of research for the future and provide insight into the contemporary environment.

The characteristics of the logboat suggest use within the lower reaches of the Tay and Earn and, travelling by the tides, along the shoreline of the estuary (Chapter 13, pp 168–70; Fig 157). The study area for this paper (Fig 158) includes a broad swathe of countryside beyond the estuary as movement would have occurred across, as well as along, the Tay and Earn river systems. Both the historic significance of Perth and its nodal position on the modern road and rail network illustrate the geographical centrality of the study area. The study area is not as wide ranging as that of Coutts (1970; 1971) in that it does not extend up the coast of Angus or cover all of Strathmore.

## 11.2 The Late Bronze Age in Scotland

The logboat was in use at some point between the 12th and ninth centuries BC; in the Late Bronze Age. This period is known as one of change, with a shift in settlement types and the evidence of the tail-ends of complex (archaeologically visible) ritual and funerary traditions (Hingley 1998, 9; Champion 1999, 95). The transitional character of the Late Bronze Age necessitates an overview of what came before as well as after to set the logboat in context. The Bronze Age in Scotland, defined by the arrival of metallurgy, an explosion in permanent settlement and a change in funerary monuments, began in the later third millennium, *c* 2200 cal BC. Archaeological evidence is plentiful and consists of settlements of roundhouses, enclosures, field clearance and cultivation remains, often extending into upland areas. The funerary and ritual traditions of Bronze Age communities are also visible in the archaeological record. Both inhumations and cremations are known from this period, discovered in cist graves and cinerary urns, occasionally richly furnished and sometimes marked by monumental barrows or cairns. Stone circles, stone settings and standing stones, along with the decoration of boulders with cup marks, originate in the third millennium BC

*Figure 157*
Aerial view of the Tay and the Earn with Moncreiffe Hill in middle ground (© David Woolliscroft)

but are still in use, or are reinvigorated in the Bronze Age. In contrast, the Scottish Iron Age (*c* 700 cal BC to *c* 400 cal AD) is characterised by the enclosure of settlement, with the most dramatic examples found in the fortification of hilltops. This shift is accompanied by the almost complete disappearance of human remains from the archaeological record indicating a change in the disposal and commemoration of dead (Hingley 1998, 9; Cowie & Shepherd 2003, 162). The archaeological evidence for the Bronze and Iron Ages of Tayside tends to fit the picture outlined, though the transition from open settlement to enclosed settlement is less straightforward in Tayside than elsewhere in Scotland, as the settlement record is dominated by open settlement, apparently with less enclosure in the Late Bronze Age and Iron Age (Macinnes 1982; Hingley 1992, 30).

The logboat, as an artefact of a mode of transport, is indicative of movement and contact between communities. Late Bronze Age artefacts are discussed elsewhere (Chapter 12, pp 153–6), however, it is worth noting that artefacts recovered from burials, hoards and chance finds are the most tangible form of evidence for contact in the second and third millennium BC though similarities in site characteristics also imply contact between communities. Ideas of population migrations of the 'Beaker Folk' in the Early to Middle Bronze Age, tracked by the recovery of metalwork and Beaker pots within cist graves, and proposed Iron Age Celtic immigrations, also implied from metalwork, still have resonance, but are likely to have been small scale and occurring in tandem with the spread of ideas and skills with traded goods and commodities (Needham 2008, 22; Dunwell & Ralston 2008, 59–60).

Tayside is one of half a dozen wealthy areas in northern Britain in the Bronze Age, evidenced by the high status and exotic artefacts of gold, jet and bronze deposited with the dead, and this wealth is likely to have been generated from the region's fertile agricultural land (Cowie & Shepherd 2003, 153). Though missing from the study area due to subsequent land-use, Bronze Age agricultural activity is well evidenced in upland Tayside. Such field systems are indicative of control and productive use of the landscape to support a mixed subsistence economy (*ibid*, 162–5).

140

## 11.3 Reconstructing the Late Bronze Age environment

RICHARD TIPPING and PAULA MILBURN

By *c* 1000 cal BC there was still a very large amount of woodland left in Scotland (Tipping 1994). The natural woodlands on the well-drained, fertile plains of eastern Scotland were dominated by deciduous trees such as oak, elm, ash and hazel. Trees like lime may not have been able to set seed this far north (Pigott & Huntley 1981), although there are some hints that on base-rich soils, lime trees might have colonised at least the Lothian lowlands (Tipping 1996), perhaps making the cist burials and Beaker pottery from Ashgrove on the south coast of Fife, where a high proportion of lime pollen was found in Cist 1, less exotic than currently understood (Dickson 1978).

The woodland had, however, been altered by the beginning of the Bronze Age. Mesolithic disturbances do not seem to have changed the composition of the lowland woods around estuaries like the Tay, but in the early Neolithic, *c* 3800 cal BC, the population of elm trees was severely reduced by factors which are still not clearly understood (Parker *et al* 2001). This loss, or perhaps small clearings for farming within the woodland (Tipping *et al* 2009), permanently changed woodland composition, increasing the proportions of trees that were previously shaded, like hazel and birch. By the Bronze Age the scrubby elements like alder, birch and willow will have grown on and around wetlands and boggy hollows (Tipping 1994).

Pollen data do not easily describe woodlands in the detail needed to reconstruct what it was like to be inside them. Some workers have tried to imagine this (Edmonds 1998; Austin 2000; Tipping 2003) because there is an increasing recognition that much of our prehistoric ancestors' time must have been spent there (Evans *et al* 1999). Analogues are hard to come by because all modern woods have been manipulated, but being inside mature oak-dominated woodland may not have been as dank and dispiriting as some have thought (Lacaille 1954). It was probably the edges of woods, by rivers, coasts and clearings, where more light allowed shrubs and brambles to flourish, that were most frustrating for people to move through. Imagining this woodland is useful, not least at Carpow because unless the oak that was felled to make the Carpow logboat grew by the estuary, it probably had to be moved to the estuary through woodland. Perhaps a tangle of scrub had to be fought through before the open, grassy salt marsh was seen.

The large extent of woodland remaining by the Late Bronze Age does not necessarily imply a scarcity of people: the value of conserving wood and protecting what they needed from livestock is very likely to have been recognised. We probably know more about human settlement in upland landscapes than in the lowlands, both archaeologically because upland monuments are better preserved and palaeoecologically because peat is more common, but arguably there is little reason to suggest that a division between lowland and upland was relevant in the Bronze Age. People may have farmed in similar ways and with a similar balance of crops and livestock everywhere, with specialisms postulated (Halliday 1985; Cowley 1998; McCullagh & Tipping 1998; Toolis 2005) but as yet unproven.

Within deciduous woodland, anthropogenic woodland clearance in the Scottish Bronze Age is often described as 'small' and 'temporary' (Turner 1975; Tipping 1994 forthcoming). This impermanence of settlement discerned in the palaeoecological record seems to accord with observations on the continent of 'wandering settlements', mobile not at short timescales as, for instance, in shifting cultivation, but at the scale of human generations (Gerritsen 1999). In lowland eastern Scotland, however, clearings for farming may have been more long-lasting, though they remained small. The most detailed pollen record close to Carpow is that at Black Loch (Whittington *et al* 1990), a small loch only two km south of the Tay Estuary, in the folds of the Ochil Hills south-west of the larger Lindores Loch. On the rich volcanic soils of these slopes, the spatial extent of grazed grassland seems to have increased at the expense of trees after *c* 1950 cal BC, and by *c* 1480 cal BC pollen grains that might be of barley (*Hordeum* type) suggest crop cultivation as well. After *c* 1250 cal BC the evidence for agriculture becomes more apparent around Black Loch, sustained until around 50 cal AD.

Methven Moss in south-east Perthshire also has a pollen record that covers the later prehistoric period (Milburn 1996). It shows an increase in the area of open land during the Bronze Age which broadly corresponds to that recorded at Black Loch (Whittington *et al* 1990). Between *c* 2450–2000 cal BC an increase in the diversity of herbs, together with fluctuations in tree and shrub pollen types, probably indicate human activity, but percentages of grass pollen remain generally low, suggesting that clearings in the woodland were either small or some distance away. From *c* 2000 cal BC the re-establishment in the area of alder may reflect the drift of farming communities farther away, but after *c* 1,760 cal BC the occurrence of cereal-type pollen (*Hordeum* type) suggests that arable agriculture was being undertaken close to the moss, albeit in small clearings in the wood. There is no suggestion of extensive woodland loss. Between *c* 1600 and 230 cal BC a sharp increase in the representation of grass pollen may reflect, in the absence of cereal type pollen, the expansion of more grazing land and a pastoral agricultural base. High levels of charcoal are recorded throughout this period, and fire may have been used as a means of land management. However, there is no evidence in eastern Scotland for the fully integrated agrarian landscapes proposed in both lowland and upland landscapes in the south and west of England (Fleming 1988; Yates 2007).

In addition to being cleared by farmers, oak trees were vulnerable to short-lived population declines; dying-off events, when lots of older trees died more or less synchronously across north-west Europe. The cause is unclear but human activity does not explain the scales of these events. They can be precisely dated through dendrochronology, and in the Bronze Age occurred at 1550, 950 and 720 cal BC, each event

lasting for less than a century (Leuschner *et al* 2002). Young oak trees regenerated after these events but a long-term effect of these declines may have been the expansion of hazel and birch trees in their place. The date of the Carpow boat is of interest in regard to these dying-off events, because prior to these regeneration failures, as that between 1200 and 1000 cal BC, oak trees in Germany and Ireland in general lived much longer than in other periods of the Holocene epoch, in woodlands undisturbed by stresses, and these trees, one of which became the Carpow boat, would have been correspondingly bigger and taller.

The tree which became the Carpow boat died close to the end of the Bronze Age, near to the transition to the Iron Age, and close to a turning-point in later prehistoric climate. The period around 900–800 cal BC includes within it a phase of global abrupt climate change (Chambers *et al* 2007). Interpretations from northern British landscapes have focused on the downward depression of agricultural limits and so the abandonment of upland landscapes (Burgess 1985; 1989; Barber 1998), although this is still disputed (Young 2000; Tipping 2002). Across the North Sea

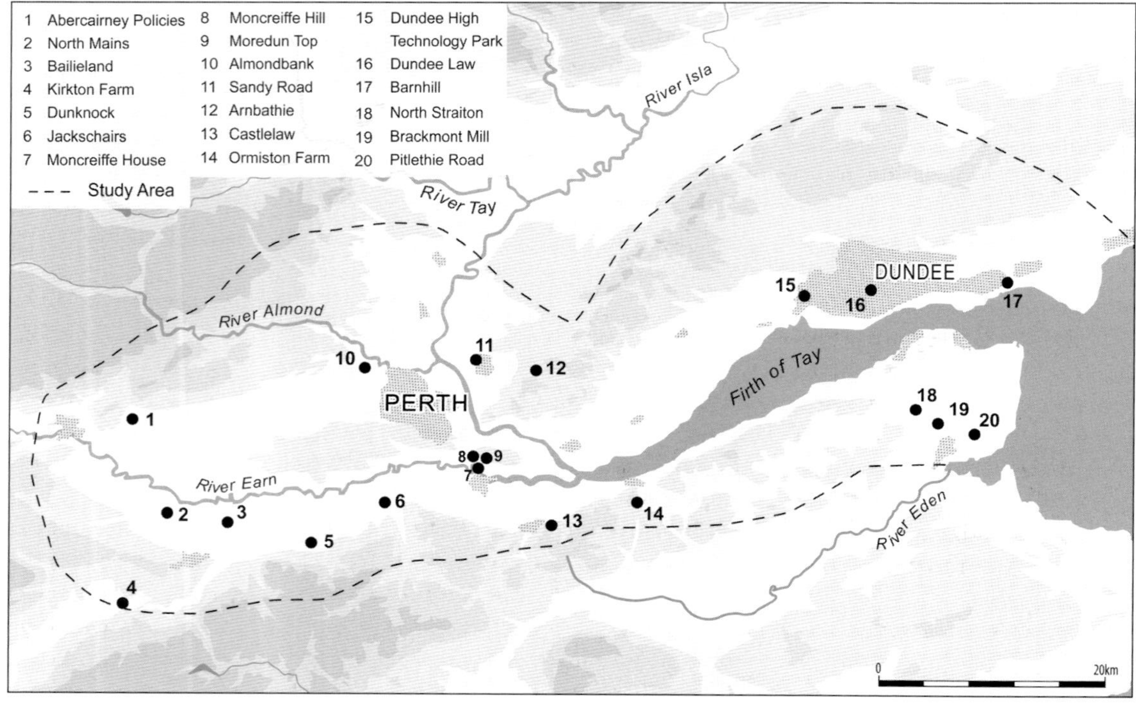


*Figure 158*
Key sites within the study area (© Crown copyright and database right (2009). All rights reserved. Ordnance Survey Licence number 100016971)

from Carpow, however, in the Netherlands, van Geel and colleagues have argued for a major climatic deterioration to have occurred around 850 cal BC that induced rising ground water tables in lowland soils and forced populations away from established farmland and out onto the extensive Dutch salt marshes (van Geel, Buurman & Waterbolk 1996; van Geel *et al* 1998; van Geel & Berglund 2000). There is no evidence at Methven Moss, in a boggy landscape not too dissimilar to the Netherlands, to suggest that land was abandoned close to the end of the Bronze Age, however, nor at Black Loch, and it remains to be seen how correct this intriguing interpretation is.

### 11.4 Nature of the archaeological evidence

The nature of the evidence is central to any archaeological discussion. The type of archaeological sites, and their survival, is largely determined by the lowland and upland geologies of the Tayside region. Lowland sites have been heavily impacted upon with the result that only truncated remains survive beneath the plough soil. As noted above, upland sites tend to be better preserved both because of their more durable construction and less intensive land-use. Conversely more is known about the lowlands, particularly funerary monuments, due to the record of accidental discoveries during ploughing and the long-established, antiquarian interest in these sites. In more recent times, excavation in advance of development has begun to address this imbalance.

Archaeological information has been drawn from the Historic Environment Records of Perth and Kinross, City of Dundee, Angus and Fife and key sites are marked on Fig 158. Sites have been selected for inclusion based on their characteristics and, as with all archaeological syntheses, certain limitations should be noted. The classification of remains, particularly from cropmarks and from antiquarian accounts, will never be entirely accurate and, without excavation and analysis, the chronology and date ranges of site types remain very broad. There are gaps within the distributions where the underlying geology or land-use has impeded the recording of archaeological sites through aerial survey.

### 11.5 Late Bronze Age settlement

Bronze Age settlements are typically made up of a single or a small group of roundhouses with the area around the house used for storage and husbandry.

Bradley suggests the physical landscape begins to be more intensively exploited in the Late Bronze Age, evidenced by the establishment of large field systems, the development of settlement with increased capacity for storage, and the appearance of forts, although it is acknowledged that this evidence of 'prosperity' accumulates more gradually in northern Britain (2007, 224). Further it has been suggested that the apparent density of Bronze Age settlement may be a product of re-use over millennia with occasional rather than continuous occupation creating the 'archaeological landscapes' visible today (Halliday 2007, 49–56). The complexity of prehistoric settlement development in northern Britain has been acknowledged and the model whereby unenclosed settlement was thought to be replaced by enclosed settlement has been recognised as over simplistic (Hill 1982). Tayside is particularly rich in open settlement with fewer enclosed settlements known in comparison to other parts of Scotland, such as East Lothian (Macinnes 1982; Hingley 1992, 30). When and why some settlements are enclosed, and the relationship between the two settlement types, remains ambiguous, primarily as the evidence stems from aerial photographic survey with relatively few settlements excavated.

Figure 160 reveals that settlement is spread more or less continuously throughout the study area but is noticeably absent from the lower parts of Strathearn and the Carse of Gowrie. Analysis of prehistoric, Roman, Early Historic and medieval settlements reveal that activity occurs above the 5m contour, above the Flandrian marine clay, presumably because these areas were too boggy to support permanent settlement prior to large scale drainage. A recent review of the apparent absence of settlement on these low lying Carse clays has raised the possibility that the blanks perceived may in fact be the result of survey bias (Cowley & Dickson 2007, 47), however, the lack of other, more durable forms of archaeological evidence (eg cist graves) within these areas substantiates the notion that these low-lying areas were salt marsh and coastal pasture in the Late Bronze Age. There are clusters of settlements at North Straiton and Leuchars; St Madoes and Errol; Invergowrie; Monifieth and Carnoustie; and to the north of Blackford. It is likely these agglomerations of houses illustrate the density with which prehistoric settlement would have populated the landscape, though it is unlikely that these houses were long-established and contemporary settlements; rather they represent multi-period and transitory occupation (Halliday 2007).

Hut circles, ring ditches, ring grooves and post rings are all forms of roundhouse known from the study area. Excavation of these various types of roundhouse within eastern Scotland (eg Douglasmuir, Monikie Burn and Culhawk Hill) has illustrated the ubiquity of construction type and it is difficult to create chronologies from house construction, particularly based on analysis of cropmarks. As such, no distinction has been made between post ring, ring groove and ring ditch houses on Fig 160. Settlements with evidence for souterrains have been excluded from this map as these have consistently been dated to the later Iron Age (RCAHMS 1994, 70–1).

### Open settlement

The majority of settlements that have been excavated are open settlements. At North Straiton, a succession of three post-built houses, dating from the Middle to Late Bronze Age, were constructed on the same site (Watkins 1987; RCAHMS 1994, 71). A group of houses at Pitlethie Road, all post-built and some with ring grooves, have also been dated to the Middle to Late Bronze Age (Cook 2007). Six of the houses formed an arced row with some showing signs of reconstruction. A similar row of five ring groove houses have recently been excavated at Kirkton Farm with pottery indicating a Bronze Age date (O'Connell & Gray 2008a). Discovered during evaluative trial trenching, this group is one of five newly discovered settlement sites that have been excavated prior to the construction of a new golf course (*ibid*), the analysis of which will provide useful chronological information.

Three-quarters of open settlements include two or more roundhouses. It is unknown as to whether agglomerations of roundhouses are contemporary with each other or represent consecutive development. The life expectancy of a prehistoric roundhouse is thought to be a generation (Cook 2007, 18–19). At Pitlethie Road at least 11 houses (some rebuilt on the same spot) spanned a period of 800 years (*ibid*). Settlements may have migrated across the landscape, with abandonment and re-establishment of settlements over generations (Halliday 2007, 49–56). Good examples of seemingly large settlements include Paddockmuir Wood, Invergowrie and Leuchars. Of the 20 or so ring ditches recorded at Leuchars, three have been excavated (Stevenson 1953). At least one represented the remains of an occupied house, with the other two returning less certain evidence other than the suggestion of a pre-Iron Age date.

Two roundhouses and external cooking pits were recorded at Dundee High Technology Park (Gibson & Tavener 1989). The heavily truncated remains were not dateable; however, fragments of Bronze Age pottery were recovered from the vicinity of one of the houses. Late Bronze Age pottery has also been recovered from Craigie Hill and Drumoig (Freeman 1997; Halliday & Simpson 1997) as well as from Tentsmuir Sands (Longworth 1968). Unfortunately little is known of occupation attested by this material.

Hut circles have been excavated at Ormiston Farm (Sherriff 1988) and Arnbathie (Stewart 1950). Both sites represent open settlement and though construction materials differ from the houses discussed above, it is unlikely that this represents any real division between upland and lowland lifestyles. The Ormiston Farm hut circle has been dated to the Late Bronze Age and consists of the remains of a house 10m in diameter defined by a stone and earth wall. The Arnbathie hut circle, one of a group of five, is slightly larger and more substantial but remains undated. The number of hut circles within the study area is relatively low. This is particularly striking in comparison with dense prehistoric remains found at similar landscape settings in the southern Grampians. The lack of prehistoric settlement in the Ochils, North Fife Hills and Sidlaws is likely a result of medieval and later agriculture and (lack of) archaeological reconnaissance (RCAHMS 1994, 9–10). Prehistoric settlement at Craigowl Hill (Greig 2002) and Prieston (Currie 2005) has been recorded from relatively recent survey and similar discoveries may be anticipated in future.

### Enclosed settlement and forts

Evidence from elsewhere in Britain suggests a shift to enclosed settlement beginning in the Late Bronze Age. Macinnes, however, notes a difference between the settlement record for north-east Fife and Angus in comparison with East Lothian, with less evidence for palisaded settlement recorded north of the Forth (1982, 57–73). Little progress has been made since the publication of Macinnes' paper, other than the confirmation that for much of the Carse of Gowrie, open settlements outnumber enclosed and fortified settlements (RCAHMS 1994, 41–75), and the distribution of settlement on Fig 160 confirms these observations. When the loose and varied category of 'enclosures', a type of site that may be indicative of defined settlement, are added to the distribution this imbalance is somewhat addressed. However, the recent

*Figure 159*
Aerial view of Moredun Top, with the smaller hillfort on Moncreiffe Hill in the background to the left of the frame
(photo: David Strachan © Perth and Kinross Heritage Trust)

excavations of a circular ditched enclosure at Burnside, where the evidence for internal activity had either been truncated or alternatively the enclosure had not been used for settlement, demonstrate the pitfalls of drawing conclusions from such a diverse group of sites classified by aerial survey (O'Connell & Neighbour forthcoming).

The excavation of a large elliptical, plank-built palisaded enclosure, some 50m by 36m containing two successive and substantial houses at Kirkton Farm (O'Connell & Gray 2008b) will help refine the chronology of this type of enclosed settlement within Tayside. Excavation of palisaded settlements outwith the study area (eg at Bannockburn and Ironshill East, where enclosure occurred in the early Iron Age and later Iron Age respectively) illustrate the potential range of enclosed settlement (Dunwell & Ralston 2008, 97). Enclosure of slighter scale, where the area immediately outside the house is surrounded by a palisade some 20m in diameter, also occurs, for example, at Mains of Murie, Errol and Middlebank, Inchture. At Pitlethie Road, one house was more

substantial than the other roundhouses with a ring groove 15m in diameter. Dated to the Late Bronze Age, this structure has been interpreted as either a larger ring groove house or one with similar 8m to 10m diameter dimensions as the rest, but enclosed by a palisade (Cook 2007, 7).

Over 60 examples of forts are recorded within the study area. Forts are defined as having substantial ditches, ramparts and walls on a larger scale than a simple enclosing palisade. The sites within the study area fit well into the three broad categories of hillforts, lowland forts and promontory forts outlined by Dunwell and Ralston (2008, 64). Hillforts are found in prominent locations along the Ochils, North Fife Hills and Sidlaws with good examples including Moredun Top (Fig 159), Ben Effrey, Forgandenny Castle Law, Clatchard Craig, Norman's Law, Evelick and Kinpurney. Lowland forts are situated on prominent knolls and rises within the straths with defences that follow the lie of the land and usually elaborately define the approach to the fort with multiple ditches and ramparts. Good examples recorded by aerial survey include Hilton House and Dunknock while Jackschairs and Danes' Camp survive as earthworks. Promontory forts modify naturally defensive lowland sites such as river terraces, coastal headlands and glacial landforms. Examples of promontory forts include Rait and Hurly Hawkin.

The date and development of forts in eastern Scotland remains uncertain (Armit & Ralston 2003, 174–82) and many have evidence for multiple phases of design and use. A number have been investigated although the majority of excavations took place in the 18th and 19th centuries AD. The dating evidence from more recent excavations is not, as yet, comprehensive enough to begin to build a chronological model of fort development, though the Late Bronze Age dates from North Mains (Barclay & Tolan 1990) and the Dunknock (Poller pers comm) indicate early fortification. The results of recent investigations that place the Caterthun hillforts in Angus (Dunwell & Strachan 2007), Jackschairs and the later use of the Dunknock (Poller pers comm) firmly in the Iron Age suggest only a few of the 60 forts within the study area would have been contemporary with the logboat.

The investigation of the cropmarks of a double-ditched lowland fort at North Mains was small scale yet revealed significant information (Barclay & Tolan 1990). The terminal of the inner ditch was found to be a substantial defensive feature some 2m deep and 4m wide with vertical sides. Lines of postholes along the inside edges of both ditches suggest some form of palisade or retaining feature. A radiocarbon date of 1300 ± 80 BC (GU-2682) returned from the upper layers of the inner ditch indicates substantial infilling had taken place by the Late Bronze Age. The Strathearn Environs and Royal Forteviot project has investigated the Dunknock, a multivallate fort situated on a large sandy knoll. The northern defences of the fort would have been impressive with up to four ramparts, and five defining the north-east entrance to the fort. A trench positioned on the prospective line of the inner ditch uncovered a U-shaped palisade trench at least 2m wide that has returned three Late Bronze Age dates (Poller pers comm). Features uncovered in the interior of the fort and at the north-east entrance have returned middle Iron Age dates, indicating a second phase of use.

A number of the forts within the study are 'oblong' forts, so named for their massive ramparts or timber laced stone walls that define a relatively small, oblong area of hilltop (Dunwell & Ralston 2008, 67). Examples include Abernethy Castlelaw, Dunsinnan, Machany

and probably Dundee Law. This type of fort often has evidence for vitrification, where the rock of the rampart is deformed as a result of intense firing, though as the fragments of vitrified material found at the Dunknock (Donaldson *et al* 2004) demonstrate vitrification does not occur solely at oblong forts. The dating of these oblong forts is controversial; the Angus fort of Finavon (the only fort studied in modern times) returned dates from the Late Bronze Age, Iron Age and the Pictish period (Alexander 2002). The archaeomagnetic dating of the vitrification of Finavon (*ibid*, 53–4) to the later Iron Age is perhaps more realistic particularly given that the majority of these forts appear to be multi-phase, with the oblong fortifications later in the sequence. Promontory forts on the Angus coast have been dated to the later Iron Age (Dunwell & Ralston 2008, 86–8). The excavations at Hurly Hawkin did not date the promontory fort though it is clear it predated the secondary broch and souterrain, built and occupied in the first centuries AD (*ibid*, 88).

The fort at Moredun Top on Moncreiffe Hill at the head of the estuary, above the confluence of the Tay and Earn is central to the study area (Figs 157 and 159). A large multivallate fort, Moredun Top has expansive views east along the estuary, north to Strathmore and Strathtay and west along Strathearn. Moredun Top has not been accurately surveyed, however, it appears to show two main phases of construction beginning with two stone and earth ramparts enclosing a large oval enclosure *c* 175m east–west by *c* 100m north–south. The summit of the hill is defined by two further stone ramparts, now much eroded, enclosing an area *c* 50m NW–SE by *c* 35m transversely. To the north, an annexe can be traced on a lower terrace of the hill. The footings of at least five circular houses have been recorded within the inner enclosure. Whilst the confluence is not visible from Moredun Top, its significance lies in its position at the only point at which much of Strathearn, the Carse of Gowrie, the Firth of Tay, north Fife and, most importantly, Strathtay (and the fording point at Perth) are visible. A smaller fort lies 0.5km to the west and consists of a single walled defence for much of its circuit with an entrance defined by at least two further ramparts parallel to the steep cliffs on the fort's south east side (Fig 159). It encloses an area *c* 110m east–west by *c* 70m north–south. The date of these forts is as yet unknown, however, their juxtaposition is interesting.

### *Activity at settlements*

A characteristic of Late Bronze Age settlement is the increasing evidence for husbandry, field systems and

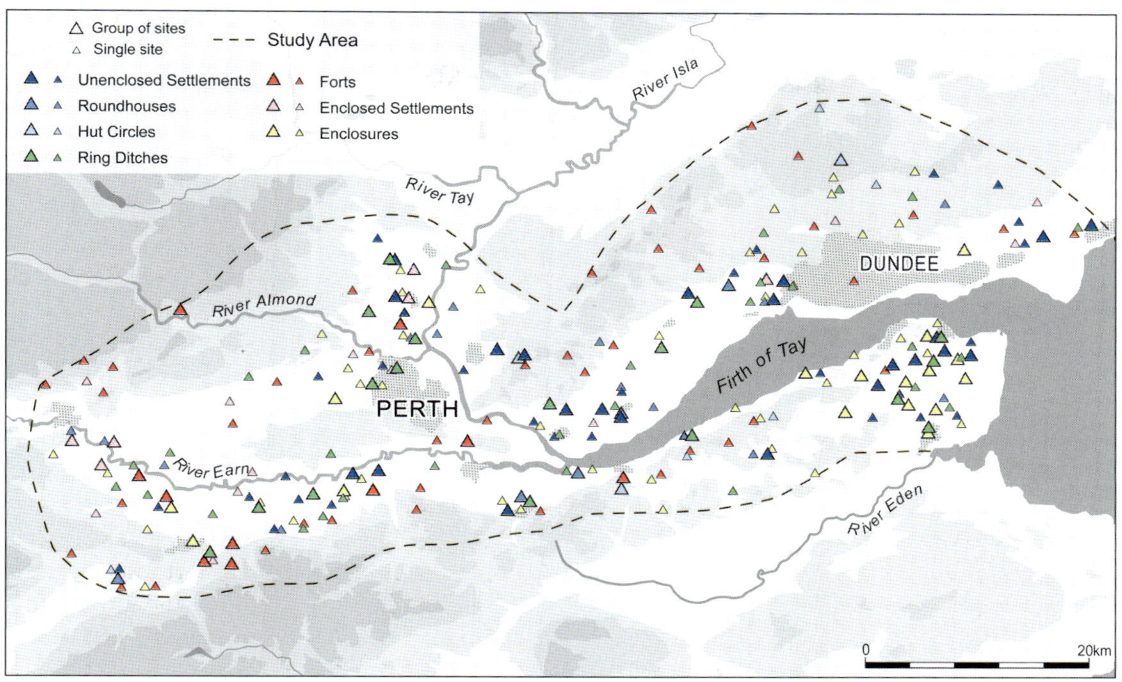


*Figure 160*
Distribution of settlement sites (© Crown copyright and database right (2009). All rights reserved. Ordnance Survey Licence number 100016971)

storage (Bradley 2007). Evidence for Late Bronze Age field systems is sparse within the study area but plentiful farther afield in Highland Perthshire and Angus. Recent interpretation suggests that rather than operating as a coherent and contemporary system, upland 'archaeological landscapes' are the result of periodic exploitation (Halliday 2007, 47). At Ormiston Farm, stone field walls abut the hut circle and have been interpreted as evidence of a contemporary field system (Sherriff 1988). Pit alignments associated with the settlement at Dundee High Technology Park may be evidence for control of stock (Gibson & Tavener 1989, 88). Evidence of storage within houses is forthcoming with semi-subterranean chambers within and outwith roundhouses excavated at Kirkton Farm (O'Connell & Gray 2008a) and Pitlethie Road (Cook 2007). Evidence for burnt mounds, a Late Bronze Age site-type associated with the heating of large quantities of water, has been recorded at Drumoig (Halliday & Simpson 1997) and Kirkton Farm (O'Connell 2008).

Evidence for human burial within settlements has been found in well-preserved Late Bronze Age houses at Cladh Hallan on South Uist (Parker Pearson *et al* 2005). The only recorded instance of funerary deposits within a domestic context from the study area is the secondary cremation deposit discovered during the investigation of Arnbathie hut circle (Stewart 1950), though burnt bone was recovered from a small circle of postholes, either the remains of a house or timber circle, at Broich, Crieff (Haines 2008). A Late Bronze Age date has been recovered from a posthole of this structure (Barton pers comm).

### 11.6 Funerary remains

Recent research has reflected the complexity of Bronze Age burial traditions (eg Sheridan 2007). The development of burial rites, in particular the supposed shift from inhumation to cremation, is not so clear cut, with overlap occurring between practices; cremation practiced early and inhumation never totally superseded (Dunwell & Ralston 2008, 49–50). A recurring characteristic of Late Bronze Age funerary practices is burial at older ritual monuments of the Neolithic and earlier Bronze Age (Hingley 1998, 52) and the only evidence for funerary activity contemporary with the logboat takes this form (Stewart 1966; Barclay 1983; Stewart *et al* 1985). It may be the case that funerary

147

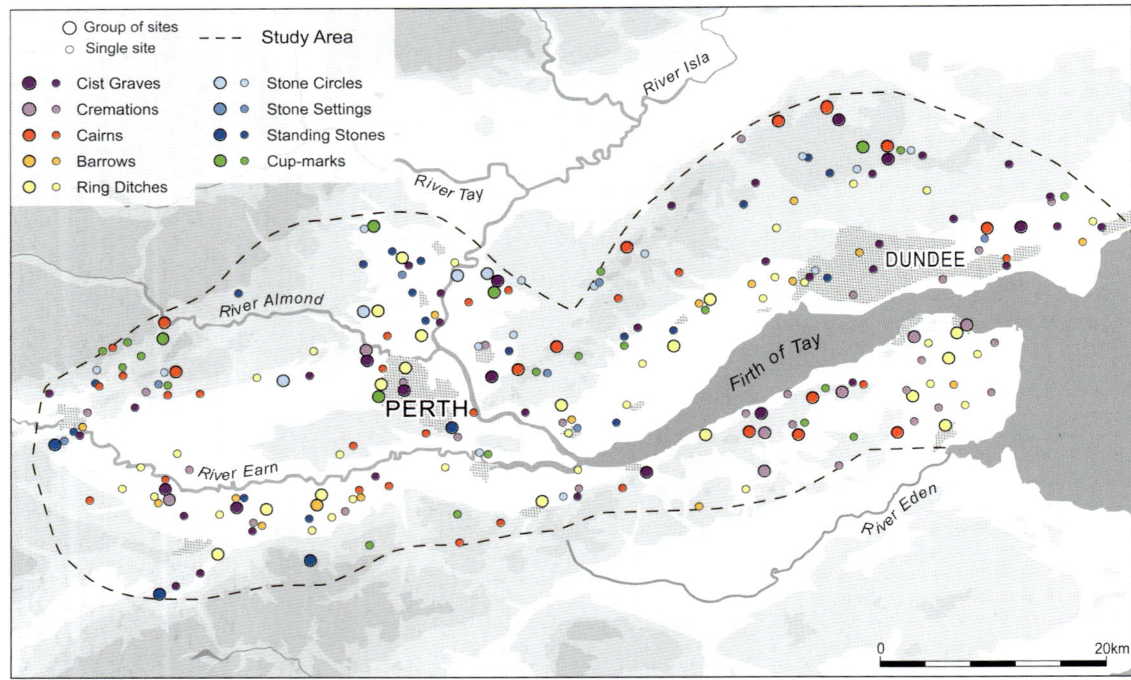



*Figure 161*
Distribution of funerary and ritual sites (© Crown copyright and database right (2009). All rights reserved. Ordnance Survey Licence number 100016971)

traditions involved practices that left little physical trace, for example, the deposition of (cremations or remains) in watery places.

Funerary sites depicted on Fig 161 consist of individual burials and cremation deposits, larger cemeteries and multi-phase sites, reflecting the complexity of Bronze Age funerary practices. The majority of sites are known from antiquarian accounts of chance discoveries during the 19th century AD although a smaller number of more recent excavations provide more detail, including some radiocarbon dates, with which to interpret the relative chronology of practices.

### Barrows and cairns

The majority of excavations of barrows and cairns took place in the 19th century (eg Stayt of Crieff (Headrick 1914); West Mains Hill (Hutcheson 1898); and Barnhill (Warden 1876)). Cists beneath barrows and cairns have been found to contain both inhumations and cremations. Dates from these burials, such as the cremation from West Mains Hill at 2030–1880 cal BC (Sheridan 2007, 179 and 185),

support the notion of an earlier Bronze Age date for these larger burial monuments. However, given the later Bronze Age re-use of earlier funerary and ritual monuments, this type of site is included on Fig 161, where their distribution is relatively even. Further evidence for these types of monument can tentatively be derived from the cropmark evidence in the form of ring ditches. While such sites will not always be ploughed-out burial mounds, it is assumed that some of these sites are the surviving remains of funerary monuments.

### Cists and cist cemeteries

Evidence for funerary deposits in the form of cists, containing inhumations, cremations or both, is widespread throughout the study area. Cists have been recorded both as individual sites, but also in larger cemeteries and it is likely that these graves were originally marked by barrows or cairns (RCAHMS 1994, 15–16). Most appear to date to the earlier part of the Bronze Age, as the cists contain Beakers and Food Vessels (Sheridan 2007). A large number of antiquarian accounts, however, often refer to the accompanying pottery simply as urns, making it difficult to ascertain the nature of these vessels and attempt to provide a date for them. Early Bronze Age Beakers have been recorded at a number of sites including Upper Muirhall (Reid *et al* 1986) and Bailieland (Reid 1899). Interestingly, at Bailieland a bronze sword was recovered *c* 200m away in the same field seven years later (*ibid*), and has been identified as Late Bronze Age (Henderson 1938). This sword may be part of a wider practice of burying or depositing metalwork on land in the Late Bronze Age with the best local example consisting of three socketed axeheads, a handled vessel and fragments of a sword deposited in boggy ground at Corrymuchloch, near Amulree (Cowie *et al* 1996). Cists containing Food Vessels and cremations have been recorded at many sites, including Battle Law (Hutcheson 1901) and Almondbank (Stewart & Barclay 1997). Cists need not contain pottery as demonstrated at Noah's Ark, Perth where the cist contained the remnants of both a crouched inhumation and a deposit of cremated bone dated to *c* 1700 cal BC (Cook *et al* 2004).

### Cremation cemeteries

A number of cremation cemeteries, where remains are interred in pottery vessels or in small pits without stone cists have been recorded from the study area, with a particularly dense distribution noted in north-east Fife. At North Straiton Quarry, the remains of five heavily truncated cremations have been dated to the Middle Bronze Age, with the best preserved cremation pit containing an intact undecorated accessory vessel and some decorated sherds from a bucket urn (Stronach *et al* 2006). At Westwood, Newport, a circle of cremation urns containing human bones was uncovered by workmen (Jervise 1866). Three collared urns and a cordoned urn identified suggest a Middle Bronze Age date. A cremation cemetery was first discovered in the 1930s at Brackmont Mill (Mears 1937; Childe & Waterston 1942). Further discoveries of cremation deposits at this site were made in the following decades (Spence 1951; Longworth 1968), with at least 70 burials, including cremation deposits in a number of different cinerary urns, reflecting long-term use of this site for funerary practices from the Neolithic well into the Bronze Age.

### Cremation at ritual sites

A key feature of Bronze Age funerary traditions which appears to continue into the Late Bronze

Age is interment at Neolithic and Early Bronze Age monuments, for example, at Loanleven (Lowe 1989) and Belhie (Ralston 1988). Further evidence for re-use has been found at North Mains Henge, with 31 cremation deposits and inhumations, both in dug graves and cists (Barclay 1983). To the immediate north of the henge and cist cemetery, four cremation pyre burials were discovered. These unusual pyres consisted of elongated and backfilled pits, with the cremations deposited in hollows in the uppermost fill of the pits and in one instance defined by a stone setting. The cremation pyre burials have been dated to *c* 1000 cal BC (*ibid*, 187), roughly contemporary with the logboat

At Sandy Road, Scone, excavation of the stone circle uncovered a large bucket urn containing a cremation set upright in a pit close to the centre of the circle (Stewart 1966). The cremation within this urn has been redated to 1190–890 cal BC (GrA-23985) (Sheridan 2007, 184). Excavation of a stone circle at Moncreiffe House uncovered four phases of activity at the site (Stewart *et al* 1985). The third phase, beginning *c* 1200 cal BC, which incorporated the grading of stones in the circle, was accompanied by cremated burials in pits and bucket urns. Four cremations interred in small pits, dated to the end of the second millennium BC, have been found within a 10m radius of the Bogleys standing stone, near Kirkcaldy. It is unknown as to whether the stone itself was erected in the Late Bronze Age, or the small cemetery is a further example of re-use of an earlier monument (Lewis & Terry 2007).

### Grave goods

As noted earlier, grave goods recovered from burial sites reflect the wide network of contacts within and between Bronze Age communities. Daggers found in cists at Barnhill (Hutcheson 1887) and West Mains Hill (Hutcheson 1898) draw parallels with examples from southern Britain; the two gold discs from Barnhill are similar to examples found at Hengistbury Head in Dorset (Dunwall & Ralston 2008, 47). Other exotic grave goods including jet necklaces and a bronze armlet have been recovered from cists at Abercairney (Gibson and Rideout 1984), Almondbank (Stewart & Barclay 1997) and Williamston, St Martins (Callander 1919).

## 11.7 Conclusions

The discussion above gives an indication of potential contemporary land-use and environment in the Late

Bronze Age. The distribution maps reflect the plentiful resource of the study area. While chronologies for settlement types and funerary remains are limited at present, results of recent commercial and academic research have provided a glimpse of the evolution of such sites through the Late Bronze Age. It is clear, however, that this resource, as a whole, remains untapped. Given the density of remains, the study area has the potential to make a significant contribution to understanding the diversity of prehistoric settlement development. Equally, the limited nature of the funerary remains for this period reflects a need for further enquiry to gain a better understanding of funerary and ritual practices during the period.

# Chapter 12

# A new look at the Late Bronze Age metalwork from the Tay

TREVOR COWIE and MARK HALL

### 12.1 Introduction

This review of the predominantly Late Bronze Age metalwork from the River Tay presents a range of material that helps to contextualise the broader use of the river. Reference is made to earlier and later objects found in the Tay to try and gain a fuller understanding of the dynamics of deposition in, and recovery from, the river. While the amount of material from the river is very small in comparison with the large quantities from the Thames or the Trent, the Tay nevertheless ranks among the more archaeologically productive rivers in Britain and is the only significant source of river finds in Scotland (Coombs 1996, 102, figs 1–2; Cowie and Hall 2001).

In the particular case of the Bronze Age metalwork, the limited number of finds from the Tay is compounded by the sparseness of the information relating to their circumstances of discovery. While this means that the Tay has a much weaker archaeological signature than more productive rivers, and the extent and nature of the activities that led to the loss or deposition of those artefacts is correspondingly more elusive, some patterns can nevertheless be teased out.

Although our main focus is on the Bronze Age material, some consideration is also given to the material of other periods that has been recovered from the river, for the waters of the Tay have received and given up a diverse range of artefacts ranging from a Neolithic stone axe to a post-medieval seal matrix. Although this

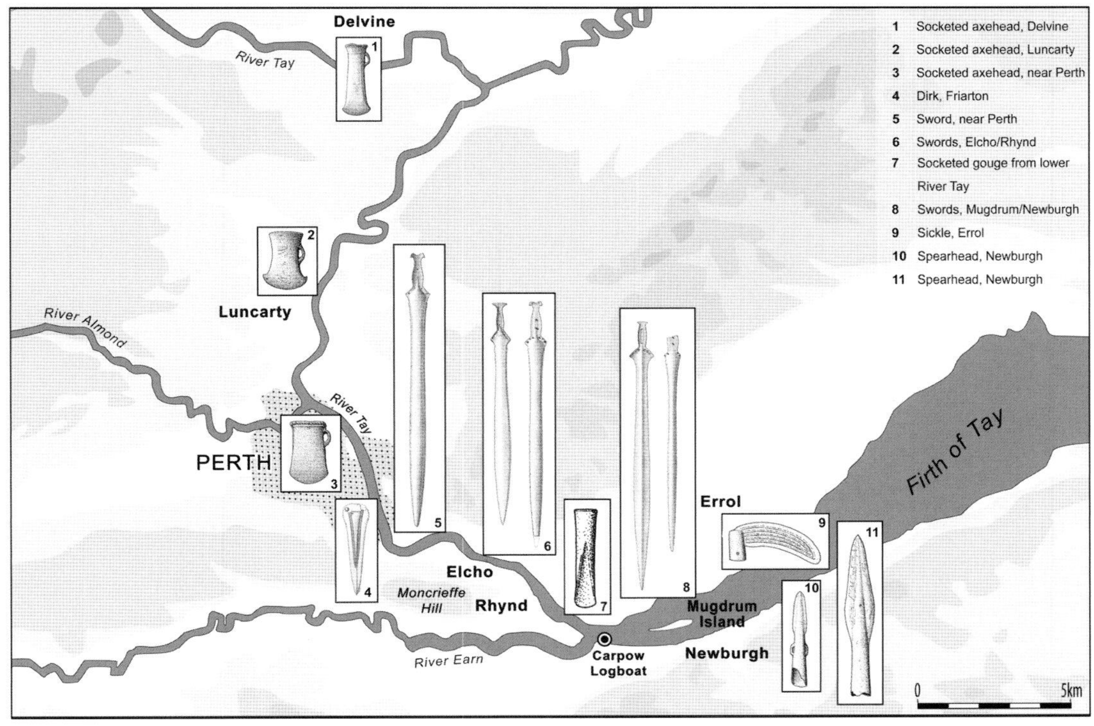


*Figure 162*
The lower Tay showing the range of Bronze Age metalwork recovered from the river

is not the place for a definitive catalogue, comparison of the character and circumstances of discovery of these finds may indirectly aid understanding of how and why material came to be deposited in or recovered from the river at certain points.

The review of the finds of Late Bronze Age metalwork from the River Tay also provides a starting point for a brief survey of contemporary artefacts from the wider Tayside and Fife region, highlighting variation in their treatment and context, the evidence they provide for the region's national and international connections, and finally the sideways light they shed on craftsmanship.

Our focus of interest is mainly on the lower Tay, extending from around the bend of the Tay at Delvine, to the north of Perth, downriver to approximately Ballinbreich to the east of Newburgh. It is therefore a stretch that neatly embraces Carpow Bank (Fig 162).

## 12.2 Middle Bronze Age metalwork from the Tay

In August 2008 Mr Ian Robertson of Perth brought into Perth Museum a very fine example of a Middle Bronze Age bronze dirk, which he had found in the river some 10 or 12 years earlier while scuba diving near Friarton (O'Connor *et al* forthcoming). The dirk (Fig 163) has a low trapezoidal butt, with somewhat rounded rather than angular shoulders and a fairly straight heel. It has had two rivet-holes; one still has a plug-rivet with domed heads in place, although the finder's account suggests that the other rivet may still have been present when the blade was first discovered. The outer rim of the damaged rivet-hole is now missing and there appear to be signs of both ancient and more recent damage. The blade has an elegant ogival outline with a central rib, broad at the butt-end and becoming more rounded and pronounced as it tapers towards the tip of the blade. The upper portion of the midrib is bordered by incised grooves which converge on the midrib approximately three-quarters down the length of the blade. On one face just below the butt end of the midrib, there are worn traces of two incised pendant triangles, probably originally forming a transverse band all the way across. The blade has a number of nicks and notches, some of them with the appearance of ancient damage. Otherwise the dirk is overall in excellent condition. A small area of the lower blade has been cleaned to reveal the underlying golden metal but otherwise the dirk has an even glossy

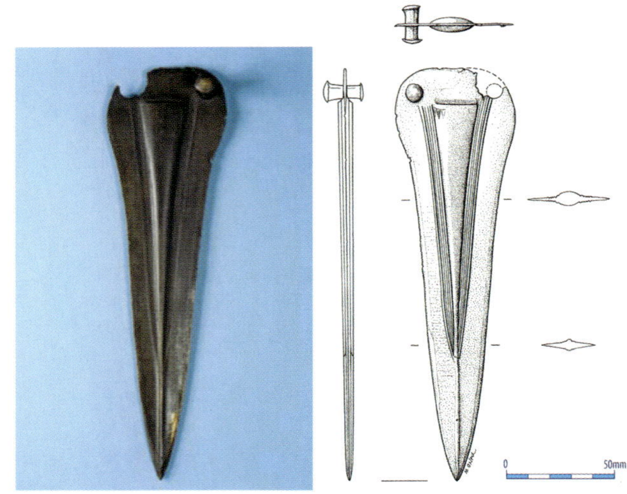

*Figure 163*
The Middle Bronze Age dirk from the Tay at Friarton
(photo: PMAG; drawing © NMS by Marion O'Neil)

dark brown patina in keeping with recovery from a benign watery environment.

Allowing for the finder's uncertainty as regards the condition of the weapon when found, the circumstantial evidence suggests that the weapon had suffered some damage in antiquity but was intact at the time of deposition. At the time of writing, the dirk is in the care of Perth Museum and Art Gallery pending a decision on ownership by the Receiver of Wreck.

The Friarton dirk is a type characterised by the presence of complex ornament bordering the pronounced, rounded midrib, with a date range from the late 16th to the 15th century cal BC. Such weapons are rare in Scotland and most common in Ireland, but it is closely paralleled by another local find from Pitkeathly, near Bridge of Earn (Burgess & Gerloff 1981, 8–9, no 18). Indeed, metal analysis seems to confirm its Irish origin (unpublished information from Dr Peter Northover). The find circumstances of the Friarton dirk are in keeping with the pattern of recovery of the majority of dirks and rapiers from watery contexts such as rivers, lakes, bogs and fens. In our present context, it has added significance since it marks the earliest item of Bronze Age metalwork from the Tay discovered in circumstances suggestive of deliberate deposition.

The only other item of Middle Bronze Age date from the river is a side-looped spearhead, recovered through metal-detecting at low tide on the foreshore at Newburgh in 1997 (Laing Museum, Newburgh; unpublished). The worn and damaged condition of this example may be more in keeping with the loss or discard of an artefact near the end of its functional life rather than votive deposition (although a combination of these factors cannot be ruled out). It may be noted that very few items of archaeological significance of any period have been recovered despite reasonably active metal detecting along the foreshore.

## 12.3 Late Bronze Age metalwork from the Tay

In the context of this volume, our focus is naturally concentrated on the later Bronze Age metalwork.

For convenience these will be grouped by types, beginning with the swords, and discussed in terms of the circumstances of recovery where known, typology, date and condition.

### Swords

Five, or just possibly six, bronze swords have been recovered from the Tay. All are 19th-century AD finds, and in the four instances where fuller details are known, the findspots lie between Perth and Newburgh. The significance of this will be discussed further below.

In terms of Late Bronze Age chronology, the earliest of the swords from the Tay is the superb specimen found in 1889 to the north of Mugdrum Island, near Newburgh on Reekit Lady sandbank (Fig

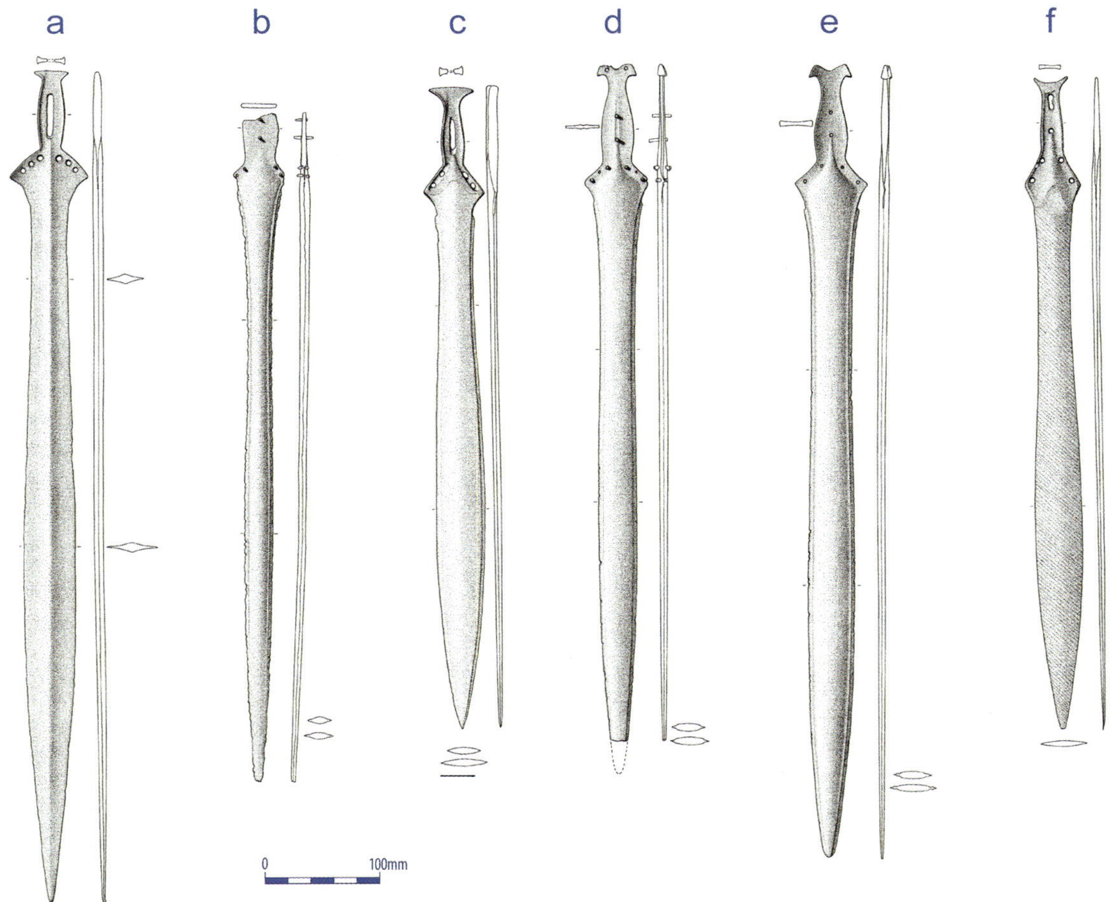

*Figure 164a–f*
Late Bronze Age swords from the river: (a–b) Mugdrum/Newburgh; (c–d) Elcho/Rhynd; (e) 'the Tay near Perth'; and (f) an
unprovenanced sword formerly alleged to be from the Tay opposite Elcho (line drawings after Colquhoun & Burgess 1988)

164a). Probably dating to *c* 11th century BC, the sword represents a variant form of the so-called Limehouse type of sword, itself a regional or insular form of flange-hilted sword of continental type (Erbenheim swords) (Colquhoun & Burgess 1988, 33–6, no 113). Although none of the rivets which would have held the organic hilt plates in place remain *in situ*, the sword is generally intact and in excellent condition, suggesting loss or deliberate deposition of a fully serviceable sword.

Also dating from the earlier part of the Late Bronze Age (Wilburton phase 11th/10th centuries BC, is the fine Wilburton type sword (*ibid*, 51–2, no 226) recovered from the river at Seggieden, which is on the north bank opposite Elcho (Fig 164c). It was found by the fishermen of Darry Island and was presented to the Perth Literary and Antiquarian Society in November 1854. Darry Island was also known as Darien or Incherrat and, along with the islands known as Sleepless Inch and Balhepburn (or Inchyra) was joined to the shore during river-deepening operations in the 1830s and 1840s (Robertson 1998, 4). The sword was deposited in good condition, complete apart from the loss of the rivets from hilt and shoulder. Once again, the overall condition hints at loss or deliberate deposition of a fully serviceable sword.

Considerable doubt surrounds the provenance of a second sword in Perth Museum reputed to be from this stretch of the Tay (Fig 164f). In their report on the Perth Museum collection undertaken as part of their survey of Scottish local museums, Joseph Anderson and George Black refer to a 'Bronze Sword, found in the Tay opposite Elcho, 23¾ inches in length, the handle-plate concealed by a handle of wood put on' (1888, 337). One of the extant swords in Perth Museum has modern alterations consistent with this description, having a black patina in keeping with a watery context, while filing of the edges of the hilt and the high polish of the blade suggest addition of a hilt (since removed) and much recent handling (Colquhoun & Burgess 1988, 106, no 630: 'provenance unknown, possibly from Perthshire'). While we can be reasonably confident that we have identified the sword described by Anderson and Black, their list was compiled in the course of a wide-ranging and relatively rapid survey and may not be wholly error-free, and it is probably wise to sound a note of caution in the absence of independent verification of the Tay provenance. None of the 19th-century records held by Perth Museum give a place-name and the later records of the 1920s and 1930s list the sword but give it no provenance.

The sword in question belongs to the Ewart Park type, the classic Late Bronze Age leaf-shaped sword (Colquhoun & Burgess 1988, 55–68). Despite the modifications to the weapon, the sword has clearly been complete at the time of deposition. It is unfortunate that the provenance of the sword is in some doubt, because despite being numerically the most common type of Late Bronze Age sword from Scotland, this is the only sword from the river of Ewart Park type. However, in view of the relatively small overall numbers of finds from the river, and the recovery of such swords from other wet locations such as bogs and lochs, it would be unwise to read too much significance into this.

Instead, numerically the most common swords from the river are the three examples of Gündlingen type, dating from the Llyn Fawr phase, marking the transition from the Late Bronze Age to the Early Iron Age around the eighth century BC. Gündlingen swords (*ibid*, 114–16) are frequently found as river finds but given the small overall numbers from Scotland this is a significant concentration.

Two of the swords belong to a particular variant of the Gündlingen type (*ibid*, variant d). One of these is a magnificent weapon purchased for the national collection in 1877 (Fig 164e); it is said to be from the Tay, near Perth, but unfortunately nothing is known of the circumstances of its discovery (*ibid*, no 739). Apart from loss of the rivets in hilt and shoulders, the sword is in excellent condition and shows little sign of wear. The other sword (Fig 164d) belonging to this variant was recovered from the river near Elcho Castle (Rhynd) in 1865 (*ibid*, no 743). The sword is in extremely good condition, and undamaged apart from loss of the tip and some distortion of one of the shoulders. All six of the serviceable rivet holes retain rivets *in situ* on the hilt and shoulders, presumably indicating the grip plates were still in place until close to the time of deposition (a further two rivet holes remain imperforate). While it is uncertain whether the damage to the tip and shoulder was incurred during combat or the result of deliberate destruction or decommissioning, the overall condition hints at loss or deliberate deposition of a sword that had until that point been in a fully serviceable condition.

The third of the Gündlingen-type swords was brought up from the bottom of the Tay in a salmon net at Mugdrum Island, some time before 1899 (Fig 164b). Loss of the upper part of the hilt precludes detailed classification. At least four pin rivets remain *in situ* in the surviving portion of the hilt, possibly suggesting that the remains of the grip were still in place when the

154

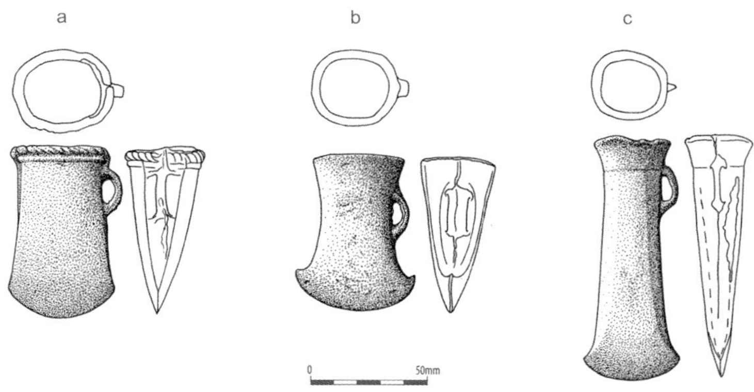



*Figure 165a–c*
Socketed axeheads from: (a) near Perth; (b) Luncarty; and (c) Delvine
(line drawings after Schmidt & Burgess 1981)

sword was deposited in the river. While it is uncertain whether fracture of the hilt-plate was the result of accidental damage during use or deliberate destruction, the presence of intact rivets and the general condition hint at loss or deposition of a sword that had till then been in a serviceable condition.

## Spearheads

The other weapon type frequently represented in riverine and other wetland deposits is the spearhead. While Late Bronze Age spearheads occur as single finds or as a component of hoards in the surrounding region; they are noticeable by their relative absence from the Tay itself. Only two examples are known to the writers. One, which has been rather overlooked, is in the collections of Dundee Museum. It was a casual find found lying in a bank of stones and mud at the head of a sandbank in the River Tay near Newburgh (Coutts 1971). A more recent discovery, made by a metal detectorist several years ago, is the tip of a further leaf-shaped spearhead of Late Bronze Age form, alleged to have been found on the Tay foreshore, but the precise location is not known.

## Socketed axeheads

Turning now to what would conventionally be classed as tools; three socketed axeheads appear to have been found in the river (Fig 165a–c). An axehead from Luncarty was found by pearl fishers prior to 1914 in the bed of the Tay at Thistle Bridge, and later acquired by Perth Museum in 1923 (Schmidt & Burgess 1981, cat 1162). That from Delvine, near Caputh is said to have been found in the bed of the Tay, again by pearl fishers, *c* 1913 and acquired by Perth Museum in 1925 (*ibid*, cat 1214). The third axehead was discovered in 1946 in sand dredged from the Tay below Perth; the axehead belongs to a relatively rare type with rope-moulding around the mouth (*ibid*, cat 1036).

## Other tools

The remaining Bronze Age metalwork recorded as being from the river includes a bronze sickle and a gouge (Fig 166a–b). The socketed sickle, a rare find,

*Table 10*

A summary of Middle and Late Bronze Age metalwork from the River Tay (metalwork assemblages after Rohl & Needham 1998)

| Phase | Date cal BC | Dirk | Sword | Spearhead | Axehead | Gouge | Sickle |
|---|---|---|---|---|---|---|---|
| Acton Park | 1500–1400 | ● | | ● | | | |
| Taunton | 1400–1300 | | | | | | |
| Penard | 1275–1140 | | | | | | |
| Wilburton | 1140–1020 | | ● ● | | | | |
| Ewart | 1020–800 | | ●? | ● ●? | ● ● ● | ● | |
| Llyn Fawr | 800–650 | | ● ● ● | | | | ● |

155

*Figure 166a–b*
(a) socketed gouge from R Tay (no location) (NMS);
(b) sickle from Tay at Errol (PMAG)

the later Bronze Age and were probably linked to development of more specialised craftsmanship.

In summary, whatever the recovery dynamics from the river, the items of Bronze Age metalwork are all in good condition, a condition suggestive of deposition close to where they were found and consistent with not having been moved by river flows and sediment deposition. Though the number of swords found is modest, nevertheless the fact that early and late swords occur together hints further at a non-random pattern, one of deposition of swords several centuries apart into the same stretch of river and so suggestive of on-going, traditional, conservative community practices.

The big problem with regard to the Late Bronze Age metalwork is whether we are looking at patterns of deposition or recovery biases, or rather what is the balance between the two? Clearly both are in operation and to look more closely at the latter we now turn to a brief exploration of other finds from the river.

## 12.4 Other archaeological finds from the Tay

On the Tay, as elsewhere in Britain and Ireland and indeed most of north-west Europe, the recovery of riverine finds in the past has been governed almost entirely by the nature of the economic life of the river in modern times. Discoveries in the Tay and the Forth have principally been made in the course of traditional pearl fishing or salmon fishing with nets, with a lesser contribution from navigation-dredging. Pearl fishing is known to have taken place as far up river as Logierait, while the scale of the Tay salmon netting is well known (Fig 167). The pattern of netting-recovery does echo the use of nets on particular parts of the river. The stretch of the Tay between Moncreiffe Island and the mouth of the Earn, some 6km, 'follows a broad single channel with sloping banks particularly suitable to the use of salmon nets. This part of the river was known to the old salmon fishers as 'the throat of the river' as, being below any of the spawning beds all returning salmon had to traverse it' (Robertson 1998, 4). Netting then was more concentrated here and perhaps more likely to favour the recovery of material than dredging: with netting, Bronze Age metalwork would much more readily stand out amongst the salmon than it would in dredged sediment. The dredging of the river has continued into this century to maintain access to the harbour at Friarton, but this has not resulted in the reporting of any archaeological discoveries.

was dredged up from the Tay near Errol in 1840 (Anderson 1886, 203–4). This marks the easterly limit of finds from the river with known locations. The sickle also represents the earliest recorded artefact found in the course of dredging operations, which invariably took place to maintain the shipping channel to Perth harbour. Finally Anderson records a fine socketed gouge in the national collection as having been dredged up from the Tay (*ibid*, 201–2, fig 218). Under the circumstances, we may assume that it came from the lower reaches of the river below Perth where the main 19th-century dredging activity was undertaken in order to improve navigation. Gouges appear in

*Figure 167*
Pearl fishers on River Tay, 1911 (PMAG)

Further elucidation of the meaning of artefact deposition and recovery from the river may also be gained from looking at what else has been recovered. The Bronze Age metalwork forms part of a diverse inventory of artefacts recovered from the river ranging from a possible Mesolithic logboat to a post-medieval seal matrix. The overall inventory of finds of other periods is not large, but a full illustrated catalogue is beyond the scope of this paper and our aim is primarily to convey its range and the varying modes of discovery for comparison and contrast with the Bronze Age record. For simplicity, the different categories are dealt with in broadly chronological order.

The artefact record associated with the river is also enriched by finds of boats and parts of boats (Chapter 9, pp 129–30). However, it may be noted that like the majority of finds from the river, they mostly owe their discovery to activity associated with the economy of the river or its immediate environs – for example,

one of the medieval logboats from Errol (Errol 2) was found by salmon fishermen in 1895 when it obstructed their fishing nets, while the logboat from Dalmarnock at Dalguise, near Dunkeld (NN c. 998 458) was found during construction work for the A9 (Mowat 1996, 21, no 25). And finally excavations at Friarton brickworks led to the discovery of the fragment of a possible Mesolithic logboat prior to 1878 (*ibid*, 34–5, no 50), placing it among the earliest artefacts associated with the story of the Tay.

### Neolithic and Early Bronze Age finds

Only two early Neolithic artefacts definitely appear to have been found in the river. One is a ground-and-polished stone axehead found in the Tay at Aberfeldy (NMS: X.AF 632), making it an exception to the general pattern of discovery; otherwise, all of the recorded prehistoric finds have been downstream of Delvine. The other early Neolithic item is a lozenge-

*Figure 168a–b*
Neolithic and Early Bronze Age finds: (a) carved stone balls from the River Tay at Mugdrum Island and the River Forth at Gargunnock; (b) flint
macehead from the Tay at Newburgh and battle-axes from the river near Mugdrum Island and at Ballinbreich (© NMS)

shaped flint arrowhead (PMAG: 1810), possibly unfinished, found in the course of dredging the river in the vicinity of Perth prior to 1920 (Asher 1923, 143).

Material of late Neolithic date includes an unusual flint macehead discovered on a sand and gravel bank in the Tay at Newburgh (Roe 1974) while a carved stone ball was found in the bed of the river during dredging and donated to the Museum in 1841 (PMAG, 1290A; Smith 1876a, 47–8 and 1876b, 316). Although not necessarily from the river itself, two further carved stone balls from Mugdrum Island (NMS: X.AS 74; Marshall 1977, 66) and Newburgh (NMS: X.AS 201; Marshall 1977, 68) possibly reinforce this local cluster of finds closely associated with the river and its margins.

Early Bronze Age material from the river includes two examples of the shaft-hole implements known as battle-axes (Roe 1966; Clough & Cummins 1988) recovered in the course of dredging near Mugdrum Island (Anderson 1886, 315–16, fig 294; NMS: X.AH 44) and at Ballinbreich near Newburgh (*ibid*, 312–13, fig 291; NMS: X.AH 57). A further battle-axe was

found, in what could be significantly close proximity to the river, on the west bank under the last arch of the railway bridge in Tay Street, Perth (Clough & Cummins 1988, 239 no. PER 36; PMAG 22/1974).

Stone artefacts such as the carved stone balls and the battle-axes are distinctive objects, with unusual shapes and forms that will perhaps have led to them being more easily spotted than more mundane artefacts and perhaps resulting in a recovery bias. Nevertheless, these are relatively special artefacts which have had considerable amounts of time and energy invested in their manufacture. In relative terms the numbers recovered from the river between Perth and Newburgh seem disproportionate – and perhaps hint at the possibility of deliberate deposition rather than casual disposal or accidental loss or erosion of riverside deposits. In view of the range of rather special late Neolithic and Early Bronze Age artefacts it is tempting to wonder if the tradition of deposition in the river had even earlier origins (Fig 168a–b).

Although not closely dateable mention may also be made of a saddle quern found below the high waterline of the Tay among stones on the east bank of the

158

river, opposite the northern end of Moncreiffe Island (PMAG, 1983.426: King 1993a, 103). Its discovery highlights the continuing potential for discovery along a river that has been the focus for settlement and activity for millennia.

### After the Bronze Age: later finds from the river

Turning to later periods, Iron Age material is absent, but in view of the relatively small numbers of artefacts of all periods, it would be unwise to read much into this when it is clear that so much depends on the vagaries of recovery and recognition. The only finds of Roman Iron Age material are a fine Romano-British trumpet brooch with traces of blue enamel (Hunter 1996, 116–17) and a hoard of six Roman denarii deposited in the late second century AD (Bateson & Hall 2002) both discovered in the Tay at Inchyra, through metal-detecting. Their loss/deposition may have been linked to a crossing point of the river.

Here we are limiting our examples to material known or believed to have been retrieved from the river itself: however, a comprehensive review would also need to take account of sites and finds from the wider riparian zone. The 'Celtic' carved stone head found at North Muirton, Perth, lies at the northern end of the North Inch, part of the Tay flood plain and set near the junction of the rivers Almond and Tay – in turn, close to the findspot of a series of pits near Bertha containing portions of Roman glass and pottery vessels (NMS, X. FR 200–203: Stuart 1852, 205; Ross 1966, 36; Hall et al 2005, 276). Also relevant in this context is the altar of Antonine date recovered from the River Almond beside Bertha Roman fort and only metres from its junction with the Tay (Keppie 1983, 402 no 16). Taken together such finds may suggest more than simple loss or discard and may hint at ritual activity associated with the banks of the river; just as in the case of Bronze Age artefact distributions, they suggest we should be wary of too simple a distinction between riverine and dry-land finds.

Turning briefly to medieval and later discoveries from the river, mention may be made of a fine socketed iron spearhead (PMAG: 191) found in the River Tay directly below Kinclaven Castle (King 1991, 72). The spearhead has recently been dated to the late 11th to early 12th century AD as a result of radiocarbon dating of a fragment of wooden shaft still present in the socket. Another weapon find was what was described as a 'cutlass' from the River Tay at Newburgh, said to have been donated to Elgin Museum in 1913 but now no longer traceable in their collections.

*Table 11*
Summary of the range of finds from the River Tay

| | Tools | Weaponry | Personal ornaments etc | Domestic vessels (pottery etc) | Boats/ boat parts | Other |
|---|---|---|---|---|---|---|
| Mesolithic | | | | | ✓? | |
| Neolithic | ✓ | | | | | |
| Late Neolithic/Early Bronze Age | ✓ | | | | | ✓ |
| Middle/Later Bronze Age | ✓ | ✓ | | | ✓ | |
| Iron Age | | | | | | |
| Roman IA | | | ✓ | | | |
| Early Historic | | | | | | |
| Medieval | | ✓ | | ✓ | ✓ | |
| Post medieval/modern | ✓ | ✓ | ✓ | | ✓? | |

Yet another chance find is the leg of a bronze cauldron or pot discovered in the bed of the river at Thistle Bridge, Luncarty in 1914 by tinkers (also responsible for the discovery of the bronze socketed axe described above – although in that case the finders were described as pearl fishers!). The object was eventually presented to Perth Museum in 1926, where it was initially accessioned as a bronze ingot (Tylecote 1974). Chance also accounts for the discovery of a lead seal bearing the arms of Orange-Nassau found at Aberfeldy (NMS: H.NM 264). As with prehistoric artefacts, the details of the circumstances of its discovery are frustratingly sparse. As a general observation then, it may be noted that as in the case of the Bronze Age record, chance lies behind most of the discoveries; metal detecting has *not* significantly added to the inventory of finds from the banks or inter-tidal zone. A copper alloy crucifix reliquary found by a detectorist on Carpow Bank (Hall 2007) is a rare exception and may be interpreted as a later reflex of votive deposition (*ibid*, 83–6).

A rare ceramic find from the river is a late-medieval, glazed, redware jug with rod handle (PMAG: 1993.427.1) dredged from the Tay at Perth (King 1993b, 103). While the circumstances of the Tay find are uncertain, it recalls the splendid cache of near-intact post-medieval earthenware jugs discovered in the Forth near Throsk, plausibly interpreted as a cargo lost following a capsize or similar accident (Caldwell & Dean 1992, 31).

An unusual discovery is the wheel (PMAG: 2007.195) found in the west bank of the River Tay, immediately south of Inchtuthil. Composed of four planks made from Scots pine and fitted with an iron tyre, the wheel is likely to date to the 18th century AD. It was found protruding from river gravel after flooding in 1996 – not only a reminder of the power of the river when in spate but also the potential for artefacts to be removed from their original depositional context through erosion of the banks and adjacent flood plain. As ever, the few reasonably well-provenanced finds flag up just how little we know about the detailed context of the majority of artefacts retrieved from the Tay, and a full review of the medieval and later discoveries would also need to take account of sites and finds from the adjacent haughlands, particularly around Perth itself. For example, an early medieval sword was found during construction work in the mid-19th century in the Watergate, Perth in what has been identified as an area of low-lying riverbank before the town became established (Hall *et al* 2005, 277 and note 12). On the other hand, an iron spearhead and a fragment

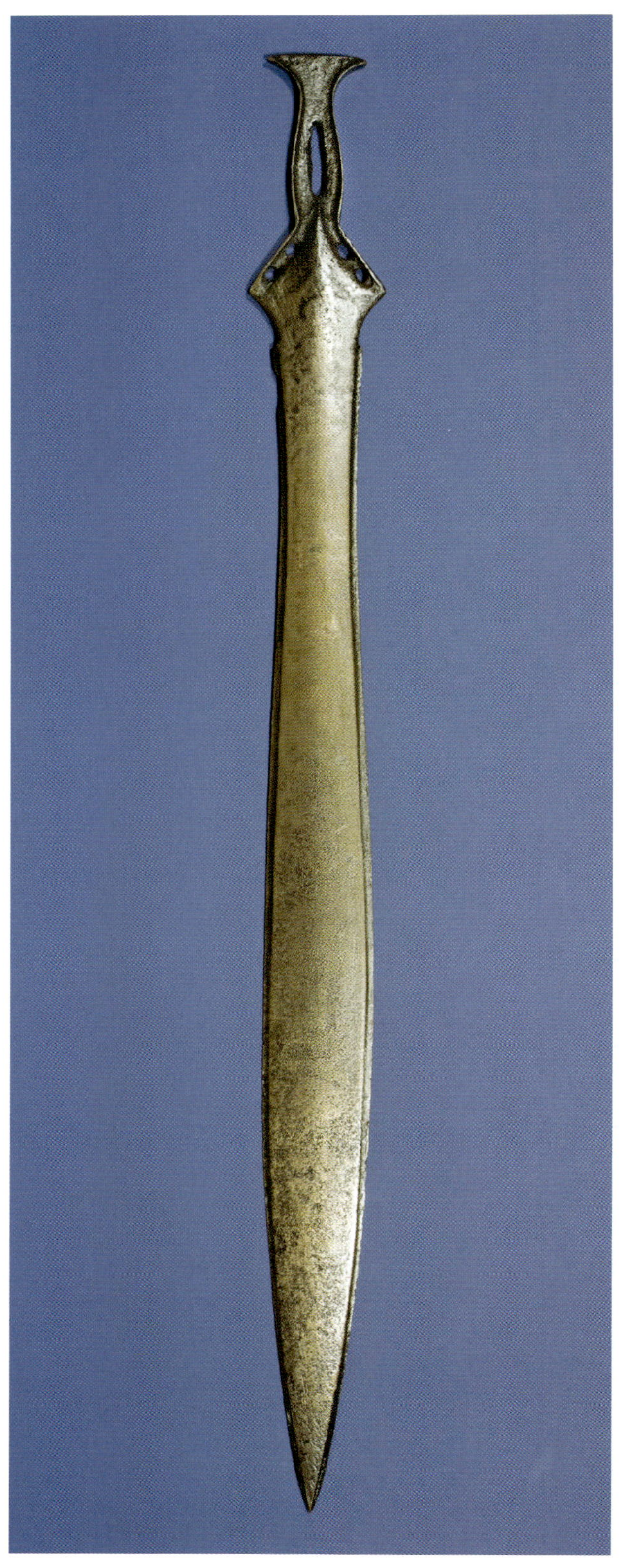

*Figure 169*
The sword from Seggieden (PMAG)

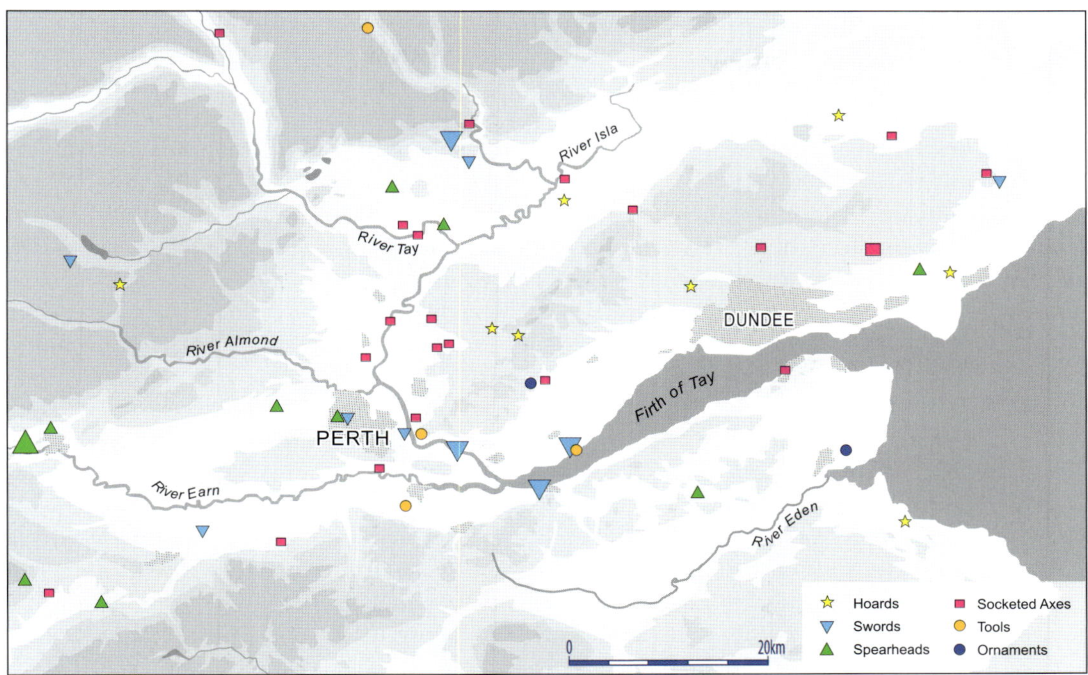


*Figure 170*

Distribution map of Late Bronze Age finds from the region. (© Crown copyright and database right (2009). All rights reserved. Ordnance Survey Licence number 100016971)

of a spur found in Tay Street, Perth may have been actual medieval losses or deposits into the river, as Tay Street was constructed in the 1870s on reclaimed land (Bowler (ed) 2004, 120 (Appendix 8 on CD)).

In summary, although not especially large in quantity, the medieval and later record of finds from the Tay is marked by a greater variety of types that may be more in keeping with an interpretation of accidental loss or disposal in the course of more mundane activities on or alongside the river.

## 12.5 Discussion: patterns of discovery?

By considering all the artefacts recovered from the Tay, we may be able to shed more light on patterns of retrieval of the Late Bronze Age artefacts. This variety has a bearing on the interpretation of the Late Bronze Age finds since the presence or absence of a range of artefacts may strengthen the possibility that the distribution of a particular type actually reflects an ancient pattern of deposition rather than being the result of biased recovery. It has already been observed that this seems likely with the swords given their focus

in one area of the river and their condition. They form a sharp contrast with the finds of socketed axes from the stretch of river north of Perth. Given that both stretches were being worked using traditional methods, it is difficult to account for this pattern of recovery if material was reaching the riverbed randomly.

In the case of the Tay, how then are we to account for this pattern of recovery? Theoretically some feature of the hydrology of the river could have promoted concentration of relatively large objects such as swords in these areas at the expense of other types. This requires further investigation but seems unlikely. Another possibility is that differences in economic activity on the river have promoted differential recovery. This again seems unlikely because, as noted above, broadly comparable contact with the river-bed has resulted in rather different patterns of recovery. As we know relatively small objects such as axeheads were being recognised and retained in one stretch, it seems unlikely that swords were being kept selectively at the expense of smaller artefacts on another. However, it is possible that changes in the dredging regime – for example, to accommodate modern navigation – have

161

altered the overall pattern of recovery downstream from Perth (as is known for other rivers, including the Thames). Or perhaps there was something about the topography of the river which promoted a concentration of activity in this area at various times in antiquity? As with other finds from wet locations, the likelihood is that the metalwork has accumulated in the river episodically. Although the amount of Bronze Age metalwork from the Tay is not great compared with rivers in England, the presence of the Friarton dirk and the range of Gündlingen swords show deposition at the *beginning* and the *end* of the sequence of Bronze Age river finds. Whatever the 'attraction of the place', it clearly persisted over a considerable time.

We believe a strong case can be made for seeing these finds of Late Bronze Age metalwork from the river – at the very least, the swords – as the result of votive offerings rather than day-to-day activities or casual losses (Figs 169–70). And we should not forget that it may have been just such a craft as the Carpow logboat that was used as the floating vehicle or platform from which to cast votives in the river. But we should not close our minds entirely to more prosaic explanations. Elcho and Inchyra were ferry crossing points in medieval and later times, and the crossing of the Tay–Earn confluence near Abernethy was on a key pilgrimage route (Fig 170). Nor should the possibility of accidental loss, as a result of capsize or wreck, be entirely overlooked. In our own minds though, seen against the body of evidence for deposition of fine metalwork in wet places such as bogs, rivers and lochs, we are confident that the concentration of swords warrants explanation in terms of votive offerings. And of course, there is no reason why some of these explanations should be mutually exclusive. Work on understanding the Late Bronze Age use of the River Tay (particularly between Perth and Newburgh) from a material culture perspective continues and a future contribution will seek to set that material in its regional, national and international contexts – including the notion of the Tay as a nodal point for networks of contact, trade and exchange.

# Conclusions: the Carpow logboat in context

DAVID STRACHAN

### 13.1 Taphonomy

An important question when considering the logboat in context is whether the location at which the boat was found was the primary deposition spot of the vessel, or whether Carpow Bank is secondary, with the vessel being relocated from an initial position at some later time. Pertinent to the circumstances and processes of how the boat was deposited, is the story of another Tay vessel, *The Larches*, built in 1905 from larchwood by the Atholl Estate, for the purpose of transporting livestock along the River Tay. The Dukes of Atholl, known as the 'Planting Dukes', experimented widely by introducing different trees, and had been trialling European and Japanese larches since the mid-18th century, giving rise to the Dunkeld larch in 1904. With the best combination of the parents' qualities, the Dunkeld larch was widely planted on Atholl lands and elsewhere throughout Britain, and *The Larches* was constructed to display the versatility of the timber. It was a relatively substantial ferry boat, measuring *c* 15m in length with a maximum width of 6m, and had an unusual oval plan. In 1922, during a spate flood of the river, it broke free from its moorings at Burnmouth, Stanley, and after being carried by the strong currents around six miles downstream, the boat crashed into the Victoria Bridge, Perth and jammed under the eastern arch before being pulled free by a fire brigade engine (*Perthshire Advertiser*, 1 March 1922, 20). Although severely damaged, the boat was later transported downstream again, and was used as a ferry to transport sheep onto Mugdrum Island at Newburgh, a practice that continued until 1972 when the boat was replaced by an iron vessel called the 'Iron Duke', at which time *The Larches* was towed to the inter-tidal marsh at Insherrit Island, on the north bank of the Tay opposite Elcho for preservation, where it remains today (Newburgh residents pers comm).

The story of *The Larches* dramatically illustrates two points: the tendency for floatable objects to make their way downstream over time; and the fact that robust historic watercraft usually had at least two (and often more) working lives, often in different locations.

As Carpow was found without a recognisable archaeological context, such as a crannog or landing stage, and without any sizable artefacts which were deposited with it, it is very possible that the findspot may not be the location of initial deposition. There are three main factors that are relevant when considering this question: the deposits from which the boat was recovered, the angle at which the boat lay *in situ*, and the condition of vessel.

*Figure 171*
*The Larches* becomes jammed under Victoria Bridge, Perth
(*Perthshire Advertiser*, 1 March 1922, A K Bell Library,
Local Studies Department)

While the stern of the vessel was found quite deeply buried in the inter-tidal sands and gravels, the highly dynamic nature of the inter-tidal environment, involving regular physical scouring and accrual of these deposits, cannot be seen as a secure context (Chapter 4, pp 40–1). Context 106, the organic rich deposit containing small hazel and birch round-woods, including carpentry waste, and the rodent damaged hazelnut shells, was found to be contemporary with the boat. It was found inside the boat and immediately beneath it, predominately at the stern, however, it was not possible to determine whether the deposit was itself *in situ*, or whether it had been transported with the logboat; the result largely of the difficulties of inter-tidal excavation (Chapter 4, p 42). A important fact, however, is that the stern of the vessel lay directly on top of a thick (*c* 300mm) block of tabulated peat (Context 107) and the boat itself lay at significant angle, with the bow exposed above Carpow Bank and the stern buried *c* 1.75m below the surface (Chapter 4, p 41, Fig 43). This is most convincingly explained through gradual process of subsidence of the heavier stern of the vessel into inter-tidal or riverine sediments, whether sands, gravels or mud, pushing the peat down beneath it, while the lighter weight of the bow of the hull sunk less. The stern is, and always has been, by far the heaviest end of the boat, and it is likely that additional weight would have been added at the stern as deposits accrued inside the hull, which survived as Context 106, increasing the differential weight of the bow and stern and promoting further subsidence. Indeed, a scenario can be envisaged whereby as the heavier stern subsided, the lighter bow would be slowly raised. There are, however, other possible scenarios as outlined in Fig 172.

Finally, it is the condition of the hull which is perhaps the most informative factor. The process of decay of exposed boats can be through physical impact, either at the level of collision or through scouring, wear and grinding, or chemical processes, notably the decay of the wood. The majority of recovered logboats are already in a poor state of preservation when discovered, and it is usually very difficult to differentiate between erosion prior to deposition and that which occurs once the boat becomes buried (Mowat pers comm). This is not the case with Carpow however, as the excellent preservation of the hull and stern, and the survival of the transom with its toolmarks, strongly suggest that the boat was buried soon after it went out of use. For example, there are no signs of the physical and chemical processes resulting in the rotting of the numerous eroding hulks visible around the coast of the UK. Indeed, the poor condition of the vast majority

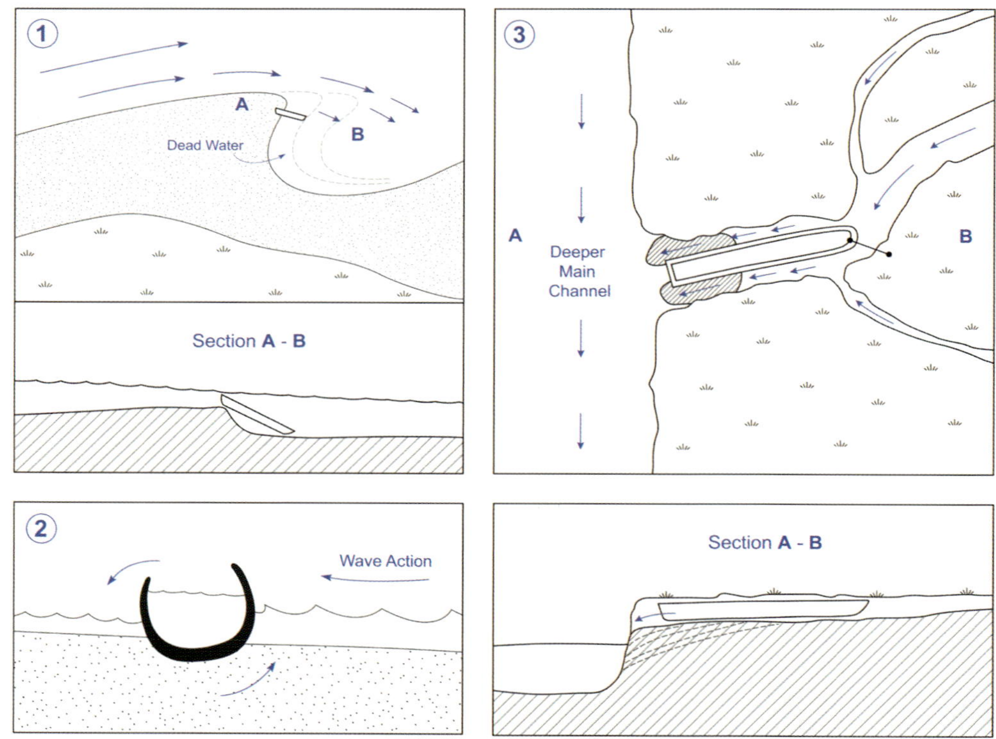


*Figure 172*
Schematic plans and sections showing some possible processes of deposition: (1) gradual movement over Carpow Bank results in the final angle of the boat; (2) wave action promotes the transverse angle of the hull; and (3) deposition at a mooring in a creek

of 19th- and 20th-century hulks indicates how rapid this process of decay occurs, despite the fact that logboats are arguably more robust that these plank-built vessels.

In contrast the erosion of the bow of the vessel clearly indicates a different history, where exposure for a relatively long period of time has resulted in significant loss and decay through both physical and chemical processes. While post-abandonment damage in logboats can be more pronounced at the more delicate bow (Mowat pers comm) the notable difference in the condition of bow and stern may suggest that the bow has become exposed and eroded in the relatively recent past, perhaps to be measured decades rather than centuries. The combined abrasive effects of the tidal waters, particularly pronounced when carrying considerable quantities of sand or silt in suspension, and rotting as a result of exposure to air at low tide are considerable, as confirmed by the condition monitoring in the few years of the project.

While it can be argued that the good condition of the hull suggests that the findspot was the initial place of deposition, it is possible that the boat was initially deposited somewhere else, where it was protected from erosion, then released from that location only to be redeposited and again fairly rapidly buried at Carpow. The story of *The Larches* is a reminder of how quickly such a journey may have taken place. The position and orientation of the boat could suggest that it was deposited on the bank having been carried downstream from either the Tay or the Earn. It is noticeable that Carpow Bank acts as a weir, collecting items washed downstream during ebb tides, and it is possible that the logboat became lodged in its current position when it was a muddy riverbank, before Carpow Bank itself was truncated and it became the inter-tidal flat that survives today. In conclusion, we cannot say with certainty, largely as a result of the constraints and challenges of inter-tidal archaeology, whether the logboat was originally deposited at Carpow Bank, or whether it floated to this spot at some later date. However, the actual findspot at Carpow, between rivers and estuary offers the opportunity to consider the nature of the vessel and how it operated, in both possible environments, riverine and estuarine.

### 13.2 Tayside in the Late Bronze Age

#### *Environment*

In general terms, the Late Bronze Age saw an abrupt deterioration of climate, beginning around the time of

the logboat, which may have contributed to a reduction in the agricultural limits of farming in the uplands, and potentially also changes in the littoral (Chapter 11). In terms of vegetation cover and land-use, there was still a significant amount of woodland in the area by *c* 1000 cal BC, despite small-scale and temporary woodland clearance since the early Neolithic. The analysis of pollen remains from Moncreiffe suggests agricultural activity in the area in the late third millennium BC (Caseldine 1983). The pollen records for Black Loch and Methven Moss suggest an increase in grazed grassland and arable cultivation, at the expense of woodland, through the second millennium BC, though for much of that period there was no extensive clearance of woodland, suggesting peripatetic settlement with associated arable agriculture in small woodland clearings (Chapter 11). It is possible that scatters of small, more permanent settlements in areas of open grazing and forest were developing around the rich ecotones of the Tay Estuary by this time, however, which may have resulted in increased grazing and cereal production. The importance of the rich riverine and estuarine environments of the Earn and the Tay, as documented on other east coast estuaries (eg Van de Noort & Ellis 1995, and Wilkinson & Murphy 1995) cannot be overstressed. The topography of the Tay Estuary, with the coastal plain of the Carse of Gowrie, and large inter-tidal mudflats, is in many ways reminiscent of Fenland or parts of the low-lying coast of East Anglia. Further, this similarity would have been far more pronounced in prehistoric and medieval periods prior to dredging, coastal and flood defences, reclamation, drainage, and conversion to arable land of low-lying areas where salt marsh and coastal grasses would have existed (Chapter 3, pp 20–4). The gradual rise in sea level since the early Holocene (Chapter 10) will have resulted in the inland shift of salt tolerant plants with the 'drowning' of previously vegetated areas, and this effect would have been augmented by embankment (Cressey pers comm). The woodland in the region included pockets of mature, dark, oak-dominated wildwood, with tall, straight oaks of a size and shape no longer found in western Europe. It is from one of these ancient woods, within portage distance of the estuary or one of the rivers, that the parent log of the Carpow boat came.

#### *The cultural landscape*

The Late Bronze Age is seen as a period of social and economic change against the backdrop of significant and rapid change in climate, reflected in a shift from open to enclosed settlement, an increase in field systems and exploitation of the landscape, and the possible development of hillforts. In terms of settlement, there are indications that the contemporary archaeology of the area is rich; however, the lack of dating for the majority of probable sites has seriously hindered any synthesis and understanding of chronology (Chapter 12). While it has been suggested that in Tayside, unlike other areas of Scotland, unenclosed settlement may have continued into the first millennium BC (Hingley 1992), it has been possible to demonstrate, largely through drawing together the results of recent developer funded archaeology, that there is no consistent picture, with both unenclosed and enclosed sites from this period (Chapter 12). This may simply, however, support the idea of the Late Bronze Age as a period of transition. The general picture however, is of small dispersed settlements, occupied for a few generations before being replaced elsewhere, leaving deserted settlements and relic landscapes, possibly with an overall trend from unenclosed to more fortified settlements.

There is no doubt that the region was prosperous in the Bronze Age, as a result of both its fertile agricultural lands and the rich coastal and estuarine environments that would have afforded additional resources from the sea. While it seems likely that there was little division between lowland and upland settlement throughout much of the Bronze Age (Chapter 11), climatic deterioration in the later Bronze Age would have resulted in new pressures on suitable agricultural land. It would appear that the apparent lack of evidence for upland settlement in the study area in comparison to, for example, the higher ground in north-east Perthshire, is simply a reflection of the nature and level of improvement, which has destroyed most of the remains of settlement on, for example, the Sidlaws (Chapter 11, p 143). A significant question is whether hillforts were in development at this time, as they are an important and numerous site type featuring along the Sidlaws, Ochil and north Fife Hills. In particular, the dominance of Moncreiffe Hill over both the head of the estuary and the rivers Tay and Earn would make for a key power centre in the landscape. It is conceivable that one or more of the hillforts in the area may have had origins in the Late Bronze Age, as has already been suggested at Moncreiffe (Cowie & Hall 2001, 10). Further, it would appear likely that developments on these key sites began not as defended hill-top forts, or densely occupied hill-top

towns, but, as at the Caterthuns (Dunwell & Strachan 2007) as hill-top enclosures with many entrances, with trysting functions in a similar vein to Neolithic causewayed enclosures. It is possible that there was a shift from more unenclosed settlement, to increasingly defended sites further upslope, and that the eventual development of hillforts is part of this process. Until palisaded enclosures and hillforts in the area are dated, however, this process will remain unclear.

In terms of ritual and funerary monuments, the Tayside region appears to fit with the broader picture. While the traditional view saw a shift from inhumation to cremation completed by the Late Bronze Age, an overlap of both methods is now thought more likely, again highlighting the transitional nature of the period. The continued Late Bronze Age use of earlier Neolithic and Early Bronze Age monuments for the deposition of cremation burials, as at North Mains and the stone circles at Moncreiffe and Scone, may be part of a wider picture of acknowledging and connecting with ancestrally important locations in the landscape through the continuity of earlier practice at revered sites. In common with the rest of Scotland, however, by the beginning of the Iron Age there is a notable lack of human remains from the area, perhaps reflecting excarnation or cremation followed by disposal, and this raises the possibility of disposal in the major rivers. Indeed, it is possible that, as with hillforts, this trend had its origins in the Late Bronze Age, or possibly before.

Finally, the concentration of Late Bronze Age metalwork from the Tay between Perth and Mugdrum Island, and the swords in particular, were most probably votive offerings (Chapter 12; Cowie & Hall 2001, 8–11). In common with metalwork from other wet places such as bogs and lochs at this time, the material from the Tay, including at least six swords of differing types, two spearheads, socketed axes, and a socketed gouge and chisel, appears to have been deposited ritually. Much of this material is broadly comparable in date to the Carpow logboat, and intriguingly, included the very tools used to fashion the boat: socketed axes, a socketed gouge and chisels. While the mutually exclusive distribution of the swords and socketed axes (Chapter 12, pp 161–2) remains enigmatic, the overall assemblage, covering much of the Bronze Age, suggests that this lower part of the Tay, where the rivers join and become the estuary, was considered a special place. Such behaviour may well be founded in a practical reverence of these waterways, as much as in any symbolic or religious meaning that the water body may have had. The scale of the Tay estuary, river, and its tributaries, connecting land from the sea to the mountainous regions around Loch Tay, would have made it of great importance in terms of contact and trade. With the added economic value of the river and estuary itself, providing so many resources that were scarce or unavailable elsewhere, the possibility of a sacred dimension to these important waterways can be considered. Indeed, the small group of Middle Bronze Age, and potentially earlier material, may suggest that ritual deposition in the river was well-established by this period. The evidence suggests that in addition to being natural boundaries, perhaps indicating political divisions, the waters of the Earn and the Tay may have had a sacred meaning to Bronze Age people which transcended both of these.

## 13.3 Reconstructing the Carpow logboat

### *Land versus water in prehistory: the ancient Tay*

The simple fact that prehistoric people moved along rivers and waterways remarkably still struggles alongside the prevalent assumption that communication was predominantly land-based and dominated by long-distance routes along higher ground (Bradley 2007, 16). The fact is that little is known about terrestrial transport in Bronze Age Scotland, but while individuals may have crossed the heavily wooded landscape with relative ease, transporting heavy cargos by land over long distances would clearly have been problematic. The earliest preserved wheel from Scotland, made of ash and discovered in 1830 in the peat of Blair Drummond Moss (Piggott 1957) has been shown to be broadly comparable in date with Carpow, having produced a date of 1255–815 cal BC (Cowie & Shepherd 2003, 156). There has been little discussion of the cart or wagon that the wheel belonged to and how such vehicles may have been used, however. In particular, the question of what distances they would have travelled, and on what surfaces remains unanswered. The association of the find with undated lengths of wooden track, reminiscent of the trackways of Ireland (Raftery 1990) and the Somerset Levels (Coles & Coles 1986) has been noted (Cowie & Shepherd 2003, 157) and may offer some insight.

In prehistory, the Tay Estuary was clearly a major boundary, and may have marked the limit of cultural borders, as today. It was clearly also, paradoxically, a conduit for transport and communication both north-south, across the estuary, and east to west,

from the sea and deep inland along both Strathearn and up Strathtay. Key to the movement of coastal and estuarine watercraft is tidal range and flow, which are made up of two components: the astronomical effects of the moon, sun and planets, and to a lesser extent the weather. The astronomical tide is predictable in advance and the semi-diurnal pattern of two high and two low waters each day would have been well understood by prehistoric people, and would have afforded them multiple opportunities to move widely both along and across the estuary on a regular basis. The Tay Estuary is one of the most widely studied in the country, and numerous studies of flow patterns have been published, from the 19th century (Cunningham 1895) to modern numerical models (Gunn & Yenigun 1987). While the general trends of these studies remain relevant, the detail of flow patterns is likely to have changed considerably since the prehistoric period, as a result of factors such as dredging and land reclamation (Chapter 3, pp 21–3).

The location of Perth on the River Tay is at both the highest navigable point and, until Victorian times, the lowest bridging point (Bowler 2004, 8). The Tay is tidal as far upstream as the confluence of the River Almond, *c* 4km north of Perth, where the Roman fort of Bertha, located on the north bank of that confluence, would have received small river boats, while larger ocean-going vessels were unable to progress beyond Perth as a result of the shallowness of the river. This process continued through the medieval and post-medieval periods, as boats and ships increased in size, and resulted in the eclipsing of Perth by Dundee which provided much easier access for larger ships. On the south shore of the estuary, only *c* 1km south-east of logboat site, the Severan-period Roman fortress of Carpow was accessed by large vessels, acting as a transhipment point and logistics base. It may have functioned alongside a small site, often interpreted as a temporary camp, at St Madoes on the opposite (north) shore of the estuary, which could be a fortified harbour site (Woolliscroft & Hoffman 2006, 147). It is possible that, to some degree, these parameters, including tidal extent and amplitude, and river width and depth, reflect restraints as relevant to prehistoric boats as Roman and medieval ones.

The cartographic and historical accounts indicate large-scale change to the banks and bathymetry of the estuary beginning in the mid-18th century and with increasing impact until the early 20th century. The overall effect of the extensive improvements was to speed the flow of the Tay (Chapter 3, p 24), by constraining it within a narrowed channel, and removing small islands with associated back channels and inlets. The reclamation by embankment, for example, at Parkhill, to the east of Newburgh, would have reduced the area within which floodwater could be dissipated, thus speeding the seasonal flow downstream to a similar degree. Probably more significantly, the widespread land drainage works, and presumably also the reduction or removal of the remaining peat cover, that characterised this area of advanced agricultural development, may be assumed to have rendered the regime significantly more variable between seasons, by speeding the flow of rainwater from agricultural land into the river. The current increased propensity of the Perth area to flooding, as result of forestry planting and peat reduction in the Upper Tay area reflects the same process. As a result, in tidal terms, the prehistoric Tay would have been a slower, gentler, watercourse, fringed with much softer and less definable boundaries between water and land. Equally both the rivers Earn and the Tay would have been broader, shallower and less clearly defined than now apparent, flowing within extensive reed swamps which extended across most, if not all, of the widths of the two straths, as defined by the hills on each side. The heavy nature of the carse on both sides of the rivers suggests a general similarity with the 'alluvial', or 'silt', fen that forms the northern part of the English fenland (Godwin 1978 *passim*). In their pre-drained form, the floodplains and river fringes would have supported a much more diverse fauna and flora than now, with salmon as a major element during the migration season.

### Parameters of operation

As a large and utilitarian artefact, we can infer much about how the logboat operated, however, its real value is as a catalyst for discussion of what it was used for, and life in the Late Bronze Age in the area more generally. As reconstructed it was *c* 10m long, with an average width and height of *c* 0.8m and just under 0.6m respectively. It would have weighed in the region of 1,300kg to 1,700kg, depending on the degree to which the green oak seasoned over time (Chapters 7 and 8), and was fashioned from a single oak tree, probably on the Tay Estuary or in the lower Strathearn area. With a volume of timber of *c* 1.6m³, it would have had an internal volume, up to the sheerline, of *c* 3.5m³. The resulting unladen freeboard (the distance between the water and the sheerline of the boat) would have been in the region of 350mm.

With a minimum safe freeboard, of around 150mm, and based on an average height of 1.8m and weight of 70kg, it is estimated that the boat could have carried a crew of up to 14, sitting in single file and paddling on alternate sides of the boat (Appendix II), although of course it could have carried fewer more comfortably. It is reasonable to suggest as many as 12 inactive passengers. With a similar freeboard, it is estimated that the boat could have a carried between *c* 750kg to *c* 900kg of cargo, again depending on the degree to which the green oak seasoned over time. The performance calculations for the reconstructed vessel suggest that it could, theoretically, have reached a maximum speed of around 7.5 knots (Appendix II), although if possible this would only have been achievable for short periods. The theoretical approach to performance must also be tempered with the more pragmatic considerations of tidal power: the boatmen would have certainly used the tide to carry the vessel, which would dictate departure and arrival times. While the theoretical maximum speed is impressive, Carpow appears to have been constructed for volume, not speed.

It would have taken a team of as many as ten boatbuilders, with fewer numbers at times, about 20 days to manufacture the boat, representing a considerable investment in time and labour. It is clear that the boat required a number of repairs and alterations to prolong its life (Chapter 5, p 64 and pp 80–6); an indication of the value of the vessel once made. Carpow was probably one of many such boats operating in the lower Strathearn and Tay Estuary however, and this must be borne in mind in the following discussion. Having ascertained, as far as possible, the parameters of the logboat in terms of how it would have operated, the questions remain: what was it used for, and where? The geographical extent in which the boat would have been used along with options for the *modus operandi* of the boat, whether as a working boat for fishing and wildfowling, a barge or ferry for transporting cargo and people, or as a prestige warrior vessel, are considered below.

### Where was the boat used? Estuary, river or both?

The sizeable group of recorded logboats from the Tay Estuary (Chapter 9) reflects the suitability of this type of craft to the shallow sheltered waters that existed here. The Carpow boat was probably less stable than many of its flat-bottomed contemporaries, and logboats of this size, unlike modern canoes, have limited manoeuvrability (Chapter 8, pp 121–2). While logboats were not sea-going vessels, the relative instability of Carpow would also have constrained its use within the estuary itself, although the degree to which different waters were utilised would naturally depend very much on tidal and weather conditions. It is probable that the vessel would have generally hugged the land and shallow waters around the estuary. Voyages across open water, such as across the full width of the estuary or in the coastal region beyond the Tayport Narrows, if conducted at all, could only have occurred in calm weather and when tides allowed, for example, in slack water or during favourable ebb or flood tide. The areas around the estuary in which the boat would have been sufficiently stable are: the head of the estuary (around Carpow Bank), along the Carse of Gowrie and the north Fife coast, and, possibly, the crossing at the Tayport Narrows (Fig 173). In addition to nearshore activity on the estuary, it is reasonable to assume that the boat was used on both the rivers Tay and Earn to at least their tidal limits (at Inveralmond and Kirkton of Mailer respectively) and possibly further. In the case of the Tay, while the river is tidal as far as Inveralmond, the shallow waters at Perth itself may have been a constraining factor with Moncreiffe Island, just to the south of Perth, perhaps being a more realistic limit for activity. Indeed, as the historic maps evidence suggests there would have been a network of small islands and creeks between Carpow and Perth (Chapter 3, pp 21–4), which would have provided rich and varied opportunities for fishing and wildfowling.

The importance of the use of tides by the boat (Chapter 8, p 122) cannot be over-stressed. Given the strength of tidal currents in the estuary, and the rivers, it is very probable that the helmsman would use the action of the tide to his favour (as the project team did when refloating the excavated boat and towing it downstream on a spring ebb tide). Slack water would offer the potential to move around the estuary with

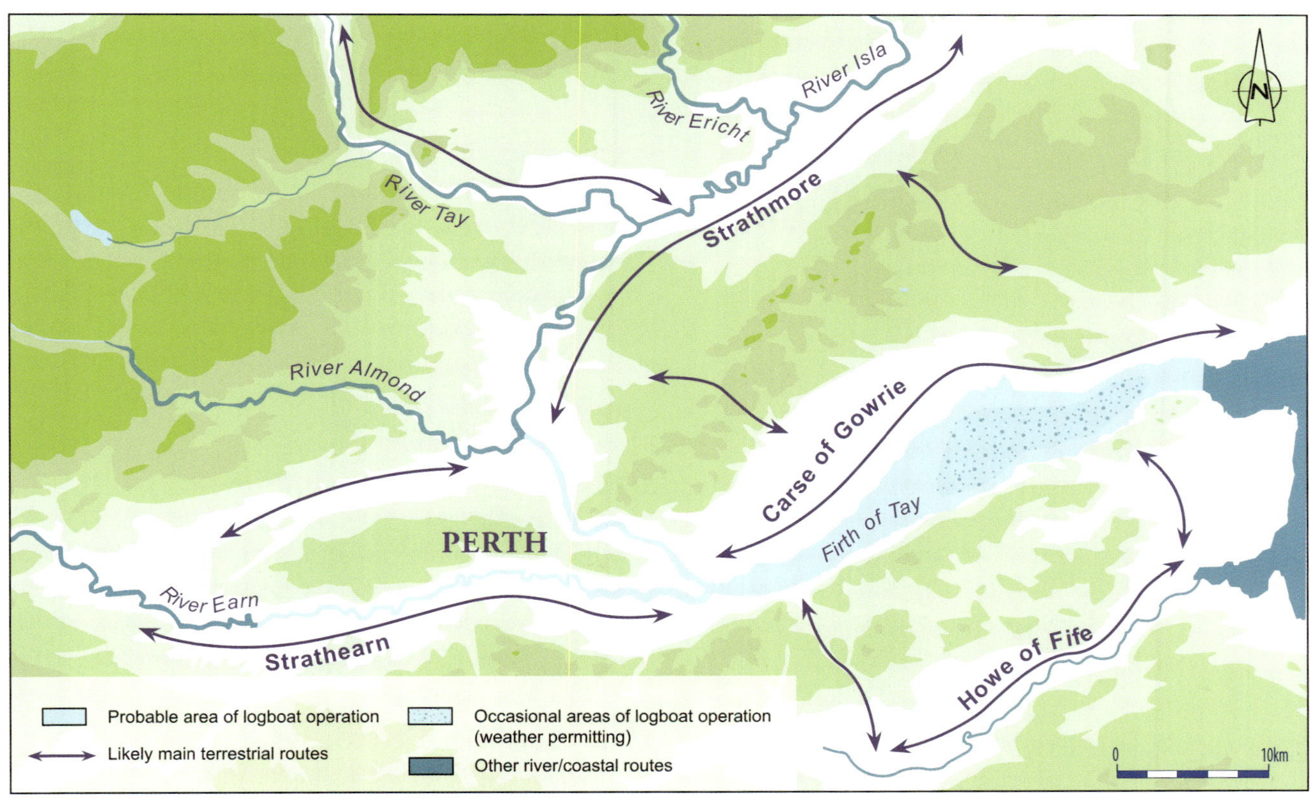


*Figure 173*
A map showing the probable areas of activity of the logboat, along with important terrestrial routes in the area © Crown copyright and database right (2009). All rights reserved. Ordnance Survey Licence number 100016971

more freedom, in any direction. Flood and ebb tides would provide a largely naturally powered journey upstream and downstream respectively, requiring the crew to mainly steer the vessel rather than propel it. Attempting to propel the vessel against a strong tidal flow would have been futile, and conversely a maximum speed, if desired, would have involved paddling in the same direction as the tide.

The concept of a 'maritime cultural landscape' – the view of the land from the sea, as much as from a terrestrial perspective – has been widely explored (eg Cooney 2003 *passim*), and one approach to studying the relationship between the littoral and boatmen has involved the identification of key coastal locations where beneficial physical characteristics, such as favourable tides and sheltered beaching and mooring locations, indicate transit points (Wilkes 2007). At this scale of study, the Tay Estuary would feature as a 'coastal node' on the east coast of Scotland, along with the Firth of Forth, Eden Bay and so on. At a more local level, however, key sites for contemporary shipping can be identified in the Tay Estuary and its associated water-routes, including, for example, the Tayport Narrows, Mugdrum Island and the confluence of the rivers Tay and Earn. In addition, many of the more general physical characteristics of the watercourses and the surrounding landscape that would have been experienced by the logboat's crew will have changed little and notable landmarks, such as unusual hilltops, bends in rivers and creeks and inlets around islands, would have been intimately known by the boatmen and used as navigational aids to well-used routes.

### Other boats in use

As artefacts, logboats are relatively unusual in that they are inherently constrained in size and form, being made through reduction from a single parent log. This may have been restrictive in Scotland where oak (*Quercus* sp), the timber pre-eminent among the surviving examples, is at the limit of its range and so prone to limited growth. It is important to consider how Carpow may have fitted in with other contemporary vessels operating in the area, and question whether logboats were even the predominant vernacular watercraft. The reality is that there would undoubtedly have been many smaller craft than Carpow in use in the area, probably taking many forms from much smaller logboats, or dug-out canoes, to skin and possibly even reed built vessels, ranging in size from between *c* 2–10m in length, with the smaller craft being more common

on the rivers. McGrail (1998, 163–72) has summarised the characteristics of small reed craft ('bundle boats' and 'rafts') emphasising their low cost, portability and simplicity of manufacture. More recently, Mac Philib (2008) has described the use of timber-framed reed boats (*cliath thulca*) around the upper River Shannon, in the Irish midlands, well into the 20th century AD. These were built of bulrushes (known locally as 'reeds') by non-specialists and used both for fishing and transport. Even more simple forms have been documented, such as at Enniskillen, Co Fermanagh, where, in the early 19th century, there was noted '… a man crossing to his fishing station, with no better mode of conveyance than a large bundle of rushes, on which he sat, moving it along by means of a small paddle' (quoted Mac Philib 2008, 603).

At the other end of the scale, it is possible that the Tay also saw much larger and more capacious sewn-plank boats, evidenced in Britain at this time through 11 examples from the Humber region, the Severn Estuary and Dover. They are all of oak and range in date from *c* 1900 cal BC to *c* 400 cal BC, and include the Ferriby boats (Wright 1990), Brigg (McGrail 1981) and Kilnsea (van de Noort *et al* 1999) examples from the Humber region, Caldicot (Nayling & Caseldine 1997; Nayling & McGrail 2004) and the Dover boat (Clark 2004c). Redating of the Humber examples has shown that they include the earliest known boats from north-west Europe (van de Noort 2004, 91), and they no doubt developed from the long-established tradition of logboat manufacture in Europe, which was already at least 6,000 years old by the time that the Carpow vessel was made (Chapter 1, pp 1–2). Indeed, the sewn-plank boats continued to share many characteristics in terms of manufacture, but importantly offered increased volume and stability. For example, the reconstructed Ferriby 1 would be 15.4m in length and have a 2.6m maximum breadth, able to carry a cargo of up to 5.5 tonnes. Within a broadly similar date range as Carpow are Dover (*c* 1550 cal BC) and Brigg (c 800 cal BC), and while debate continues as to the degree to which these larger boats were sea-going, they would clearly have offered the capacity for the transportation of much larger cargoes and numbers of passengers across greater distances.

### Who built the boat? The question of specialists

The question of specialisation is critical for vessels the size of Carpow where a team of five or six, and possibly as many as ten to 12 at some stages, may have worked on manufacture (Chapter 7, p 110). Building the boat

*Figure 174*
A 19th-century view of the Tay, taken from *Sketches of Scenery in Perthshire* by D O Hill (1821), with Kinnoull Hill, showing a variety of boat types working the water (A K Bell Library, Local Studies Department)

may have been undertaken by an extended family, possibly with additional support required at times. The main question is whether the level of expertise involved for a boat like Carpow required specialist advisors or craftsmen. As outlined above, there would certainly have been many smaller craft in use in the area, from reed and skin vessels to smaller logboats. These smaller craft of up to *c* 5m were probably constructed by individuals from within one family unit and the techniques for constructing boats of this scale is likely to have been widely known to people living on the edges of the estuary and along the rivers, for which the use of watercraft would have been an everyday experience. At the other extreme, one can envisage the larger sewn-plank boats, such as Ferriby, Brigg and Dover requiring a higher level of cooperation, at least on the level of several extended families that might translate to a larger local political unit (Clark 2004d, 4–6). Not only is the scale of the operation and the resources and manpower required significantly increased, however: the complexity of design and far more complicated wood-working techniques required suggests the need for specialist master boat-builders, who would have spent most, if not all, of their time working with boats, if not solely building them.

While the manufacture of Carpow would clearly have been a smaller operation, it is possible that specialist craftsmen, like those in charge of the manufacture of the sewn-plank boats, were called in for the more complex stages of construction, involving the more unusual tools of the recently expanded Late Bronze Age toolkit. The existence of specialist craftsmen and highly skilled woodworkers, with a new range of specialist tools, can be seen in a variety of surviving artefacts and in a hoard from Loughbown, Co Galway. This consisted of a socketed bronze axe head, a socketed bronze gouge, a narrow tanged chisel and a broad tanged and has been interpreted as the toolkit of such a specialist worker, and gives insight into the range of tools used (Eogan 2007). For example, the fashioning of the stern and the insertion of the transom may have required some advice and guidance, while the more basic hollowing out process – a technique unchanged since the Neolithic and before involving wooden edges and mallets – could have been carried out by non-specialists. Irrespective of who built a large logboat such as Carpow, the scale of the raw materials used and the investment of labour required, must have made it fairly notable compared to many of the more ephemeral contemporary smaller craft.

### Who used the boat?

The question of specialism permeates into the use of the boat. It is possible that the boatmen also subsistence farmed and that the boat was only part of their life. The Old Statistical Account for Newburgh notes that in the 18th century, the population of the burgh were effectively both fishermen and weavers, and shifted the emphasis of their activities according to the seasons and conditions (OSA 1791–99 viii, 180). It also seems reasonable, however, to assume that running a ten-metre working boat could be a full-time job regardless of whether the boat was tasked to a single function, as fishing boat or ferry, or employed on a variety of tasks. It is fair to suggest that the boatmen lived in the lower reaches of Strathearn or the Tay, or on the estuary itself, most probably within walking distance of where the boat was moored. Small jetties and trackways, similar to contemporary examples found on the Essex coast (Wilkinson & Murphy 1995 *passim*), would have provided easy and safe access from dry ground to the water.

### Other uses of the wildwood resource

The use of a large wildwood oak for the hull of Carpow indicates that such woodland still existed in the area, despite the introduction early metal axes well over 1,000 years before. There would have been numerous uses for large oak timbers and the size of the log used for Carpow can be compared with the recorded diameters of logs used in heavy timber construction revealed by excavation. Typically, timbers used in such structures as Neolithic long barrows, later prehistoric and Early Historic fort defences, and medieval and later waterfront works have a maximum diameter of no more than *c* 0.5m. There are exceptions however, such as the 'prepared timbers' of exceptional size within the massive Neolithic 'house' at Balbridie, Aberdeenshire (Fairweather & Ralston 1993, 314) and within the long barrow at Haddenham, Cambridgeshire (Evans & Hodder, 2006). At the latter, a turf long barrow was found to cover a 'mortuary house' or 'burial chamber' of similar form to that of a megalithic chambered tomb, but using large timber baulks in place of stone slabs. These were apparently of oak (*Quercus* sp) throughout; the surviving timbers included planks up to 4m long, 1.3m broad and 0.25m thick in the mortuary structure, and split oak trunks measuring up to 1.2m in diameter in both the mortuary structure and the façade (*ibid*, 117, fig 3.40 and 139, fig 3.48). The recorded presence of post-pipes, which apparently contained substantial timbers, in the mortuary structure at Wayland's Smithy, Oxfordshire (Whittle 1991, 70) further indicates the potential value in this context of a compilation of the sizes and species of the large timbers recorded in structural contexts across British prehistory. The exceptional parent log of the Hasholme logboat, estimated to measure 5.4m in girth and so about 1.7m in diameter (Millett & McGrail 1987, 106), puts both the scale of the above examples, and Carpow, in some context. Indeed, the fact that a spiral grained tree was used for Carpow might be a subtle indicator that the very best trees were being reserved for other purposes, such as for planked boats, and radially cleft boards in terrestrial monuments.

## 13.4  What was it used for?

A rich and varied array of natural resources would have been abundant in the Tay Estuary in prehistoric times. The varied estuarine environments that survive today, including the extensive inter-tidal mudflats and sandbanks, and large areas of reed-beds with smaller pockets of salt marsh, support an internationally important assemblage of wintering waterfowl. Further, while the Tay is renowned as a salmon river, it is also has plentiful supplies of sea-trout and other fish. Prior to the littoral improvements around the estuary, the more extensive and diverse habitats of prehistory would have provided bountiful supplies of fish, wildfowl, shellfish and mammals (Chapter 3, p 26). While the logboat was most probably a working-vessel, there are a number of ways in which it may have operated and not all of these necessarily relate to collecting resources. Its capacity to transport cargo and people is an equally possible function; while there is archaeological evidence for the use of logboats to carry materials, their ability to transport people and possibly livestock remains compelling. It is also possible, however, that the boat was a prestige warrior vessel, built to impress and for ceremony.

### Fishing and wildfowling

The Tay is renowned for its salmon and the economic importance of this resource is both widely reported and illustrated by the numerous fishing lodges along the Tay and the lower reaches of the Earn. For example, the Old Statistical Account for Newburgh notes that 'the Tay furnishes great quantities of excellent salmon, the fishing of which has, especially of late years, become a considerable source of wealth to all who have property in the river' (OSA 1791–99 viii, 172).

Fish would undoubtedly have been a major resource to be exploited through a variety of methods including line- and net-fishing, and probably the use of inter-tidal fish weirs.

Small-scale line- or, more probably, net-fishing requires only simple equipment and no specific adaptation of the vessel, however, a net-fishing related function for the sheerline holes on Carpow is arguably as feasible as any of the other possible explanations. Equally the logboat could provide a mobile and secure platform from which to carry out sweep netting (Fig 174), allowing a variety of locations to be harvested when conditions were suitable. There is understandably no archaeological evidence for the above methods of fishing. The use of fish weirs is, as yet, not demonstrated on the Tay Estuary although they do have an extensive distribution and are documented at numerous similar estuaries throughout Britain and Ireland. Fish weirs consist of strategically positioned stationary fish traps, comprising two, or more, artificial walls in a V- or

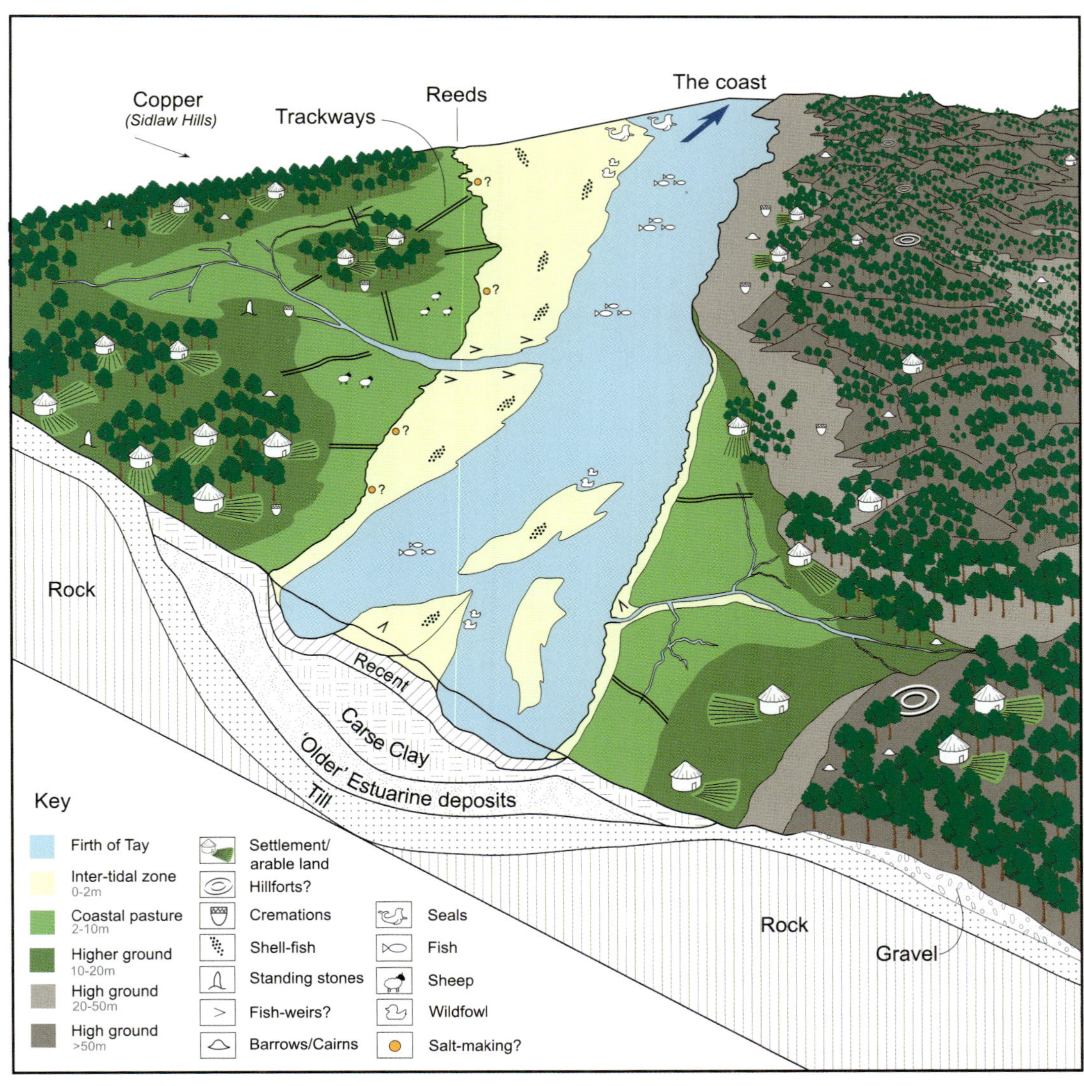


*Figure 175*
A schematic section through the Tay Estuary (looking east) illustrating how the geology and topography of the area resulted in various ecotones, with diverse natural resources, and determined human land-use. Note the scale of marsh and open water on the Carse of Gowrie, which has been subsequently reclaimed and drained

*Figure 176*
A reconstructed scene showing the Carpow boat sweep netting from Mugdrum Island with the prominent Clatchard Craig, now quarried away, dominating the horizon above what is now Newburgh (artist: David Hogg)

L-shaped configuration, with a trap at the narrow point, on the seaward side, designed to collect fish during ebb tides. The traps are then regularly accessed at low tide to collect the fish. They can be made from stone and/or wood, with the latter consisting of wattle panels secured to timber uprights, with basketry made from small round-woods. Examples of these have been recorded in similar estuaries on the Essex coast, where they were found to date to the Saxon period and constructed on an impressive scale, having walls in excess of 100m in length and traps areas of around 5–10m, which would clearly have collected high volumes of fish (Strachan 1998). Indeed, similar studies of Early Historic and medieval fish weirs exist from almost all areas of coast with suitable estuaries (eg Godbold & Turner 1994; Hale 2005), usually with monastic associations.

Some of the earliest proposed inter-tidal fish traps are from Quarr beach on the Isle of Wight and date to

the Neolithic (Tomalin *et al* forthcoming). Located in key tidal locations, they survive as V-shaped settings of upright posts which are thought to have held large conical traps like those set at the points of fish weirs. Similar settings of upright posts have tentatively been interpreted as fish traps of Bronze Age date on the Essex coast (Wilkinson & Murphy 1995 *passim*; Wilkinson *et al* forthcoming). While these prehistoric examples are much smaller than the Early Historic and medieval weirs, they do illustrate that the technology was well established and employed in British estuaries well before the Bronze Age.

Accessing fish weirs by foot at low tide would have been possible though transporting the large quantities of fish trapped would be difficult, particularly on muddy flats, and the use of small boats at slack water would offer a far easier way to transport the catch. This relationship between logboats and fish weirs is suggested at a lake in Der Andresee, Germany where

174

both fish weirs, the oldest from that country and dating from *c* 2671 cal BC, and numerous logboats of various periods were recovered (Leineweber & Lübke 2007). Accessing inter-tidal fish weirs may also have provided access to shellfish at the lower reaches of the inter-tidal zone. Both these activities would most likely have involved both basketry and wattle making, and it is possible that the numerous round-woods and carpentry waste from Context 106 within the Carpow vessel related to these activities (Chapter 5, p 43). The lack of recorded fish weirs on the Tay Estuary may be in part due to the reduction of the inter-tidal deposits in the 19th century (Chapter 3, p 24), but it is equally possible that examples await discovery.

The Tay Estuary has long been noted for its variety and frequency of wildfowl (NSA x 1834–45, 841 and 1121), and while there are no records for the area that indicate the intensive exploitation of this resource through duck decoy ponds, as in parts of England (Payne-Gallwey 1886), non-commercial wildfowling has always existed, and indeed, is still popular today. Another possible resource for food, oil and skins is the seal. Both grey seals (*Halichoerus grypus*) and common seals (*Phoca vitulina*) are common visitors to the estuary today, particularly around the mouth of the estuary and Abertay Sands, and they were ubiquitous at least until the 19th century AD. Local newspaper accounts of seal hunting in the lower reaches of the estuary continue into this period, accounting for the sandbank still named 'Dog Bank' (Fothergill pers comm), however, by the mid-19th century, the sale of five large seals in Perth was described as a 'curiosity' (*Perthshire Advertiser*, 27 June 1850). In prehistory, the oil and skins of seals would have been a resource not easily obtained from surrounding coastal environments.

## Salt

The extraction of salt from sea water in the British Isles is first recognised in the Late Bronze Age at Mucking, Essex, through the survival of *briquetage*, the debris of clay-lined tanks used in the boiling process (Barford 1990, 81). An important preservative in prehistory, salt was extracted from the sea through the open pan process, where sea water was collected and then boiled in containers to produce a solid block of salt. In the Bronze Age, it is likely natural pools were exploited, and gradually modified, to collect sea water, with shallow artificial clay lined tanks being introduced in

the Iron Age and Roman periods (Fawn *et al* 1990). Medieval salt extraction is well documented on the Lincolnshire coast (Hallam 1960) and from the post-medieval periods from a number of major estuaries around the British Isles (de Brisay & Evans 1975). While the earliest records of salt production on the Fife coast come from Dysart in the 15th century AD (Sibbald 1803, 322), it is recognised that established salt industry on the Forth was aided by the introduction of coal as early as the 13th century AD (Murdoch & Lewis 1999, 5). The coal and salt industries continued hand in hand, often operated by the same owners, over subsequent centuries becoming of considerable import in the post-medieval period, as at St Monans (Lewis *et al* 1999). While there is no direct evidence for prehistoric salt-working on the Tay, it must remain a possibility, given that the conditions of the coast would appear ideal: extensive, flat, south facing, inter-tidal areas, with a plentiful supply of Carse clay for the production of *briquetage* if the open pan method was used, in addition to solar evaporation in artificial pools and tanks. Logboats would have proved very useful for transporting salt from such sites, located as they were, in the upper reaches of the tidal limit. The alternative would have been to transport the blocks of salt across salt marsh, reed-beds and muddy creeks which, even with the provision of timber walkways would have been an onerous task.

### *Other possible cargos*

In addition to goods collected from source, such as fish, wildfowl, shellfish, seal, and, possibly, salt, the ability of the boat to transfer heavy objects, of any kind, significant distances with minimal effort, has to be considered as a primary function. Water transport has been identified as a significant factor in the development of the Iron Age Glastonbury lake village, constructed in the Somerset Levels within a comparable environment to that of the area of the Late Bronze Age inner Tay Estuary. For the Glastonbury Village, it has been suggested that some 1,000 tonnes of construction clay was brought from at least 1km away, Lias (stone) rubble from a greater distance, and selected hearth slabs weighing up to 50kg each from sources 10km away. The only available transport was 'raft, logboat, mud sled or peat sled, depending on the conditions at the time of need' (Coles & Minnitt 1995, 115). The Shardlow logboat, with its load of quarried stone is probably the clearest example of a cargo from a logboat. The five large blocks of Bromsgrove sandstone, along with many smaller pieces, from a few kilometres upstream from the findspot, have been interpreted as being ferried to the site to strengthen a causeway that crossed the River Trent.

The Carpow vessel, with a crew of two and carrying a maximum cargo of around one tonne, could have transported significant quantities of materials over relatively short periods of time. Cargoes transported around the estuary, and perhaps more importantly to and from the estuary inland along either river, could have included estuarine products, as described above, as well as stone, timber, wheat grain, reeds, peat or carcasses. In this simplified model, the boat would transport surplus resources from one area to the other, with coastal and estuarine products transported inland, and upland and inland commodities returned downstream, with the additional possibility of transporting goods from outwith the immediate environs of the estuary farther inland (Fig 175; Figs 178 and 179).

The question of longer distance movement of materials should also be considered, however. The Tay's basic waterways from the coast inland along the rivers were part of a much lager network of coastal and riverine routes off-shooting from the east coast and branching out inland from the major estuaries, such as the Thames, the Humber and the Firth of Forth, ultimately making contact with the near-Continent (Bradley 2007, 18, fig 1.7). Such a network is only surprising from a terrestrially based view of communication and transport and would have been completely familiar to 19th-century fishermen operating along the east coast from Shetland to Dover.

One ultimate material requiring transportation in the period is bronze itself. There was clearly significant movement of the raw materials – copper and tin – from the Middle Bronze Age, and the larger sewn-plank boats, like Dover, may well have been involved in these connections (Clark, 2004d, 6). Copper is available locally (Dunwell & Ralston 2008, 52); for example, at Milton Den, near Abernyte in the Sidlaw Hills, *c* 10km from the Carpow Bank, a copper mine was considered in the late 18th century AD, although

*Figure 177*
Carpow as a ferry, crossing the River Tay beneath Kinnoull Hill near the site of where Elcho Castle stands today. A ferry crossed from here to Seggieden during the medieval period and into the 19th century AD (artist: David Hogg)

the quality of the ore was found subsequently to be too poor (OSA 1791–99 ix, 153). Generally, however, the raw materials for bronze required importing from the far west of Britain, Ireland or the Continent (Nash Briggs 2003, fig 1), and it is possible to envisage larger plank-sewn vessels, travelling greater distances, hugging the coasts, and decanting materials to be transported farther inland on rivers by logboats like Carpow. Once again, descriptions from the Statistical Accounts, in this case of recent shipping, may contain echoes of more ancient practices:

> As far up as Newburgh, the Tay admits vessels of 500 tons burden; but above the confluence with the Earn, beyond which Perth is situated, vessels of 200 tons

burden, when deep laden, proceed with difficulty. Vessels, however, of about 90 or 100 tons (in which the trade with Perth is usually carried on), easily make the shore of Perth; and when larger vessels are employed in that trade, part of their cargo is distributed among lighters, on their arrival at the shore of Newburgh (OSA 1791–99 viii, 172).

This practice continued into the mid-19th century when larger boats would unload part of their cargo at Newburgh before proceeding up river.

### Carpow as a ferry

Finally, given the key location of Carpow and the associated rivers for ferries, operating until the 19th

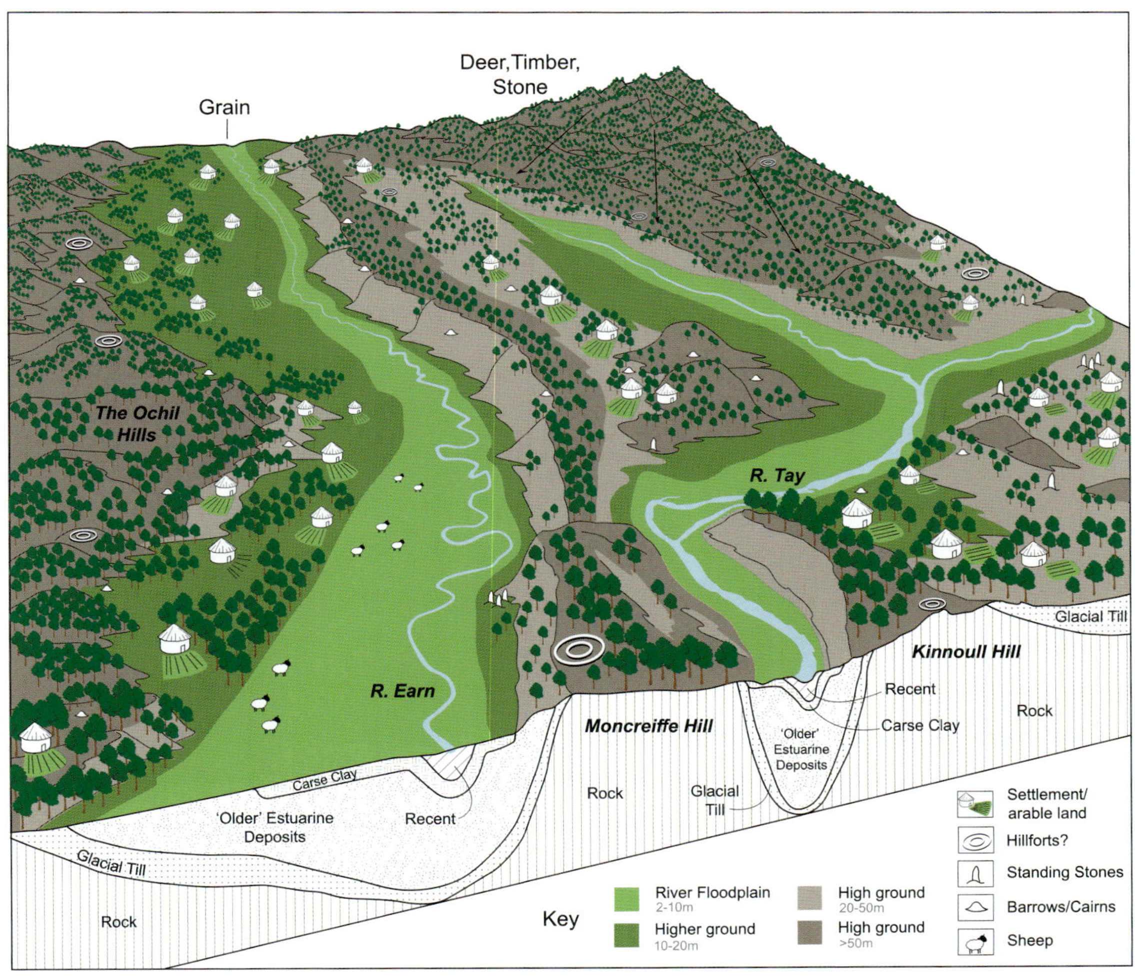


*Figure 178*
A schematic section through lower Strathearn and Strathtay (looking west) illustrating the various environments, natural resources and human activities

century AD (Chapter 9, p 128 and 131), it is possible that the boat operated as a ferry instead of, or in addition to, carrying cargo (Fig 177). The boat could have transported as many as 12 people safely, and this simple function may have been the boat's primary occupation. It is striking that the findspot of the boat is in such close proximity to the Ferryfield of Carpow (see Fig 23) and what would have been one of the busiest crossing points in the region in the medieval period.

### *Ritual*

While there may be problems associated with the taphonomy of the Late Bronze Age metalwork from the Tay (Chapter 12, pp 161–2) there is clearly a genuine concentration of material from between Perth and Mugdrum Island. The fact that the river here was the focus of ritual activity associated with the deposition of swords and other metalwork should come as no surprise, given the importance of this mighty river, into which most of modern Perthshire drains. Indeed, the ritual importance of the Tay may have been connected to its direct economic value and importance in terms of communication and transport. It is understandable that the significant bend of the river to the south of Perth at Moncreiffe Island, set dramatically under the near vertical cliffs beneath Kinnoull Hill, was a focus of interest. Historic maps indicate that pre-Improvement there were many more small islands with reeds and shallows (Chapter 3, pp 21–4), and the significance of this stretch may be that it is where the river ends, meets it partner, the Earn, and becomes the open estuary. The ritual and funerary monuments of the period in this area appear to be set on the edge of what would be lower-lying, probably much wetter, land in prehistory (Fig 161). In terms of stone circles, stone settings and standing stones, the evidence for these is concentrated more around lower Strathtay and Glenalmond, above Perth, with the notable exceptions of Moncreiffe stone circle and the linear stone setting at St Madoes, while the distribution of cist graves, cremations, cairns and barrows is less easily read.

While no direct association can be made, a possible ritual aspect to Carpow should be considered, and there are examples where logboats clearly have been ritually deposited. For example, at Fiskerton, Lincolnshire a votive deposition has been interpreted for one of two logboats recently excavated at an Iron Age timber causeway. The vessel was apparently deposited in pristine condition, set between two clusters of posts and pegged into position. A large assemblage of other artefacts interpreted as votive offerings were discovered, including a sword, an iron dagger, a spear, numerous pieces of bronze and a socketed axe, the latter being a skeuomorph of Late Bronze Age examples (Field *et al* 2003; Field & Parker-Pearson 2004). With a ritual focus demonstrated for this section of the Tay it is possible, if not likely, that logboats were involved, even if not as a primary function. Indeed, given the example of Fiskerton, then deliberate sinking of the vessel, at some point, cannot be ruled out.

### 13.5 Final thoughts

The significance of the Carpow vessel is not only its early date and good state of preservation, but the fact that it is one of a very few Scottish logboats to be recorded, recovered and conserved using modern techniques of archaeology and conservation. In addition to its contributions to logboat studies, this artefact has allowed a long overdue review of our understanding of the Late Bronze Age of the area, and in particular the relationship between the land and the waterways. We can only consider the possible options for how the natural resources of the estuary were exploited and distributed, both at a subsistence level and as a generator of 'wealth', however, increasing our understanding of such questions aids debate around whether the estuary promoted or inhibited social, political and economic unity or diversity.

Equally, we will never be sure how the boat was used, and are again left with a series of options to consider. It could have been a specialist craft concentrating on one of many possible functions: a fishing and wildfowling boat; a barge to transport cargos large distances; or a ferry carrying people across fixed ferry points or perhaps operating more broadly as a sort of river taxi. It is possible that as a multi-tasking general working boat, it was used for a combination of these functions, perhaps at different times of year. Alternatively her use changed over time: for example, from a barge in her early years of life while in prime condition, followed by a later period of time served as a ferry once repairs were required and the boat was fit only for shorter journeys with a lighter load. The reality of Carpow is very probably a pragmatic one, as a simple working vessel, of middling size operating as part of a busy fleet of vessels of various sizes, with the backdrop of the ritual importance of the rivers.

*Figure 179*

The River Earn, as it may have appeared *c* 1000 cal BC, showing the logboat transporting a full cargo upstream near what is now Forteviot. The familiar landmark of Craig Rossie in the top left of the picture dominates the landscape, and settlement, indicated by smoke, on the higher ground around what is now Dunning (artist: David Hogg)

The helmsman and crew of the logboat would have been more than aware than most about the power and importance of the two rivers and the estuary. Their lives depended on it and they would have felt its power daily as it effortlessly transported them from one destination to another. They were probably aware of the rituals of depositing metalwork, even if they were not carrying them out themselves. In the Bronze Age, however, a ritual dimension to life is likely to have infiltrated into every aspect of life, and even the very mundane tasks, as those proposed above would have involved associated rituals, arguably more so if the river was seen as sacred. So while perhaps it is unlikely that a simple boatman crewing the Carpow vessel would have deposited a broken sword, perhaps he witnessed, or contributed, to the ceremony this must have involved.

# Chapter 14

# Afterword: the wet, the dry and the in-between

PETER CLARK

## 14.1 Tales of the riverbank

The discovery and publication of the Carpow logboat is a huge contribution to the corpus of knowledge about mankind's relationship with the waters of the world in the distant past. Although many hundreds of ancient logboats have been discovered in Britain and Ireland, less than 20% have been scientifically dated, and less than 5% of those from Scotland (Lanting 2000, tables 1–2; fig 1). Of these only a fraction are prehistoric, but even this convenient categorisation masks the fact that they are separated by gulfs of time and space; close scrutiny reveals that our understanding of the construction and use of boats in prehistory is based on infinitesimal amounts of data, rarely recorded to modern professional standards. In this context, discoveries such as Carpow will remain of great significance for the foreseeable future.

My interest in the Carpow boat was piqued when the date of the vessel emerged in 2002; at 1130–970 cal BC it was a product of the Bronze Age, a period that has long been a focus of my own work. My involvement in the excavation, analysis and display of the Dover Bronze Age boat (*c* 1550 cal BC; Bayliss *et al* 2004) had made me very aware of the rarity and importance of such finds, and so I was delighted to be invited to speak on the Dover experience at the conference, entitled *Tales of the Riverbank: the Carpow Bronze Age Logboat in Context*, held at Abernethy in September 2007. I knew little about the find before the conference, but as the story of the discovery unfolded I experienced a burgeoning sense of delight. Those who have had the privilege of excavating prehistoric boats form a pretty select crew and I felt an instant camaraderie with the Carpow team as the images of mud, wet wood and electric pumps appeared on the screen. I was transported back to 1992 and the excavation of the Dover boat; a very different vessel found in completely different circumstances, but the similarities between the two projects resonate powerfully (Fig 180). By 2007 I was in the privileged position of having completed my work on the Dover boat (or so I thought; Clark 2008) and the vessel had been successfully excavated, conserved

and placed on display in a specially designed gallery at Dover Museum, along with the publication of a detailed monograph setting out the results of analysis by a large multi-disciplinary team over several years (Clark 2004a). David Strachan's team were only part way along their own odyssey of nautical archaeology, a voyage that will no doubt continue long after the publication of this volume.

The conference venue was situated on the southern bank of the River Tay, overlooking the findspot of Carpow. It is a stunningly beautiful and peaceful place, with the blue waters of the Tay meandering eastwards toward Dundee, alive with wildfowl and overshadowed by the green slopes of Kinnoull Hill on the opposite bank. The photographs of the excavation and recovery of the Carpow boat all had this glorious vista as their backdrop, and I reflected on the stark contrast between this and the noise, grime and pollution of the major road works in central Dover in 1992 when we first stumbled across the Dover Bronze Age boat (Fig 180). A major new road was being built to link the Eastern Docks of Dover with the newly constructed Channel Tunnel, some 10km to the west, and it cut right through the historic town.

## 14.2 The discovery of the Dover boat

This new dual carriageway effectively cut the citizens of Dover off from the seafront, and so a pedestrian underpass was planned to allow access from the town to the sea. This required the excavation of a 7m deep shaft for the insertion of a pump to keep the underpass dry; and this work was monitored by the Canterbury Archaeological Trust. It was midday on Monday 28 September 1992; the construction workers had temporarily ceased work for lunch. My friend and colleague Keith Parfitt seized the opportunity to inspect the shaft (which by now had reached a depth of 6m below modern street level) and clambered down the ladder. There, in the side of the hole dug for the de-watering sump, he found a 'thin band of wood' exposed in section, along with a 'carved, semi-circular fitting' and 'twisted fibre rope' (Parfitt 2004,

14). Keith remembered being shown similar features during a lecture he attended as an undergraduate by Ted Wright, describing his excavations of the first Bronze Age sewn-plank boat at Ferriby in North Yorkshire. Keith had found another. Immediately recognising the importance of the find, construction work was halted for the day, whilst a call to the head office in Canterbury alerted others to the discovery and 'phones began to ring as the news spread rapidly through the archaeological community and beyond. Keith and his team continued cleaning up the timbers through the day and by 9 o'clock that night the nature of the find had become clear; a substantial, largely

*Figure 180*
The Dover boat *in situ*; by complete coincidence, the second excavation neatly exposed the southern end of the boat (© Canterbury Archaeological Trust)

complete section of a prehistoric sewn-plank boat in a perfect state of preservation lay revealed at the bottom of the cramped (4m × 5m) shaft.

The next morning, the team continued the excavation and recording of the boat. The find lay below the water table, and pumps had to be running continually to cope with the water gushing through the sides of the sheet piling lining the sides of the shaft. A routine of work was established; a start at around 8:00 am working through to around 9:30–10:00 pm when the pumps were turned off; the boat was thus submerged every night in a metre or so of water which helped stop the timbers drying out. Remarkably, by 11:30 am the day after the discovery, a group of maritime archaeologists and conservation experts had

gathered at the site to discuss the best course of action, including Ted Wright. On his recommendation, it was agreed that the best way to salvage the vessel was to cut it into sections and remove the pieces by crane. The contractors agreed to allow us a further two days for our work.

On the third day, a press briefing and photo call was held at Dover Museum; with so many people eager to witness the boat being excavated, the bottom of the narrow shaft often became very crowded. This occasionally tested the patience of the excavation team who were very aware of the ticking clock; however, as the importance of the discovery began to sink home, a further three days were granted; we now had until Sunday to record and rescue the boat.

By Friday we had completed the recording of the vessel and were ready to cut the boat into sections and lift it out of the shaft. Dover Harbour Board had made available a crane and had also constructed a large water-filled holding tank in a nearby warehouse to receive the boat pieces. One of the contractor's staff cut the boat using a diamond-tipped rotary saw; there was much discussion about where we should make the cuts, though the guiding principle was to preserve as best we could the complex jointing between the planks (see below). Working alongside conservation experts from English Heritage, our first idea was to encase the timbers in polyurethane foam to protect them as they were manhandled onto a timber pallet ready for lifting (Fig 181). This did not prove very successful; the hardened foam obstructed our view of the plank as we tried to extricate the first boat piece from the suction of the underlying sediments, meaning that we might damage the boat piece without knowing it. Nevertheless, the first section of the boat was lifted out of the shaft at around 6:00 pm on Friday 2 October. Another drawback of the foam became apparent when we placed the boat piece in its water-filled holding tank. The foam was lighter than water, and so the boat piece simply bobbed around on the surface; we had to cut the foam away before the timbers could be completely immersed.

The next day the remaining part of the boat was cut into sections and lifting continued. We had abandoned the foam, but it still proved very difficult to free the boat timbers from the underlying sediments, and there was a great deal of trial and error finding an effective way of freeing the timbers without damaging them. In the end we undercut the underlying deposits with bare hands, water jets and metal rods, inserting plywood supports under the boat piece and dragging it to the lifting cradle with sediment still adhering to the bottom of the timbers. On Sunday the final recording of the shaft was undertaken, including the drawing of the cross-section of a part of the vessel that had been left *in situ* on the southern side of the shaft. This last piece was recovered on the morning of Monday 5 October; the contractors took charge of the shaft once more and concrete was poured into the base of the hole at midday.

*Figure 181*
Excavating the Dover boat; the first boat piece being manhandled on to a wooden pallet prior to lifting by crane (© Canterbury Archaeological Trust)

The weary diggers were not given much time to recover, however; on Friday 9 October the Department of Transport gave instructions to excavate a second shaft, immediately adjacent to the southern side of the first, with the sole purpose of recovering more of the boat. Late on Monday 12 October the timbers of the vessel were revealed; miraculously the second shaft neatly exposed the complete southern end of the vessel.

By now we were a little more accustomed to excavating prehistoric boats and more confident about how to go about things. It is hard to describe the exhilaration and tactile pleasure one feels when excavating such an object; working with wooden or plastic tools – often just with bare hands – one carefully peels backs the adhering sediments to reveal the timber itself, initially a beautiful golden honey-brown (the colour of fresh oak), that turned black in front of one's eyes in a matter of seconds (the result of ferrous ions reacting to residual tannins in the wood). Somehow the feel of organic finds like the boat timbers has a different quality to the usual staples of archaeological excavation – silts, sands, gravels, masonry, or stone. It was not enough to see the boat, it was important to touch it, to run one's fingertips over the beautifully preserved toolmarks, to feel the grain of the ancient oak. It is only now when I see the reassembled boat safely preserved in its display case behind 19mm thick toughened glass panels that I truly appreciate how privileged we were to be able to come into contact with the boat itself.

Recording and excavation was less frenetic in the second shaft, but we were still under some time pressure. Although from the start were given a reasonable window of opportunity to excavate the vessel (unlike the first shaft, when our deadline was extended intermittently), and in spite of the boat being submerged every night and the torrential rain that fell during the latter stages of the excavation, the boat timbers were visibly degrading before our eyes as each day passed. It was essential to get the boat into the holding tanks as quickly as possible. In the end, the whole operation took just nine days from the moment we first glimpsed the boat timbers until the last boat piece was lifted from the bottom of the shaft.

### 14.3 Aftermath: finding a way forward

Thus, on 20 October 1992, the exhausted excavation team could stand down and reacquaint themselves with their friends and families. Two days later a meeting was held between representatives of the Canterbury Archaeological Trust, English Heritage and the site contractors when the fateful decision was made not to sink a third shaft in an attempt to retrieve the northern end of the boat. Whatever the rationale behind this decision, it has proved most regrettable. To this day we have no idea how the northern end of the boat was closed or how long the original boat was; controversy and debate continues about the original form of the vessel to this day (eg Boon & van Rietbergen 2009; Coates 2005a; 2005b; Crumlin-Pedersen 2006; Fenwick 2006; 2007; Roberts 2006a; 2006b; Sanders 2007; Von der Porten 2006; Ward 2005). Otherwise the whole operation had been a great success despite the unexpected nature of the discovery, the uncertainty about the time allowed for the excavation, and the necessity to develop new methodologies of excavation, recording and salvage on a trial and error basis under extreme time pressure and under the eyes of the world's media. I was intensely proud of the achievement of all of those who worked on the Dover boat excavations, in difficult working conditions and perforce being reactive to the novel challenges that the project seemed to throw up on an almost daily basis. Nevertheless, at the conference in Abernethy I confess to a stab of envy as I listened to David Strachan's account of the conduct of the Carpow boat project from its discovery in 2001 up until its eventual salvage in 2006; a perfect model of professional archaeological planning and execution from evaluation to excavation, allowing the appropriate skilled personnel and specialist equipment to be assembled, to make provision for conservation, post-excavation analysis and display and most importantly to secure the funds necessary for the work. What more could we have done with Dover if we had had the luxury of time?

In late 1992, whilst we had rescued the boat from certain destruction, the way forward was far from clear. Although we were fairly confident that English Heritage would fund the post-excavation analysis, they quite rightly would not do so unless they were in receipt of a rigorous, detailed project design. However, although we had a substantial portion of a Middle Bronze Age sewn-plank boat in an astonishing state of preservation, none of us had any experience of dealing with such things. Indeed, the only person who could truly claim to be experienced in this field was Ted Wright, who was generous with valuable advice. Furthermore, we had seen the boat timbers start to degrade from the moment they were exposed to the air; whilst this hopefully would be minimised by their immersion in water in the holding tanks, it was imperative that the boat should be properly conserved. We assumed that conservation technology had greatly improved since the days of the Ferriby discoveries (the planks of Ferriby 1 are now so badly decayed they are not even on display); but what method should be used? And how could we fund the conservation? English Heritage was uncertain if they would be able to fund such an endeavour, particularly considering the potentially significant costs involved. Finally, from the moment of discovery, there an intense desire that the boat should be put on display in Dover, but this posed further challenges. The boat is a huge artefact, over 9m long and 2.3m broad that would need a specially built environmental case for

its display without overwhelming existing museum collections.

After extensive discussions with English Heritage, Dover Museum and others we decided to hold a 'study fortnight' in November 1992 when a large group of experts from many fields were invited to Dover to view the boat pieces and debate the way forward. This event proved very worthwhile, and the shape of a multi-disciplinary team to undertake the analysis of the vessel began to take form. Early in 1993 I was invited to head up the analysis team, which I gladly accepted. Although no expert on ancient boats or prehistory, the importance of the find and the assembled band of senior experts led me to believe I would hold a largely administrative role with little need to get 'hands on'. Needless to say, this did not turn out to be the case and the next ten years proved a demanding and exhilarating experience, steering the project through to publication whilst trying to maintain a holistic overview of the work of so many specialists from so many different fields of expertise.

## 14.4 Analysis of the Dover boat

We had recovered around 9.5m of the boat, 2.3m wide at its widest point, but cut into 32 pieces. Our first job was to create a 1:1 drawn record of each of the pieces, a task complicated by the requirement to prop each piece in the same position it was in the ground, so that a 'true plan' could be recorded (Fig 182). Supportive boxes were built for each piece so that they could be inverted and the adhering sediments removed from the underside and the outboard faces drawn. This also allowed for the design and manufacture of fibreglass cradles, custom built for each piece, which meant that the pieces could be moved more easily, lessening the potential for damage. At the same time we were able to study and record the rays and rings of the trees that the boat planks were made from, revealed in the cut edges of the boat pieces. This was to prove invaluable in understanding the compression of the planks and the position of the planks in their parent logs (Darrah 2004a; 2004b). After this long process (the primary recording took some eleven months), the arduous process of piecing together the individual plans could begin, so that for the first time we could see a detailed drawing of the entire section of the vessel (Fig 183). In essence, the boat remains consist of four planks, hewn from logs of huge, straight-grained oak trees (*Quercus* sp) without side branches, which must have originated in close set oak forests, with at least 11m between the

*Figure 182*
Recording the timbers; each boat piece was recorded at a scale of 1:1. Techniques such as three-dimensional laser scanning were not available in 1993 (© Canterbury Archaeological Trust)

transverse timbers and wedges hammered through the cleats and central rails. Curved side planks were stitched to the bottom of the boat with twisted withies of yew (*Taxus baccata*). These side planks also possess side cleats carved out of the solid wood. The timbers forming the end of the boat splay into a Y-shape, intricately carved from the main planks. This originally would have held a carved wooden board, reminiscent of a modern 'punt'. On the top of the curved side planks was another row of stitches, cut through in antiquity. There were clearly two further side planks, and the boat had been deliberately dismantled when abandoned. She had been made waterproof by pressing in a mixture of beeswax and animal fat into the stitch-holes and along the seams, where the stopping was overlain by pads of moss wadding, compressed and held in place by long thin laths of oak under the yew

basal buttresses and the first appearance of branches. Such trees are very rare in western Europe today. Two flat planks form the bottom, each carved out of a half log, leaving upstanding cleats and rails allowing its jointing with other boat timbers. These bottom planks were joined together along a central butt joint, with

stitches. The boat had clearly been used extensively. Tool marks on its bottom surface were differentially worn away, suggesting it had been beached regularly on a sand or gravel shore. The main timbers had split and were repaired by stitching wooden laths over the damage.

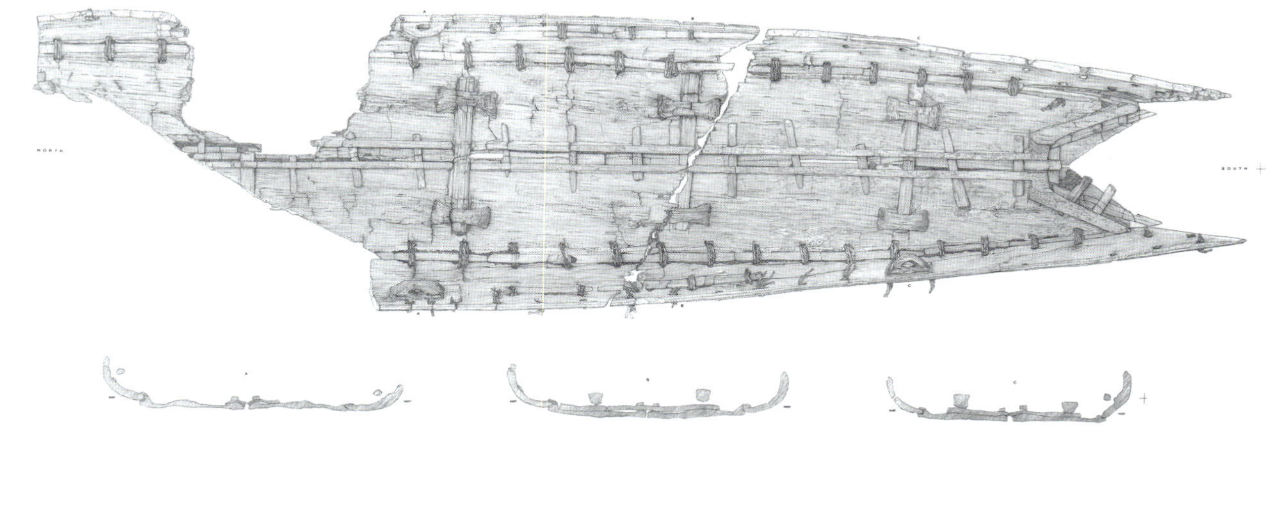

*Figure 183*
The plan of the Dover boat; this was the first time that we could see what we had retrieved in its entirety (© Canterbury Archaeological Trust)

The analysis of the find by a large multi-disciplinary team was to continue for many years; a detailed study of the hull was of course central to the exercise, including the assessment of three hypothetical reconstructions of the original boat shape and its possible performance and cargo carrying capacity. I was determined to understand the boat as a product of the Bronze Age society that constructed, used and ultimately disposed of it; to move outside of the tightly focused discipline of nautical archaeology and set the find in its broadest cultural context. This determination was reflected in the wide-ranging themes of the ultimate publication (Clark 2004a) and perhaps went some way to contributing to the growing accommodation of maritime issues in 'mainstream' (terrestrial) archaeology (Adams 2007). An appreciation of cultural context is as critical an imperative for the Carpow find as it was for Dover.

## 14.5  Conservation and display

At the same time as this campaign of analysis was taking place, which was wholly funded by English Heritage, the issues of conservation and public display of the boat needed to be addressed. The costs of this work, originally estimated at £1 million (it ultimately cost over £1,600,000), required an organisation capable of raising significant funds, and one that could take on the stewardship and long-term care of this internationally important find. To this end the Dover Bronze Age Boat Trust was created in October 1993, initially as a voluntary organisation but granted full charitable status a year later in November 1994. The amount of effort that the (unpaid) Trustees put in to the project over the next few years was (is) truly astounding. The Trust was very effective; by 1994, English Heritage had agreed a substantial sum for the conservation of the vessel, and in 1996 a successful application was made to the Heritage Lottery Fund for the lion's share of the costs of designing and building a museum gallery devoted to the Bronze Age with the boat as its centrepiece (this is not to forget the many other critical financial contributions to the project; Clark *et al* 2004, table 18.1). But this was not the only task that fell to the Trustees; they also had to co-ordinate the work of conservation, design and build the new gallery and finally install the boat in its new home, which was to be just 250m from the place where it had lain unseen for some 3,500 years.

Though there was some criticism about the decision to cut the boat into pieces at the time of excavation (though no practical alternatives were offered), the

methodology had two unforeseen advantages. First, as mentioned above, it allowed the rays and rings of the parent trees to be studied and recorded as exposed in the cuts made through the boat planks. Secondly, even the largest of the boat pieces could fit into a freeze-drying chamber; preserving the timbers by freeze-drying would drastically reduce the time (and cost) for conservation compared to that by other methods. Closely supervised by conservation experts from English Heritage and the Mary Rose Trust, the boat pieces were initially soaked in a solution of PEG for 16 months followed by freeze-drying by the Mary Rose Trust in 1995. Although not widely advertised at the time, there was some trepidation amongst the team about using the technique on such large and complex pieces of such antiquity; it had not been tried before. It was with palpable relief, therefore, that we greeted the first pieces to emerge from the freeze-drying chamber; the process had been completely successful, with only minimum distortion of the timbers.

Meanwhile plans for a new gallery at Dover Museum were being drawn up. Initial designs were submitted to the Heritage Lottery Fund at the beginning of 1996, though construction work did not begin until May 1997. As with our efforts with the analysis, the emphasis was on placing the boat in its Bronze Age context; surveys showed that less than 10% of visitors knew when the Bronze Age was and only 60% knew anything at all about the period. Thus besides telling the story of the boat; how it was built, how it was excavated and how we know what we do about it, there are also themed displays exploring the Bronze Age way of life, including a replica roundhouse, manikins in Bronze Age costume and real Bronze Age artefacts from the Museum's own collection and on loan from elsewhere (notably part of the Langdon Bay hoard from the British Museum).

The initial fitting out of the new gallery was completed in August 1998, when the 32 conserved boat pieces returned to Dover. I had been given responsibility for reassembling the boat pieces in their new home, a task that was to occupy a small team for the better part of a year, working inside an environmentally controlled 'room within a room' set up inside the new gallery and on view to the public (Clark *et al* 2004). The reassembly was completed in July 1999. Work could then begin on finishing the rest of the gallery displays, the boat hidden behind plywood panels as work progressed. The whole exhibition was finally opened to the public on November 22nd 1999 (Fig 184).

*Figure 184*
The Dover boat in the Gallery of Bronze Age Life at Dover Museum
(© Canterbury Archaeological Trust)

## 14.6 The impact of the discovery

In retrospect, one can more easily appreciate the impact of the discovery of the Dover boat has had in many areas. First, the determinedly multi-disciplinary approach to its study with an emphasis on the social significance and context of the find (Clark 2004b, 3) may be seen as part of a wider move towards a fuller appreciation and integration of maritime issues into 'mainstream' archaeology; a coming together of the 'wet' and 'dry' archaeological communities (Adams 2007, 219). It is no longer acceptable to present distribution maps of Britain standing in splendid isolation, a blank space lying where France or Ireland should be (eg Mellars 1974, fig 9; Darvill 1987, fig 77). The richly complex potential of maritime archaeology, embracing symbolic, technological, perceptual, social and economic aspects of the past is increasingly interwoven into modern narratives and explanations of early communities (eg Bradley 2007; Cooney 2003), whilst at the same time perspectives derived from studies of 'terrestrial' archaeology are contributing more satisfying explanations of boats and their context (eg Champion 2004; Pryor 2004).

Whilst we shall no doubt always be arguing about the original form of the boat and the uses to which it was put, it seems fairly clear that it did travel at sea, if only to make the short voyage to Folkestone a few miles down the coast (Green 2004). This of course has exercised our imaginations about the contacts across the sea in the transmanche area, contacts that indubitably did exist, though whether enabled by vessels similar to that from Dover remains moot. Nevertheless, the Dover boat has become symbolic of these Bronze Age connections, and its discovery has contributed to a renaissance of research into the linked communities of the Manche–Mer du Nord region in the second millennium BC (eg Marcigny & Ghesquière 2003; Marcigny & Talon 2009). In particular, this was reflected in the contributions to the first Dover boat conference celebrating the tenth anniversary of the discovery in 2002 (Clark 2004c) and even more so in those of the second conference in 2006 (Clark 2009). A most gratifying aspect of this renewed appreciation of maritime connections in the transmanche area has been the collaboration and debate it has engendered between archaeologists across national boundaries; it is increasingly commonplace that scholars from the UK, Belgium, France and the Netherlands work together in an integrated approach to studying these Bronze Age connections. Indeed, at the time of writing (2009) the Association for the Promotion of Research into the Bronze Age ('l'Association pour la Promotion des Recherches sur l'Age du Bronze' or APRAB) is planning a third conference focusing on the Dover boat in Boulogne-sur-Mer in 2012. Furthermore, this perspective is influencing studies outside of Bronze Age research; for example, in 2004 members of the Neolithic Studies Group met at the British Museum to discuss 'Cross Channel Contacts in the fourth and third millennia BC', whilst Barry Cunliffe's surveys of the archaeology of the Atlantic Zone have proved hugely influential in bringing the maritime dimension into the mainstream of enquiry in both prehistoric and historic archaeology of all periods (2001; 2008).

I use the term 'maritime' here as shorthand for the waters of the world; not just seas but lakes and river systems that require a boat of some kind to travel upon them. In the south-east of Britain we tend to focus on the sea, particularly the Strait of Dover and the Channel/southern North Sea, but these waters are only part of a much larger system. The recent publication of excavations on Thanet (a now land-locked island just north of Dover) entitled 'At the Great Crossroads' recognises that the island lies at the crossing of two major axes of communication (Bennett *et al* 2008); the first running roughly east–west from central Europe to the west of southern Britain, formed by the River Rhine and the River Thames, their estuaries facing each other across the waters of the southern North Sea. The second axis runs north–south along the western

European seaboard from Iberia to Scandinavia, another immense routeway that has been used for millennia.

Other nodal points, large and small, are not hard to find; the Orkney Isles, as just one example, lying at the junction of the sea lanes between Scandinavia, Ireland, Scotland and Iceland can also surely be described as another 'crossroads'. The interdigitation of land and water was a critical component of the physical and mental landscapes of prehistoric communities, not only juxtaposing differing resource zones but also shaping the patterns of potential movement of people and goods and the interconnections between these zones. Even until relatively recent times, travel by water was faster and more economical than by land and this was perhaps even more the case in the distant past. Modern day perceptions of bodies of water presenting an obstacle to travel and contact are not appropriate in understanding past perceptions; we find cultural connections between peoples on either side of bodies of water that are not apparent between communities on the littoral and farther inland, as at Lake Peipsi in eastern Europe during the early medieval period (Tanel Laan pers comm) or (as mentioned above) the communities in the coastal regions of the transmanche zone during the Bronze Age (Clark 2004d; 2005; Needham 2006; Marcigny & Talon 2009).

Rivers, of course, where navigable can facilitate movement over long distances, as can be seen in the distribution of material culture across the European landmass from the Neolithic onwards (eg Ellmers 1993; Teigelake 2003; Kristiansen & Larsson 2005) and control of the portages between different river systems was of great importance in the past, reflecting the critical significance of water transport (Westerdahl 2006). The great estuaries play a particularly important part in this network of routes, providing broad paths deep into the heart of the land, and in themselves being important nodal points. Thus the estuary of the River Canche in northern France was a major centre for maritime contact between southern Britain and the continent for millennia (Philippe 2009); likewise the Humber Estuary was a place of great significance in prehistory (van de Noort 2004; van de Noort *et al* 1999) and of course was the location of the other major finds of Bronze Age sewn-plank boats (McGrail 1991; Wright 1994; Wright *et al* 2001). The Carpow logboat was found at the head of the Tay Estuary, and whilst it may never have engaged in long journeys along the network of maritime routes, it can be perceived as symbolic of these connections and act as a pivot for encouraging a better understanding of waterborne

transport in prehistoric Scotland, as Dover has in south-eastern Britain.

## 14.7 Carpow and Dover: symbols of prehistoric water borne connections

The Carpow logboat is by its very nature a more modest construction than the Dover boat and can be described as rather basic in its design in comparison. The repairs to the hull and the reworking of the transom are intriguing and numerous interpretations of the stern can be entertained. The possibility of making a reconstruction of the Carpow boat (David Strachan pers comm) will allow the testing of these hypotheses; though reconstructed logboats are relatively common, focussing on specific details such as this will be of immense value. Certainly the reconstruction of a mid-section of the Dover boat gave us insights into the vessel's construction that otherwise could not have been easily achieved (Darrah 2004c).

With its unspecialised hull form and in the absence of a cargo we probably can never be certain of what the Carpow boat was used for (Chapter 13, p 178); we can guess that it was used in exploiting the riparian wetlands, and for transporting both people and cargo, but there are other possibilities and no unequivocal way to decide between them. It is the same for the Dover boat, where we cannot even be confident about the original form of the hull; was it created to operate on a shallow lagoon lying behind a bar across the mouth of the Dour valley or in the relatively sheltered waters of the Wantsum Channel to the north of Dover? Was it some kind of Bronze Age 'tramp steamer', plying regularly across the Strait of Dover to France and along the south coast of Britain to Devon or Cornwall along sea lanes thick with boats of many kinds? Or was it a 'special' boat, its sophisticated construction owing as much to conspicuous consumption as technological need, a symbol of membership of a maritime elite, only occasionally making voyages to distant lands but in so doing becoming redolent of power and knowledge? The reader may take their pick, or create an entirely new hypothesis consistent with the data; I certainly seem to change my mind about Dover on a regular basis and have published a number of different and contrasting interpretations of the role of the Dover boat in Bronze Age society (eg Clark 2004b; 2004d; 2005).

In some senses this does not really matter; as I suggested at the start of this afterword, with so little data available to us, we are unlikely to be able to be

*Figure 185*
A reconstruction drawing of the manufacture of the boat; here the lower side planks are being stitched to the bottom planks with
twisted yew withies (© Canterbury Archaeological Trust)

unequivocal regarding the nature of these prehistoric boats for some time to come. What is important is that these rare and precious discoveries are symbolic of the maritime realm and its importance in the lives of prehistoric societies, reminding us that we must not neglect this dimension in our studies of the past.

Of course, Scottish archaeologists have long appreciated the importance with water transport in understanding and explaining past societies; this is inescapable when considering a country of 'unparalleled landscape variety ... fragmented by its interpenetrative relationship with the sea' (Mercer 2004, 292). This perspective is becoming increasingly pervasive in recent studies; 'Scottish material is being placed into a wider context within the British Isles and continental Europe' (Brophy 2006, 38), but this 'wider context' must be understood in terms of maritime contacts; the Carpow logboat, like Dover, makes this dimension concrete and demands our accommodation of the world of *Pontus* with that of *Gaea*.

But this presents a challenge when attempting to convey this understanding to the general public; logboats are not particularly well served by museum displays, either being rather uninspiring, bulky lumps of desiccated and badly split wood accompanied by little (if any) interpretive material or undergoing lengthy and expensive conservation processes like that from Hasholme in Yorkshire. However, the option to preserve the Carpow logboat by freeze-drying will mean that the boat will be available for display in a relatively short period of time, and that it will not suffer splitting and distortion. The fine detail of the repairs and the transom, complete with toolmarks will survive. The boat, being largely complete, is immediately comprehensible for what it is and can be used to bring alive the richly complex world of the Bronze Age.

The Dover boat gallery, with its deliberate emphasis on Bronze Age life in addition to presenting the boat hull itself, has proved to be a popular attraction for

189

local citizens, schoolchildren and visitors alike, and has won a number of national and international awards recognising its contribution to our cultural heritage. Scotland now has another icon of the maritime dimension of prehistoric life, well preserved and excavated and conserved to the highest professional standards; Carpow is important in its own right, but its full potential can only be realised by exploring its status as a symbol of the close interrelationship between Bronze Age peoples with the land and the water, and ultimately the human connections that such vessels helped to articulate.

# Appendix I

# Conservation

THEO SKINNER

## Introduction

From the initial identification of the excellent state of preservation of the stern of the logboat, through planning, excavation, recovery, lifting and transportation, Department of Conservation and Analytical Research (C&AR) staff from the National Museums of Scotland (NMS) were involved in advising the excavation team on conservation possibilities, and potential problems and solutions. This involved assessing facilities, costs, and time-scales for potential conservation processes, as well as identifying potential threats of damage or deterioration during the excavation and lifting stages. It also included solutions appropriate to the difficult excavation situation, for example, the application of a layer of mud to prevent drying of the wood while the vessel was being excavated, rather than spraying which would have added to the water being pumped out from the trench.

This report is necessarily an interim one, as the conservation of the logboat is still in process at the time of writing. With regards to the conservation options for the logboat, a primary consideration had to be financial, as previous experience of similar situations, involving the same potential funding sources, made clear that the project would not proceed unless costs were kept low. Reburial was quickly disregarded as an option to preserve the logboat, as it would still be costly, require long-term monitoring, and offered little benefit except basic recording of the vessel. All interested parties agreed that, if excavated, the vessel should be preserved for display, rather than become an ongoing monitoring and maintenance problem, as considerable funds had already been spent on monitoring the vessel since its initial discovery. At an early stage it was agreed that the boat should be conserved by the NMS with a view to it being returned to Perth Museum and Art Gallery for display.

## The problem

The main problem with the conservation of waterlogged archaeological wood is excessive shrinkage on drying, as well as warping and cracking (Barbour & Leney 1982). The extent of shrinkage depends very much on the degree of degradation, for example, in very degraded oak the shrinkage can be as high as 90% by volume (Jones & Rule 1991). Sound oak shrinks around 20% by volume on air-drying from the waterlogged state. As oak decays in the waterlogged state it gradually loses wood polymers, and these are replaced by water. As the polymers are denser than water, as the water content increases the density of the wood decreases; there is less wood and more water. Very degraded wood therefore also requires some consolidation to provide physical strength, to replace the missing wood polymers. The Carpow logboat was found to fall into a common condition for waterlogged archaeological oak, having a sound core with a degraded outer layer. Without conservation treatment, the degraded outer layer would have shrunk by 60% by volume, destroying the integrity of the surface.

Shrinkage can be prevented by impregnating the wood with materials which penetrate the wood cell wall, and the cell cavities and wood capillaries or pores (Grattan 1988). Polyethylene glycol (PEG) of low molecular weight (PEG 200) will penetrate the cell wall of sound and degraded oak and remain there on drying, preventing cell wall shrinkage, which is about 20% by volume for sound oak and less for more degraded wood. The remaining excessive shrinkage of degraded waterlogged archaeological wood (up to 90% by volume) is caused by collapse of the cell cavities on drying. This can be prevented by filling the cell cavities with high molecular weight PEG (PEG 4000), or by turning the water into ice and removing it as water vapour under vacuum (ie freeze-drying, where the lack of any liquid phase avoids the liquid tension effects which cause collapse of the cavities in normal air-drying). Because water expands by about 10% in volume when frozen, some high molecular weight PEG is introduced into the cell cavities, preventing freezing damage, before freeze-drying (Ambrose 1990).

Following initial assessment of the logboat *in situ*, a number of conservation options, based on current standard treatments, were considered:

### Air drying

Air drying has to be carried out slowly to reduce moisture gradients and their resultant stresses, and this would probably result in the loss of most of the outer layer. Had the vessel been completely abraded and there were no tool-marks or other details, this might not be too serious a loss: the inner core would be left showing the original size and shape of the logboat, albeit with some shrinkage. It was estimated that this process would have taken around two years to complete with minimal costs, however, the results of such treatments can be seen in several museums, and are usually not acceptable. This is particularly the case with older, more degraded specimens, while more modern logboats, such as that from Closeburn (on display in the Museum of Scotland, catalogue number IN2, radiocarbon date post-AD 1000) can look quite good, as only a very thin degraded layer is lost. It was expected, from the age of the Carpow logboat, that the surface loss would be unacceptable, and the method was deemed inappropriate. Later work in the laboratory showed that the degraded outer layer on the Carpow logboat was several centimetres thick.

### PEG tank

For a tank treatment with PEG, an initial bath of 10% PEG 200 is used, the concentration being raised in stages to 50% PEG 200. This would then be removed and replaced with 50% PEG 4000. The PEG 4000 concentration is then increased to 70% in stages (Hoffman 1986). The wood is then cleaned and slowly dried to avoid drying stresses. This is a good and reliable method, but because of the high concentrations of PEG required is very expensive. It is also a lengthy process and for the Carpow example it was estimated that it would take three years for the impregnation and about 6–12 months for drying to be completed.

### PEG spraying

Spraying would reduce the amount of PEG required, but impregnation would take longer, and the results are usually not as good. It was estimated that it would have taken four years for the complete process, but the spraying equipment is costly, and can be problematic and prone to failure and blockage.

### Sugar tank

Given the expense of PEG, sugar can be used as a cheaper alternative, but it is not as good. The process demands sterile conditions, otherwise the sugar ferments and it can be difficult to achieve and maintain in a large tank, especially over the lengthy period the sugar impregnation process requires (Hutchings & Spriggs 2005).

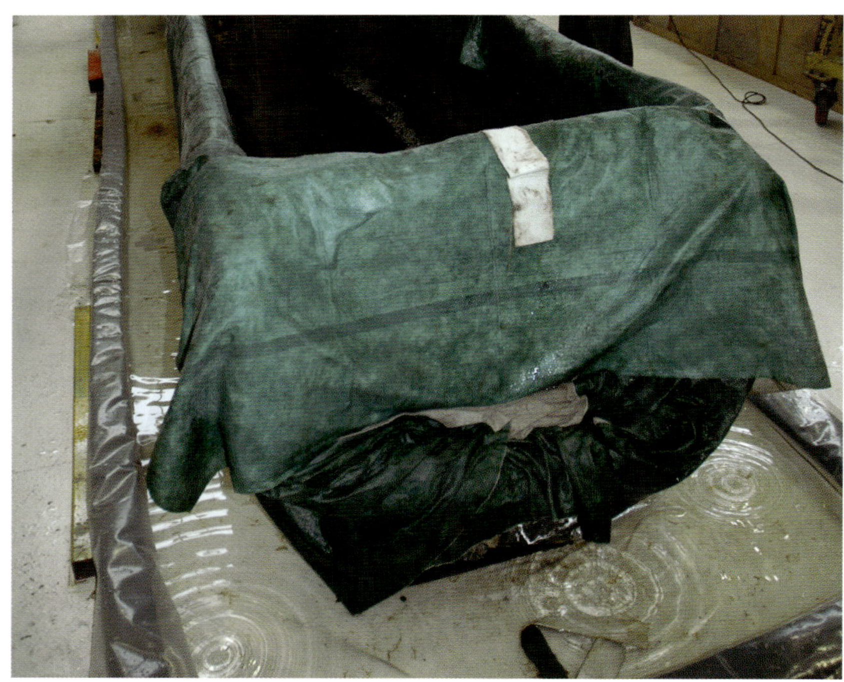

*Figure 186*
The capillary matting used to keep the hull wet during the cleaning process

### Freeze-drying

The advantage of freeze-drying is that it requires the use of much less PEG. For the logboat consideration was given to the use of 10–30% PEG 200 followed by a bath of 30% PEG 4000. It was estimated that this would take about 14 months, and drying in the freeze-drier about two months. Because of the size limit of the available freeze-drier, this required the logboat to be cut and then repaired at the end of the process, a process commonly carried out on wood that has been

*Figure 187*
The stern of the vessel showing gravel concretion (see also Fig 69)

sliced for dendrochronology, and the joins are mostly good. This was the option finally chosen, as it seemed the best compromise between cost and preservation of form and surface detail.

There was a considerable negative response to the idea of cutting the logboat from members of the public and in the press at the time of excavation. However, note was made of other logboat projects in Britain, where the option of cutting and freeze-drying was not taken, and which have run into serious difficulties. The conservation process of the Hasholme logboat has still not been completed at the time of writing, although the spraying process began in 1988. Great difficulties were experienced in health and safety aspects, due to the high temperatures needed for the spraying process with high concentrations of PEG (Foxon 1996). The Poole logboat was immersed in a bath of 67% sucrose, but lack of proper maintenance, caused by a loss of continuity of staff over the extended treatment period, resulted in this becoming the largest wasp trap in existence (Hutchings & Spriggs 2005). The dead wasps infected the sugar solution, which then fermented and

had to be replaced, with the project only eventually being completed after 12 years.

Having the logboat in sections, rather than as one *c* 9m long object, would also facilitate easier storage and transportation of the conserved vessel. As a result of these various factors, the decision to section the logboat and freeze-dry was taken.

### Initial treatment

While at one stage in the planning process, consideration was given to cutting the vessel into three parts while *in situ*, it was ultimately decided that the vessel could be recovered in one piece, allowing the cutting process to be carried out in more controlled circumstances at the NMS C&AR laboratory in Granton, Edinburgh.

The initial stages of conservation of the logboat involved facilitating the detailed recording of the vessel, while carrying out analytical work needed to assess its condition. This involved keeping the logboat accessible, and yet maintaining it in a wet state, and was accomplished, very successfully, by using 'leaky'

*Figure 188*
The logboat in the Granton laboratory

hoses and capillary matting (items used to water plants on stages in greenhouses) to distribute tap-water over the whole surface of the boat. A small pump and float switch were used to pump out the tap-water from the bund housing the boat into the drain. This continuous washing also effectively removed soluble salts from the wood (Fig 186).

A major problem that immediately became evident was the conglomerate concretion adhering to the surface of the vessel over large areas (Figs 187 and 189). This was found to be composed of gravel overlying a layer of fine silt, bound, according to scanning electron microscope (SEM) analysis, with iron and sulfur compounds. It was found to be worse on the outside of the boat, but was also found to be present on the inside. While it is possible to soften such concretions with dilute hydrochloric acid, this can only be done with small pieces of wood in a fume cupboard, as the process produces highly toxic and flammable hydrogen sulfide. Attempts to remove the concretion by local freezing of the surface were not successful, and as a result, the concretion was removed, where necessary to reveal detail, mainly around the stern and on the transom, by mechanical means, using a hammer, fine chisel, and great care. This was laborious and time-consuming, and while it revealed interesting detail in the stern, in other areas it left the impressions of the larger pebbles, that had been pressed into the softened wood surface, producing a pock-marked appearance.

The cleaning was successful in revealing well-preserved tool-marks on the transom (Chapter 5, pp 75–80) and also revealed quantities of moss in the gap between the transom and the hull, as well as details of the transom grooves (Chapter 5, pp 81–3).

## Analysis

### *The Concretion*

A scanning electron microscope (SEM) investigation of the concretion was carried out on a small sample, removed from a damaged area of the side of the hull,

*Figure 189*
The removal of the gravel concretion in progress at the stern (compare to Fig 187)

by Dr Jim Tate of NMS. The analysis showed that the concretion consisted of mineral grains cemented together by iron/sulfur compounds. The presence of sulfur and iron compounds in the concretion presented a problem, as these can oxidise in air to produce sulfuric acid, a matter of major international concern in marine conservation. In the holding operation, while the vessel was being constantly washed with running tap-water, the acid, if generated, was diluted and washed out, and therefore not a problem. Indeed, that was an ideal situation, and there is some evidence that this was occurring (Fig 190). During treatment in the PEG solutions, the lack of oxygen would prevent oxidation and no acid would be formed.

Once the wood was dried, and oxygen became available, however, acid could be generated and would become concentrated, causing deterioration of the wood. Oak timbers from HMS Dartmouth (sunk AD 1690), stored in water for about 30 years in the NMS since 1974, still contained iron sulfur compounds which produced sulfuric acid on drying and exposure to air (Skinner *et al* 2005). It was

important to determine the nature and distribution of these compounds within the wood itself. Core samples were taken with an increment borer and analysed at the Swiss Light Source using X-ray spectroscopy. This type of sampling is destructive, as the cores are usually 5mm in diameter. In large shipwrecks, such as the Vasa or Mary Rose, numerous samples are routinely taken in this way, but in this case we felt that such sampling should be limited, to only those that were absolutely essential to determine the type and distribution of sulfur compounds in the wood, and the water content distribution across the thickness of the hull. X-ray spectroscopy is a synchrotron-based technique which allowed identification of the type of sulfur compounds in the wood, and in a core sample, their distribution.

The spectra shown in Fig 190 are for one core, and show the relative amounts of reduced and oxidised sulfur compounds at various depths into the cross-section of the hull. The relative height of the lines gives an indication of the total sulfur content. The results indicate that the reduced sulfur species were found to be more prevalent on the outside of the

195

boat, but there are some on the inside of the hull. The centre of the hull, at a depth of 40mm, shows very little sulfur compared to the near-surface sample spots. The oxidised sulfur compounds appear to be more concentrated on the outer parts of the core, perhaps indicating some oxidation during the washing process in running, oxygenated tap-water.

There is a significant possibility that the reduced sulfur compounds (sulfides and thiols) will oxidise into sulfuric acid once the conservation process is complete, although it may take several years for the problem to become apparent, as happened with the Swedish warship the Vasa (Hall Roth & Malmberg 2005; Sandstrom *et al* 2005). The NMS have been

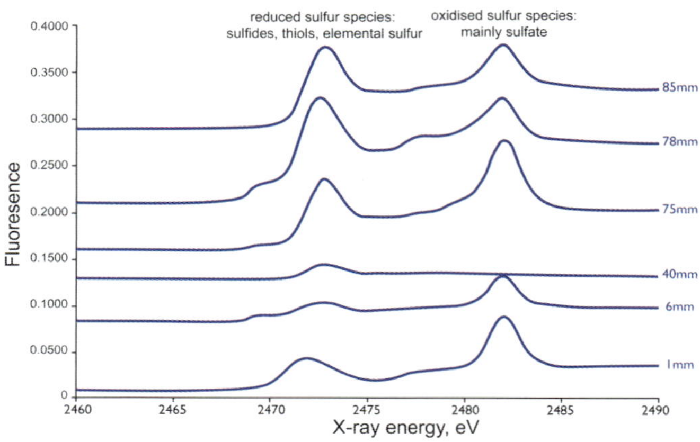


*Figure 190*

X-Ray absorption near edge spectroscopic (XANES) analysis of the sulfur compounds in a core sample across the hull of the Carpow logboat

working on this problem, in collaboration with the Mary Rose Trust, and have found at least one potential solution: treatment with calcium phytate (Skinner & Jones 2007). This is a compound found in seeds, and acts as an iron-chelating agent to prevent oxidation in the seeds, enabling them to remain dormant and viable for considerable periods of time. Results with a modern respirometer indicate that treatment of marine wood with low levels of calcium phytate dramatically reduce the oxidation rate, and should prevent acid generation. This treatment may be easily incorporated in the PEG impregnation phase.

### *Water Content*

One core was used to measure the water content distribution across the hull thickness. This was carried out by dividing the core sample into 5mm long sections, which were weighed fully waterlogged and then after oven drying. From this the water content was calculated on the basis of weight of water per dry weight of wood. Unfortunately, as is often the case, the core sample was difficult to take and the inner few centimetres were not suitable for analysis as they were too fragmentary and crushed, which would have resulted in much of the water being expelled and therefore underestimated. The results from the remainder of the core are shown below (Fig 192).

The water content information is important in establishing the amount of shrinkage expected on air drying, in specifying the amount and types of PEG needed for the treatment, and in giving some idea of the time needed for impregnation. Less degraded wood, with lower water content, needs to be dimensionally stabilised with low molecular weight PEG, as only these can penetrate and stabilise the cell walls, while high molecular weight PEG is needed to bulk the cavities of degraded wood, to provide some strength. The greater the thickness of less degraded wood the longer impregnation time, as the process is dependent on the rate of diffusion of the PEG into the cell walls and through the thickness of the un-degraded area, whereas penetration of the degraded layer is usually relatively quick.

### **Proposed treatment**

The information gained from the analyses was used to formulate the treatment plan, with the vessel being cut into three sections to fit into the freeze-drier, and this was easily accomplished with ordinary hand saws. The sections were pre-treated with polyethylene glycol before freeze-drying. An initial bath of 20% PEG of molecular weight 200 would be used to stabilise the sound inner core of the hull, with a water content of 100%. This solution would be replaced with a solution of 10% PEG 200 and 20% PEG 4000 to stabilise and strengthen the outer degraded layer. The freezing point of 20% PEG 200 is too low for successful freeze-drying with the equipment available. It was hoped that we could monitor the impregnation process by weighing the sections as the water was replaced by the PEG, but this proved impractical as the weighing process was not accurate enough. The first solution was therefore given an extended time to soak of 18 months before being replaced. This is the

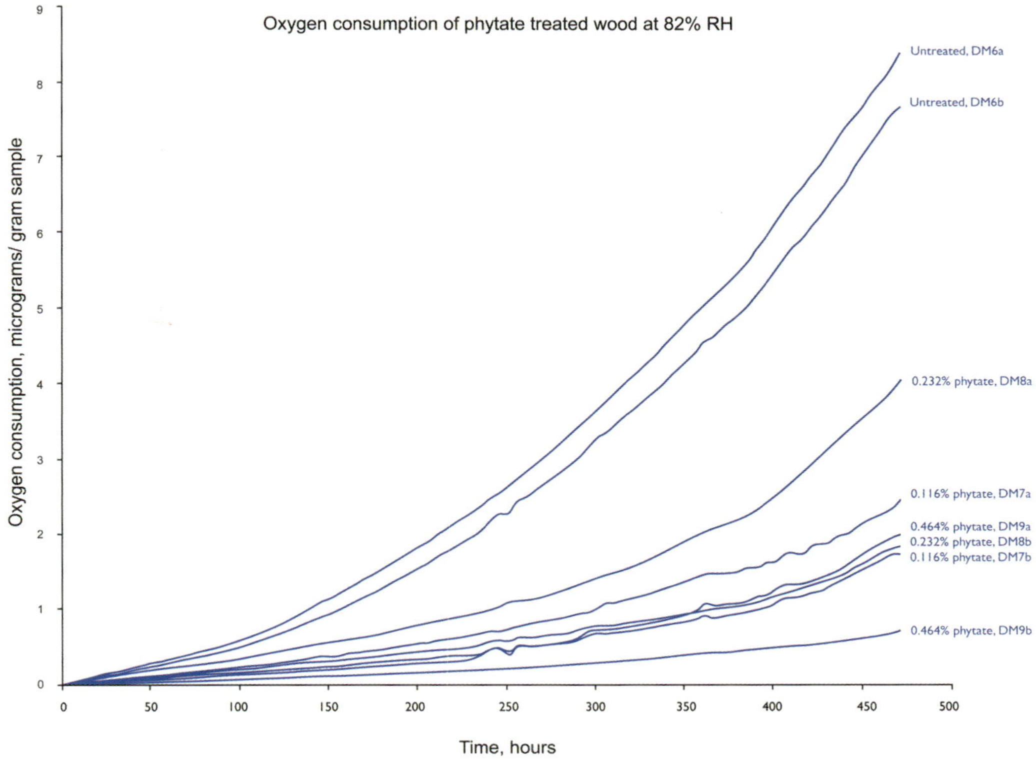



*Figure 191*

Respirometer data for the oxygen consumption of wood from a marine shipwreck showing the oxygen consumption of wood either untreated or treated with a solution of calcium phytate

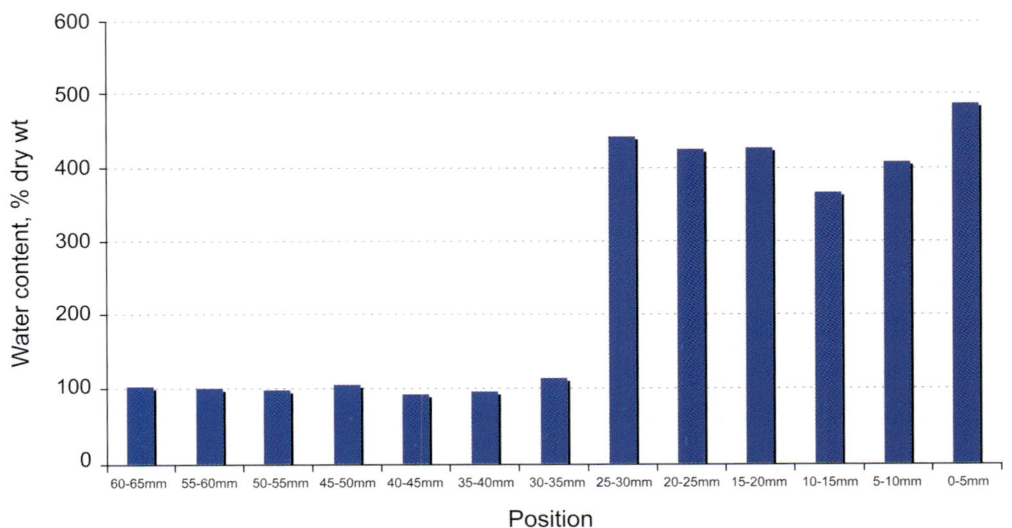



*Figure 192*

Water content distribution across the thickness of the hull

*Figure 193*
Inspection of the bottom of the hull

current state at the time of writing. A biocide, Kathon CG, was used to prevent the growth of bacteria and slime moulds, which can degrade the PEG or prevent impregnation by forming a barrier on the wood surface. This biocide is exceptionally good, often being used in sugar treatments where the growth of microbes can be disastrous.

Because the wood contains reduced sulfur compounds, the final PEG bath will contain a phytate solution, as our experiments showed this to be an effective way of reducing the rate of acidification without causing any health and safety concerns. The final baths should last about nine months, after which the sections will be freeze-dried consecutively. It is expected that each section will take about one month to dry. The bow section will be dried first, and a template taken from the cut end to be transferred to the front cut end of the middle section and screwed into place to ensure the correct shape is maintained. A similar process will be used between the middle and stern sections. A template taken from the transom, which was removed early on during the cleaning stage, will be used to fix the stern in the correct shape.

### *Rejoining*

The plan is to mount the individual section on steel frames with adjustable feet and wheels that can be raised to enable the feet to be set on the ground. The sections will then be set into the correct alignments to fit together using the adjustable feet. A biscuit jointing technique may be used between the sections. The frames, with their wheels, would make the sections moveable on site for installation, or for movement around or within a storeroom.

### Conclusion

Waterlogged wood conservation is not an exact science as yet, and this project will continue to be challenging, but the results will be worth the effort, and Scotland will have at least one well-preserved, and well-conserved, logboat to display for the benefit of the public.

**Appendix II**

# Theoretical calculations on performance

STEVEN TIMONEY

Theoretical calculations are often used to estimate the performance of early craft (eg McGrail 1988 and 1990) once reconstructions of boats have been made (Crumlin-Pedersen, 2006; Crumlin-Pedersen & McGrail 2006; McGrail 2007). The following calculations are based on a three dimensional reconstruction model of the Carpow logboat created using AutoCAD software. As the logboat does not survive as a complete vessel, certain attributes have been estimated (eg the length of the boat) to allow for the following calculations to be made.

### 1. Mass of the Carpow logboat

The model was designed with a length of 10.076m, an average width of 0.829m and an average height of 0.56m. The volume of timber of the logboat was calculated as $c$ 1.61m³, with the internal volume of the vessel (up to the sheerline) calculated to be $c$ 3.58m³. The measurements above were then used to calculate the mass of the logboat. McGrail (1978, 131) suggests calculating oak at fibre saturation point, that is 27% moisture content. Oak in this state has a specific density of 800kg/m³.

Therefore:

$$1.61\text{m}^3 \times 800\text{kg} = 1288\text{kg}$$

giving a mass of 1288kg for the Carpow logboat.

### 2. Loading capacity of the Carpow logboat

A minimum safe freeboard of 150mm (McGrail 1978) is suggested for the Carpow logboat to operate safely, though it is possible that the freeboard could have been as low as 100mm if the logboat was operating in a calm estuary (Goodburn pers comm).

a. calculating the unladen freeboard

The unladen draught for the logboat was estimated as one-third the external height of the boat's side, near amidships (McGrail pers comm):

$$\tfrac{1}{3} \times 0.56 = 0.19\text{m}$$

giving a freeboard of 0.19m.

b. Safe loading capacity

Using Fry's (2000, 30) equation to calculate safe loading capacities:

$$\left[\frac{60\%(\text{or }70\%)\,\text{H}' - \text{D}}{\text{H}'} \times \text{M}\right] \times \frac{(\text{L} \times \text{B})}{(\text{L} \times \text{B} \times \text{H})}$$

D is the unladen draught, M the mass if the hull (kg) L the hull length, B the hull breadth, and H the average hull height. Fry used 60% and 70% to relate to the hull's depth of immersion, related to freeboard of 40% and 30%.

Instead of using 60% or 70% of height, the percentage of height for the minimum safe freeboards mentioned above (150mm and 100mm) can be calculated:

   i) 150mm is 26.8% of 0.56m therefore depth of immersion = 73.2%

   ii) 100mm is 17.9% of 0.56m therefore depth of immersion = 82.1%

*i) 150mm freeboard*

$$\left[\frac{73.2\%\,\text{H}' - \text{D}}{\text{H}'} \times \text{M}\right] \times \frac{(\text{L} \times \text{B})}{(\text{L} \times \text{B} \times \text{H})}$$

$$\left[\frac{73.2\% \text{ of } 0.56 - 0.223}{0.56} \times 1755\right] \times \frac{(10.08 \times 0.83)}{(10.08 \times 0.83 \times 0.56)}$$

$$\left[\frac{0.41 - 0.223}{0.56} \times 1755\right] \times \frac{8.3664}{4.685}$$

$$\left[\frac{0.187}{0.56} \times 1755\right] \times 1.786$$

$$586 \times 1.786 = 1046.7\text{kg}$$

150mm freeboard = 1046.7kg

*ii) 100mm freeboard*

100mm freeboard = 1325.2kg

### 3. *Calculating crew of the Carpow logboat*

For crew members, McGrail (1978, 131) uses an average height of 1.65m (5'4") and weight of 60kg (9½ stone), although this may be slightly short and light. Evidence for example, from an Iron Age cist at Galson, Isle of Lewis contained the remains of an adult male who may have been up to 1.75m (5'9") tall (Ponting 1989). A suggested average of 1.75m (5'9") and 70kg (11 stone) is used for the following crew capacity calculations. The boat would not have been wide enough for more than one paddler across. McGrail (1978) suggests a minimum of 2m longitudinally between three paddlers working on alternate sides. With the length of the Carpow logboat estimated at 10.08m, this would allow for a proposed maximum of *c* 14 crew weighing 980kg.

Calculating maximum cargo capacity the Carpow logboat, McGrail (1987, 21) suggests *c* 80% of the volume of the logboat for cargo (the other 20% for crew), with the following bulk densities for cargo:

$$\text{Iron ore/stone} = 2{,}500\text{kg/m}^3$$
$$\text{Wheat grain} = 680\text{kg/m}^3$$
$$\text{Peat} = 435\text{kg/m}^3$$

Working on the assumption that the logboat would have operated with two crew (one fore and one aft), the following volume estimates have been made.

*i) 150mm freeboard*

$$1047\text{kg (safe loading capacity for 150mm}$$
$$\text{freeboard)} - 140\text{kg (crew)} = 907\text{kg}$$

$$\frac{907}{2500} = 0.36\text{m}^3$$

$$\frac{807}{680} = 1.33\text{m}^3$$

$$\frac{907}{435} = 2.09\text{m}^3$$

In this state the logboat could transport a maximum of:

0.36m³/907kg of iron ore/stone;
1.33m³/907kg of wheat grain;
2.09m³/907kg of peat.

*ii) 100mm freeboard*

$$1325\text{kg (safe loading capacity for 100mm}$$
$$\text{freeboard)} - 140\text{kg (crew)} = 1185\text{kg}$$

$$\frac{1185}{2500} = 0.47\text{m}^3$$

$$\frac{1185}{680} = 1.74\text{m}^3$$

$$\frac{1185}{435} = 2.72\text{m}^3$$

In this state the logboat could transport a maximum of:

0.47m³/1185kg of iron ore/stone;
1.74m³/1185kg of wheat grain;
2.72m³/1185kg of peat.

### 4. *Calculating speed of the Carpow logboat*

The potential maximum speed of the Carpow logboat was calculated using Marchaj's equation as used in McGrail (1988, 38–9). Accordingly drag increases greatly when the speed to length ratio

$$\frac{V}{\sqrt{L}} = 1.34$$

where V = speed in knots and L = the waterline length (in feet).

The following calculation was made to ascertain the hypothetical maximum potential speed of the Carpow logboat according to the above formula, with 10m (32.8feet) approximated for the waterline length:

$$\frac{V}{\sqrt{L}} = 1.34$$

$$\frac{7.5}{\sqrt{32.8}} = 1.31$$

According to the above formula, the potential maximum speed of the logboat would be 7.5 knots, although if this was possible it would have only been for very short sprints.

# Appendix III

# Hull features and small finds

DAVID STRACHAN and SARAH WINLOW

## Logboat Features: ordered from bow to stern
### (see Chapter 5, Figs 89, 98 and 100)

| Feature number | Description | Measurement |
| --- | --- | --- |
| F1a–c | A line of three equally spaced circular indents, of which a) is the deepest and most prominent. | (a) 45mm in diameter; 12mm deep; (b) 45mm in diameter; 4mm deep; (c) 50mm in diameter; 3mm deep. |
| F2 | A large pronounced knot with hairline crack running towards the bow, slightly raised on the inside of the hull and hollow on the exterior. | *c* 350mm in diameter; 35mm in height. |
| F3 | A prominent possible raised feature. Darker in colour than surrounding wood and trapezoidal in shape. | 50mm by 70mm; 9mm in height. |
| F4 | A large, pronounced knot, raised on the inside of vessel, and hollow on the exterior. | Internal: 170mm in diameter; 30mm in height. External: 120mm by 80mm, 50mm deep. |
| F5 | A pronounced sub rectangular daub of resin-like material on line of basal split F10, which appears to be two separate amorphous applications. | 140mm × 70mm; 30mm in height (distance between F5 and F6: 240mm). |
| F6 | An amorphous daub of resin-like material on line of basal split F10. | 60mm in diameter; 10mm in height (distance between F6 and F7: 250mm). |
| F7 | A sub-circular daub of resin-like material on line of basal split F10. | 80mm × 50mm; 15mm in height (distance between F7 and F8: 290mm). |
| F8 | A sub-circular daub of resin-like material on line of basal split F10. | 40mm in diameter; 30mm in height (distance between F8 and F9: 240mm). |
| F9 | A large sub-circular daub of resin-like material on line of basal split F10, which is made up of numerous smaller sub-circular composite daubs, around 20 of which are visible. | Overall feature: 230mm × 180mm; 30mm in height; composite daubs: 40mm diameter (average). |
| F10 | An eroded sub-circular daub of resin-like material on line of basal split F10, with a slightly raised circumference and depressed centre. | 50mm × 40mm; 9mm in height. |
| F11 | A sub circular daub of resin-like material. | 35mm × 20mm; 5mm in height. |
| F12 | An amorphous daub of resin-like material. | 40mm × 30mm; 5mm in height. |
| F13 | Numerous linear indents, possibly the result of excavation damage. | *c* 300mm in length (max). |

| Feature number | Description | Measurement |
| --- | --- | --- |
| F14 | An amorphous daub of resin-like material. | 40mm × 50mm; 7mm in height. |
| F15 | A sub circular daub of resin-like material (on line of basal split F10). | 40mm × 50mm; 5mm in height. |
| F16 | Footrest (port side) fashioned in the solid from the parent log. | 390mm × 130mm; 90mm in height (max). |
| F17 | Footrest (starboard side) fashioned in the solid from the parent log, part of the top of which has been sheared off. | 385mm × 130mm; 86mm in height (max). |
| F18a | Sheer-line hole: port side. | External: 40mm × 50mm (port to starboard, prow to stern). Internal: 40mm in diameter. Depth: 25mm. |
| F18b | Sheer-line hole: port side. | External: 40mm × 50mm (port to starboard, prow to stern). Internal: 40mm in diameter. Depth: 25mm. |
| F19 | Sheer-line hole: starboard. | External: 40mm × 50mm (port to starboard, prow to stern). Internal: 40mm in diameter. Depth: 25mm. |
| F20 | A vertically cut retaining feature (port side). It appears as a deep sub circular depression and is paired by F21. | 65mm (port to starboard) × 40mm (stern to bow); 65mm deep. |
| F21 | A vertically cut retaining feature (starboard side). It appears as a deep sub circular depression eroded on the after side and is paired by F20. | 65mm (port to starboard) × 60mm (stern to bow); 65mm deep. |
| F22 | A beam tie retaining hole, cut horizontally through the sheer-line aft the transom (port side). The afterside is missing. It is paired with F24. | 80mm (top to bottom), 90mm (stern to bow); 100mm thick at base of hole. |
| F23 | Repair transom groove lower retaining hole (port side). Roughly triangular in shape, it is angled downwards from the exterior to interior, and is paired with F25. | 50mm (top to bottom), 45mm (stern to bow); 110mm thick. |
| F24 | A beam tie retaining hole, cut horizontally through the sheer-line aft the transom (starboard). It is paired with F22. | 80mm (top to bottom), 100mm (stern to bow); 90mm thick at base. |
| F25 | Repair transom groove lower retaining hole (starboard side). It is circular and angled downwards from the exterior to interior, and is paired with F23. | 60mm (top to bottom); 60mm (stern to bow). |
| F26a | Basal split in the parent log at the stern (port side). | The split runs for _c_ 80cm from the stern. |
| F26b | Basal split along the parent log (starboard) which has a number of repairs (see F5–10 and F15 above). | The split is _c_ 7m long and runs from the stern to near F4. |
| F27a–c | Repair transom groove. Rectangular-shaped groove with vertical sides. | a: 45mm wide; 25mm deep; b: 40mm wide; 25mm deep; c: 20mm wide; 20mm deep. |

| Feature number | Description | Measurement |
|---|---|---|
| F28a–e | Main transom groove. Flat bottomed groove with angled rather than vertical sides. Forward side of groove is slightly higher than the after side. | (a) 40mm wide; 25mm deep; (b) 40mm wide (aft side 20mm deep, forward side 40mm deep); (c) 45mm wide (aft side 40mm deep, forward side 50mm deep); (d) 45mm wide (aft side 30mm deep, forward side 50mm deep); (e) 45mm wide (aft side 40mm deep, forward side 50mm deep). |
| F29 | Transom ridge, fashioned in the solid from the parent log, parallel to inner transom groove, providing a slightly raised section at the stern to receive F28. | 60mm thick at port side, 50mm thick at starboard side. |
| F30 | Repair block slot: a section cut across the inner transom groove. During excavation, an eroded timber block (SF015) would found *in situ* between the transom board and this slot. | 240mm of inner transom groove and transom ridge have been removed. |
| F31 | Sheerline transom wedge, found in F28 (starboard). | *c* 10mm × *c* 20mm head, *c* 100mm in length |
| F32 | Sheerline transom wedge, found in F28 (port side). | *c* 10mm × *c* 20mm head, *c* 95mm in length |

## Small Finds (see Chapter 4, Fig 49)

| Find No | Description/Context |
|---|---|
| SF001 | A D-shaped wooden plank with a central hole, *c* 25–30mm thick, *c* 290mm in length and *c* 80mm in height, with the hole measuring *c* 4 × 20mm). There is no reason to suggest that the find is associated with the logboat, as it came from Context 102, and it is possibly a section of a small barrel lid. |
| SF002 | A wooden peg *c* 15cm long, from Context 102; probably a modern tent. |
| SF003 | Possible worked round-wood (*c* 14 × 12 × 4cm), which appears to have been worked by a single cut. Context 103. |
| SF004 | Possible worked round-wood (*c* 23 × 15 × 6cm). Context 103. |
| SF005 | Possible worked round-wood (a) eroded and compressed round-wood, *c* 7cm in length and oval in section (*c* 2 × 1cm); (b) a roughly square section of thin wood, possibly bark (*c* 5 × 5cm); a roughly square section of thin wood, possibly bark (*c* 7 × 6cm). Context 103. |
| SF006 | Possible worked round-wood ×4 (less than *c* 10cm length). Context 104? |
| SF007 | Possible worked round-wood, slightly compressed (*c* 18 × 12 × 10cm) which appears to have been worked by a single cut. Context 106. |
| SF008 | Possible worked round-wood, *c* 11cm in length by *c* 5cm in diameter. Context 104/105? |
| SF009 | Possible worked round-woods: (a) *c* 16cm in length and *c* 3cm in diameter; (b) *c* 7cm in length by *c* 4cm in diameter; (c) compressed in diameter in diameter *c* 11cm in length × *c* 4 × 2cm in (oval) section. Only (b) may possibly be worked. Context 104/105? |
| SF010 | Possible worked round-wood, compressed; *c* 10cm in length × *c* 4 × 3cm in (oval) section. Context 104/105? |
| SF011 | Round-wood: (a) ×2 *c* 4–6cm; and (b) *c* 10cm long and *c* 5cm in diameter. Only (b) may be worked. Context 104/105? |

| Find No | Description/Context |
| --- | --- |
| SF012 | Round-wood: ×8 fragments of eroded wood *c* 10–18cm in length, none appear worked. Context 106. |
| SF013 | Round-wood: ×10 fragments of eroded wood *c* 6–9cm in length, none appear worked. Context 106. |
| SF014 | Possible worked wood: a sub-rectangular block of wood *c* 20 × 14 × 6cm) which may have been worked by a single cut. Context 106. |
| SF015 | A sub-rectangular block of worked wood, much eroded and found in two pieces, although *in situ* at the stern of the vessel on either side of the transom board and slotted into cut feature F30. Context 105. |
| SF016 | Worked wood: a probable birch stake *c* 180mm long × *c* 50mm in diameter. Context 106. |
| SF017 | Worked wood: a probable alder toggle *c* 180mm long × *c* 60mm in diameter at widest point, and *c* 40mm diameter at the narrowest point. Context 106. |
| SF018 | Worked wood sub-circular in shape *c* 90mm long × *c* 54mm at widest point: carpentry waste. Context 106. |
| SF019 | Worked wood triangular in shape *c* 96mm long × *c* 48mm at widest point: carpentry waste. Context 106. |
| SF020 | Worked wood sub-rectangular in shape *c* 54mm long × *c* 44mm at widest point: carpentry waste. Context 106. |
| SF021 | Worked wood sub-rectangular in shape *c* 64mm long × *c* 26mm at widest point: carpentry waste. Context 106. |
| SF022 | Worked wood sub-rectangular in shape *c* 112mm long by *c* 24mm at widest point: carpentry waste. Context 106. |

**Appendix IV**

# Grab samples and diatom species within Sample SP1

(see Chapter 4, pp 41–8; Chapter 10, pp 133–4; Figs 43–5 and 49)

DAVID STRACHAN and SUE DAWSON

## Grab Samples

| Sample No | Summary description | Sample Location/context |
|---|---|---|
| SAMPLE 1 | A highly compressed peat containing Phragmites stems. Two fragments of small diameter, compressed, branch wood extracted from the centre, probably *Betula*. | Beneath boat *c* 2m from bow. Context 106. |
| SAMPLE 2 | Ten hazelnut shells, four have rodent damage. One stake with two oblique facets forming a point. Abundant small twigs. | Beneath boat *c* 2m from bow. Context 106. |
| SAMPLE 3 | Gravel rich sample containing small branch wood, one fir cone. | Beneath boat *c* 0.75m from bow. Context 103. |
| SAMPLE 4 | Grey alluvial silt and sand with pea-sized gravel. | Beneath boat *c* 0.8m from bow. Context 104. |
| SAMPLE 5 | Alluvial sand and gravel. | Beneath boat *c* 12m from bow. Context 105. |
| SAMPLE 6 | Fragments of round-wood and hazelnut shells. | Inside hull *c* 2.5m from stern. Context 106. |
| SAMPLE 7 | Twigs with some identified as hazel. | Inside hull *c* 0.8m from stern. Context 106. |
| SAMPLE 8 | Alluvial sand and gravel | Above hull *c* 0.4m from stern. Context 105. |
| SAMPLE 9 | Large fragment of wood, 360 × 220 × 80mm identified as birch | Beneath stern. Context 105. |
| SAMPLE 10 | Grey estuarine clay. | At transom area of stern. Context 105? |
| SAMPLE 11 | Trunk wood identified as hazel, 160mm diameter encrusted with gravel and iron oxide | Part of a larger log beneath the boat *c* 2.5m from the stern. Context 106. |
| SP1 | Birch tree stump resting on inter-tidal peat. | *c* 25m north-east of boat. |
| SP2 | Large oak stump with eroded inter-tidal peat. | *c* 30m south-east of boat. |
| SP3 | Small birch stump resting on shallow inter-tidal peat. | *c* 100m south-east of boat. |

## Diatom species within sample SP1 (Basal Unit 4)

| | |
|---|---|
| *Achnanthes brevipes* | *Polyhalobous* (marine) |
| *Cocconeis scutellum* | *Polyhalobous* (marine) |
| *★Rhaphoneis surirella* | *Polyhalobous–mesohalobous* (brackish-marine) |
| *Diploneis smithii* | *Polyhalobous–mesohalobous* (brackish-marine) |

| | |
|---|---|
| *Rhaphoneis amphiceros | *Polyhalobous–mesohalobous* (brackish–marine) |
| Mastagloia elliptica | *Polyhalobous–mesohalobous* (brackish–marine) |
| Navicula marina | *Polyhalobous* (marine) |
| Navicula abrupta | *Polyhalobous–mesohalobous* (brackish–marine) |
| Navicula hennedyii | *Polyhalobous–mesohalobous* (brackish–marine) |
| *Paralia sulcata | *Polyhalobous* (marine) |
| Plagiogramma staurophorum | *Polyhalobous* (marine) |
| *Rhabdonema minutum | *Polyhalobous–mesohalobous* (brackish–marine) |
| Trachyneis aspera | *Polyhalobous* (marine) |
| Actinophycus senarius | *Polyhalobous* (marine) |
| Podosira stelliger | *Polyhalobous* (marine) |
| Coscinodiscus sp | *Polyhalobous* (marine) |
| Amphora marina | *Polyhalobous* (marine) |
| Caloneis westii | *Mesohalobous-polyhalobous* (brackish–marine) |
| Diploneis didyma | *Mesohalobous-polyhalobous* (brackish–marine) |
| *Diploneis interrupta | *Mesohalobous* (brackish) |
| Navicula digitoradiata | *Mesohalobous* (brackish) |
| *Navicula peregrina | *Mesohalobous* (brackish) |
| Navicula cincta | *Mesohalobous* (brackish) |
| Navicula halophila | *Mesohalobous* (brackish) |
| Navicula forcipata | *Mesohalobous* (brackish) |
| *Nitzschia sigma | *Mesohalobous* (brackish) |
| Nitzschia navicularis | *Mesohalobous* (brackish) |
| Nitzschia accuminata | *Mesohalobous* (brackish) |
| *Nitzschia punctata | *Mesohalobous* (brackish) |
| Rhopolodia musculus | *Mesohalobous* (brackish) |
| Scolioneis tumida | *Mesohalobous* (brackish) |
| Synedra tabulata | *Mesohalobous* (brackish) |
| Gyrosigma balticum | *Mesohalobous* (brackish) |
| Diploneis ovalis | *Mesohalobous-oligohalobous* (brackish–fresh) |
| Cocconeis placentula | *Mesohalobous-oligohalobous* (brackish–fresh) |
| *Fragilaria pinnata | *Mesohalobous-oligohalobous* (brackish–fresh) |

| | |
|---|---|
| *Fragilaria construens* | *Oligohalobous* (fresh) |
| *Fragilaria construens var venter* | *Oligohalobous* (fresh) |
| *Fragilaria brevistriata* | *Oligohalobous* (fresh) |
| *Navicula radiosa* | *Oligohalobous* (fresh) |
| *Rhopolodia gibba* | *Oligohalobous* (fresh) |
| *Pinnualaria borealis* | *Oligohalobous* (fresh) |
| *Pinnularia microstauron* | *Oligohalobous* (fresh) |
| *Pinnularia viridis* | *Oligohalobous* (fresh) |
| *Cymbella microcephala* | *Oligohalobous* (fresh) |

★ = dominating species

# References

The following abbreviations have been used in the references:

| | |
|---|---|
| The Antiquaries Journal | *Antiquaries J* |
| Antiquities Journal | *Antiq J* |
| Antiquity | *Antiq* |
| Archaeological Journal | *Archaeol J* |
| Conservation Science | *Conservation Sci* |
| Derbyshire Archaeological Journal | *Derbyshire Archaeol J* |
| Discovery and Excavation in Scotland | *Discovery Excav Scot* |
| Earth and Planetary Science Letters | *Earth Planet Sci Lett* |
| Lincolnshire Architectural and Archaeological Society Papers and Reports | *Lincolnshire Arch Archaeol Soc Rep* |
| International Journal of Nautical Archaeology | *Int J Naut Archaeol* |
| Journal of Archaeological Science | *J Archaeol Sci* |
| Journal of Irish Archaeology | *J Irish Archaeol* |
| Journal of Quaternary Science | *J Quat Sci* |
| Journal of Wetland Archaeology | *J Wetland Archaeol* |
| Memoir of the British Geological Survey | *Mem Br Geol Surv* |
| New Phytologist Journal | *New Phytol J* |
| Oxford Journal of Archaeology | *Oxford J Arch* |
| Proceedings of the Dorset Natural History and Antiquarian Society | *Proc Dorset Nat Hist Antiq Soc* |
| Proceedings of the Prehistoric Society | *Proc Prehist Soc* |
| Proceedings of the Royal Society of Edinburgh B | *Proc Royal Soc Edinburgh B* |
| Proceedings of the Society of Antiquaries of Scotland | *Proc Soc Antiq Scot* |
| Proceedings of the Somersetshire Archaeological and Natural History Society | *Proc Somerset Archaeol Nat Hist Soc* |
| Progress in Physical Geography | *Prog Phys Geog* |
| Quaternary Science Reviews | *Quat Sci Rev* |
| Scottish Journal of Geology | *Scott J Geol* |
| Tayside and Fife Archaeological Journal | *Tayside Fife Archaeol J* |
| Transactions of the Cumberland and Westmorland Antiquarian and Archaeological Society | *Trans Cumberland Westmorland Antiq Archaeol Soc* |
| Transactions of the East Riding Antiquarian Society | *Trans East Riding Antiq Soc* |
| Transactions of the Perthshire Society of Natural Science | *Trans Perthshire Soc Natur Sci* |
| Transactions of the Royal Society of Edinburgh | *Trans Royal Soc Edinburgh* |
| Transactions of the Thoroton Society | *Trans Thoroton Soc* |
| Ulster Journal of Archaeology | *Ulster J Archaeol* |

Adams, J 2007 Joined-up boats: maturing maritime archaeology, *Antiquity* 81, 217–220.

Aitken, J 1986 *Above the Tay Bridges*. Montrose.

Alexander, D 2002 The oblong fort at Finavon, Angus: an example on the over-reliance on the appliance of science? In Ballin Smith, B and Banks, I (eds) *In the Shadow of the Brochs: The Iron Age in Scotland*. Tempus, 44–54.

Allen, M J & Gardiner, J 2000 *Our Changing Coast: A Survey of the Intertidal Archaeology of Langstone Harbour, Hampshire*. CBA Research Report 124, York.

Ambrose, W R 1990 Application of freeze-drying to archaeological wood. In Rowell, R M & Barbour, R J *Archaeological Wood: Properties, Chemistry and Preservation*. Washington, DC, American Chemical Society, 235–261.

Anderson, C, Anderson, J & Proctor, W 1997 *Freshwater inputs and pollutant loads to the Tay Estuary. Coastal Zone Topics: Process, Ecology and Management 3 The Estuaries of Central Scotland*. Joint Nature Conservation Committee.

Anderson, J 1886 Scotland in pagan times: the Bronze and Stone Ages. *The Rhind Lectures in Archaeology for 1882*, Edinburgh, 312–13.

Anderson, J & Black, G 1888 Reports on local museums in Scotland, obtained through Dr R H Gunning's Jubilee gift to the Society. *Proc Soc Antiq Scot* 22, 331–422.

Armit, I & Ralston, I B M 2003 The Iron Age. In Edwards, K J & Ralston, I B M (eds), 169–193.

Armit, I 2006 *Anatomy of an Iron Age Roundhouse: The Cnip Wheelhouse Excavations, Lewis*. Society of Antiquaries of Scotland, Edinburgh.

Armstrong, M, Paterson, I B & Browne M A E 1985 Geology of the Perth and Dundee District. *Mem Br Geol Surv*, Sheets 48W, 48E, 49.

Arnold, B 1996 Pirogues monoxyles d'Europe centrale. *Archéologie Neuchâteloise* 20/21.

Asher, J 1923 A descriptive catalogue of stone implements in Perth Museum. *Trans Proc Perthshire Soc Nat Sci*, 7, 122–48.

Austin P 2000 The emperor's new garden: woodland, trees and people in the Neolithic of southern Britain. In Fairbairn, A S (ed) *Plants in Neolithic Britain and Beyond*. Oxford, 63–78.

Baillie M G L 1982 *Tree-Ring Dating and Archaeology*. University of Chicago Press.

Barber J W 1998 *The Archaeological Investigation of a Prehistoric Landscape: Excavations on Arran 1978–1981*. Edinburgh.

Barbour R J & Leney L 1982 Shrinkage and collapse in waterlogged archaeological wood: Contribution III, Hoko River Series. In Grattan, D W & McCawley, J C (eds) *Proceedings of the ICOM Waterlogged Wood Working Group Conference, Ottawa 1981*. Ottawa, 209–25.

Barclay G J 1983 Sites of the third millennium BC to the first millennium AD at North Mains, Strathallan, Perthshire. *Proc Soc Antiq Scot* 113, 122–281.

Barclay, G J & Tolan, M 1990 Trial excavation of a terrace-edge enclosure at North Mains, Strathallan, Perthshire. *Proc Soc Antiq Scot* 120, 45–54.

Barford, P M 1990 Appendix 2: Salt production in Essex before the Red Hills. In Fawn *et al* 1990.

Bateson, D & Hall, M A 2002 Inchyra, Perthshire. In R Abdy, I Leins & J Williams (eds) *Coin Hoards from Roman Britain XI*. Royal Numismatic Society Special Publication no 36, 119–21.

Baxter, P 1930 *Perth's Old-Time Trades and Trading*. Perth.

Bayliss, A, Groves, C, McCormac, C, Bronk Ramsey, C, Baillie, M, Brown, D, Cook, G & Switsur, R 2004 Dating. In Clark, P (ed) 2004a, 250–5.

Bell, M 1993 Field survey and excavation at Goldcliff, Gwent 1992. *Severn Estuary Levels Research Committee Annual Report 1993*. Lampeter, SELRC, 81–102.

Bell, M 1994 Field survey and excavation at Goldcliff, Gwent 1993. *Severn Estuary Levels Research Committee Annual Report 1994*. Lampeter, SELRC, 115–44.

Bell, M & Neumann, H 1999 Intertidal survey, assessment and excavation of a Bronze Age site at Redwick, Gwent 1999. *Archaeology in the Severn Estuary* 10. Lampeter, Severn Estuary Levels Research Committee 25–37.

Bennett, P, Clark, P, Hicks, A & Riddler, I 2008 *At the Great Crossroads: Prehistoric, Roman, and Medieval Discoveries on the Isle of Thanet 1994–95*. Canterbury Archaeological Trust Occasional Paper, 4, Canterbury: Canterbury Archaeological Trust.

Best, E 1976 *The Maori Canoe*. Lawrence Verry Inc.

Boon, B & van Rietbergen, E 2009 Aspects of the analysis of structure and strength of pre-historic ships. In Bockius, R (ed) *Between the Seas – Transfer and Exchange in Nautical Technology*, Proceedings of the 11th International Symposium on Boat and Ship Archaeology, Mainz, Germany, 377–85.

Bowler, D (ed) 2004 *Perth: The Archaeology and Development of a Scottish Burgh*. Tayside and Fife Archaeological Committee Monograph 3, Perth.

Bowler D P 2004 Perth and the Tay: the flood regime, 1209–1993. In Bowler, D (ed) 2004, 12–20.

Bradley, R 2007 *The Prehistory of Britain and Ireland*. Cambridge World Archaeology, Cambridge University Press.

Brennand, M & Taylor, M 2003 The survey and excavation of a Bronze Age timber circle at Holme-next-the-Sea, Norfolk, 1998–9. *Proc Prehist Soc* 69, 1–84.

Brophy, K 2006 Rethinking Scotland's Neolithic: combining circumstance with context. *Proc Soc Antiq Scot* 136, 7–45.

Brunning, R 2000 Wood Studies 1: Species composition and wood use on the crannog. In Crone, A 2000 *The History of a Scottish Lowland Crannog: Excavations at Buiston, Ayrshire 1989–90*. Historic Scotland Monograph 4, 84–99.

Buchanan, J 1854a Discovery of ancient canoes in the Clyde. *Proc Soc Antiq Scot* 1, 44–5.

Buchanan, J 1854b Notice of the discovery of an ancient boat, of singular construction, on the banks of the Clyde. *Proc Soc Antiq Scot* 1, 211–13.

Buck, A L 1993 *An Inventory of UK Estuaries Vol 4: North and East Scotland*. Joint Nature Conservation Committee, Peterborough.

Burgess, C 1985 Population, climate and upland settlement. In Spratt, D & Burgess, D (eds), 195–230.

Burgess, C 1989 Volcanoes, catastrophe and the global crisis of the late second millennium BC. *Current Archaeology* 117, 325–9.

Burgess, C & Gerloff, S 1981 *The Dirks and Rapiers of Great Britain and Ireland*. Prähistorische Bronzefunde, München.

Burgess, C Topping, P & Lynch, F (eds) 2007 *Beyond Stonehenge: Essays on the Bronze Age in honour of Colin Burgess*. Oxbow.

Caldwell, D H & Dean, V E 1992 The pottery industry at Throsk, Stirlingshire, in the 17th and early 18th century. *Post-Medieval Archaeol* 26, 1–46.

Callander, J G 1919 Discovery of (1) a short cist containing human remains and a bronze armulet, and (2) a cup-marked stone, at Williamston, St Martins, Perthshire. *Proc Soc Antiq Scot* 53, 15–19.

Caseldine, C 1983 Palynological evidence for early cereal cultivation in Strathearn. *Proc Soc Antiq Scot* 112, 39–47.

Chambers, F M, Mauquoy, D, Brain, S A, Blaauw, M & Daniell, J R G 2007 Globally synchronous climate change 2800 years ago: proxy data from peat in South America. *Earth Planet Sci Lett* 253, 439–44.

Champion, T 1999 The Later Bronze Age. In J Hunter & I Ralston (eds) *The Archaeology of Britain: An Introduction from the Upper Palaeolithic to the Industrial Revolution*. Routledge, 95–112.

Champion, T 2004 The deposition of the boat. In Clark, P (ed) 2004a, 276–81.

Childe, V & Waterston, D 1942 Further urns and cremation burials from Brackmont Mill, near Leuchars, Fife. *Proc Soc Antiq Scot* 76, 84–93.

Clark, P (ed) 2004a *The Dover Bronze Age Boat*. Swindon.

Clark, P 2004b Introduction. In Clark, P (ed) 2004a, 1–3.

Clark, P (ed) 2004c *The Dover Bronze Age Boat in Context: Society and Water Transport in Prehistoric Europe*. Oxford.

Clark, P 2004d The Dover boat ten years after its discovery. In Clark, P (ed) 2004c, 1–12.

Clark, P 2005 Shipwrights, sailors and society in the Middle Bronze Age of NW Europe. *J Wetland Archaeol* 5, 87–96.

Clark, P 2008 One step at a time: The Dover Bronze Age boat experimental research programme. In Springmann, M-J & Wernicke, H (eds) *Historical Boat and Ship Replicas: Conference-Proceedings on the Scientific Perspectives and the Limits of Boat and Ship Replicas, Torgelow 2007*. Maritime Kulturgeschichte von Bodden- und Haffwewässern des Ostseeraumes, Friedland: Steffen Verlag, 29–38.

Clark, P 2009 *Bronze Age Connections: Cultural Contact in Prehistoric Europe*. Oxford: Oxbow.

Clark, P, Corke, B & Waterman, C 2004 Reassembly and display. In Clark, P (ed) 2004a, 290–304.

Clarke R W 1986 The Hasholme Boat. *Conservation News* 31, 17–19.

Close-Brooks, J 1975 An Iron Age date for the Loch Lotus canoe. *Proc Soc Antiq Scot* 106, 199.

Clough, T & Cummins, W 1988 *Stone Axe Studies Volume 2: The Petrology of Prehistoric Stone Implements from the British Isles*. CBA Research Report 67, 236.

Coates, J 2005a Early seafaring in north-west Europe: could planked vessels have played a significant part? *The Mariner's Mirror* 91, 517–30.

Coates, J 2005b The Bronze Age Ferriby Boats: seagoing ships or estuary ferry boats? *Int J Naut Archaeol* 34, 38–42.

Coles, B & Coles, J M 1986 *Sweet Track to Glastonbury: The Somerset Levels in Prehistory*. New York.

Coles, J M 1972 Later Bronze Age activity in the Somerset levels. *Antiq J* 52, 269–75.

Coles, J M & Minnitt, S 1995 *Industrious and Fairly Civilized: the Glastonbury Lake Village*. Exeter.

Coles, J M & Orme, B 1985 Prehistoric woodworking from the Somerset Levels 2. *Somerset Levels Paper* 11, 7–24.

Collins, A E P & Seaby, W A 1960 Structures and small finds discovered at Lough Eskragh, Co Tyrone. *Ulster J Archaeol* 23, 25–37.

Colquhoun, I & Burgess, C B 1988 *The Swords of Britain*. C H Beck: München [=*Prähistorische Bronzefunde* IV.5].

Cook, M, Inglis, R & Hatherley, C 2004 Noah's Ark (Tibbermore parish). *Discovery Excav Scot* 5, 111.

Cook, M 2007 Early Neolithic ritual activity, Bronze Age occupation and medieval activity at Pitlethie Road, Leuchars, Fife. *Tayside Fife Archaeol J* 13, 1–24.

Coombs, D 1996 Aspects of ritual in the Late Bronze Age of Southern England. In P Schauer (ed) *Archäologische Forschungen zum Kultgeschehen in der Jüngeren Bronzezeit und Frühen Eisenzeit Alteuropas*, 101–15.

Cooney, G 2003 Seascapes. *World Archaeology* 35, 323–489.

Coutts H 1970 *Ancient Monuments of Tayside*. Dundee Museum and Art Gallery.

Coutts H 1971 *Tayside before History*. Dundee Museum and Art Gallery.

Cowie T, Hall, M, O'Connor, B & Tipping, R 1996 The Late Bronze Age hoard from Corrymuckloch, near Amulree, Perthshire: an interim report. *Tayside Fife Archaeol J* 2, 60–9.

Cowie, T & Hall, M A 2001 Late Bronze Age metalwork from Scottish Rivers: a rediscovered sword from the River Forth at Cambus, Clackmannanshire, in its wider context. *Tayside Fife Archaeol J* 7, 1–15.

Cowie, T & Shepherd, I A G 2003 The Bronze Age. In Edwards, K J & Ralston, I B M (eds), 151–68.

Cowley, D C 1998 Identifying marginality in the first and second millennia BC in the Strath of Kildonan, Sutherland. In Mills, C M & Coles, G (eds) *Life on the Edge: Human Settlement and Marginality*. Oxford, 165–71.

Cowley, D C & Dickson, A L 2007 Clay and 'difficult' soils in eastern and southern Scotland: dealing with the gaps. In Mills, J & Palmer, R (eds) *Populating Clay Landscapes*. Tempus, 43–54.

Crawford, O G S 1949 *Topography of Roman Scotland North of the Antonine Wall*. Cambridge University Press.

Cressey, M 2007 Small fragments of a bigger picture: coastal erosion and the Neolithic in the inner Solway Firth, south-west Scotland. In Sidell, J & Haughey, F (eds), 1–10.

Cressey, M, Bunting, M J, Dawson, A, Dawson, S, Long, D & Milburn, P 2001 Relative sea-level changes at Newbie Cottages, near Annan, Upper Solway Firth, SW Scotland. In Raftery, B & Hickey, J 2001 (eds) Recent Developments in Wetland Research WARP Occasional Paper 14, 257–270.

Cressey M, Rees, A & Dawson, S 2003 Radiocarbon determinations on marine shell from Inchture, Perth and Kinross. *Tayside Fife Archaeol J* 9, 3–5.

Crone, A 2000 The History of a Scottish Lowland Crannog: Excavations at Buiston, Ayrshire 1989–90, STAR Monograph Series 4.

Crone A 2002 The wood assemblage; species composition, woodworking and dendrochronology. In C Ellis, A Crone, E Reilly & P Hughes, Excavation of a Neolithic wooden platform, Stirlingshire. *Proc Prehist Soc* 68, 247–56.

Crone, A & Barber, J 1981 Analytical techniques for the investigation of non-artifactual wood from prehistoric and medieval sites. *Proc Sco Antiq Scot* 111, 510–15.

Crone, A & Mills, C M 2002 Seeing the wood and the trees; dendrochronological studies in Scotland, *Antiq* 76, 788–94.

Crumlin-Pedersen, O 2006 The Dover Boat: a reconstruction case-study. *Int J Naut Archaeol* 35, 58–71.

Crumlin-Pedersen, O & McGrail, S 2006 Some principles for the reconstruction of ancient boat structures. *Int J Naut Archaeol* 35, 53–7.

Cullingford, R A, Caseldine, C J & Gotts, P E 1980 Early Flandrian land and sea-level changes in Lower Strathearn. *Nature* 284, 159–61.

Cummings, V & Johnston, R (eds) 2007 *Prehistoric Journeys*. Oxford.

Cunliffe, B 2001 *Facing the Ocean: The Atlantic and Its Peoples 8000 BC–AD 1500*. Oxford.

Cunliffe, B 2008 *Europe between the Oceans: 9000 BC–AD 1000*. Yale.

Cunningham, D 1895 *The Estuary of the Tay*. Institution of Civil Engineers.

Current Archaeology 2001 Fiskerton. *Current Archaeology* 15, Nov/Dec, 327–9.

Currie, G 2005 Prieston (Tealing parish) cup-and-ring-marked rock: ?hut circles. *Discovery Excav Scot* 6, 21.

Darrah, R 2004a Illuminating the original shape of the Dover boat timbers. In Clark, P (ed) 2004a, 96–105.

Darrah, R 2004b Woodland management and timber conversion. In Clark, P (ed) 2004a, 106–23.

Darrah, R 2004c The reconstruction experiment. In Clark, P (ed) 2004a, 163–88.

Darvill, T 1987 *Prehistoric Britain*. London.

Dawson, S 2009 Relative sea-level changes at Clachan Harbour, Raasay, Scottish Hebrides. In Hardy, K & Wickham-Jones, C *Mesolithic and Later Sites around the Inner Sound, Scotland: The Work of the Scotland's First Settlers Project 1998–2004*. Scottish Archaeology Internet Report 31 (www.sair.org.uk/sair31).

Dawson, S, Dawson, A G & Edwards, K J 1998 Rapid Holocene relative sea level changes in Gruinart, Isle of Islay, Scottish Inner Hebrides. *Holocene* 8, 183–95.

Dawson, A G, Dawson, S, Mighall, T M, Waldman, G, Brown, A & Mactaggart, F 2001 Inter-tidal peat deposits and early Holocene relative sea-level changes, Traigh Eileraig, Isle of Coll, Scottish Hebrides. *Scott J Geol* 37, 11–18.

de Brisay, K W & Evans, K A (eds) 1975 *Salt: The Study of an Ancient Industry*. Report on the Salt Weekend held at the University of Essex, September 1974, Colchester.

Denys, L 1992 *A Check-list of the Diatoms in the Holocene Coastal Deposits of the Western Belgian Coastal Plain with a Survey of their Apparent Ecological Requirements*. Professional Paper 246, Geological Survey of Belgium.

Dewar, H S L & Godwin, H 1963 Archaeological discoveries in the raised bogs of the Somerset Levels, England. *Proc Prehist Soc* 29, 17–49.

Dickson, J H 1978 Bronze Age Mead. *Antiq* 52, 108–13.

Dixon, N 2004 *The Crannogs of Scotland: An Underwater Archaeology*. Stroud.

Dixon, N 2007 Crannog structure and dating in Perthshire with particular reference to Loch Tay. In Barber, J, Clark, C, Cressey, M, Crone, A, Hale, A, Henderson, J, Housley, R, Sands, R & Sheridan, A (eds) *Archaeology from the Wetlands: Recent Perspectives*. Proceedings of the 11th WARP Conference, Edinburgh, 2005. Society of Antiquaries of Scotland and WARP, 253–65.

Donaldson, C H, Allison, S & Hall, M A 2004 Vitrified rocks from Dun Knock hillfort, Dunning, Perthshire. *Tayside and Fife Archaeol J* 10, 64–72.

Duncan J, 1997 *Perth and Kinross: The Big County*. John Donald Publishers Ltd.

Dunwell, A & Strachan, R 2007 *Excavations at Brown Caterthun and White Caterthun Hillforts, Angus, 1995–1997*. Tayside and Fife Archaeological Committee Monograph 5. Perth.

Dunwell, A & Ralston, I 2008 *Archaeology and Early History of Angus*. Stroud.

Earwood, C 1990 The wooden artefacts from Loch Glashan crannog, Mid-Argyll. *Proc Soc Antiq Scot* 120, 79–94.

Edmonds, M 1998 *Ancestral Geographies of the Neolithic*. London.

Edwards, K J & Ralston, I B M (eds) 2003 *Scotland after the Ice Age 8000 BC – AD 1000*. Edinburgh University Press.

Ellmers, D 1978 Shipping on the Rhine during the Roman period: the pictorial evidence. In Du Plat Taylor, J & Cleere, H (eds) *Roman Shipping and Trade: Britain and the Rhine provinces*. CBA Res Rep No 24, 1–14.

Ellmers, D 1993 Zwei neolithische Bootsmodelle donauländischer Kulturen. In Lang, A (ed) *Kulturen zwischen Ost und West: das Ost-West-Verhältnis in vor- und frühgeschichtlicher Zeit und sein Einfluss auf Werden und Wandel des Kulturraums Mitteleuropa*. Festschrift for Kossack, G, Berlin, 9–17.

Eogan, G 2007 The tool kit of a Late Bronze Age wood-worker from Loughbown, Co Galway, Ireland. In Burgess, C Topping, P & Lynch, F (eds).

Evans, C & Hodder, I 2006 *A Woodland Archaeology: Neolithic Sites at Haddenham*. The Haddenham Project at Haddenham, Vol 1: monograph of the McDonald Institute for Archaeological Research, University of Cambridge.

Evans, C, Pollard, J & Knight, M 1999 Life in woods: tree-throws, 'settlement' and forest cognition. *Oxford J Arch* 18, 241–54.

Fairweather, A D & Ralston, I B M 1993 The Neolithic timber hall at Balbridie, Grampian Region, Scotland: the building, the date, the plant macrofossils. *Antiq* 67, 313–23.

Fawn, A J, Evans, K A, McMaster, I & Davies, G M R 1990 *The Red Hills of Essex: Salt Making in Antiquity*. Colchester.

Feacham, R W 1959 A dug-out canoe from Cambuskenneth Abbey. *Proc Soc Antiq Scot* 92, 116–17.

Fenwick, V 2006 Introduction. In *Keeping Up with the Dover Boat: IJNA's Track Record*. Oxford, 1–9.

Fenwick, V 2007 The Dover Boat: the reality of deep-mud rescue. *Int J Naut Archaeol* 36, 177–84.

Field, N & Parker-Pearson, M 2004 *Fiskerton: An Iron Age Timber Causeway with Iron Age and Roman Votive Offerings: Volume 1: The 1981 Excavations*. Oxford.

Field, N, Parker-Pearson, M & Rylatt, J 2003 The Fiskerton causeway: research – past, present and future. In Catney, S & Start, D (eds) *Time and Tide: The Archaeology of the Witham Valley*, Heckington. Witham Valley Archaeology Research Committee, 16–32.

Fleming, A 1988 *The Dartmoor Reaves*. London.

Fleming, J 1816 Observations on the junction of the fresh water of rivers with the salt water of the sea. *Trans Royal Soc Edinburgh* 8, 507–13.

Fleming, J 1822 On a submarine forest in the Frith of Tay, with observations on the formation of submarine forests in general. *Trans Royal Soc Edinburgh* 9, 419–31.

Fox, C 1926 Dug-out canoe from South Wales: with notes on the chronology, typology and distribution of monoxylous craft in England and Wales. *Antiq J* 6, 121–51.

Foxon, A 1996 The Hasholme Iron Age logboat: 17 metres of trouble. In Hoffman, P *et al* (eds), 547–53.

Freeman, P 1997 Excavations at Craigie Hill, Fife, 1991. In *Tayside and Fife Archaeol J* 3, 61–73.

Fry, M F 2000 *Coití Logboats from Northern Ireland*. Northern Ireland Archaeological Monographs 4, Antrim.

Gardiner, J (ed) 1993 *Flatlands and Wetlands: Current Themes in East Anglian Archaeology*. East Anglian Archaeology Report 50, Norwich.

Garton, D, Elliott, L & Salisbury, C R 2001 Aston-upon-Trent, Argosy Washolme (SK 431291). In Guilbert, G & Garton, D Some fieldwork in Derbyshire by Trent and Peak Archaeological Unit. *Derbyshire Archaeol J* 121, 196–200.

Geikie, J 1880 Discovery of an ancient Canoe in the old alluvium of the Tay at Perth. *The Scottish Naturalist: A Magazine of Natural History* 5, 1–7.

Gerritsen, F 1999 The cultural biography of Iron Age houses and the long-term transformation of settlement patterns in the southern Netherlands. In Fabech, C & Ringstvad, J (eds) *Settlement and Landscape*. Jutland, 139–48.

Gibson, A & Rideout, J 1984 Abercairney (Fowlis Wester p), cist, corn drying kilns. *Discovery Excav Scot* 41.

Gibson, A & Tavener, N 1989 Excavations at Dundee High Technology Park, Tayside. *Proc Soc Antiq Scot* 119, 83–9.

Gifford, E, Gifford, J & Coates, J 2006 The construction and trials of a half scale model of the Early Bronze Age ship Ferriby 1, to assess the capability of the full-sized ship. In Blue, L, Hocker, F & Englert, A (eds) *Connected By the Sea*. Proceedings of the Tenth International Symposium on Boat and Ship Archaeology, Denmark 2003. Oxford, 57–62.

Gifford, J 2007 *Perth and Kinross: The Buildings of Scotland Series*. Yale University Press.

Gillespie, J E 1876 Notice of a canoe found in Loch Lotus, Parish of New Abbey, Kirkcudbrightshire. *Proc Soc Antiq Scot* 11, 21–3.

Godbold, S, & Turner, R C 1994 Medieval Fishtraps in the Severn Estuary. *Medieval Archaeology* 37, 19–54.

Godwin, H 1967 Discoveries in the peat near Shapwick Station. *Proc Somerset Archaeol Nat Hist Soc* 111, 20–3.

Godwin, H 1978 *Fenland: Its Ancient Past and Uncertain Future*. Cambridge.

Goodburn, D 1992 Wood and woodland: carpenters and carpentry. In Milne, G (ed) *Timber Building Techniques in London c 900–1400*. London and Middlesex Archaeological Society Special Paper 15, 106–31.

Goodburn, D 2002 *An Archaeology of Early English Boatbuilding Practice c 900–1600 AD: Based mainly on Finds from SE England*. Unpublished PhD thesis, UCL London.

Goodburn, D 2003 Prehistoric woodwork. In Masefield, R, Branch, N, Couldrey, P, Goodburn, D & Tyers, I A later Bronze Age well complex at Swalecliffe, Kent. *Antiquaries J* 83, 98–105.

Goodburn, D 2004 Assembly and construction techniques. In Clark, P (ed) 2004a, 124–62.

Goodburn, D 2007 *Woodwork from the Timber Henge Site at Old Hall, Essex*. Unpublished Museum of London Specialist Services report for Essex County Council.

Goodburn, D forthcoming Prehistoric woodwork from the Ebbsfleet Valley. In Stafford, E C, Wenban-Smith, F F *Prehistoric Ebbsfleet: Excavation and Research in advance of the Channel Tunnel Rail Link and South Thameside Development Route 4 1989–2003*. Oxford Wessex Archaeology Monograph.

Goodburn, D & Minkin, J 1999 *Bronze Age Woodwork found at Atlas Wharf, Isle of Dogs, London*. Unpublished Museum of London Specialist Services report.

Goodburn, D & Redknap, M 1988 Replicas and wrecks from the Thames area. *London Archaeologist* 6, 7–10, 19–22.

Grattan, D W 1988 Treatment of waterlogged wood. In B Purdy (ed) *Wet Site Archaeology*. Gainesville, 237–54.

Green, C 2004 Evidence of a marine environment associated with the Dover boat. In Clark, P (ed) 2004c, 13–16.

Greenhill, B 1971 *Boats and Boatmen of Pakistan*. Newton Abbot.

Greig, M 2002 Craigowl Hill (Tealing parish) (Sites recorded during winter aerial reconnaissance, Angus). *Discovery Excav Scot* 3, 12.

Guido, C M 1974 A Scottish crannog redated. *Antiq* 48, 54–5.

Gunn, D J & Yenigun, O 1987 A model for tidal motion and level in the Tay Estuary. *Proc Royal Soc Edinburgh B*, 257–73.

Haines, K 2008 *Archaeological Excavation, Crieff High School, Broich Road, Crieff CF08*. Unpublished Data Structure Report. SUAT Ltd.

Hale, A 2005 Fish-traps in Scotland: construction, supply, demand and destruction. In Klápste, J (ed) *Water Management in Medieval Rural Economy*. Památky archeologické – supplementum, 17, Prague, Institute of Archaeology, 119–26.

Hall, M A 2007 Crossing the pilgrimage landscape: some thoughts on a holy rood reliquary from the River Tay at Carpow, Perth & Kinross, Scotland. In S Blick (ed) *Beyond Pilgrim Souvenirs and Secular Badges: Essays in Honour of Brian Spencer*. Oxford, 75–91.

Hall, M A, Hall, D & Cook, G 2005 What's cooking?: new radiocarbon dates from the earliest phases of the Perth High Street Excavations and the question of Perth's early medieval origin. *Proc Soc Antiq Scot* 135, 273–85.

Hallam, H E 1960 Salt-making in the Lincolnshire Fenland during the Middle Ages. *Lincolnshire Arch Archaeol Soc Rep* 8, 85–112.

Halliday, S P 1985 Unenclosed upland settlement in the east and south-east of Scotland. In Spratt, D & Burgess, C (eds), 231–51.

Halliday, S & Simpson, B 1997 Drumoig (Forgan: Leuchars parishes); watching brief and excavation. *Discovery Excav Scot* 38–9.

Halliday, S 2007 Unenclosed round-houses in Scotland: occupation, abandonment and the character of settlement. In Burgess, C, Topping, P & Lynch, F (eds), 49–56.

Hall Roth, I & Malmberg, L 2005 Save the Vasa – an introduction. In Hoffman, P *et al* (eds), 171–80.

Harding, D W 1982 (ed) *Later Prehistoric Settlement in South-East Scotland*. University of Edinburgh Dept of Archaeology Occasional Paper No. 8.

Hartley, B 1986 A check-list of the freshwater, brackish and marine diatoms of the British Isles and adjoining coastal waters. *Journal of the Marine Biological Association of the United Kingdom* 66, 531–610.

Headrick, M 1914 The 'Stayt' of Crieff: A Bronze-Age burial site. *Proc Soc Antiq Scot* 48, 365–9.

Hedges, J 1975 Excavation of two Orcadian burnt mounds at Liddle and Beaquoy. *Proc Soc Antiq Scot* 106, 39–98.

Henderson, W 1938 Scottish Late Bronze Age axes and swords. *Proc Soc Antiq Scot* 72, 150–77.

Hendey, N I 1964 *An Introductory Account of the Smaller Algae of British Coastal Waters Part V: Bacillariophyceae (Diatoms)*. London, HMSO.

Hill, P 1982 Settlement and Chronology. In Harding, D W (ed), 4–43.

Hillam, J 1987a Dendrochronology: 20 years on. *Current Archaeology* 107, 358–63.

Hillam, J 1987b Tree ring dating of oak timbers from the Hasholme logboat. *Ancient Monuments Laboratory Report*. 35.87 (microfiche).

Hillam, J, Morgan, R & Tyers, I 1987 Sapwood estimates and the dating of short ring sequences. In Ward, R G W (ed) *Applications of Tree-ring Studies*. BAR Int Ser 333, 165–85.

Hingley, R 1992 Society in Scotland from 700 BC to AD 200. *Proc Soc Antiq Scot* 122, 7–56.

Hingley, R 1998 *Settlement and Sacrifice: The Later Prehistoric People of Scotland*. Canongate Books with Historic Scotland.

Hoffman, P 1986 On the stabilisation of waterlogged oakwood with PEG. *Studies in Conservation* 31, 103–13.

Hoffmann, P, Straetkvern, P, Spriggs, J & Gregory, D (eds) 2005 *9th ICOM Group on Wet Organic Archaeological Materials, Copenhagen*. ICOM Committee for Conservation Working Group on Wet Organic Archaeological Materials.

Hunter, F 1996 Recent Roman Iron Age metalwork finds from Fife and Tayside. *Tayside and Fife Archaeol J* 2, 113–25.

Hutcheson, A 1887 Notice of a burial place of the Bronze Age at Barnhill, near Broughty Ferry. *Proc Soc Antiq Scot* 21, 316–24.

Hutcheson, A 1897 Notices (1) of an ancient canoe found in the River Tay, near Errol; (2) a grinding-stone found on the Sidlaw Hills; (3) a beggar's badge of sixteenth century found in Dundee; and (4) a spear-head of flint found in the carcass of a whale. Being recent additions to the Dundee Museum. *Proc Soc Antiq Scot* 31, 265–81.

Hutcheson, A 1898 Notice of the discovery of a burial of the Bronze Age on the Hill of West Mains of Auchterhouse, the property of D S Cowans, Esq. *Proc Soc Antiq Scot* 32, 205–20.

Hutcheson, A 1901 Notice of the discovery of a series of cairns and cists, and urns of the Bronze Age, at Battle Law, Naughton, Fifeshire, the property of Mrs C H Anstruther Duncan. *Proc Soc Antiq Scot* 35, 301–9.

Hutchings, J & Spriggs, J 2005 The Poole logboat: a treatment update and investigation into a suitable drying regime for large-scale sucrose impregnated waterlogged wood. In Hoffman, P *et al* (eds), 333–53.

Inglis, H R G 1912–13 The roads and bridges of the Early History of Scotland. *Proc Soc Antiq Scot* 47, 303–33.

Jane, F W 1970 *Structure of Wood*. 2nd edn. London.

Jardine, W G & Masters, L S 1977 A dugout canoe from Catherinefield Farm. *Transactions of the Dumfriesshire and Galloway Natural History and Antiquarian Society*, 3rd series 52, 56–65.

Jervise, A 1866 Account of the discovery of a circular group of cinerary urns and human bones at Westwood, near Newport on the Tay. *Proc Soc Antiq Scot* 6, 388–95.

Jones, A M & Rule, M H 1991 Preserving the wreck of the Mary Rose. In Hoffman, P (ed) *4th ICOM Group on wet organic archaeological materials, Bremerhaven*. ICOM Committee for Conservation Working Group on Wet Organic Archaeological Materials 25–48.

Keppie, L 1983 Roman inscriptions from Scotland: some additions and corrections to RIB I. *Proc Soc Antiq Scot* 113, 391–404.

King, M 1991 Kinclaven socketed iron spearhead. *Discovery Excav Scot* 72.

King, M 1993a Saddle quern River Tay, Bellwood Gardens. *Discovery Excav Scot* 103.

King, M 1993b Late medieval jug, River Tay, Perth. *Discovery Excav Scot* 103.

Kristiansen, K & Larsson, T 2005 *The Rise of Bronze Age Society: Travels, Transmissions and Transformations*. Cambridge University Press.

Lacaille, A D 1954 *The Stone Age in Scotland*. Edinburgh.

Laing, A 1876 *Lindores Abbey and Its Burgh of Newburgh: Their Tales and Annals*. Edomston and Douglas. Edinburgh.

Lanting, J N 2000 Dates for origin and diffusion of the European logboat. *Palaeohistoria* 39/40, 627–50.

Lanting, J N & Brindley A L 1996 Irish logboats and their European context. *J Irish Archaeol* 7, 85–95.

Leineweber, R & Lübke, H 2007 Unterwasserarchäologie in der Altmark. In Landesamt für Denkmalpflege und Arcäologie Sachsen-Anhalt und der Archäologischen Gesellschaft in Sachsen-Anhalt eV. *Archäologie in Sachsen-Anhalt*, 127–39.

Lerche, G 1977 Double paddle-spades in prehistoric contexts in Denmark. *Tools and Tillage* 3, 111–24.

Lerche, G & Steensberg, A 1973 Observations on spade cultivation in the New Guinea Highlands. *Tools and Tillage* 2, 87–104.

Leshikar, M 1975 Construction of a dugout canoe in the parish of St Ann, Jamaica. In Johnston, P (ed) *Proceedings of the 16th Conference on Underwater Archaeology*. Society for Historical Archaeology, special publication series 4, Glasboro, 48–51.

Lett, H W 1895 Ancient canoe found near Loughbrickland, Co Down. *Ulster J Archaeol* 7, 85–95.

Leuschner, H H, Sass-Klaassen, U, Jansma, E, Baillie, M G L & Spurk, M 2002 Subfossil European bog oaks: population dynamics and long-term growth depressions as indicators of changes in the Holocene. *Holocene* 12, 695–706.

Lewis, J & Terry, J 2007 Excavations at the Bogleys Standing Stone, Kirkcaldy, Fife. *Tayside and Fife Archaeol J* 13, 81–90.

Loader, R D 2007 The Wootton-Quarr Archaeological Survey, Isle of Wight. In Sidell, J & Haughey, F (eds), 48–58.

Longworth, I 1968 Further discoveries at Brackmont Hill, Brackmont Farm, Tentsmuir, Fife. *Proc Soc Antiq Scot* 99, 60–92.

Lowe, C 1989 Loanleven Gravel Quarry (Methven Parish). *Discovery Excav Scot*, 63.

Lyell, C 1829 On a recent formation of freshwater limestone in Forfarshire, and on some recent deposits of freshwater marl; with a comparison of recent with ancient freshwater formations; and an appendix on the grygonite or seed-vessel of the chara. *Transactions of the Geological Society of London*, 2, 73–96.

MacCormick, A G, Dickson, J H, Ransom, M & Alvey, R C 1968 Three dugout canoes and a wheel from Holme Pierrepont, Nottinghamshire. *Trans Thoroton Soc* 72, 14–31.

Macinnes, L 1982 Pattern and purpose: the settlement evidence. In Harding, D W (ed), 57–74.

Mac Philib, S 2008 Bundle Rafts in Ireland. In Mac Cárthaigh, C (ed) *Traditional Boats of Ireland: History, Folklore and Construction*. Wilton, Cork, 598–603.

Marcigny, C & Ghesquiere, E 2003 *L'Île Tatihou (Manche) à l'Âge du Bronze: Habitats et Occupation du Sol*. Documents d'Archéologie Française, 96, Paris: Éditions de la Maison des Sciences de l'Homme.

Marcigny, C & Talon, M 2009 Sur les rives de la Manche: Qu'en est-il du passage de l'âge du Bronze à l'âge du Fer à partir des découvertes récentes? In Roulière-Lambert, M-J, Daubigney, A Milcent, P-Y, Talon, M & Vital, J (eds), *De l'Âge du Bronze à l'Âge du Fer en France et en Europe occidentale (Xe–VIIe siècle avant J-C); la moyenne vallée du Rhône aux âges du Fer, Actes du XXXème colloque international de l'Association Française pour l'Étude de l'Âge du Fer, co-organisé avec l'Association pour la Promotion des Recherches sur l'Âge du Bronze, Saint-Germain-en Gal, 26–28 mai 2006*. Dijon, Revue Archéologique de l'Est, supplément 27, 385–403.

Mapleton, R J 1868 Notice of the discovery of an Artificial Island in Loch Kielziebar, in a letter to Mr Stuart, Secretary. *Proc Soc Antiq Scot* 6, 322–4.

Marsden, P, Branch, N, Evans, J, Gale, R, Goodburn, D, Juggins, S, Marsden, P, McGrail, S, Rackham, J, Tyers, I, Vaughan, D & Whipp, D 1989 A Late Saxon logboat from Clapton, London borough of Hackney. *Int J Nautical Archaeol* 18.2, 89–111.

Marshall, D N 1977 Carved stone balls. *Proc Soc Antiq Scot* 108, 40–72.

McCullagh, R P J & Tipping, R 1998 *The Lairg Project 1988– 96. The Evolution of an Archaeological Landscape in Northern Scotland*. Edinburgh.

McGrail, S 1978 *Logboats of England and Wales with Comparative Material from European and Other Countries*. British Archaeological Reports British Series 51. Oxford.

McGrail, S (ed) 1981 *The Brigg 'raft' and her prehistoric environment*. British Archaeological Reports, British Series 89. Oxford.

McGrail, S 1987 *Ancient Boats in NW Europe: The Archaeology of Water Transport to AD 1500*. London.

McGrail, S 1988 Assessing the performance of an ancient boat – the Hasholme logboat. *Oxford J Arch* 7, 35–46.

McGrail, S 1990 The theoretical performance of a hypothetical reconstruction of the Clapton logboat. *Int J Naut Archaeol* 19, 129–33.

McGrail, S 1991 Early sea voyages. *Int J Naut Archaeol* 20.2, 85–93.

McGrail, S 1998 *Ancient Boats in North-West Europe: The Archaeology of Water Transport to AD 1500*. Revised paperback edition. London.

McGrail, S 2007a The reassessment and reconstruction of excavated boats. *Int J Naut Archaeol* 36, 254–64.

McGrail, S & Switsur, R 1979 Medieval logboats of the River Mersey: a classification study. In McGrail, S (ed) *The Archaeology of Medieval Ships and Harbours in Northern Europe: Papers based on those presented to an International Symposium at Bremerhaven in 1979*. BAR international series 66 and National Maritime Museum archaeological series 5. Oxford, 93–112.

McLaren, T 1944 *From the Royal Seat of Scone to Falkland Palace: Map and Note*. Unpublished archive held at the Local Studies Section, A K Bell Library, Perth.

Mears, J 1937 Urn burials of the Bronze Age at Brackmont Mill, Leuchars, Fife. *Proc Soc Antiq Scot* 71, 252–78.

Mellars, P 1974 The Palaeolithic and Mesolithic. In Renfrew, C (ed) *British Prehistory: A New Outline*. London: Duckworth, 41–99.

Melville, L 1986 *The Fair Land of Gowrie*. William Culross & Son.

Mercer, R 2004 Summary and Conclusion. In Shepherd, I & Barclay, G (eds) *Scotland in Ancient Europe: The Neolithic and Early Bronze Age of Scotland in their European Context*. Edinburgh: Society of Antiquaries of Scotland, 283–93.

Merchant Shipping Act 1995. HMSO. Chapter 21, Part IX, Sections 224–49.

Milburn, P 1996 *Palaeoenvironmental Investigations into Aspects of the Vegetation History of North Fife and South Perthshire*. Unpublished PhD thesis, University of Edinburgh.

Millett, M & McGrail, S 1987 The Archaeology of the Hasholme Logboat. *Archaeol J* 144, 69–155.

Mowat, R J C 1996 *The Logboats of Scotland, With Notes on Related Artefact Types*. Oxbow monograph 68, Oxford.

Munro, R 1882 *Ancient Scottish Lake-Dwellings or Crannogs*. Edinburgh.

Munro, R 1885 Lake Dwellings of Wigtonshire. *Ayrshire Collections* 5, 73–8.

Murdoch, R & Lewis, J 1999 Excavations at the St Monans saltpans 1990–96. In Lewis, J, Martin, C, Martin, P & Murdoch, R *The Salt and Coal Industries at St Monans, Fife in the 18th and 19th Centuries*. Tayside and Fife Archaeological Committee monograph 2.

Nash Briggs, D 2003 Metals, salt, and slaves: economic links between Gaul and Italy from the eighth to the late sixth centuries BC. *Oxford J Arch* 22, 243–260.

Nayling, N & Caseldine, A 1997 *Excavations at Caldicot, Gwent: Bronze Age Palaeochannels in the Lower Nedern Valley*. CBA Research Reports 108.

Nayling, N & McGrail, S 2004 *The Barland's Farm Romano-Celtic Boat*. CBA Research Report 138.

Needham, S 2006 Networks of contact, exchange and meaning: the beginning of the Channel Bronze Age. In Needham, S, Parfitt, K & Varndell, G (eds) *The Ringlemere Cup: Precious Cups and the Beginning of the Channel Bronze Age*. British Museum Research Publication, 163. London, 75–81.

Needham, S 2008 In the Copper Age. *British Archaeology*, July/ August. Council for British Archaeology.

Nicolaisen, W F H 1976 *Scottish Place-Names*. New edition. Edinburgh 2001.

Nilsson, M, Klarqvist, M, Bohlin, E, Possnert, G 2001 Variation in C14 age of macrofossils and different fractions of minute peat samples dated by AMS. *The Holocene* 11, 579–86.

O'Connell, C 2008 gWest (Golf Development): Watching brief, evaluation and excavation. *Discovery Excav Scot* 139– 40.

O'Connell, C & Gray, H 2008a *gWest, Kirkton Farm, Blackford, Perth and Kinross. Archaeological Excavation Golf Area P (Houses) Report No 1509*. Unpublished Data Structure Report. CFA Archaeology Ltd.

O'Connell, C & Gray, H 2008b *gWest, Kirkton Farm, Blackford, Perth and Kinross. Archaeological Excavation Golf Area P (Palisaded Enclosure) Report No 1508*. Unpublished Data Structure Report. CFA Archaeology Ltd.

O'Connell, C & Neighbour, T forthcoming Excavation of Burnside Enclosure, Blairgowrie, Perth and Kinross. *Tayside Fife Archaeol J*.

O'Connor, B, Cowie, T & Hall, M A forthcoming A Middle Bronze Age Dirk from the River Tay, at Perth.

O'Sullivan, A 1996 Neolithic, Bronze Age and Iron Age woodworking techniques. In Raftery, B (ed) *Trackway*

*Excavations in the Mountdillon Bogs, Co Longford, 1985–1991.* Irish Archaeological Wetland Unit Transactions, vol 3, 291–342.

OSA 1791–9 *[The Old] Statistical Account of Scotland.* Edinburgh.

Osler, A 1983 *The Shetland Boat: South Mainland and Fair Isle.* Maritime Monographs and Reports 58, Nat Maritime Museum, Greenwich.

Owen, O & Dalland, M 1999 *Scar: A Viking Boat Burial on Sanday, Orkney.* East Linton.

Parfitt, K 2004 Discovery and excavation. In Clark, P (ed) 2004a, 9–22.

Parker, A G, Goudie, A S, Anderson, D E, Robinson, M A & Bonsall, C 2001 A review of the mid-Holocene elm decline in the British Isles. *Prog Phys Geog* 26, 1–45.

Parker Pearson, M & Sharples, N 1999 *Between Land and Sea: Excavations at Dun Vulan.* SEARCH, Sheffield.

Parker Pearson, M, Chamberlain, A T, Collins, M J, Craig, O E, Marshall, P, Mulville, J, Smith, H, Chenery, C, Cook, G, Craig, G, Evans, J, Hillier, J, Montgomery, J, Schwenniger, J L, Taylor, G & Wess, T 2005 Evidence for mummification in Bronze Age Britain. *Antiquity* 79, 529–56.

Payne-Gallwey, R 1886 *The Book of Duck Decoys: Their Construction, Management and History.* London.

Peers, R N R 1964 Archaeology and history [reports and papers]: Dugout canoe from Poole Harbour, Dorset. *Proc Dorset Nat Hist Antiq Soc* 86, 131–4.

Perry, D 2005 *Dundee Rediscovered: The Archaeology of Dundee Reconsidered.* Tayside and Fife Archaeological Committee Monograph 4.

Peterken, G 1996 *Natural Woodland.* Cambridge.

Petersen, E 2000 *Jukung-Boats from the Barito Basin, Borneo.* Viking Ship Museum, Roskilde.

Philippe, M 2009 The Canche Estuary (Pas-de-Calais, France) from the early Bronze Age to the emporium of Quentovic: a traditional landing place between south-east England and the continent. In Clark, P 2009, 68–79.

Piggott, S 1957 A tripartite disc wheel from Blair Drummond, Perthshire. *Proc Soc Antiq Scot* 90, 238–41.

Pigott, C D & Huntley, J P 1981 Factors controlling the distribution of *Tilia cordata* at the northern limits of its range. II History in north-west England. *New Phytol J* 84, 145–64.

Pontin, R A & Reid, J A 1975 The freshwater input to the Tay Estuary. *Proc Royal Soc Edinburgh B* 75, 1–9.

Ponting, M 1989 Two Iron-Age cists from Galson, Isle of Lewis. *Proc Soc Antiq Scot* 119, 91–100.

Pryor, F 2004 Some thoughts on boats as Bronze Age artefacts. In Clark, P (ed) 2004c, 31–4.

Rackham, O 1977 Neolithic woodland management in the Somerset Levels: Garvin's Walton Heath and Rowland's tracks. *Somerset Levels Papers* 3, 65–71.

Raftery, B 1990 *Trackways through Time: Archaeological Investigations on Irish Bog Roads, 1985–9.* Dublin.

Ralston, I B M 1988 Belhie (Auchterarder parish) enclosed cremation cemetery, minihenge and other cropmarked features. *Discovery Excav Scot*, 27.

RCAHMS 1994 *South-East Perth: An Archaeological Landscape.* HMSO.

Reed, N 1976 The Scottish campaigns of Septimus Severus. *Proc Soc Antiq Scot* 107, 92–102.

Reid, A G 1899 Notice of an urn and bronze sword found on the farm of Balielands in the parish of Auchterarder. *Proc Soc Antiq Scot* 33, 314–16.

Reid, A G, Shepherd, I A G & Lunt, D A 1986 A beaker cist from Upper Muirhall, Perth. *Proc Soc Antiq Scot* 116, 63–8.

Roberts, K, & Shackleton, P 1983 *The Canoe.* Toronto.

Roberts, O 2006a Interpretations of prehistoric boat remains. *Int J Naut Archaeol* 35, 72–8.

Roberts, O 2006b The Dover Boat: Steady as she goes! *Int J Naut Archaeol* 35, 334.

Robertson, I A 1998 *The Tay Salmon Fisheries since the Eighteenth Century.* Glasgow.

Roe, F E S 1966 The battle-axe series in Britain. *Proc Prehist Soc* 32, 199–245.

Roe, F E S 1974 A flint macehead from the River Tay. *Proc Soc Antiq Scot* 103, 225.

Rohl, B & Needham, S 1998 The circulation of metal in the British Bronze Age: the application of lead isotope analysis. British Museum, London (= British Museum Occasional Paper 102).

Ross, A 1966 A Celtic(?) stone head from Perthshire. *Trans Perthshire Soc Natur Sci* 11, 31–7.

Rudolph, W 1974 *Boats, Rafts, Ships.* London.

Salemke, G 1972 Der Einbaum vom Mondsee, Osterreich. *Das Logbuch* 8, 4–8.

Sanders, D 2007 The Dover Boat; some responses to Ole Crumlin-Pedersen & Seán McGrail, concerning its propulsion, hull form, assembly and some observations on the reappraisal process. *Int J Naut Archaeol* 36, 184–92.

Sands, R 1997 Prehistoric woodworking: the analysis and interpretation of Bronze and Iron Age toolmarks. *Wood in Archaeology* 1. London.

Sandstrom, M, Fors, Y, Jalilehvand, F, Damian, E & Gelius, U 2005 Analyses of iron and sulfur in marine archaeological wood. In P Hoffman *et al* (eds), 181–99.

Schmidt, P K & Burgess, C B 1981 *The Axes of Scotland and Northern England.* Prähistoriche Bronzefunde IX. 7. Munchen, Beck.

Schweingruber, F H 1990 *Microscopic Wood Anatomy.* 3rd edition. Swiss Federal Institute for Forest, Snow & Landscape Research.

Scott, W L 1934 Excavation of Rudh'an Dunain Cave, Skye. *Proc Soc Antiq Scot* 68, 200–23.

Scottish Executive Education Department 1999 *Treasure Trove in Scotland: Information on Treasure Trove Procedures – Criteria for Allocation and the Allocation Process.* Edinburgh.

Sheppard, T 1901 Notes on the ancient model of a boat and warrier crew found at Roos in Holderness. *Trans East Riding Antiq Soc* 9, 62–74.

Sheridan, A 2007 Dating the Scottish Bronze Age: There is clearly much the material can still tell us. In Burgess, C, Topping, P & Lynch, F (eds), 162–85.

Sherriff, J 1988 A hut-circle at Ormiston Farm, Newburgh, Fife. *Proc Soc Antiq Scot* 118, 99–110.

Shore, J S, Bartley, D D, Harkness, D D, 1995 Problems encountered with the $^{14}$C dating of peat. *Quat Sci Rev* 14, 373–83.

Sibbald, R 1803 *The History, Ancient and Modern, of the Sheriffdoms of Fife and Kinross . . .* New edition. Cupar.

Sidell, J & Haughey, F (eds) 2007 *Neolithic Archaeology in the Inter-tidal Zone.* Neolithic Studies Group Seminar Paper 8. Oxford.

Skinner, T, Erpenbeck, S, McConachie, G, Jones, M & Smith, A D 2005 A XANES spectroscopic study of changes in sulfur speciation in waterlogged archaeological wood in response to high humidity. In Hoffman, P *et al* (eds), 213–24.

Skinner, T & Jones, M 2007 Respirometry: a technique to assess the stability of archaeological wood and other materials containing sulfur compounds. *Conservation Sci.*

Smith, A G 1958 The context of some Late Bronze Age and Early Iron Age remains from Lincolnshire. *Proc Prehist Soc* 25, 78–84.

Smith, J A 1876a Notes of small ornamental stone balls found in different parts of Scotland, etc; with remarks on their supposed age and use. *Proc Soc Antiq Scot* 11, 29–62.

Smith, J A 1876b Additional notes on small ornamented stone balls found in different parts of Scotland etc. *Proc Soc Antiq Scot* 11, 313–19.

Spence, L 1951 Burials at Brackmont Mill and Brackmont Farm, Leuchars. *Proc Soc Antiq Scot* 83, 224–9.

Spratt, D & Burgess, C 1985 *Upland Settlement in Britain. The Second Millennium BC and After.* Oxford.

Stevenson, D 1845 *Remarks on the Improvements of Tidal Rivers.* London.

Stevenson, R B K 1953 *Fifeshire Leuchars 37/445216.* Council for British Archaeology 8th Report, Scottish Regional Group.

Stewart, M 1950 *Perthshire, Arnbathie, Scone 27/170260.* Council for British Archaeology 5th Report, Scottish Regional Group.

Stewart, M 1966 Excavation of a circle of standing stones at Sandy Road, Scone, Perthshire. *Trans Perthshire Soc Natur Sci* 11, 7.

Stewart, M & Barclay, G 1997 Excavations in burial and ceremonial sites of the Bronze Age in Tayside. *Tayside Fife Archaeol J* 3, 22–57.

Stewart, M, Close-Brooks, J, McKerrell, H, Thorns, L 1985 The excavation of a henge, stone circles and metal-working area at Moncrieffe, Perthshire. *Proc Soc Antiq Scot* 115, 125–50.

Strachan, D 1998 Inter-tidal stationary fishing structures in Essex: some radiocarbon dates. *Essex Archaeology and History* 29, Colchester.

Strachan, D 2001 Carpow logboat. *Discovery Excav Scot*, 74.

Strachan, D 2004 A Late Bronze Age logboat from the Tay estuary at Carpow, Perth and Kinross. *Tayside Fife Archaeol J* 10, 58–63.

Strachan, D 2006 *The Carpow Logboat, Perth and Kinross. Method Statement for Low Tide Survey, Environmental Sampling, Excavation and Lifting.* Unpublished method statement. Perth and Kinross Heritage Trust.

Strachan, D & Glenndinning, B 2002 Carpow Logboat. *Discovery Excav Scot* 90.

Strachan, D & Glenndinning, B 2003 Carpow Logboat. *Discovery Excav Scot* 104.

Stronach, S, Sheridan, A & Henderson, D 2006 A Bronze Age cremation cemetery at North Straiton, Fife. *Tayside Fife Archaeol J* 12, 1–13.

Stuart, J 1866 Notice of a group of artificial islands in the Loch of Dowalton, Wigtonshire, and of other artificial islands or 'crannogs' throughout Scotland. *Proc Soc Antiq Scot* 6, 114–78.

Stuart, R 1852 *Caledonia Romana.* Edinburgh.

Stuiver, M, Reimer, P J, Braziunas, T F 1998 High-precision radiocarbon age calibration for terrestrial and marine samples. *Radiocarbon* 40, 1127–51.

Tay Estuary Forum 2009 *Management Plan: Tay Estuary and Adjacent Coastline, River North Esk to Fife Ness, 2009–14.*

Taylor, M 1992 Flag Fen: the wood. *Antiq* 66, 476–98.

Teigelake, U 2003 Boat on the river: developing and applying alternative methods of tracing shipping traffic in inland waters. In Rönnby, J (ed) *By the Water: Archaeological Perspectives around the Baltic Sea.* Södertörn Academic Studies 17, 37–64.

Tipping, R 1994 The form and fate of Scottish woodlands. *Proc Soc Antiq Scot* 124, 1–54.

Tipping, R 1996 The Neolithic landscapes of the Cheviot Hills and hinterland – palaeoenvironmental evidence. In Frodsham, P (ed) *The Neolithic of Northern England.* Northern Archaeology Special Edition, Newcastle, 17–35.

Tipping, R 2002 Climatic variability and 'marginal' settlement in upland British landscapes: a re-evaluation. *Landscapes* 3, 10–28.

Tipping, R 2003 Living in the past: woods and people in prehistory to 1000 BC. In Smout, T C (ed) *People and Woods in Scotland: A History.* Edinburgh, 14–39.

Tipping, R forthcoming 'I have not been able to find anything of interest in the peat': landscapes and environment in the Later Bronze and Iron Ages in Scotland. In Ralston, I & Hunter, F (eds) *Scotland in Later Prehistoric Europe.* Edinburgh.

Tipping, R, Bunting, M J, Davies, A L, Murray, H & Fraser, S 2009 Modelling land use around an early Neolithic timber 'hall' in north-east Scotland from high spatial resolution pollen analyses. *J Archaeol Sci* 36, 140–9.

Tomalin, D J, Loader, R D & Scaife, R G forthcoming *Coastal Archaeology in a Dynamic Setting: a Solent Case Study*. Oxford, BAR.

Toolis, R 2005 Bronze Age pastoral practices in the Clyde Valley: excavations at West Acres, Newton Mearns. *Proc Soc Antiq Scot* 135, 471–504.

Trump, B A V 1962 The origin and development of British Middle Bronze Age rapiers. *Proc Prehist Soc* 28, 80–102.

Turner, J 1975 The evidence for land use by prehistoric farming communities: the use of three-dimensional pollen diagrams. In Evans, J G, Limbrey, S & Cleere, H (eds) *The Effect of Man on the Landscape: The Highland Zone*. London, 86–95.

Tyers, I 1989 Dating by tree-ring analysis. In P Marsden *et al* 1989, 104.

Tylecote, R 1974 *Specimens of Copper-base Alloy removed from a Cauldron Leg found near Perth*. In published note in PMAG object history files.


Van de Noort, R 2004 *The Humber Wetlands: The Archaeology of a Dynamic Landscape*. Macclesfield.

Van de Noort, R & Ellis, S (eds) 1995 *Wetland Heritage of Holderness: An Archaeological Survey*. Kingston upon Hull.

Van de Noort, R, Middleton, R, Foxton, A & Bayliss, A 1999 The 'Kilnsea-boat' and some implications from the discovery of England's oldest plank boat remains. *Antiquity* 73, 131–5.

Van der Werf, A & Huls, H 1957–74 *Diatomienflore van Nederland*, 8 parts, Koenigstein, Otto Koeltz Science Publishers.

van Geel, B & Berglund, B E 2000 A causal link between a climatic deterioration around 850 cal BC and a subsequent rise in human population density in NW-Europe? *Terra Nostra* 7, 126–30.

van Geel, B, Buurman, J & Waterbolk, H T 1996 Archaeological and palaeoecological indications of an abrupt climate change in The Netherlands, and evidence for climatological teleconnections around 2650 BP. *J Quat Sci* 11, 451–60.

van Geel, B, van der Plicht, J, Kilian, M R, Klaver, E R, Kouwenberg, J H M, Renssen, H, Reynaud-Ferrara, I & Waterbolk, H T 1998 The sharp rise of $\Delta^{14}C$ *c*800 cal BC: possible causes, related climatic teleconnections and the impact on human environments. *Radiocarbon* 40, 535–50.

Vinson, S 1994 *Egyptian Boats and Ships*. Princes Risborough.

Von der Porten, E 2006 Minimal, intermediate and maximum reconstructions of the Dover Boat. *Int J Naut Archaeol* 35, 332–3.

Vos, P C & de Wolf, H 1993 Diatoms and a tool for reconstructing sedimentary environments in coastal wetlands; methodological aspects. *Hydrobiologia* 269/270, 285–96.


Ward, J E 1974 Wooden objects uncovered at Branthwaite, Workington, in 1956 and 1971. *Trans Cumberland Westmorland Antiq Archaeol Soc* 74, 18–28.

Ward, C 2005 Dover Bronze Age Boat. *Int J Naut Archaeol* 34, 347–8.

Warden, A J 1876 Notice of stone cists etc, found on Barnhill links, near Broughty-Ferry. *Proc Soc Antiq Scot 11,* 310–12.

Watkins, T 1987 North Straiton (Logie p), Settlement. *Discovery Excav Scot* 15–16.

Watson, A 2002 *Place-names, Land and Lordship in the Medieval Earldom of Strathearn*. Unpublished PhD thesis, University of St Andrews.

Watson, W J 1926 *The History of the Celtic Place-names of Scotland*. Edinburgh (reprinted with an Introduction by Simon Taylor, Edinburgh 2004).

Weir, M 1988 *Ferries in Scotland*. Edinburgh.

Westerdahl, C (ed) 2006 *The Significance of Portages. Proceedings of the First International Conference of the Significance of Portages, 29 September–2 October 2004, in Lyngdal, Vest-Agder, Norway, arranged by the County Municipality of Vest-Agder, Kristiansand*. British Archaeological Reports (International Series), 1499.

Whittington, G, Edwards, K J & Cundill, P R 1990 *Palaeoenvironmental Investigations at Black Loch, in the Ochil Hills of Fife, Scotland*. O'Dell Monograph 22.

Whittle, A W R 1991 Wayland's Smithy, Oxfordshire: excavations at the Neolithic tomb in 1962–3 by R J C Atkinson & S Piggott. *Proc Prehist Soc* 57, 61–101.

Wilkes, E 2007 Prehistoric sea journeys and port approaches: the south coast and Poole Harbour. In Cummings, V & Johnston, R (eds), 121–30.

Wilkinson, T J & Murphy, P L (eds) 1995 *Archaeology of the Essex Coast, Volume 1: The Hullbridge Survey*. East Anglian Archaeology Report 71. Chelmsford.

Wilkinson, T J & Murphy, P L, Heppell, E & Brown, N forthcoming *Archaeology of the Essex Coast, Volume 2: The Stumble*. East Anglian Archaeology Report.

Williams, J & Brown, N 1999 *An Archaeological Research Framework for the Greater Thames Estuary*. Essex County Council.

Woolliscroft, D J & Hoffmann, B 2006 *Rome's First Frontier: The Flavian Occupation of Northern Scotland*. Tempus.

Wright, E 1978 Artefacts from the boat-site at North Ferriby, Humberside, England. *Proc Prehist Soc* 44, 187–202.

Wright, E 1990 *The Ferriby Boats: Seacraft of the Bronze Age*. London.

Wright, E 1994 The North Ferriby boats: A final report. In Westerdahl, C (ed) *Crossroads in Ancient Shipbuilding*. Oxbow Monograph 40. Oxford, 29–34.

Wright, E, Hedges, R, Bayliss, A & Van de Noort, R 2001 New AMS dates for the Ferriby boats; a contribution to the origin of seafaring. *Antiquity* 75, 726–34.

Yates, D H 2007 *Land, Power & Prestige: Bronze Age Field Systems in Southern England*. Oxford.

Young, R 2000 Continuity and change: marginality and later prehistoric settlement. In Harding, J & Johnston, R (eds) *Northern Pasts: Interpretations of the Later Prehistory of Northern England and Southern Scotland*. Oxford, 71–80.

<h1 style="text-align:center">Index</h1>